D0837369

THE EXISTENTIALIST TRADITION

SELECTED WRITINGS

Nino Langiulli, who holds an M.A. degree in English from Hunter College of the City University of New York and an M.A. degree in philosophy from New York University where he is also pursuing a Ph.D. degree, studied with Professor Nicola Abbagnano under Fulbright and Italian government grants during the academic year 1960–61. In 1966 he was nominated to the Danforth Associateship for his commitment to the personal dimension of teaching. He is the translator and editor of *Critical Existentialism*. Mr. Langiulli presently teaches philosophy at St. Francis College in Brooklyn.

THE EXISTENTIALIST TRADITION

SELECTED WRITINGS
EDITED BY
NINO LANGIULLI

ANCHOR BOOKS

DOUBLEDAY & COMPANY, INC.

GARDEN CITY, NEW YORK

1971

REMOVED FROM THE
ALVERNO COLLEGE LIBRARY

142.7
L284

102606

The Anchor Books edition is the first publication
of *The Existentialist Tradition*

Anchor Books edition: 1971

Library of Congress Catalog Card Number 78–150930
Copyright © 1971 by Nino Langiulli
All Rights Reserved
Printed in the United States of America

The kindness of authors and publishers who gave permission
for the inclusion of material in this book is gratefully acknowledged.

"The Interlude," from *Philosophical Fragments or A Fragment of Philosophy*, by Søren Kierkegaard, orig. transl. by D. Swenson, new Introduction and Commentary by N. Thulstrup, rev. trans. by H. V. Hong (Copyright © 1936, 1962 by Princeton University Press). Reprinted by permission of Princeton University Press.

From *Concept of Dread*, by Søren Kierkegaard, transl. by Walter Lowrie (Copyright © 1944 by Princeton University Press). Reprinted by permission of Princeton University Press.

Friedrich Nietzsche. "On Truth and Falsity in Their Ultramoral Sense," from *Early Greek Philosophy and Other Essays*, transl. by Maximilian A. Mügge, Vol. II of *The Complete Works of Friedrich Nietzsche*, ed. by Oscar Levy (1909–1911). New York: Russell & Russell, 1964.

Friedrich Nietzsche. Pp. 30–33, 55–58, 63, 64, from *The Will to Power*, transl. by Anthony M. Ludovici, Vol. XV of *The Complete Works of Friedrich Nietzsche*, by Oscar Levy (1909–1911). New York: Russell & Russell, 1964.

Wilhelm Dilthey, *The Essence of Philosophy*, pp. 1–6, 25–26, 66, 73–76. Transl. into English by Stephen A. and William T. Emery. University of North Carolina Studies in the Germanic

Alverno College Library

Languages and Literatures, XIII. Chapel Hill: The University of North Carolina Press, 1954.

Edmund Husserl, "Author's Preface to the English Edition," pp. 5–22. Reprinted with permission of The Macmillan Company from *Ideas* by Edmund Husserl. First Collier Books Edition, 1962.

From *Philosophical Perspectives* by Max Scheler, Ch. 1, "Philosopher's Outlook," pp. 1–12. Reprinted by permission of the Beacon Press, copyright © 1958 by Beacon Press. Transl. from the German edition in the series *Dalp Taschenbucher,* Vol. 301 (Bern: A. Francee, and Munich: L. Lehnen, 1954). First published in *Müncher Neueste Nachrichten* (May 5, 1928).

"Philosophizing Starts with Our Situation" and "The Search for Being" by Karl Jaspers, reprinted from *Philosophy*, Vol. I, transl. by E. B. Ashton. Chicago: The University of Chicago Press, 1969.

"Letter on Humanism," by Martin Heidegger, from *Philosophy in the Twentieth Century*, by William Barrett and Henry D. Aiken, editors. Copyright © 1962 by William Barrett and Henry D. Aiken. Reprinted by permission of Random House, Inc.

Reprinted from *What Is Philosophy?* by José Ortega y Gasset. Transl. from the Spanish by Mildred Adams. By permission of W. W. Norton & Company, Inc. Copyright © 1960 by W. W. Norton & Company, Inc.

"Existentialism Is a Positive Philosophy," from *Critical Existentialism,* by Nicola Abbagnano. Copyright © 1969 by Doubleday & Company, Inc. Reprinted by permission of the publisher.

Martin Buber, "Dialogue," reprinted with permission of The Macmillan Company from *Between Man and Man* by Martin Buber. Copyright © by Martin Buber, 1965. Copyright © by The Macmillan Company, 1965.

"An Outline of a Concrete Philosophy" reprinted with the permission of Farrar, Straus & Giroux, Inc., from *Creative Fidelity* by Gabriel Marcel, copyright © 1964 by Farrar, Straus & Company.

Chapter III in *The Beginning and the End* by Nicholas Berdyaev, copyright © 1952, by YMCA Press. Reprinted by permission of Harper & Row, Publishers.

Reprinted by permission of The Philosophical Library from *Existentialism Is a Humanism* by Jean-Paul Sartre, The Philosophical Library, New York, 1947.

"Interrogation and Intuition," by Maurice Merleau-Ponty from *Visible and Invisible*. Reprinted by permission of Northwestern University Press, Evanston, 1969.

From *The Myth of Sisyphus,* by Albert Camus. Copyright © 1955 by Alfred A. Knopf, Inc. Reprinted by permission of the publisher.

PERSONAL ACKNOWLEDGMENTS

I am grateful to those persons who have contributed to the realization of this anthology: to Francis Slade, a colleague, who discussed with me the selections that have been included; to Joseph Carpino, another colleague, whose suggestions have made the manuscript more readable; to Yvonne Noether, Sal Rasa, Peter Donohue and Louis Cappellino, students, who assisted me with the bibliographies; and to my sister-in-law, Frances, and my wife, Elizabeth, for typing the manuscript.

Contents

THE EXISTENTIALIST TRADITION

SELECTED WRITINGS

Introduction

1. *The Existentialist Tradition*

Most of the authors whose selections are included in this anthology are classified as Existentialists. The classifiers have been philosophers or historians of philosophy; or they have been historians of ideas, literary critics, or even journalists. The remaining authors, on the other hand, are regarded as forerunners or antecedents of the alleged Existentialists. The irony of this matter is that several of these writers, such as Heidegger, Marcel, and Jaspers, have for different reasons repudiated the label. Even Sartre has disowned the essay chosen for this anthology to represent his formulation of the problems of Existential philosophy. The added irony of the matter is that those who have done the classifying are aware of these repudiations, repeat them, approve of them, but nevertheless stick to the classification. They are correct in doing so, for it does seem that there is a set of distinguishing characteristics that justifies their tactic.

There is a nagging temptation merely to point out what experts or authorities on Existentialism say about it and to rely simply on their selection of philosophers for its representatives. It is the measure of reasonableness that makes the temptation so attractive. But a credulous endorsement of convention neither explains satisfactorily the principle of unity in this anthology nor does it illuminate the sound reasons that support the convention. Part of the temptation is to fall back on the affectation of claiming to allow the philosophers to speak for themselves. Which philosophers? About what? How? And why? The title of the anthology is already a commitment to a specific group of philosophers, concerned about a certain set of problems, formulated and elaborated in a given way. There are conditions, for which Existentialism is the name, that must be satisfied.

The term "tradition" was chosen for the title in order to suggest that the book aims at greater intelligibility of its theme by providing samples from antecedents of and influences upon it. Consequently, although Existentialism is regarded here and elsewhere as an example of twentieth-century philosophizing, nineteenth-century thinkers such as Kierkegaard and Nietzsche are presented as its forerunners. Furthermore, thinkers frequently associated with other trends in philosophy such as Historicism and Phenomenology are included because of their influence upon the Existentialists. Dilthey, Husserl, and Scheler, therefore, have their places in the book.

2. *Omission of Literary Figures*

This is a book of *philosophical* readings, hence the omission of authors frequently mentioned in discussions of Existentialism and even found in anthologies devoted to it. There is no doubt that Dostoevsky, Kafka, Rilke, and Tolstoy have written about the human condition in all its finite, problematic, and fragile manifestations. Saul Bellow even baptizes the Existential conception of man with the label "dangling man" to express the radical contingencies of human life. In *Notes from Underground,* Dostoevsky strikes at the romance and myth of humanism by describing the world of infected livers, toothaches, nasty smells, and spite. He portrays with irony the dreams of science to eliminate error, evil, and suffering through calculation and tabulation. The edifice of complete predictability, the "Palace of Crystal," cracks and shatters under the pressure of uncalculated incident, the misadventure, the reactionary move to kick over the whole affair. Freedom, the correlate of contingency, has spoiled the show.

In *The Brothers Karamazov,* Dostoevsky pits the grandiose project of the Grand Inquisitor to make men happy and secure through bread, mystery, and miracle against the silent stare of Christ, who would not descend from the Cross lest man's freedom be destroyed. It is that freedom from which every possible good or evil derives.

Human finitude receives its due in Tolstoy's *Death of Ivan Illich*. The protagonist becomes dreadfully aware that a paradigmatic syllogism employed in his logic textbook has another twist. The conclusion, "Caius is mortal," refers to him. Dread and death are the ciphers of that finitude.

In Rilke's *Notes of Malte Laurids Brigge*, time, another bedfellow of contingency, turns out to be the context wherein every aspect of human existence is played out. Authenticity and inauthenticity, awareness and dying take time.

Kafka expresses the contingency and finitude of human existence in *The Trial* by placing man under an imminent accusation. The threat is unclear and inexplicable yet certain and irremovable at the same time. The senselessness and groundlessness of the accusation are a metaphor for the possibly absurd and groundless nature of human existence itself. It is a threat whose menace is interrupted and ends with death. Kafka places in counterpoint the theme of the fundamental insecurity of life for which there is no insurance or refuge (*The Burrow*) and the theme of a bright stable and secure existence whose promise tantalizes man but constantly eludes him (*The Castle*). The only escape Kafka supplies in *The Metamorphosis* is the descent into the wretchedness of daily banality which ultimately deprives man of his human character.

The masterful treatments of these themes by the aforementioned authors are the fictional expression of the finite and contingent character of human existence which Existentialist philosophers try to elucidate conceptually and at the level of rational argument. They are omitted here only because this anthology is intentionally restricted to philosophical literature with one exception—Camus's "Myth of Sisyphus." The exception is ambiguous because, although it is a piece of imaginative fiction, it belongs to a larger piece of philosophical argument, much as "The Myth of the Cave" does in Plato's *Republic*.

There is a hope related to this omission—the hope that the distinction between fictional discourse and philosophical discourse remains intact in the mind of the reader. The chances against such a hope being fulfilled are great, however, because of the blithe facility of this era, or of any era probably, to blur distinctions and to ignore differences.

3. Defining Existentialism

The problem discussed in the first section of this introduction is necessarily related to the problem of defining Existentialism. The selection of authors to be included as well as the choice of a title depend on what the concept of "Existentialism" includes.

Although historians of philosophy or authorities on Existentialism differ in formulating the definition of "Existentialism," a certain set of features recurs in their formulations such that a fairly adequate notion of this kind of philosophizing can be reached. A task of this introduction will be to make this notion as clear as possible by discussing what has often remained unsaid in the formulations alluded to.

F. C. Copleston claims modestly to give a "rough generalization at least" when he defines Existentialist philosophies as those which have "Man as their principal theme."[1] He then specifies this principal theme by referring to the ways in which the various Existentialists play the theme. Kierkegaard, says Copleston, was not so much concerned with the problem of God's existence and nature but rather with "man's relationship to God," i.e., with "man's possible attitudes to God," especially the attitude of faith and the problem "of how one becomes a Christian."[2] Jaspers, he continues, dwells on man's general quest for the Transcendent which is apprehended as the unreachable goal acting as the boundary of every particular quest (such as knowledge, truth, value, justice, etc.). Gabriel Marcel, according to Copleston, is clearly concerned with the "description of and analysis of personal relationships" and the ground of those relationships.[3] Heidegger, too, although concerned with the "problem of Being in general," concentrates on "man himself and man's own apprehension of Being."[4] And for Sartre, says Copleston, Existentialism is a humanism.

John Passmore in the second edition of his *A Hundred Years*

[1] F. C. Copleston, *Existentialism and Modern Man* (Aquinas Paper, No. 9). London: Blackfriars, 1948, p. 4.
[2] *Ibid.*   [3] *Ibid.*, p. 5.
[4] Copleston, *op. cit.*, p. 5.

of Philosophy is very much in concert with Copleston. When he musters the strength as a student and devotee of analytical philosophy to stifle his contempt for Existentialism, he characterizes it as a "violent reaction against that view of man and his world which is enshrined in Plato's *Republic*."[5] What Passmore refers to when he speaks of the view of man and his world in Plato's *Republic* is, of course, the Neoplatonic interpretation of Plato—an interpretation which has its adherents among Plato's bitter opponents as well as among his staunch supporters.

Passmore elaborates his characterization of Existentialism by saying that "for Plato, 'existence' is a paltry, second rate manner of being; existent entities are real only in so far as they manifest a 'form' or 'essence.'" He repeats the opinion that the real world, for Platonists, is an "intelligible system of essences" and as a result "individuality is a defect." A man achieves his authentic nature only if he accomplishes a "function," i.e., the function of a philosopher, a guardian, a citizen. Just as the "good ruler is dominated by the forms," so "the good citizen" is ruled "by force of habit." Passmore says that according to the Existentialists, neither the ruler nor the citizen need "suffer the agony of choice"; neither "has to commit himself"; neither "knows what it is to be a person."[6]

Apart from a questionable interpretation of Plato which is employed as the foil to Existentialism in his presentation, Passmore has singled out an important feature of Existential philosophy, namely, the argument that what is particular or individual is important. This argument, moreover, is rightly contrasted with classical thought, as represented by Plato, for which importance was attached to what is general or universal.

But Passmore has other important comments on Existentialism. He points out that Jaspers insists on the clear distinction between philosophy and science.[7] Not to do so, according to Jaspers, is a confusion that bedevils modern philosophy from Descartes to Husserl. The attitude of the disinterested spectator, of the objective observer—an attitude essential for scientific inquiry—is

[5] John Passmore, *A Hundred Years of Philosophy*. 2nd ed. Baltimore: Penguin, 1968, p. 467.
[6] *Ibid.*   [7] *Ibid.*, p. 471.

incompatible with philosophy. Thus Passmore touches on another important feature of Existentialism, that is, the sharp cleavage between science and philosophy.

Passmore's discussion of Heidegger illuminates still another feature of Existentialism—the argument that human existence is, by definition, existence in the world.[8] The discussion refers to the fact that in modern philosophy (Descartes, Kant) there was much ado about proving the existence of an external world, whereas for Heidegger and a considerable part of contemporary (twentieth-century) philosophy, especially Existentialism, it was much ado about nothing. In addition to the not so obvious abuse of metaphor in regarding the world as "external," the very raising of the question leads either to a self-contradiction if denied or to a truism if affirmed.

Sartre's point, according to Passmore, is made emotionally in the novel *La Nausée* and bombastically in the ontological essay *Being and Nothingness*—namely "that contingency, brute factuality, cannot be explained away as necessity in disguise."[9] Passmore gives what he calls a technical summary of that point in the following way: " 'By definition, existence is not necessity. To exist is *to be there,* simply; existents appear on the scene, let themselves be met but can never be deduced.' To lose sight of contingency by absorbing the world into a set of rational functions is to blind oneself, Sartre argues, to what the world is really like."[10]

Despite his antipathy for Existentialism, Passmore has, it seems, illuminated its essential characteristics. A more sympathetic commentator as well as an expert in Existential philosophy, William Barrett, says that "Existentialism is a philosophy that confronts the human situation in its *totality* to ask what the basic conditions of human existence are and how man can establish his own meaning out of these conditions."[11] This schematic statement is fleshed out by Barrett when he shows how Existential philosophy begins with the ordinary, common, and concrete aspects of human existence and tries to understand them in their

---

[8] *Ibid.,* p. 478.   [9] *Ibid.,* p. 491.   [10] *Ibid.,* pp. 491–492.
[11] William Barrett, *Philosophy in the Twentieth Century.* New York: Random House, 1962, Vol. 3, p. 143.

ordinariness, their commonness, and their concreteness. The aim is to grasp reality before it is understood at a technical level where it is fixed in the categories of matter-spirit, body-soul, subject-object, and the even more sophisticated language of the sciences.

Barrett refers, moreover, to the twofold revolt of Existentialism: the revolt against modern philosophy, on the one hand, which had severed man from the world in the effort to establish a certain foundation for the emerging physical sciences; and the revolt against ancient and medieval philosophy, on the other hand, which had argued for the priority of actuality over possibility, i.e., the priority of actual existence over possible existence. Both of these will be explained later in the introduction.

It is the feature of revolt that Walter Kaufmann in his popular anthology, *Existentialism from Dostoevsky to Sartre,* counts as the core of Existentialism.[12] He claims that the Existentialists refuse to belong to a school of thought; that they reject as inadequate any body of beliefs or rational syntheses and that they are dissatisfied with traditional philosophy as a trivial academic venture that is far removed from concrete events. Kaufmann is correct about the revolt but is overstating the case; he blurs its character and tends to regard differences among the philosophers as affairs of psychology and temperament.

The next sample definition of Existentialism is taken from a historian of philosophy and an Existentialist in his own right. In his *Dizionario di Filosofia,* Nicholas Abbagnano says that the term refers to a group of philosophers who, while differing in their presuppositions and conclusions, employ the same instrument, namely the analysis of existence.[13] He clarifies the statement by saying that these philosophers mean by "existence" the mode of being proper to man inasmuch as it is a mode of being in the world, that is, always in a determinate situation that can be analyzed in terms of *possibilities.*[14] Abbagnano goes on to say that Existential analysis is of the most common and ordi-

[12] Walter Kaufmann, *Existentialism from Dostoevsky to Sartre.* Cleveland: World, 1956, p. 12.

[13] Nicholas Abbagnano, *Dizionario di Filosofia.* Turin: UTET, 1960, p. 311.

[14] *Ibid.*

nary human situations. He does not add, though, that it is the very ordinariness and commonness of these situations that make them difficult to understand as, for example, it is difficult to see the lines and shape of one's hand when it is placed next to one's eyes. Hence the principal reason for the difficulty in understanding the writings of these or any other philosophers.

To exist, says Abbagnano, means to be in relationship with the world, that is, with things and with other men. The term "transcendence" found in the writings of the Existentialists who appropriated it from Husserl's Phenomenology means precisely this: that the relationships of knowing, willing, producing, possessing, etc., as well as their contraries, are the ways in which man and the world are constantly configured. The analysis of existence is not only the clarification and interpretation of the ways in which man is related to the world in his cognitive, emotive, and practical possibilities, but it is at the same time the clarification and interpretation of the ways in which the world manifests itself to man and conditions his possibilities.[15]

Abbagnano warns that, although the man-world theme is a fundamental theme of Existentialism, it should not be understood in an idealistic sense whereby the world is *in* man or *in* consciousness. Nor is it posited by man or his consciousness, but it has the characteristic of transcendence whereby it manifests itself as such in the structures that constitute man. These structures, however, are none other than the ordinary and extraordinary possible ways in which man himself relates to the world. Thus, Abbagnano concludes, the other fundamental characteristic of Existentialism is the use of the concept of possibility in the analysis of existence. Human existence is constitutively possibilities, its constituents being the various ways in which the man-world relationship can occur.[16]

These sample definitions are not intended to cover the entire range of opinion on Existentialism. They do reflect, however, the prevailing conventions about its fundamental characteristics —conventions, it should be noted, with which the definition to

[15] Nicholas Abbagnano, *Storia della Filosofia*, 2nd ed. Turin: UTET, 1969, Vol. III, p. 824.
[16] *Ibid.*

be given in this introduction is in agreement. It excludes, therefore, the definition arrived at by Peter Hare in an analysis wherein Existentialism is regarded primarily as a value system and is defined as the philosophy which "takes the following to be the *only* intrinsic values: commitment, intensity of experience, and uniqueness of experience."[17]

The mention of these various definitions serves to show how the one given here is not idiosyncratic with respect to the literature on Existentialism but draws on it and not merely in an eclectic manner. Thus the following features distinguish Existentialism: It is an inquiry that understands philosophy itself as characteristic of man in the sense that he is concerned with and asks about the meaning of his existence in particular and as a whole. It is in and through discourse that this meaning is sought. Parenthetically it is the metaphilosophical question, i.e., the question of what philosophy is, that is the mark of every serious and mature philosopher. Most of the selections in this anthology explicitly reflect that concern.

Discourse, through the question about the meaning of existence, reveals a world to be understood. The sciences, whether physical, social, or behavioral, and the arts describe, predict, and create within that world but the ultimate grounds for describing, predicting, or creating are not answered by the sciences or the arts themselves. The question about ultimate grounds is a philosophical one. It is the case that questions about the foundations of the different arts and sciences are philosophical ones but they are intermediate to the question of the meaning of existence in general.

Discourse, furthermore, in its primary spoken mode, is immediately a common world—a world of objects and persons—objects *about* which we speak and use in science, technology, and in ordinary life; persons *with* whom we speak, frequently about objects or other persons as we do in science, technology, and in ordinary affairs. The difference between an object's mode of being and a person's is revealed in the act of speech. (The question discussed among Analytical philosophers about

[17] Peter Hare, "On Defining Existentialism," *Buffalo Studies,* Vol. IV, No. 4, December 1969, p. 14.

which predicates refer to persons and which ones refer to objects is an aspect of this issue.)

This common world, however, is not revealed all at once in an eternal now. Just as the question of the meaning of existence occurs within the space of the world, so too does it occur within the time of the world. Time, whose meaning is revealed in the relationship of past, present, and future, is the context within which every aspect of existence shows up. In the myth, Chronos devours his children; so, too, time is the context where every facet of existence ends or fails. Knowing and understanding take time, but there is also failure in knowing and understanding. Willing and loving take time but there is also failure in willing and loving. Taking and holding power take time, but there is also failure in taking and holding power.

Dissatisfied with the descriptions and predictions of science on one hand and the creative activity of the arts on the other, the philosophic quest for the meaning of existence is thwarted in its effort to achieve its goal, namely a statement about the whole of existence. But making a true and valid statement about the whole requires that there be a disinterested spectator of that whole. Obviously, however, a statement that does not include that statement itself is not a statement about the whole. Likewise the attempts to find satisfactory meta-statements or meta-systems lead to infinite regress, i.e., to endless circularity.

The stance of the detached objective observer is essential to scientific inquiry. How else can reports about states of affairs be presented as true? But philosophic inquiry in the effort to make a true statement about the whole is such that the inquirer is lodged in that whole about which he labors to know and utter the truth. And without a true statement about the whole, there can be no *necessarily* true statements about particulars. In whatever field they are made, whether they be in the sciences, in history, or in ordinary everyday discourse, they are contingent in the absence of a true statement about the whole. Things, events, persons, and relations among them present themselves as possibilities, not as necessities. When they occur, necessities are relative to a given field or to a given system of discourse. Mathematical necessities are the classical example. The axioms, definitions, and postulates of mathematical discourse with respect to the whole of existence are contingent, unless, of course, the whole itself is said to be essentially mathematical. Then, of course, the truth of that statement about the whole is in question. The history of philosophy, however, is strewn with just these kinds of statements whose disparate character illustrates in a radical way the finitude of man.

This does not mean that philosophy leads to relativism, to skepticism, or to eclecticism. Rather, discussion with other standpoints in the history of philosophy leads to the source of philosophy in the act of distinguishing between the statements about the whole of existence.

Here again the philosophical question is the paradigm for the question of the meaning of existence in general. The multiple and brittle answers to the question in the history of philosophy are possibilities of choice for the inquirer. His commitment to and responsibility for his chosen response are the conditions that correlate with the condition of those responses as possibilities of choice. It is these conditions that define the freedom of the inquiry and of the inquirer.

Similarly if things, events, persons, and the relations among them are possibilities, it is a correlate of their being possibilities that they be free. In the human mode of being this freedom consists first of all in the possibility to be and not to be and, secondly, as the character of the choices made in the moral, political, scientific, and artistic domains. The choices are free in the sense that they are not infallibly predictable from the conditions in which they are made, not in their being absolutely unconditioned. They are free in their being possibilities of choice, not in their actually being chosen, because it is the character of possibility that involves alternatives. It is the presence of alternatives and consequently the absence of compulsion that guarantee the freedom to the choice.

Finally, since discourse by questioning the meaning of existence entails a world, then a revolt against a major presupposition of modern philosophy has taken place. And since that world is discovered to be *primarily* a structure of possibilities rather than *primarily* a structure of actualities, then a revolt against a presupposition of the whole tradition of philosophy begun by the Greeks and continued by the medievals has also taken place. The term "revolt," however, is too strong. The better metaphor to employ with respect to the differences among philosophers is that of "a lover's quarrel" (as Heidegger puts it) rather than that of a political divorce.

Descartes, in the attempt to place philosophy and science on a firm foundation, as he puts it, found that he could doubt all his ordinary beliefs about the things of the world except that he was doubting them. The result, of course, is the famous *cogito ergo sum*. Since he could not doubt that he was doubting, he must exist. It is thought reflecting on itself that yields certainty and nothing else. Consequently human thought is severed from the world. Knowledge has "ideas" or concepts as its immediate object—the point of departure for subsequent theories of knowledge. The results are grave. If knowledge has as its immediate object only ideas, how could there be knowledge of anything other than ideas? Or how can there be certainty that an object or reality corresponds to the idea, thereby testing or confirming its truth? Descartes himself says in the *Meditations on First Philosophy* that there is nothing easier for him to understand than his own mind. In his investigation of a piece of wax, the example he employs to explicate his theory of knowledge, he concludes that all the reasons which helped him to know and conceive the nature of the wax, or of any body whatsoever, served much better to show the nature of his mind. He also concludes later in the *Meditations* that among all the ideas which exist in him, besides that which represents himself to himself concerning which there can be no difficulty (doubt), there is another which represents a God, others corporeal and inanimate things, others angels, animals, and still other ideas which represent men similar to himself. Descartes's quest for certitude led him to separate man from the world, thought from objects, minds from bodies, with the result that the divergent paths of skepticism and solipsism have opened up before him.

In *modern* Western philosophy, two major traditions are Rationalism and Empiricism. Historians of philosophy usually place Descartes at the head of the Rationalist tradition and regard Empiricism as its contrast. Although this contrast is correct, there is a level at which their similarities are more important. Take

Hume, for example, as representative of the Empiricist tradition. He argues that the immediate objects of knowledge are sense impressions (currently called sense-data), and divides all the objects of human reason into two radically different kinds, namely "relations of ideas," to which necessary truth belongs, and "matters of fact," to which probability belongs.

As with Descartes, so for Hume; it is not things and persons that are known directly but sense-impressions somehow arising or caused by objects that are known. The dualism of thought and nature (or mind and body; or man and world) in Descartes has its counterpart in the dualism between thought and states of affairs in Hume. Skepticism and solipsism are again in the offing.

A descendant of these modern traditions has expressed the consequences of their arguments in such a clear manner that a glance at what he says would make it obvious what it is that Existentialism is in revolt against. Bertrand Russell in his book *The Problems of Philosophy* states: "Thus when we are trying to show that there must be objects independent of our own sense-data we cannot appeal to the testimony of other people, since this testimony itself consists of sense-data, and does not reveal other people's experiences unless our own sense-data are signs of things existing independently of us. We must, therefore, if possible, find, in our own *purely private experiences*,[18] characteristics which show, or tend to show, that there are in the things other than ourselves and our private experiences. In one sense it must be admitted that we can never *prove* the existence of things other than ourselves and our experiences. No logical absurdity results from the hypothesis that the world consists of myself and my thoughts and feelings and sensations, and that everything else is mere fancy."[19]

The question of the meaning of existence, it has been pointed out, reveals, in and through discourse, a world that is structured as the place and time of existence. Kant thought it a scandal that no one had proved the existence of the external world. The Existentialists think it a scandal that anyone should

18 Editor's italics.
19 Bertrand Russell, *The Problems of Philosophy*. London: Oxford University Press, 1912, pp. 21–22.

have to or want to. If the hypothesis that the world consists of myself and my thoughts and feelings and sensations and that everything else is mere fancy is correct, to whom could I prove the existence of the external world? Doubting and proving imply a world wherein such activities take place. The pathetic aspect of the use of the phrase "external world" in modern philosophy is that the adjective "external" is regarded literally. There is not the slightest hint that it is being used either loosely or metaphorically.

The last sentence from Russell's passage is particularly worthy of attention. The Existentialists would object to the claim that no logical absurdity results from such a hypothesis. If logic is the correct and public form of discourse (and not mere consistency since it is possible to be consistently wrong), then the hypothesis that the *world* consists of myself and my thoughts, feelings, and sensations, and that *everything else* is mere fancy *is* logically absurd. If the hypothesis is true, then the words "world" and "everything else" are either not permitted or they are meaningless. Even the term "myself" would be meaningless, for its meaning depends in part upon its contrast with the terms "yourself," "himself," "ourselves," "themselves." The questions of and about the meaning of existence disclose a world of persons and things and relations between them that is prior to the doubts about it either in part or as a whole.

Existentialism's "revolt" against ancient and medieval philosophy is more difficult to understand than that against modern philosophy. The reason is that against modern philosophy Existentialism seems to have common sense or ordinary experience on its side, but against ancient and medieval philosophy the converse seems to be true. Apart from the question of Existentialism stressing the importance of the particular or the individual in contrast to their apparent neglect from Plato on (Kierkegaard as an antecedent of Existentialism made much of this, influenced as he was by his Christian belief in the Incarnation which asserts that God became man—the particular made important by the universal), there is the insistence that the possible is logically and ontologically prior to the actual.

The classical locus for the traditional and apparently common-sensical argument that actuality is logically, ontologically, and even temporally prior to possibility is the eighth chapter of Book Theta (Nine) of Aristotle's *Metaphysics*. The argument was repeated in the scholastic axiom, *actus melius ac prius est quam potentia*. (Act is better than and prior to potency.) Aristotle's argument and his examples are persuasive enough. He says that what is possible in the primary sense is so because it can become actual. What has the capacity to build means what can *build*; what has the capacity to see means what can *see*, etc. Reason or knowledge of the actual must occur before there is knowledge of the possible.

Aristotle also argues that the actual is temporally prior also, in the sense that an actual being precedes another being of the same kind that is merely possible. Whenever something possible becomes actual it always does so by means of some actual being. Aristotle goes on to say that it is held to be impossible for one who has never built anything to be a builder, or for one who has never played the harp to be a harpist. Gilbert Ryle, good Aristotelian that he is, remarks in his chapter on dispositions in *The Concept of Mind* that the statement "He is smoking a cigarette now" differs from the statement "He is a cigarette smoker." Ryle's agreement with the Aristotelian tradition on the priority of the actual over the possible is disclosed by his conclusion that "unless statements like the first were sometimes true, statements like the second could not be true."[20] Ryle's position here, although argued in the manner of contemporary analytic philosophy, is fundamentally that of Aristotle's. Mentioning Ryle in this context is intended to point out the strength of the tradition as it appears in the work of an important contemporary philosopher.

Aristotle says, furthermore, that actuality is prior to possibility in being. A reason is that what comes later in genesis is prior in form and being. The adult is prior to the child; the oak prior to the acorn. Everything that is produced proceeds according to its end or purpose. Actuality is the end or purpose of beings, and it is in virtue of the purpose that powers or possibilities are possessed. Thus animals do not see in order that

20 Gilbert Ryle, *The Concept of Mind*. London: Hutchinson University Press, 1949, p. 117.

they may have the possibility of sight; they have the possibility of sight in order that they may in fact see. Likewise men have the capacity of knowing in order that they may in fact know. The presence of the actual is the justification of the possible.

The results of asserting the priority of the actual over the possible is, with respect to time, to assert the priority of the present over the past and the future. Pushed to the extreme, this view amounts to both the destruction of the concept of possibility and the destruction of the concept of time. The possible ends up as a kind of preformation of the actual, a mere abstraction. But the consequences for the actual are equally disastrous. For actual things come into existence and cease to exist regardless of the type of existent they may be. Their coming into existence and their ceasing to exist are not explained by the purely positive and present character of the mode of actuality which does not account for the negative or for the temporal aspects of existence. The mode of existence that does account for them is, according to the Existentialists, the mode of possibility. For the possible includes by definition the positive and negative features of existence. Consequently the positive and actual features are not absolute or necessary; nor are negations or failures to exist actual things themselves. If it is that existence includes contrary features, then it is that modality of existence which includes contrariness in itself that is the primary mode of existence. That mode is possibility. As Aristotle himself says in Book Gamma (IV), Chapter 5: "It is possible for the same thing to be potentially contraries, but not actually." If it is so that existence includes active and passive features, then it must be the mode of existence that includes in itself both the power to act and to be acted upon that is the primary mode of existence. That mode is possibility. Plato apparently reached this conclusion in the *Sophist* where he claims that the mark of existence is "the possibility of acting or being acted upon."

It is the foregoing set of characteristics that defines Existentialism.

4. *The Selections*

The pieces selected for this anthology are in one way or other the references, the extensions, the denotations of the Existentialist tradition, while the above "definition" is its sense, its intention, its connotation. An attempt has been made to have as many self-contained pieces as possible. Some of them, however, belong to larger works. Where this is the case, the selection is a unit that can be read by itself as, for example, the "Interlude" from Kierkegaard's *Philosophical Fragments;* the sections from Nietzsche's *Will to Power;* "An Outline of a Concrete Philosophy" from Marcel's *Creative Fidelity;* the "Preface" to the English edition of Husserl's *Ideas;* "Interrogation and Intuition" from Merleau-Ponty's *The Visible and Invisible;* and "The Myth of Sisyphus" from Camus's *Myth of Sisyphus.*

There is *some* order to the selections. The first part of the book is devoted to those philosophers who are commonly regarded either as antecedents of Existentialism or as having profoundly influenced it. Kierkegaard, Nietzsche, Dilthey, Husserl, and Scheler fall into this class. Of this earlier group of Existentialists, there are those whose arguments arise from philosophic considerations alone, as is the case with Jaspers, Heidegger, Ortega y Gasset, and Abbagnano; and there are those whose arguments are conditioned by religious considerations, as is the case with Buber, Berdyaev, and Marcel. Two of the three remaining thinkers who make up the later group, though not much later, are largely responsible for the popularity of Existentialism outside of purely philosophical circles and even academic circles. Sartre and Camus, more than any other figures in the book, are associated with Existential philosophy in the popular mind. Merleau-Ponty, a less popular and less dramatic though an equally legitimate practitioner of the Existentialist trade, is the remaining thinker included in the anthology. His essay provides a kind of recapitulation of the themes that constitute this manner of philosophizing.

Finally, without predigesting them, the selections themselves could bear some comments to show how they are related to each other or how they satisfy the theme of the book as argued in the previous section.

The first selection from Kierkegaard is the "Interlude" from the *Philosophical Fragments*. It is an argument for the free, possible, and historical nature of existing things. Kierkegaard draws important distinctions between the terms "possible," "actual," and "necessary"; he challenges Aristotle's view that "the necessary is possible" and Hegel's understanding of what it means to come into existence. An implication of the argument is that the primary mode of existing things is their possibility rather than their actuality; for while they exist it is possible for them not to exist. Past events, too, remain tied to the mode of possibility by virtue both of their coming into existence and the fact that there is no contradiction in saying that they need not have occurred.

The two selections from *The Concept of Dread* probe into a pair of concepts associated with the view that the structure of existence is a structure of possibilities, namely, the concepts of temporality and of dread. Kierkegaard places stress on the future, thereby regarding time as the measure of the possibilities that constitute existence. Dread, therefore, is also a structural concept; it does not refer to a particular fear of this or that thing or event, but to the emotive grasp of the meaning of existence as a whole.

Nietzsche, in a brilliantly seductive argument, portrays the radical finitude of man. He is the being, according to the essay *Truth and Falsity in the Ultramoral Sense,* who dissimulates and fabricates. Logic, science, religion, and history are the instruments with which man keeps the horror of existence at bay. The selections from *The Will to Power*—on the principle of non-contradiction (the principle of meaningful discourse), on the principle of causality (the principle of scientific explanation), and on the "thing-in-itself" (the object and objective of knowledge)—illustrate a later modification of Nietzsche's argument. The shift is from dissimulating to dominating. Logic, science, religion, and history are no longer just sub-sets of art; they are sub-sets of power. In Nietzsche's thought the cleavage between man and nature, so optimistically carried out in modern philosophy for the purpose of establishing the foundations of science, has reached its hollow depths.

The clever reader will pick up Nietzsche's ambiguity when he argues that existence is irrational and horrible and also that truth is a fiction. To put it in philosopher's terms, he both employs the correspondence theory of truth and then discards it in favor of the pragmatic theory of truth. It is hoped that the same reader will not miss the disclosure of that ambiguity, and even inconsistency, as a mark of final statements of the meaning of existence.

Dilthey's place within the Existentialist tradition can readily be grasped from the way he argues for the basic historicity of the human world whose fundamental units are individuals as "living psychophysical unities." The aim of what Dilthey calls the sciences of the spirit, in contrast to the natural sciences, is to discover what is singular and particular (rather than universal or general) in the historical human world and to describe how social convergences operate in the formation of individuals. The characteristic that distinguishes human reality from other entities is a lived-through historical consciousness which Dilthey calls *Erlebnis*. It is Dilthey's conception of man as a historical being that is the thread that runs through the fabric of the Existentialist tradition. Furthermore his concept of *Erlebnis* plays an influential role in Ortega y Gasset's claim that "the basic reality is our life." Heidegger, however, while prepared to use what is positive in Dilthey's analyses, such as the historicity of human being, finds him too uncritically committed to Descartes's point of departure—a point of departure which is possible, according to Heidegger, if and only if the world discloses itself.

For Dilthey, the historicity of the human world invests philosophy itself as a particular form of living through the world. In *The Essence of Philosophy* he argues that art, religion, science, and philosophy are all ways of expressing the "lived experience" of the world. But this "lived experience" is not only a cognitive matter; it also involves values, passions, and purpose. Philosophy differs from the other ways of experiencing the world in virtue of its claim of universal validity—a claim that conflicts with historical consciousness attesting to the historical conditioning of all philosophical doctrines. When the claim of universal validity is made, it takes the name of metaphysics. Dilthey attempts to resolve the conflict between historical consciousness and metaphysics and to avoid the relativistic implications of his argument by appealing to the sovereignty of the mind over against the various world-views or metaphysical schemes, i.e., to "the positive consciousness of how in the various attitudes of the mind the one reality of the world exists for us." It should come as no surprise, however, that this attempt has been branded a failure by Heidegger, who in other respects has benefited by Dilthey's analyses.

The selection chosen to illustrate Edmund Husserl's relationship to the Existentialist tradition contains within it discussions of points of convergence with and divergence from that tradition. The ways in which Husserl's Phenomenology figures in the Existentialist scheme is by means of the concepts of "intentionality" and "transcendence." For Husserl the nature of consciousness lies in its intentionality; i.e., consciousness is always consciousness *of* or *about* something. The acts of consciousness or the ways in which objects are given in consciousness are its "intentions." In simpler language, the intentions of consciousness are its objects as *meant*. The relation between consciousness and its object is such that the object is not a creature of consciousness nor is consciousness merely a member of the world of objects. Essential to the world of objects is transcendence; the relationship between consciousness and its objects (not only at the level of cognition but also at the levels of emotion and volition) is such that the objects themselves are not "within" consciousness but must remain "outside" it so as to present themselves in "flesh and bones."

The concept of "intentionality" is appropriated by the Existentialists in the following way. In the question of the meaning of existence, discourse has a referring character; it entails a world wherein questions arise. And the concept of "transcendence" stands for the relationship between man and the world insofar as the world is the structure of possibilities constituting his existence.

Husserl placed ever greater emphasis on the primacy of consciousness by affirming the ontological supremacy of the "transcendental ego" while in the Existentialist tradition the term consciousness is studiously avoided (by Heidegger) or regarded as pure negation (by Sartre) or translated as *the* mode of being in the world (by Merleau-Ponty). In this selection, Husserl is critical of those who have minimized the importance of the Phenomenological reduction (i.e., the leaving in abeyance of the question of the existence or non-existence of an object so as to discover its essence as a datum constituted in consciousness). Husserl regards this minimizing as both a betrayal of Phenomenology as an attempt to organize philosophy into a strict science and as a retrogression of philosophy toward anthropologism and psychologism. He is referring especially to Heidegger and Scheler.

It is precisely on the question of the nature of philosophy that the divergence between Phenomenology and Existentialism is most sharply articulated. Existentialism forswears as an objective the turning of philosophy into a strict science or into the science of the foundations of science, whereas this objective is constitutive of Husserl's Phenomenology. It also forswears the point of view of the disinterested spectator—because the question of the meaning of existence would render that point of view simply impossible—whereas that point of view, according to Husserl, is the *only* way of avoiding philosophical naiveté and the anthropomorphizing and psychologizing of the data of consciousness.

Scheler's influence in the Existentialist tradition moves in two directions. In the first place his Phenomenological investigation of man's emotive experience provides an example for some of the analyses in Heidegger, Ortega y Gasset, Sartre, and Merleau-Ponty. But even more important is the theme he sets for philosophy as the inquiry into the meaning of man—the theme played by Jaspers, Abbagnano, Ortega y Gasset, Sartre, Merleau-Ponty, and Camus; entertained by Heidegger only to get at the meaning of Being itself and subsumed by Buber,

Marcel, and Berdyaev under the wider investigation into the meaning of God.

Scheler clearly intones the theme in the selection included here with the words: "Man is the only locus in which and through which original being grasps and recognizes itself, but man is also the being in whose free decision God can *realize* and sanctify his pure essence." Need Scheler point out that "modern metaphysics is no longer cosmology and metaphysics of concrete objects but metanthropology and metaphysics of action"?

Jaspers's *Philosophy* contains some of his most important formulations. The excerpt anthologized here touches upon nearly all the features affirmed in this Introduction as essential to Existentialism: philosophy as the inquiry into the meaning of existence; existence as possibility, as freedom, as historical, and as being in situation.

Philosophical questions, argues Jaspers, situate man in the world. That situation establishes him in the quest for being but what he encounters is this or that being, i.e., particular beings. Being as a whole is always beyond the quest. It encompasses every particular being, every mode of being, and every attempt to grasp it as a whole. Being comprehends and encompasses but is never comprehended or encompassed.

Since Jaspers employs the concept of "transcendence," it is necessary to point out that it differs from the way Husserl, Heidegger, Abbagnano, and Merleau-Ponty use it. Transcendence, for Jaspers, refers to the whole of being as absolutely beyond the reach of *existenz* (human existence) but without which human existence cannot be understood.

Heidegger is both the pivotal figure of this anthology and of the tradition from which the anthology gets its name. The first selection chosen to illustrate Heidegger's place in the tradition does not even come from Heidegger's hand. It is a stenographic report of a "workshop" on Kant by Heidegger and Ernst Cassirer held at Davos in Switzerland in March of 1929. Although doubts about the reliability of that report may immediately arise, it must be said that the statements made by the two philosophers in the report are perfectly consistent with their published writings.

There are three levels to their discussion. The first is about Heidegger's thesis that Kant's *Critique of Pure Reason* is primarily an ontology, i.e., an analysis of the structure of existence and is only secondarily an epistemology, i.e., an analysis of the structure of knowledge so as to establish the foundations of natural science. Cassirer supports the conventional view that *The Critique* is primarily an affair of the possibility of knowledge. In the discussion, Heidegger makes the important remark that the best argument for the finitude of man is the infinity of his understanding of Being. "Ontology is an index of finitude. God does not have it."

The second level of the discussion is concerned with Heidegger's statements about his major work, *Being and Time*. He says that the problem of *Being and Time* is that "if the possibility of the understanding of 'that-which-is' is based on an understanding of Being, and if this ontological understanding is in some sense in terms of time, then the task is to expose the temporality of *Dasein* [being-in-the-world] in terms of the possibility of the understanding of Being."

The third level of the discussion reveals subtle differences between Heidegger and Cassirer on the nature of philosophy itself. Heidegger argues that it is in philosophy that the finitude of man discloses itself in the most radical way.

It is the *Letter on Humanism* that was chosen as the example of Heidegger's published work. The piece exemplifies in various ways Heidegger's position within the Existentialist tradition. It is, at one level, an excellent companion piece to Sartre's *Existentialism Is a Humanism* insofar as it is an explicit challenge to Sartre's positions. At another level it is an analysis of the relations between thought, language, and Being which rest on Being as "the quiet power of the possible." Heidegger reviews, moreover, the themes of *Being and Time* and makes some interesting remarks about the relation of that work to a part of it that he suppressed, i.e., the part called "Time and Being." The remarks are interesting insofar as they refer to "reversal" in his thought, which, according to Heidegger, deals with "the dimension from which *Being and Time* is experienced; and, indeed, experienced from the basic experience of Being. But the main thrust of the essay, as the title indicates, is the question of humanism, which Heidegger regards as an expression of the perversion indulged in by the whole of Western philosophy from Plato to Nietzsche, namely the anthropomorphizing of Being.

It would have been needless for Heidegger to insist, in the course of the *Letter,* that although he argues against "humanism," he does not defend the inhuman or glorify barbaric cruelty, had there not been a thoroughgoing vilification of both his person and his philosophy.

The curiously interesting slogan that "man does not have a nature, but a history" was formulated by Ortega y Gasset who drank deeply from Dilthey's cup. The meaning of the slogan is elucidated in the characteristics that have been suggested as definitive of the Existentialist tradition in general, namely, the temporal and historical conditions of man rather than some eternal property; human existence as structured by possibilities rather than a single essential feature, the finitude of man as disclosed in the question of the meaning of existence. In the chapter taken from *What Is Philosophy* and included here, Ortega y Gasset wishes to conserve part of the modern tradition by saying that the first problem of philosophy consists in finding which reality is "the most sure, the one beyond any trace of doubt." He breaks with that tradition by arguing that the fundamental datum is not the conscious self, the subject, but *life, "our life,"* which includes "both the subject and the world."

According to Ortega y Gasset, the Aristotelian categories belong to being in general, but "our life" is different. He goes on to enumerate and analyze its categories in the course of the essay. The structure of "our life" defined by those categories discloses its finitude—a finitude to be stressed with irony as the fairy queen Titania, "in Shakespeare's enchanted forest, caressed the head of a donkey."

The thought of Abbagnano lies within the Existentialist tradition insofar as it attempts to establish a critical hold on that tradition. Existentialism is born, says Abbagnano, from the recognition of the very problematic nature of philosophy itself, that is to say, that the meta-philosophical question is whether the form, features, and defense of philosophy should fall outside of philosophy or whether they should be the "heart and soul" of philosophy itself.

The essay *Existentialism Is a Positive Philosophy* ties the problematic character of philosophy to the problematic and finite character of existence itself such that the stance of the disinterested spectator is inconsistent with philosophical inquiry. Philosophy, claims Abbagnano, is not contemplation.

Consequently the categorial perspective within which Existentialism moves is what Abbagnano calls the category of possibility. It is this category and the way that it is related to existence, transcendence, time, history, and freedom that is the analytic tool and concern of a rigorous Existentialism. It is the consistent use of this category that differentiates the positive from the negative expressions of Existential philosophy. Hence it is the standard by which Abbagnano measures those other expressions.

Religious considerations enter the picture with the work of Buber, Marcel, and Berdyaev. In the case of Buber, the selection chosen to indicate his place within the Existentialist tradition is "Dialogue" from *Between Man and Man*. The argument of the work places it in opposition to a basic trend in modern philosophy. Buber's argument is that the primary mode of discourse is not self-consciousness, or the soul talking to itself, but dialogue between persons which is expressed in the formula "I-thou." The plurality of persons is preserved in the unity of dialogue, and conversely dialogue is impossible without a plurality of persons. Dialogue is the place where persons get a toehold in existence.

The paradigm of the I-thou relationship for Buber, of course, is derived from the central event of Jewish history, namely the contract made on Mount Sinai between the Lord and Israel—the event at which Israel becomes possible and the Lord becomes its God.

For Marcel, a Catholic, the central event of history is the Incarnation, that is to say, the Word of God becoming flesh in

Jesus Christ. But as is the case with Buber, philosophical reflection, although influenced by religious considerations, is not theology. "An Outline of a Concrete Philosophy," the third chapter of *Creative Fidelity*, was selected for this anthology not only because it contains a discussion of the two most important themes in Marcel's thought (namely, the distinction between problem and mystery, and incarnation as the mode of being in the world), but also because it argues for the relationship between these themes and the nature of philosophy.

If it were not for this discussion of the nature of philosophy, Marcel's reflections could be construed as a kind of personalism oozing outrage over contemporary man's depersonalization, like the moralizing popular sociology found in the pages of the New York *Times Magazine*. The discussion contains an attack upon the starting point of modern philosophy—Descartes's *cogito* —suggesting that its seductiveness lies in its *apparent* transparency. The starting point that Marcel claims is logically and ontologically prior to the *cogito* is "incarnation," the situation of a being which appears to itself as tied to a body. In the strict sense, he says, "incarnation" is not a fact but the ground "with respect to which a fact becomes possible."

Marcel's philosophical point of departure, "incarnation," pulsates in Merleau-Ponty's "body-subject" as the ground for the primacy of perception.

In the Russian Orthodox thinker, Berdyaev, one finds a rebellious clamor against the traditional metaphysics of being. Like Heidegger, Berdyaev claims that the ancient and medieval metaphysics of "being" are a kind of philosophical physics, i.e., an objectified and naturalistic account of actual and presently determined beings—an account which obliterates the "contradictory, suffering, and flamingly tragic character" of existence. Bombast aside, Berdyaev is arguing the Existential theme of the priority of possibility and its correlates, freedom and temporality, over actuality and its correlates, necessity and the timeless. He maintains that deeper than "being" lies the *Ungrund*, a concept he explicitly borrows from Boehme, a late sixteenth-early seventeenth-century German mystic, which signifies "the bottomless abyss, irrational mystery and primordial freedom." At this point Berdyaev's comments are a reweaving of the Nietzschean threads running through Existentialism's tradition. Nietzsche called Dionysian those primordial sources of being which are irrational and voluntaristic and which Apollonian rationality and intelligence hold at bay.

For Berdyaev, the ordering principle of the irrational and voluntaristic sources of being is Logos, i.e., meaning, as a historical event. Meaning and direction are *conferred* (not discovered) by the entrance of God historically into the existence of the world. It is the belief that meaning in and of the world is conferred historically that leads Berdyaev to conclude that history is the only possible way out of the objectification of traditional metaphysics. If the meaning of existence is conferred historically, then metaphysics, says Berdyaev, is located at its proper level as *eschatology*.

Through the life and writing of Jean-Paul Sartre, the Existentialist tradition achieved a kind of popularity and even a touch of notoriety. Although it must be frankly acknowledged that *Existentialism Is a Humanism* is not his best piece from a purely philosophical standpoint, it is the best selection for the purposes of this anthology. On the one hand it is the corresponding piece to Heidegger's *Letter on Humanism,* and on the other it has the virtue of intelligibility, which is sometimes compromised in Sartre's other philosophical writings. Furthermore, it is an integral piece, while *Being and Nothingness,* his complete statement within the tradition, would have to have been excerpted. Still further, Sartre attempted in the essay to give a more positive cast to the themes of *Being and Nothingness,* albeit a somewhat more popularized and fetching cast. Lastly, after the publication of the essay, he moved away from those themes toward a Marxist subsumption of them in his *Critique de la raison dialectique.*

It is in this essay that Sartre intones the slogan "existence precedes essence" and then attempts to clarify its meaning. He says that if God does not exist, then there is at least one being that exists before his nature is determined—man. The concept of "God" is self-contradictory for Sartre, insofar as it implies absolute being and absolute consciousness. If consciousness is other than its object, then absolute consciousness would be negation pure and simple (nothingness). Thus the combined concept of absolute being and absolute consciousness is self-canceling. Man is, therefore, what he *wills* himself to be. His existence is characterized by freedom. Since man's acts constitute his existence, his nature or essence is the set of his acts and the freedom of those acts entails his responsibility for them. Sartre then produces arguments against various kinds of determinism—compulsion by instinct, compulsion by society, compulsion by physiology.

There are, moreover, no *a priori*, i.e., intrinsic, values according to Sartre because there is no infinite and perfect consciousness, i.e., no God to think of them. Values are such simply because they are chosen. It is choosing that confers value upon actions. Sartre adds that it is impossible to choose the worse and that the choices are a commitment for others as well, insofar as they are the chooser's *will* for everyone.

The doubtful consistency of Sartre's concepts of freedom and choice is not what is important about his analysis. It is the assumption that what would constitute an intrinsic value is that there be an infinite and perfect consciousness to conceive of it. This is the parallel, in the moral order, of his assumption, in the ontological order, that what constitutes an objective essence or nature is that there be a God to conceive of it. What makes these assumptions important as far as the Existentialist tradition is concerned is that it indicates in Sartre's case his failure to tear loose from the basic assertion of modern philosophy, Descartes's "I think, therefore I am." As a matter of fact Sartre is not interested in tearing loose from it inasmuch as he explicitly affirms it as his own point of departure and even tries to salvage it from its skeptical and solipsistic consequences. And the way he does so is by trying to marry the "cogito" to Heidegger's *Dasein* (being-in-the-world), a marriage whose chances of even taking place are doubtful, not to speak of the chances of its working out.

Sartre disavows the mawkish humanism of "*homo* the magnificent"—suggested in the Renaissance, developed by the Enlightenment, and worshiped in nineteenth-century Positivism. Instead he affirms a humanism whose meaning is that man is able to exist by pursuing transcendent aims. The relation of transcendence and subjectivity as constitutive of man is the Sartrian sense of humanism.

For Merleau-Ponty, modern philosophy began with the quest for certitude only to end with the discovery of ambiguity. The selection anthologized here is part of the work that Merleau-Ponty was writing at the time of his death. It was an editor who saw it through to publication, not the author himself.

In the essay "Interrogation and Intuition" from *The Visible and the Invisible,* Merleau-Ponty opens with the meta-philosophical issue of what kind of questions philosophical questions turn out to be. In their attempt to be radical questions, that is, to reach the root of questioning itself, they not only cannot cut the umbilical cord that binds them to their matrix—"Being" —but must grasp it in order even to reach that matrix. Consequently Merleau-Ponty avails himself of the concept of "flesh" in order to understand the coincidence of man's body with the world. With echoes of Marcel and Heidegger ringing through his analysis, he argues that the mode of human being in the world is perception, that the condition of perception is incarnation, and that the structure of incarnation is spatial and temporal. Perception, however, is not brute sensation but sensation threaded by discourse. Language, says Merleau-Ponty, is not "a mask over Being" but the witness of existence inasmuch as perceptions and thoughts are structured in and through discourse.

Philosophy, argues Merleau-Ponty, is language; it is language that *cares* about language—language that can be known only through its exercise, as it articulates, fails to articulate, or even simply keeps its peace before the structure of Being.

It should not seem mischievous or perverse to bring this book of philosophical readings to a close with a myth. There is sound precedent for doing so if the example of a certain well-known writer of dialogues is allowed. The myth selected for this anthology, therefore, is Camus's "Myth of Sisyphus." If this myth is taken with a very strict reservation, it can serve both as the myth of human existence for which Camus intended it *and* as a myth of philosophy itself. No reason is given in the myth for Sisyphus persisting in his futile effort. His attitude is simply one of willful obstinacy—a courage in the face of the absurd. The reservation might be put in the form of questions. Can Sisyphus' obstinacy be regarded as courage if it is completely pointless? Or if courage in the face of the absurd is the only point in a pointless world—then is it a pointless world?

Classical philosophy was always concerned to discover the necessities of existence; the "philosophy of the absurd" makes philosophy and meaningful existence quite *impossible*. In this Introduction an effort has been made to present Existentialism as a genuine tradition within the history of philosophy, a tradition whose question about the meaning of existence discloses the possibility of existence—not its necessity or impossibility.

Søren Kierkegaard (1813–1855)

Søren Kierkegaard was born in Copenhagen on May 5, 1813. He was the youngest child of an elderly father who, though he had come to the city in poverty, succeeded in achieving substantial financial security as a merchant. The father, a man of intelligence, austerity, passion, and piety, constituted a major personal influence on Kierkegaard's life by giving him a strict religious formation. Kierkegaard entered in his *Journal* the following comment about his father: "the terrible thing about the man who once, when he was a little boy tending his sheep on the Jutland heath, suffering greatly, hungry and in want, stood up on a hill and cursed God—and this man could not forget this even when he was eighty-two years old."

When he entered the University of Copenhagen in 1830, Kierkegaard tried to enroll in the Royal Life Guards but was rejected because of physical unfitness. During the years spent at the university, he claims to have led a disorderly life in revolt, apparently, against his father and against God. There was, however, both a reconciliation with his father and a religious reconciliation which he refers to in his *Journal* as an "indescribable joy." His father died shortly thereafter, leaving him a substantial fortune.

In 1837 Kierkegaard met Regine Olsen, a girl of fourteen with whom he fell in love. She was another major influence on his life. He did not begin to court her until she was seventeen. After winning her affection, he subsequently questioned the authenticity of the relationship. It seems that he loved her more at a distance than up close. He felt that it would be a betrayal of Regine and a rejection of his destiny to enter into the happy ordinariness of married life. Although he retained a kind of idealized affection for her, he had her break the engagement.

Later, the Philosophical Faculty at the university accepted his thesis on *The Concept of Irony* and awarded him the degree in philosophy in 1841. He left Copenhagen for Berlin in order to avoid the scandal of his broken engagement. While in Berlin he pursued his philosophical studies and completed *Either/Or,* and from that time to his death, writing became an absorbing activity.

In 1846 a series of events led to a scurrilous attack upon Kierkegaard in the pages of the *Corsair,* a satirical weekly owned and edited by Meir Goldschmidt. The highly popular journal claimed to serve the aims of political liberalism by ridiculing the prominent people of Denmark. The caricatures of Kierkegaard in its pages included references to his physical disabilities (he seems to have been a hunchback) such that to the end of his life he had to endure jibes from people in the streets as well as the malicious laughter from those in the drawing rooms.

Kierkegaard devoted the last six years of his life to what he believed was his religious duty to "introduce Christianity into Christendom." His biting criticism of "Christendom" (institutionalized Christianity) was specifically directed against the person of Bishop Mynster, an official of the Lutheran State Church of Denmark and against Protestantism in Denmark.

On October 2, 1855, Kierkegaard collapsed on a Copenhagen street and was taken to Fredericks Hospital, where he died on November 11, 1855.

Interlude from *Philosophical Fragments*

Translated by David Swensen and revised by Howard Hong

> Is the past more necessary than the future? or, When the possible becomes actual, is it thereby made more necessary than it was?

1. Coming into Existence

In what sense is there change in that which comes into existence? Or, what is the nature of the coming-into-existence kind of change (κίνησις)? All other change (ἀλλοίωσις) presupposes the existence of that which changes, even when the change consists in ceasing to exist. But this is not the case with coming into existence. For if the subject of coming into existence does not itself remain unchanged during the change of coming into existence, that which comes into existence is not *this* subject which comes into existence, but something else. Then the question involves a μετάβασις εἰς ἄλλο γένος in that the inquirer in the given case either sees another change copresent with the change of coming into existence, which confuses the question for him, or he mistakes the nature of what is coming into existence and therefore is not in position to ask the question. If a plan in coming into existence [in being fulfilled or carried out] is in itself changed, it is not this plan which comes into existence; but if it comes into existence without being changed, what then is the change of coming into existence? This coming-into-existence kind of change, therefore, is not a change in essence but in being and is a transition from not existing to existing. But this non-being which the subject of coming into existence leaves behind must itself have some sort of being. Otherwise "the subject of coming into existence would not remain unchanged during the change of coming into existence," unless it had not been at all, and then the change of coming into existence would for another reason be absolutely different from every other kind of change, since it would be no change at all, for every change always presupposes something which changes. But such a being, which is nevertheless a non-being, is precisely what possibility is; and a being which is being is indeed actual being or actuality; and the change of coming into existence is a transition from possibility to actuality.

Can the necessary come into existence? Coming into existence is a change, but the necessary cannot be changed, since it always relates itself to itself and relates itself to itself in the same way. All coming into existence is a *suffering*, and the necessary cannot suffer; it cannot undergo the suffering of the actual, which is that the possible (not only the excluded possibility but also the accepted possibility) reveals itself as nothing in the moment it becomes actual, for the possible is made into nothing by the actual. Everything which comes into existence proves precisely by coming into existence that it is not necessary, for the only thing which cannot come into existence is the necessary, because the necessary *is*.

Is not necessity then a synthesis of possibility and actuality? What could this mean? Possibility and actuality do not differ in essence but in being; how could there from this difference be formed a synthesis constituting necessity, which is not a determination of being but a determination of essence, since it is the essence of the necessary to be. If possibility and actuality could be united to become necessity, they would become an absolutely different essence, which is not a kind of change; and in becoming necessity or the necessary, they would become that which alone of all things excludes coming into existence, which is just as impossible as it is self-contradictory. (Compare the Aristotelian principle: "it is possible," "it is possible that not," "it is not possible."—The theory of true and false propositions—Epicurus— tends only to confuse the issue here, since essence and not being is reflected upon, and in this way no help is given with respect to the characterization of the future.)

The necessary is a category entirely by itself. Nothing ever comes into existence with necessity; likewise the necessary never comes into existence and something by coming into existence never becomes the necessary. Nothing whatever exists because it is necessary, but the necessary exists because it is necessary or because the necessary is. The actual is no more necessary than the possible, for the necessary is absolutely different from both. (Compare Aristotle's doctrine of the two kinds of possibility in relationship to the necessary. His mistake lies in his beginning with the principle that everything necessary is possible. In order to avoid having to assert contradictory and even self-contradictory predicates about the necessary, he helps himself out by two kinds of possibility, instead of discovering that his first principle is incorrect, since possibility cannot be predicated of the necessary.)

The change involved in coming into existence is actuality; the transition takes place with freedom. No coming into existence is necessary. It was not necessary before the coming into existence, for then there could not have been the coming into existence, nor after the coming into existence, for then there would not have been the coming into existence.

All coming into existence takes place with freedom, not by necessity. Nothing comes into existence by virtue of a logical ground, but only by a cause. Every cause terminates in a freely effecting cause. The illusion occasioned by the intervening causes is that the coming into existence seems to be necessary; the truth about intervening causes is that just as they themselves have come into existence they point back ultimately to a freely effecting cause. Even the possibility of deducing consequences from a law of nature gives no evidence for the necessity of any coming into existence, which is clear as soon as one reflects definitively on coming into existence. The same is the case with manifestations of freedom, provided we do not let ourselves be deceived by the manifestations of freedom but reflect upon the coming into existence.

2. The Historical

Everything that has come into existence is *eo ipso* historical. For even if it accepts no further historical predicate, it nevertheless accepts the one decisive historical predicate: it has come into existence. That whose coming into existence is a simultaneous coming into existence (*Nebeneinander*, Space) has no other history than this. But even when viewed in this light (*en masse*), and abstracting from what an ingenious speculation calls the history of nature in a special sense, nature has a history.

But the historical is the past (for the present pressing upon the confines of the future has not yet become historical). How then can it be said that nature, though immediately present, is historical, except in the sense of the said ingenious speculation? The difficulty comes from the fact that nature is too abstract to have a dialectic with respect to time in the stricter sense. This is nature's imperfection, that it has no history in any other sense; but it is a perfection in nature that it nevertheless has this suggestion of a history, namely that it has come into existence. (This constitutes its past, the fact that it exists is its present.) On the other hand, it is the perfection of the Eternal to have no history and, of all that is, the Eternal alone has absolutely no history.

However, coming into existence may present a reduplication, i.e., the possibility of a second coming into existence within the first coming into existence. Here we have the historical in the stricter sense, subject to a dialectic with respect to time. The coming into existence which in this sphere is identical with the coming into existence of nature is a possibility, a possibility which for nature is its whole reality. But this historical coming into existence in the stricter sense is a coming into existence within a coming into existence, which should constantly be kept in mind. The more specifically historical coming into existence occurs by the operation of a relatively freely effecting cause, which in turn points ultimately to an absolutely freely effecting cause.

3. The Past

What has happened has happened, and cannot be undone; in this sense it does not admit of change (Chrysippus the Stoic—Diodorus the Megarian). Is this immutability identical with the immutability of the necessary? The immutability of the past has been brought about by a change, namely the change of coming into existence; such an immutability does not exclude all change, since it did not exclude this change. All change is excluded (subjecting the concept to a temporal dialectic) only by being excluded in every moment. If the past is conceived as necessary, this can happen only by virtue of forgetting that it has come into existence; is such forgetfulness perhaps also necessary?

What has happened has happened as it happened; in this sense it does not admit of change. But is this immutability identical with the immutability of the necessary? The immutability of the past consists in the fact that its actual "thus" cannot become different; but does it follow from this that its possible "how" could not have been realized in a different manner? The immutability of the necessary, on the contrary, consists in its constant relating itself to itself, and in its relating itself to itself always in the same manner, excluding every change. It is not content with the immutability that belongs to the past, which as we have shown is not merely subject to a dialectic with respect to a prior change from which it emerges, but must even suffer a dialectic with respect to a higher change which annuls it. (Repentance, for example, which seeks to annul an actuality.)

The future has not yet happened. But it is not *on that account* less necessary than the past, since the past did not become necessary by coming into existence, but on the contrary proved by coming into existence that it was not necessary. If the past had become necessary it would not be possible to infer the opposite about the future, but it would rather follow that the future also was necessary. If necessity could gain a foothold at a single point, there would no longer be any distinguishing between the past and the future. To assume to predict the future (prophesy) and to assume to understand the necessity of the past are one and the same thing, and only custom makes the one seem more plausible than the other to a given generation. The past has come into existence; coming into existence is the change of actuality brought about by freedom. If the past had become necessary it would no longer belong to freedom, i.e., it would no longer belong to that by which it came into existence. Freedom would then be in a sorry case, both an object of laughter and deserving of tears, since it would be responsible for what did not belong to it, being destined to bring offspring into the world for necessity to devour. Freedom itself would be an illusion, and coming into existence no less so; freedom would be witchcraft and coming into existence a false alarm.[1]

[1] A prophesying generation despises the past, and will not listen to the testimony of the scriptures; a generation engaged in under-

4. The Apprehension of the Past

Nature, as the spatial order, has only an immediate existence. But everything that admits of a dialectic with respect to time is characterized by a certain duality, in that after having been present it can persist as past. The essentially historical is always

standing the necessity of the past does not like to be reminded of the future. Both attitudes are consistent, for each would have occasion to discover in the opposite the folly of its own procedure. The Absolute Method, Hegel's discovery, is a difficulty even in Logic, aye a glittering tautology, coming to the assistance of academic superstition with many signs and wonders. In the historical sciences it is a fixed idea. The fact that the method here at once begins to become concrete, since history is the concretion of the Idea, has given Hegel an opportunity to exhibit extraordinary learning, and a rare power of organization, inducing a quite sufficient commotion in the historical material. But it has also promoted a distraction of mind in the reader, so that, perhaps precisely from respect and admiration for China and Persia, the thinkers of the middle ages, the four universal monarchies (a discovery which, as it did not escape Geert Westphaler, has also set many a Hegelian Geert Westphaler's tongue wagging), he may have forgotten to inquire whether it now really did become evident at the end, at the close of this journey of enchantment, as was repeatedly promised in the beginning, and what was of course the principal issue, for the want of which not all the glories of the world could compensate, what alone could be a sufficient reward for the unnatural tension in which one had been held—that the method was valid. Why at once become concrete, why at once begin to experiment *in concreto?* Was it not possible to answer this question in the dispassionate brevity of the language of abstraction, which has no means of distraction or enchantment, this question of what it means that the Idea becomes concrete, what is the nature of coming into existence, what is one's relationship to that which has come into existence, and so forth? Just as it surely might have been cleared up in the Logic what "transition" is and means, before going over to write three volumes describing its workings in the categories, astounding the superstitious, and making so difficult the situation of one who would gladly owe much to the superior mind and express his gratitude for what he owes, but nevertheless cannot over this forget what Hegel himself must have considered the matter of principal importance.

the past (it is over, but whether years since or only a matter of days ago makes no difference), and has as past its own actuality; for the fact that it has happened is certain and dependable. But the fact that it has happened is on the other hand the ground of an uncertainty, by which the apprehension will always be prevented from assimilating the past as if it had been thus from all eternity. Only in terms of this conflict between certainty and uncertainty, the distinguishing mark of all that has come into existence, and hence also of the past, can the past be understood. When the past is understood in any other manner, the apprehension has misunderstood itself in the role of apprehension; and it has misunderstood its object, as if anything such could be the object of an apprehension. Every apprehension of the past which proposes to understand it better by construing it, has only the more thoroughly misunderstood it. (A manifestation theory instead of a construction theory is at first sight deceptive, but the next moment we have the secondary construction and the necessary manifestation.) The past is not necessary, since it came into existence; it did not become necessary by coming into existence (which is a contradiction); still less does it become necessary through someone's apprehension of it. (Distance in time tends to promote an intellectual illusion, just as distance in space provokes a sensory illusion. A contemporary does not perceive the necessity of what comes into existence, but when centuries intervene between the event and the beholder he perceives the necessity, just as distance makes the square tower seem round.) If the past became necessary through being apprehended, the past would be the gainer by as much as the apprehension lost, since the latter would come to apprehend something else, which is a poor sort of apprehension. If the object of apprehension is changed in the process of apprehension, the apprehension is changed into a misapprehension. Knowledge of the present does not confer necessity upon it; foreknowledge of the future gives it no necessity (Boethius); knowledge of the past confers no necessity upon the past; for no knowledge and no apprehension has anything of its own to give.

Whoever apprehends the past, *historico-philosophus*, is therefore a prophet is retrospect (Daub). That he is a prophet expresses the fact that the certainty of the past is based upon an uncertainty, an uncertainty that exists for the past in precisely the same sense that it exists for the future, being rooted in the possibility (Leibniz and the possible worlds) out of which it could not *emerge* with necessity, *nam necessariam se ipso prius sit, necesse est.* The historian thus again confronts the past, moved by the emotion which is the passionate sense for coming into existence: wonder. If the philosopher never finds occasion to wonder (and how could it occur to anyone to wonder at a necessary construction, except by a new kind of contradiction?) he has *eo ipso* nothing to do with the historical; for wherever the process of coming into existence is involved, as is the case in relation to the past, there the uncertainty attaching to the most certain of events (the uncertainty of coming into existence) can find expression only in this passion, which is as necessary to the philosopher as it is worthy of him. (Plato, Aristotle.) Even if the event is certain in the extreme, even if wonder offers its consent in advance, saying that if this had not happened it would have had to be invented (Baader), even then the passion of wonder would fall into contradiction with itself if it falsely imputed necessity, and thereby cheated itself.—As for the Method, both the word itself and the concept sufficiently show that the progress connoted is teleological. But in every such movement there is each instant a pause (where wonder stands *in pausa* and waits upon coming into existence), the pause of coming into existence and of possibility, precisely because the τέλος lies outside. If there is only one way possible, the τέλος is not outside, but in the movement itself, and even behind it, as in the case of an immanent progression.

So much for the apprehension of the past. We have in the meanwhile presupposed that a knowledge of the past is given; how is such knowledge acquired? The historical cannot be given immediately to the senses, since the *elusiveness* of coming into existence is involved in it. The immediate impression of a natural phenomenon or of an event is not the impression of the historical, for the *coming into existence* involved cannot be sensed immediately, but only the immediate presence. But the presence of the historical includes the process of coming into existence, or else it is not the presence of the historical as such.

Immediate sensation and immediate cognition cannot deceive. This is by itself enough to show that the historical cannot be the object of either, because the historical has the elusiveness which is implicit in all coming into existence. As compared with the immediate, coming into existence has an elusiveness by which even the most dependable fact is rendered doubtful. Thus when the observer sees a star, the star becomes involved in doubt the moment he seeks to become aware of its having come into existence. It is as if reflection took the star away from the senses. So much then is clear, that the organ for the historical must have a structure analogous with the historical itself; it must comprise a corresponding somewhat by which it may repeatedly negate in its certainty the uncertainty that corresponds to the uncertainty of coming into existence. The latter uncertainty is two-fold: the nothingness of the antecedent non-being is one side of it, while the annihilation of the possible is another, the latter being at the same time the annihilation of every other possibility. Now faith has precisely the required character; for in the certainty of belief[2] [Danish: *Tro, faith* or *belief*] there is always present a negated uncertainty, in every way corresponding to the uncertainty of coming into existence. Faith believes what it does not see; it does not believe that the star is there, for that it sees, but it believes that the star has come into existence. The same holds true of an event. The "what" of a happening may be known immediately, but by no means can it be known immediately that it has happened. Nor can it be known immediately that it happens, not even if it happens as we say in front of our very noses. The elusiveness pertaining to an event consists in its having happened, in which fact lies the transition from nothing, from non-being, and from the manifold possible "how." Immediate sensation and immediate cognition have no suspicion of the uncertainty with which belief approaches its object, but neither do they suspect the certainty which emerges from this uncertainty.

Immediate sensation and immediate cognition cannot deceive. This is important for the understanding of doubt, and for the

[2] *Tro* is translated here and in the following three pages as *belief* or "faith . . . in a direct and ordinary sense," as distinguished from Faith "in an eminent sense." Trans. note.

assignment to belief of its proper place through a comparison
with doubt. This thought underlies Greek scepticism, strange as
it may seem. Yet it should not be so difficult to understand, nor
to perceive the light that this throws upon the nature of belief,
provided one has escaped being altogether confused by the
Hegelian doctrine of a universal doubt, against which it is certainly not necessary to preach. For what the Hegelians say about
this is of such a character as rather to encourage a modest little
doubt of how far it can be true that they have ever doubted
anything at all. Greek scepticism was of the retiring kind
(ἐποχή). The Greek sceptic did not doubt by virtue of his
knowledge, but by an act of will (refusal to give assent—
μετριοπαθεῖν). From this it follows that doubt can be overcome only by a free act, an act of will, as every Greek sceptic
would understand as soon as he had understood himself. But
he did not wish to overcome his scepticism, precisely because he
willed to doubt. For this he will have to assume the responsibility; but let us not impute to him the stupidity of supposing that
doubt is necessary, or the still greater stupidity of supposing that
if it were, it could ever be overcome. The Greek sceptic did not
deny the validity of sensation or immediate cognition; error, he
says, has an entirely different ground, for it comes from the conclusions that I draw. If I can only refrain from drawing conclusions, I will never be deceived. If my senses, for example,
show me an object that seems round at a distance but square near
at hand, or a stick bent in the water which is straight when taken
out, the senses have not deceived me. But I run the risk of being
deceived when I draw a conclusion about the stick or the object.
Hence the sceptic keeps his mind constantly in suspense, and it
was this frame of mind that he *willed* to maintain. In so far as
Greek scepticism has been called φιλοσοφία ζητητική,
ἀπορητική, σκεπτική, these predicates do not express its distinctive feature, for Greek scepticism had recourse to knowledge
only for the sake of protecting the state of mind which was its
principal concern, and therefore did not even express its negative
cognitive results θετικῶς, for fear of being caught in a conclusion. The state of mind was the sceptic's chief concern.
(τέλος δέ οἱ σκεπτικοί φασι τὴν ἐποχήν, ἦ σκιᾶς τρόπον

ἐπακολουθεῖ ἢ ἀταραξία, Diogenes Laertius, IX, 107.)[3]
—By way of contrast it now becomes easy to see that belief is not a form of knowledge, but a free act, an expression of
will. It believes the fact of coming into existence, and has thus
succeeded in overcoming within itself the uncertainty that corresponds to the nothingness of the antecedent non-being; it believes the "thus" of what has come into existence, and has consequently succeeded in annulling within itself the possible
"how." Without denying the possibility of another "thus," this
present "thus" is for belief most certain.

In so far as that which through its relation to belief becomes
historical and as historical becomes the object of belief (the one
corresponds to the other) has an immediate existence, and is
immediately apprehended, it is not subject to error. A contemporary may then safely use his eyes and so forth, but let him
look to his conclusions. He cannot know, as a matter of immediate cognition, that his fact has come into existence, but neither
can he know it as a matter of necessity; for the very first expression for coming into existence is a breach of continuity. The
moment faith believes that its fact has come into existence, has
happened, it makes the event and the fact doubtful in the process
of becoming, and makes its "thus" also doubtful through its
relation to the possible "how" of the coming into existence. The
conclusion of belief is not so much a conclusion as a resolution,
and it is for this reason that belief excludes doubt. When belief
concludes: this exists, *ergo*, it must have come into existence, it
might appear to be making an inference from effect to cause.
However, this is not quite the case; and even if it were so it must
be remembered that the cognitive inference is from cause to
effect, or rather, from ground to consequent (Jacobi). But it is

---

[3] Both Plato and Aristotle insist on the principle that immediate
sensation and immediate cognition cannot deceive. Later also
Descartes, who says precisely as do the Greek sceptics, that error has
its root in the will, which is over-hasty in drawing conclusions. This
also throws light on faith; when faith resolves to believe it runs the
risk of committing itself to an error, but it nevertheless believes. There
is no other road to faith; if one wishes to escape risk, it is as if one
wanted to know with certainty that he can swim before going into
the water.

not accurate to say that the conclusion of belief is an inference from effect to cause; I cannot sense or know immediately that what I sense or know immediately is an effect, since for the immediate apprehension it merely is. I believe that it is an effect, for in order to bring it under this category I must already have made it doubtful with the uncertainty implicit in coming into existence. When belief resolves to do this, doubt has been overcome; in that very instant the indifference of doubt has been dispelled and its equilibrium overthrown, not by knowledge but by will. Thus it will be seen that belief is the most disputable of things while in process of approximation; for the uncertainty of doubt, strong and invincible in making things ambiguous, *dis-putare*, is brought into subjection within it. But it is the least disputable when once constituted, by virtue of its new quality. Belief is the opposite of doubt. Belief and doubt are not two forms of knowledge, determinable in continuity with one another, for neither of them is a cognitive act; they are opposite passions. Belief is a sense for coming into existence, and doubt is a protest against every conclusion that transcends immediate sensation and immediate cognition. The sceptic does not, for example, deny his own existence; but he draws no conclusion from fear of being deceived. In so far as he has recourse to dialectics in order to make the opposite of any given conclusion seem equally probable, it is not on the foundation of these dialectical arguments that he sets up his scepticism. They are but outworks, human accommodations. He has no result, therefore, not even a negative result; for this would be to recognize the validity of knowledge. By an act of will he resolves to keep himself under restraint, and to refrain from every conclusion (φιλοσοφία ἐφεκτική).

One who is not contemporary with the historical, has, instead of the immediacy of sense and cognition, in which the historical is not contained, the testimony of contemporaries, to which he stands related in the same manner as the contemporaries stand related to the said immediacy. Even if the content of the testimony has undergone in the process of communication the change which makes it historical, the non-contemporary cannot take it up into his consciousness without giving it his assent, thus making it historical for himself, unless he is to transform it into something unhistorical for himself. The immediacy of the testimony, i.e., the fact that the testimony is there, is what is given as immediately present to him; but the historicity of the present consists in its having come into existence, and the historicity of the past consists in its having once been present through having come into existence. Whenever a successor believes the past (not its truth, which is a matter of cognition and concerns not existence but essence), whenever he believes that the past was once present through having come into existence, the uncertainty which is implicit in coming into existence is present in the past that is the object of his belief. This uncertainty (the nothingness of the antecedent non-being—the possible "how" corresponding to the actual "thus") will exist for him as well as for a contemporary; his mind will be in a state of suspense exactly as was the mind of a contemporary. He has no longer a mere immediacy before him; neither does he confront a necessary coming into existence, but only the "thus" of *coming into existence.* A successor believes, to be sure, on account of the testimony of some contemporary; but only in the same sense as a contemporary believes on account of his immediate sensation and immediate cognition. But no contemporary can believe by virtue of this immediacy alone, and neither can any successor believe solely by virtue of the testimony to which he has access.

Thus at no time does the past become necessary, just as it was not necessary when it came into existence nor revealed itself as necessary to the contemporary who believed it, i.e., believed that it had come into existence. For belief and coming into existence correspond to one another, and are concerned with the two negative determinations of being, namely the past and the future, and with the present in so far as it is conceived from the point of view of a negative determination of being, namely as having come into existence. Necessity, on the other hand, is wholly a matter of essence, and thus it is of the essence of the necessary to exclude coming into existence. The possibility from which that which became actual once emerged still clings to it and remains with it as past, even after the lapse of centuries. Whenever a successor reasserts its having come into existence, which he does by believing it, he evokes this potentiality anew, irrespective of whether there can be any question of his having a more specific conception of it or not.

Supplement: Application

What has here been said applies to the historical in the direct and ordinary sense, whose only contradiction is that it has come into existence, which contradiction is implicit in all coming into existence.[4] Here again one must guard against the illusion of supposing that it is easier to understand after the event than before the event. Whoever thinks this does not yet grasp the fact that what he apprehends has come into existence; he has before him only the present content of a sensory and cognitive immediacy, in which coming into existence is not contained.

Let us now return to our story, and to our hypothesis that the God *has been*. As far as the direct and ordinary form of the historical is concerned, we have seen that this cannot become historical for immediate sensation or cognition, either for a contemporary or for a successor. But this historical fact which is the content of our hypothesis has a peculiar character, since it is not an ordinary historical fact, but a fact based on a self-contradiction. (This is sufficient to show that in relation to this fact there is no difference between an immediate contemporary and a successor; for over against a self-contradiction, and the risk involved in giving it assent, an immediate contemporaneity can yield no advantage.) Yet it is an historical fact, and only for the apprehension of Faith. Faith is here taken first in the direct and ordinary sense [belief], as the relationship of the mind to the historical; but secondly also in the eminent sense, the sense in which the word can be used only once, i.e., many times, but

[4] The word "contradiction" must not here be taken in the frothy sense into which Hegel has beguiled himself and others and the concept—that it has the power to produce something. As long as nothing has come into existence, the contradiction is merely the impulsive power in the passion of wonder, its *nisus*; but it is not the *nisus* of the process of coming into existence itself. When the process of coming into existence has occurred, the contradiction is again present as the *nisus* of the wonder in the passion which reproduces the coming into existence.

only in one relationship. From the eternal point of view, one does not *have Faith* that the God exists [eternally is], even if one assumes that he does exist. The use of the word Faith in this connection enshrines a misunderstanding. Socrates did not have faith that the God existed. What he knew about the God he arrived at by way of Recollection; the God's existence was for him by no means historical existence. If his knowledge of the God was imperfect in comparison with his who according to our supposition receives the condition from the God himself, this does not concern us here; for Faith does not have to do with essence, but with being [historical existence], and the assumption that the God is determines him eternally and not historically. The historical fact for a contemporary is that the God has *come into existence*; for the member of a later generation the historical fact is that the God has been present through *having come into existence*. Herein precisely lies the contradiction. No one can become immediately contemporary with this historical fact, as has been shown in the preceding; it is the object of Faith, since it concerns coming into existence. No question is here raised as to the true content of this; the question is if one will give assent to the God's having come into existence, by which the God's eternal essence is inflected in the dialectical determinations of coming into existence.

Our historical fact thus stands before us. It has no immediate contemporary, since it is historical in the first degree, corresponding to faith [belief] in the ordinary sense; it has no immediate contemporary in the second degree, since it is based upon a contradiction, corresponding to Faith in the eminent sense. But this last resemblance, subsisting between those who are most diversely situated temporally, cancels the difference which in respect of the first relation exists for those of diverse temporal situations. Every time the believer makes this fact an object of his Faith, every time he makes it historical for himself, he re-instates the dialectical determinations of coming into existence with respect to it. If ever so many thousands of years have intervened, if the fact came to entail ever so many consequences, it does not on that account become more necessary (and the consequences themselves, from an ultimate point of view, are only relatively necessary, since they derive from the freely effecting cause); to say nothing of the topsy-turvy notion that the fact might become necessary by reason of the consequences, the consequences being wont to seek their ground in something else, and not to constitute a ground for that of which they are the consequences. If a contemporary or a predecessor saw ever so clearly the preparations, perceived intimations and symptoms of what was about to come, the fact was nevertheless not necessary when it came into existence. That is to say, this fact is no more necessary when viewed as future, than it is necessary when viewed as past.

From *The Concept of Dread*

Translated by Walter Lowrie

Dread as the Consequence of that Sin which is
the Default of the Consciousness of Sin

[In the first two chapters of *The Concept of Dread*] it was constantly affirmed that man is a synthesis of soul and body which is constituted and sustained by spirit. Dread—to use a term which says the same thing that was said in the foregoing discussion but points forward to what is to follow—dread was the instant in the individual life.

There is a category which is constantly used in modern philosophy—no less in logic than in historico-philosophical investigations—and that is "transition." What it means more precisely we are never told. It is employed without more ado, and while Hegel and the Hegelian School startle the world by the mighty thought of the presuppositionless beginning of philosophy, or that nothing must precede philosophy but the most complete absence of presuppositions, no embarrassment is felt in employing the terms "transition," "negation" and "mediation," i.e. the principles of movement in Hegelian thought, in such a way that no place is definitely assigned to them in the systematic progression. If this is not a presupposition, I do not know what a presupposition is; for to employ something which is nowhere explained is in effect to presuppose it. One might think that the System must have such marvelous transparency and introspectiveness that like the omphalopscychoi[1] it would gaze immovably at the central Nothing for so long a time that everything would explain itself and its whole content would of its own accord come into existence. This openness to public inspection the System surely must have. Such, however, is not the case, and the Systematic thought seems to be vowed to secretiveness with respect to its inmost motions and emotions. Negation, transition, mediation, are three masked men of suspicious appearance, the secret agents (*agentia*), which provoke all movements. Hegel would hardly call them "hot heads," for it is by his sovereign permission they carry on their game so brazenly that even in logic terms and expressions are employed which are drawn from the observation of transition in time: "thereupon," "when," "this is like being," "this is like becoming."

But let that be as it will, and let logic tend to its own affairs. The word "transition" cannot be anything but a witty conceit in logic. It belongs in the sphere of historical freedom, for transition is a *state*, and it is actual.[2] Plato clearly enough perceived the difficulty of introducing transition into pure metaphysics, and for this reason the category of "the instant"[3] cost him so

---

[1] The name which describes certain Greek monks who, like the Buddhists, gazed at the navel as an aid to profound meditation.

[2] Therefore when Aristotle says that the transition from possibility to actuality is a κίνησις, this is not to be understood logically but with reference to the historical freedom.

[3] By Plato the instant was conceived in a purely abstract way. To orient oneself in its dialectic one must take into account the fact that the instant is non-being under the category of time. Non-being (τὸ μὴ ὄν; τὸ κενόν, of the Pythagoreans) preoccupied the ancient philosophers much more than it does the modern ones. Non-being was conceived ontologically by the Eleatic philosophers, to the effect that what is affirmed about it can only be affirmed in contradictions, that only being *is*. If one would follow this further, one will see that it recurs in all spheres. In metaphysical propaedeutics the proposition is expressed thus: He who affirms non-being says nothing at all. (This misunderstanding was combatted in the *Sophist*, and in a more mimic way it was combatted already in an earlier work, *Gorgias*). Finally, in the practical spheres the Sophists made use of non-being in such a

much effort. To ignore the difficulty is certainly not to "go further" than Plato; to ignore it by a pious fraud against thought in

---

way that they annulled all moral concepts: non-being *is* not, *ergo*
everything is true, *ergo* everything is good, *ergo* a deceit, etc., does
not exist. Socrates combats this in several dialogues. Plato, however,
dealt with it principally in the *Sophist*, which, like all Plato's dialogues, elucidates at the same time by art the doctrine it teaches
formally; for the Sophist, whose definition and concept the dialogue
is seeking to discover while it follows its principal theme of non-
being, is himself a non-being, and thus both the concept and this
example of it come into existence at the same time in the course of
the argument in which the Sophist is attacked and which ends with
his not being annihilated but brought into existence, which was the
worst thing that could befall him, seeing that in spite of his sophistic
which, like the armor of Mars, is able to make him invisible, he must
come out openly. Modern philosophy has not yet got any further in
the apprehension of non-being, in spite of its pretense to be Christian. Greek philosophy and modern philosophy alike take the position
that everything depends upon getting non-being to come into existence; for to do away with it and cause it to vanish seems to them
too easy. The Christian view takes the position that non-being is
everywhere present as the Nothing out of which all is created, as appearance and vanity, as sin, as sensuousness divorced from the spirit,
as the temporal forgotten by eternity; wherefore the whole point is
to do away with it and get being in its stead. Only with this orientation does the concept of atonement receive an historically correct
interpretation, in the sense in which Christianity brought it into the
world. If the interpretation is carried out in the opposite sense (the
starting point of the movement being derived from the conception
that non-being does not exist), then the Atonement is volatilized and
turned inside out.—It is in *Parmenides* Plato propounds "the instant."
This dialogue is engaged in showing the contradiction within the
concepts themselves, and Socrates expresses this with such precision
that it does not exactly redound to the discredit of that beautiful
old Greek philosophy, but may well serve to put to shame a new and
boastful philosophy which does not make, like the Greek, great demands upon itself, but upon men and their admiration. Socrates remarks that it would not be wonderful if a man were able to demonstrate the contradictoriness (τὸ ἐναντίον) involved in a particular
thing which is made up of diversities, but if one were able to show
the contradiction in the concepts themselves, that would be something to wonder at (ἀλλ' εἰ ὅ ἐστιν ἕν, αὐτό τοῦτο πολλά ἀποδείξει

order to get speculation afloat and start movement again is to treat speculation as a rather finite affair. I remember, however,

---

καί αὖ τὰ πολλὰ δὴ ἕν, τοῦτο ἤδη θαυμάσομαι. καὶ περὶ τῶν ἄλλων ἁπάντων ὡσαύτως. §129 B.C.). The method as usual is that of experimental dialectics. It is assumed that unity (τὸ ἕν) *is* and *is not*, and then it is shown what the consequence will be for it and for the rest. The instant appears now to be that strange being (ἄτοπον— the Greek word is admirably chosen) which lies between movement and repose, without occupying any time; and to this and out of this "the moving" passes over into rest, and "the reposing" into movement. The instant therefore becomes the general category of transition (μεταβολή); for Plato shows that the instant is related in the same way to the transition from unity to plurality and from plurality to unity, from likeness to unlikeness, etc., it is the instant in which there is neither ἕν nor πολλά, neither discrimination nor integration (οὔτι διακρίνεται οὔτι ξυγκρίνεται, §157,A). Now with all this Plato has the merit of making the difficulty clear, but nevertheless the instant remains a mute atomistic abstraction, which is not any further explained when one ignores it. Now if logic is willing to affirm that there is no transition in it (and if it has this category, it surely must have its place assigned to it in the System, seeing that in fact it is already operative there), then it will become clearer that the historical sphere and all the knowledge which reposes upon a historical presupposition has the category of the instant. This category is of great importance as a barrier against the philosophy of paganism and the equally pagan philosophy in Christianity. Another passage in the dialogue *Parmenides* makes evident the consequence of the fact that the instant is such an abstraction [in Plato's conception of it]. It is shown then how under the category of time there emerges the contradiction that unity (τὸ ἕν) becomes younger and older than itself and than plurality (τὰ πολλά), and then in turn, that it is neither younger nor older than itself and plurality (§151,E). Unity nevertheless must exist, it is said, and now it is defined thus: participation in a being or an essence in the present (τὸ δὲ εἶναι ἄλλο τί ἐστι ἡ μέθεξις οὐσίας μετὰ χρόνου τοῦ παρόντος §151,E). In the further development of the contradiction it then appears that the present (τὸ νῦν) wavers between meaning the present, the eternal, the instant. This "now" (τὸ νῦν) lies between "was" and "will be," and unity, as it strives forward from the past to the future, cannot leap by this "now." So then it comes to a stop with the "now," does not become older but is older. In modern philosophy the abstraction culminates in "pure being"; but pure being is the most abstract expression once hearing a speculator say[4] that one ought not to think too much about difficulties beforehand, for with that one would never get to the point of speculating. If the important thing is merely to begin to speculate, and not that one's speculation might really become speculation, then it was said with a fine spirit of resolution that one must merely try to get to the point of speculating, just as it would be laudable in a man who had not the means to drive to the Deer Park[5] in his own carriage to say, "One ought not to be troubled by such things, one can quite well ride in the charabanc."[6] Quite true. It is to be hoped that both conveyances will reach the Deer Park. On the other hand, that man will hardly reach speculation who was so firmly resolved not to trouble himself about the mode of conveyance, if only he could barely get to the point of speculating.

In the sphere of historical freedom transition is a state. However, in order to understand this affirmation one must not forget that the new situation comes about by the leap. For if this is not kept in mind, transition acquires a quantitative preponderance over the elasticity of the leap.

So then, man was said to be a synthesis of soul and body; but he is at the same time *a synthesis of the temporal and the eternal*. I have no objection to recognizing that this has often been said; I have no wish to discover novelties, but rather it is my joy and my darling occupation to think upon things which seem perfectly simple.

---

for eternity, and in turn, like "nothing," it is the instant. Here it is evident again how important "the instant" is, because only by this category can one succeed in giving eternity its proper significance. Eternity and the instant are the extreme terms of the contradiction, whereas otherwise conceived the dialectical witchcraft makes eternity and the instant signify the same thing. It is only with Christianity that the sensuous, the temporal, the instant, are to be understood, precisely because it is only with it the eternal becomes essential.

[4] Cf. *Papers* IV B 1, p. 143; V B 55, 3.

[5] The *Dyrehaven* is a vast park surrounded by forests at a considerable distance from Copenhagen, to which the citizens commonly resorted on holidays.

[6] "Coffee-mill" was the disparaging name bestowed upon this popular means of conveyance.

As for the latter synthesis, it evidently is not fashioned in the same way as the former. In the former case the two factors were soul and body, and the spirit was a third term, but was a third term in such a sense that there could not properly be any question of a synthesis until the spirit was posited. The other synthesis has only two factors: the temporal and the eternal. Where is the third term? And if there be no third term, there is really no synthesis; for a synthesis of that which is a contradiction cannot be completed as a synthesis without a third term, for the recognition that the synthesis is a contradiction is precisely the assertion that it is not a synthesis. What then is the temporal?

When time is correctly defined as infinite succession, it seems plausible to define it also as the present, the past and the future. However this distinction is incorrect, if one means by it that this is implied in time itself; for it first emerges with the relation of time to eternity and the reflection of eternity in it. If in the infinite succession of time one could in fact find a foothold, i.e. a present, which would serve as a dividing point, then this division would be quite correct. But precisely because every moment, like the sum of the moments, is a process (a going-by) no moment is a present, and in the same sense there is neither past, present, nor future. If one thinks it possible to maintain this division, it is because we *spatialize* a moment, but thereby the infinite succession is brought to a standstill, and that is because one introduces a visual representation, visualizing time instead of thinking it. But even so it is not correctly thought, for even in this visual representation the infinite succession of time is a present infinitely void of content. (This is the parody of the eternal.) The Hindus speak of a line of kings which has reigned for 70,000 years.[7] About the kings nothing is known, not even their names (as I assume). Taking this as an illustration of time, these 70,000 years are for thought an infinite vanishing; for visual representation they widen out spatially into an illusive view of a nothing infinitely void.[8] On the other hand, so soon

[7] See Hegel, *Philosophie der Geschichte* (*Werke* IX [2nd ed.], p. 200).

[8] Moreover, this is space. Just here the practiced reader will see the proof that my representation is right, since for abstract thinking

as we let one moment succeed the other we posit the present.

The present, however, is not the concept of time, unless precisely as something infinitely void, which again is precisely the infinite vanishing. If one does not give heed to this, then, however swiftly one may let it pass, one has nevertheless posited the present, and having posited that, one lets it appear again in the definition of the past and the future.

On the contrary, the eternal is the present. For thought, the eternal is the present as an annulled [*aufgehoben*] succession (time was succession, going by). For visual representation, eternity is a going-forth, yet it never budges from the spot, because for visual representation it is a present infinitely rich in content. Likewise in the eternal there is not to be found any division of the past and the future, because the present is posited as the annulled succession.

So time is infinite succession. The life which is in time and is merely that of time has no present. It is true that to characterize the sensuous life it is commonly said that it is "in the instant" and only in the instant. The instant is here understood as something abstracted from the eternal, and if this is to be accounted the present, it is a parody of it. The present is the eternal, or rather the eternal is the present, and the present is full. In this sense the Roman said of the Deity that He is *praesens* (*praesentes dii*), and in using this expression for the Deity His powerful aid was indicated at the same time.

The instant characterizes the present as having no past and no future, for in this precisely consists the imperfection of the sensuous life. The eternal also characterizes the present as having no past and no future, and this is the perfection of the eternal.

If one would now employ the instant to define time, and let the instant indicate the purely abstract exclusion of the past and the future, and by the same token of the present also, then the instant precisely is not the present, for that which in purely abstract thinking lies between the past and the future has no existence at all. But one sees from this that the instant is not a mere

time and space are absolutely identical (*nacheinander* and *nebeneinander*), and they become so for visual representation, and so it is with the definition of God as omnipresent.

characterization of time, for what characterizes time is only that it goes by, and hence time, if it is to be defined by any of the characteristics revealed in time itself, is the passed time. On the other hand, if time and eternity are to touch one another, it must be in time—and with this we have reached the instant.

"The instant" [in Danish, *Øjeblikket*—"a glance of the eye"] is a figurative expression, and for that reason not so easy to deal with. Yet it is a pretty word to reflect upon. Nothing is so swift as a glance of the eye, and yet it is commensurable with the content and value of eternity. Thus when Ingeborg[9] gazes out over the sea to descry Frithiof, this is a picture of what the figurative word signifies. An outburst of her emotion, a sigh, a word, has, as a sound, more the character of time, as a thing that vanishes it is more like the present, and has not so much the presence of the eternal in it, and for this reason a sigh, a word, etc., has power to help the soul to get rid of the weight which oppresses it, precisely because the oppression, if only it finds utterance, begins already to become a past. A glance is therefore a designation of time, but note that this means, of time in the fateful conflict when it is touched by eternity.[10] What we call "the instant," Plato calls ἐξαίφνης ["the sudden"]. However it may be explained etymologically, it is related at all events to the notion of invisibility, because by the Greeks time and eternity alike were conceived abstractly, since the Greeks lacked the concept of the temporal owing to the fact that they lacked the concept of spirit. In Latin it is called *momentum*, which by derivation (from *movere*) merely expresses the vanishing of time.[11]

[9] She figures in Tegnér's *Frithiofs Saga* IX, but here it evidently is a picture S. K. has in mind.

[10] It is noteworthy that Greek art culminates in statuary, in which it is precisely the glance that is lacking. This, however, has its deep reason in the fact that the Greeks did not in the profounder sense comprehend the concept of spirit, and therefore did not in the profoundest sense comprehend the sensuous and the temporal. How striking is the contrast that in Christianity God is pictorially represented as an eye!

[11] In the New Testament there is a poetical paraphrase of the instant. Paul says that the world will pass away "in an instant, in the

Thus understood, the instant is not properly an atom of time but an atom of eternity. It is the first reflection of eternity in time, its first effort as it were to bring time to a stop. For this reason Hellenism did not understand the instant; for even if it comprehended the atom of eternity, it did not comprehend that it was the instant, did not define it with a forward orientation but with a backward, since for Hellenism the atom of eternity was essentially eternity, and so neither time nor eternity had true justice done it.

The synthesis of the eternal and the temporal is not a second synthesis but is the expression for the first synthesis in consequence of which man is a synthesis of soul and body sustained by spirit. No sooner is the spirit posited than the instant is there. For this reason it can be said reproachfully of man that he lives only in the instant, since this comes about by an arbitrary abstraction. Nature does not lie in the instant.

As it is with the sensuous, so it is also with the temporal; for the temporal seems even more imperfect, and the instant still more insignificant, than the apparently secure persistence of nature in time. And yet it is exactly the converse, for nature's security is due to the fact that time has no significance for it.

---

twinkling of an eye" (ἔν ἀτόμῳ καὶ ἐν ῥιπῇ ὀφθαλμοῦ). By that he also expresses the thought that the instant is commensurable with eternity, because the instant of destruction expresses at the same instant eternity. Allow me to illustrate what I mean, and forgive me if there is found anything offensive in the parable I employ. Here in Copenhagen there once upon a time were two actors, who perhaps hardly reflected that a deeper significance might be found in their performance. They came on the stage, placed themselves opposite one another, and then began a pantomime representation of some passionate conflict. When the pantomimic play was in full swing, and the spectators were following the play with keen expectancy of what was to come after, the actors suddenly came to a stop and remained motionless, as though they were petrified in the pantomimic expression of the instant. This may produce a most comical effect, because the instant becomes accidentally commensurable with the eternal. The effect of sculpture is due to the fact that the eternal expression is expressed eternally; the comic effect, on the other hand, by the fact that the accidental expression was eternalized.

Only in the instant does history begin. Man's sensuousness is by sin posited as sinfulness, and therefore is lower than that of the beast, and yet this is because here the higher life begins, for now begins spirit.

The instant is that ambiguous moment in which time and eternity touch one another, thereby positing *the temporal*, where time is constantly intersecting eternity and eternity constantly permeating time. Only now does that division we talked about acquire significance: the present, the past, and the future.

In making this division, attention is at once drawn to the fact that in a certain sense the future signifies more than the present and the past; for the future is in a sense the whole of which the past is a part, and in a sense the future may signify the whole. This is due to the fact that the eternal means first of all the future, or that the future is the incognito in which the eternal, as incommensurable for time, would nevertheless maintain its relations with time. Thus we sometimes speak of the future as identical with eternity: the future life = eternal life. Since the Greeks did not have in a deeper sense the concept of the eternal, neither did they have the concept of the future. One cannot therefore reproach the Greek life for losing itself in the instant, or rather we cannot even say that it was lost; for by the Greeks the temporal was conceived just as naïvely as was the sensuous, because the category of spirit was lacking.

The instant and the future posit in turn the past. If the Greek life might be supposed to define time in any sense, it is as time past, yet without defining this by its relation to the present and the future, but defining it, like the definition of time in general, as a going-by. Here the significance of the Platonic recollection[12] is evident. The Greek eternity lies behind, as the past into which one enters only backwards.[13] However, to say that eternity is the past is to present a perfectly abstract concept of it, whether

---

[12] In his *Phaedo* Plato draws a proof of the immortality of the soul from the fact that in this life we have conceptions, such as the good and the beautiful, which can only be explained as recollections of a previous existence.

[13] Here again one must bear in mind the category I maintain, i.e. repetition, by which one enters eternity forwards.

this be further defined philosophically (by the philosophical dying to the world)[14] or historically.[15]

In general, by seeing how the past, the future, the eternal are defined, one can see how the instant has been defined. If there is no instant, then the eternal appears to be behind, like the past. It is as though I were to picture a man walking along a road but do not assume that he takes a step, then the road behind him appears to be the distance traveled. If the instant is posited, but merely as a *discrimen*, then the future is the eternal. If the instant is posited, so is the eternal—but also the future, which comes again like the past. This appears clearly in the Greek, the Jewish, and the Christian conceptions. The concept around which everything turns in Christianity, the concept which makes all things new, is the fullness of time, is the instant as eternity, and yet this eternity is at once the future and the past. If one does not give heed to this, one cannot save any concept from heretical and treasonable admixtures which destroy the concept. One does not get the past as a thing for itself but in simple continuity with the future—and with that the concepts of conversion, atonement, redemption, are resolved in the significance of world-history, and resolved in the individual historical development. One does not get the future as a thing for itself but in simple continuity with the present—and with that the concepts of resurrection and judgment come to naught.

Let us now picture to ourselves Adam, and then remember that every subsequent individual begins exactly the same way, only within the quantitative difference which is the consequence of the fact of generation and of the historical situation. For Adam then, just as much as for every subsequent individual, there is the instant. The synthesis of the soulish and the bodily is to be posited by spirit, but the spirit is the eternal, and therefore this is accomplished only when the spirit posits at the same time along with this the second synthesis of the eternal and the temporal. So long as the eternal is not posited, the instant *is* not, or

---

[14] In the *Phaedo* Plato recommends to the philosopher the ascetic discipline of dying from the sensible world, a thought which is prominent also in the New Testament—and not merely in ascetic theology.

[15] It appears from *Papers* V B 56, 7, that S. K. had in mind "the Ancient of Days" in Daniel 7:9, 13, 22.

is only as a *discrimen*. Therefore, seeing that in the state of innocence the spirit is characterized merely as a dreaming spirit, the eternal manifests itself as the future, for this, as I have said, is the first expression of the eternal, is its incognito. Just as in the foregoing chapter the spirit when it was about to be posited in the synthesis or rather was about to posit the synthesis, as the spirit's (freedom's) possibility in the individual, expressed itself as dread, so here in turn the future, the possibility of the eternal (i.e. of freedom) in the individual is dread. When then the possibility of freedom manifests itself before freedom, freedom succumbs, and the temporal now emerges in the same way as did sensuousness with the significance of sinfulness. Here again I say that this is the last psychological approximation to the qualitative leap. The difference between Adam and the subsequent individual is that by the latter the future is conceived more reflectively than by Adam. Psychologically speaking, this "more" may have a terrible significance, but in relation to the qualitative leap its significance is unessential. The highest maximum of difference in comparison with Adam is that the future seems to be anticipated by the past, or, in other words, it is the dread that possibility has been lost before it has been lost.

The possible corresponds precisely to the future. For freedom the possible is the future; and for time the future is the possible. Corresponding to both of these in the individual life is dread. A precise and correct linguistic usage associates therefore dread and the future. It is true that one is sometimes said to be in dread of the past, and this seems to be a contradiction. Nevertheless, upon closer inspection it appears that this manner of speaking points in one way or another to the future. The past of which I am supposed to be in dread must stand in a relation of possibility to me. If I am in dread of a past misfortune, this is not in so far as it is past, but in so far as it may be repeated, i.e. become future. If I am in dread of a past fault, it is because I have not put it in an essential relation to myself as past, and have in some way or another prevented it from being past. For in case it is really past, I cannot be in dread but only repentant. If I do not repent, then I have first taken the liberty of making my relation to it dialectical, but thereby the fault itself has become a possibility and not something completely passed. If I am in dread of punishment, it is only when this is put in a dialectical relation with the fault (otherwise I bear my punishment), and then I am in dread of the possible and the future.

So again we have reached the point where we were in Chapter I. Dread is the psychological state which precedes sin, comes as near as possible to it, and is as provocative as possible of dread, but without explaining sin, which breaks forth first in the qualitative leap.

The instant sin is posited, the temporal is sin.[16] We do not

---

[16] From the characterization of the temporal as sinfulness death in turn follows as punishment. This is a progression, an analogy of which, *si placet*, may be found in the fact that, even in relation to the external phenomenon, death is more terrible in the degree that the organism is more perfect. Thus, whereas the death and decay of a plant diffuses an odor almost more delicious than its spicy breath, the decay of an animal, on the other hand, infects the air. It is true in a deeper sense that the more highly we value man, the more terrible death appears. The beast cannot properly be said to die; but when the spirit is posited as spirit, death appears terrible. The dread of death therefore corresponds to that of childbirth, though with this I do not subscribe to what in part is said truly, in part only wittily, in part enthusiastically, in part lightly, about death being a metamorphosis. At the instant of death man finds himself at the extremest point of the synthesis; the spirit cannot, as it were, be present, and yet it must wait, for the body must die. The pagan view of death—as the pagan's sensuousness was more naïve and his sense of time more carefree—was milder and more attractive, but it lacked the highest element. Let one read the beautiful essay by Lessing* on the representation of death in classical art, and one cannot deny that one is put in a mood of pleasurable sadness by this picture of the sleeping genius, or by observing the beautiful solemnity with which the genius of death bows his head and extinguishes the torch. There is, if one will, something indescribably persuasive and alluring in the thought of trusting oneself to such a guide, who is as tranquilizing as a recollection in which nothing is recollected. But on the other hand there is in turn something uncanny in following this mute guide; for he conceals nothing, his form is no incognito, as he is, so is death, and therewith all is over. There is an unfathomable sadness in seeing this guide with his friendly figure bend over the dying man and with

* *Wie die Alten den Tod gebildet* (*Werke* VIII [Maltzahn's ed.], pp. 197–248).

say that the temporal is sinfulness, any more than that the sensuous is sinfulness; but for the fact that sin is posited the temporal signifies sinfulness. Therefore that man sins who lives merely in the instant abstracted from the eternal. If Adam (to speak again by way of "accommodation" and to speak foolishly) had not sinned, he would the same instant have passed over into eternity. On the other hand, so soon as sin is posited it does not avail to want to abstract oneself from the temporal, any more than it would from the sensuous.

Dread as a Saving Experience by Means of Faith

In one of Grimm's Fairy Tales[1] there is the story of a youth who went out in search of adventures for the sake of learning what it is to fear or be in dread. We will let that adventurer go his way without troubling ourselves to learn whether in the course of it he encountered the dreadful. On the other hand I would say that learning to know dread is an adventure which every man has to affront if he would not go to perdition either by not having known dread or by sinking under it. He therefore who has learned rightly to be in dread has learned the most important thing.

If a man were a beast or an angel, he would not be able to be in dread. Since he is a synthesis he can be in dread, and the greater the dread, the greater the man. This, however, is not affirmed in the sense in which men commonly understand dread, as related to something outside a man, but in the sense that man himself produces dread. Only in this sense can we interpret the passage where it is said of Christ that he was in dread [ængstes] even unto death, and the place also where he says to Judas, "What thou doest, do quickly." Not even the terrible word upon

---

the breath of his last kiss extinguish the last spark of life, while all he has experienced has already vanished little by little, and death only is left, which, itself unexplained, explains that the whole of life was a game in which all, the greatest and the least, went out like tapers, one by one, and at last the soul itself. But then there is implied by it also the muteness of annihilation, because the whole thing was only a childish game, and now the game is finished.

[1] *Kinder- und Hausmärchen*, I, No. 4; II, No. 121.

which even Luther dreaded to preach, "My God, my God, why hast thou forsaken me?"—not even this expresses suffering so strongly. For this word indicates a situation in which Christ actually is; the former sayings indicate a relation to a situation which is not yet actual.

Dread is the possibility of freedom. Only this dread is by the aid of faith absolutely educative, consuming as it does all finite aims and discovering all their deceptions. And no Grand Inquisitor has in readiness such terrible tortures as has dread, and no spy knows how to attack more artfully the man he suspects, choosing the instant when he is weakest, nor knows how to lay traps where he will be caught and ensnared, as dread knows how, and no sharp-witted judge knows how to interrogate, to examine the accused, as dread does, which never lets him escape, neither by diversion nor by noise, neither at work nor at play, neither by day nor by night.

He who is educated by dread is educated by possibility, and only the man who is educated by possibility is educated in accordance with his infinity. Possibility is therefore the heaviest of all categories. One often hears, it is true, the opposite affirmed, that possibility is so light but reality is heavy. But from whom does one hear such talk? From a lot of miserable men who never have known what possibility is, and who, since reality showed them that they were not fit for anything and never would be, mendaciously bedizened a possibility which was so beautiful, so enchanting; and the only foundation of this possibility was a little youthful tomfoolery of which they might rather have been ashamed. Therefore by this possibility which is said to be light one commonly understands the possibility of luck, good fortune, etc. But this is not possibility, it is a mendacious invention which human depravity falsely embellishes in order to have reason to complain of life, of providence, and as a pretext for being self-important. No, in possibility everything is possible, and he who truly was brought up by possibility has comprehended the dreadful as well as the smiling. When such a person, therefore, goes out from the school of possibility, and knows more thoroughly than a child knows the alphabet that he can demand of life absolutely nothing, and that terror, perdition, annihilation, dwell next door to every man, and has learned the profitable lesson that every dread which alarms [*ængste*] may the next instant become a fact, he will then interpret reality differently, he will extol reality, and even when it rests upon him heavily he will remember that after all it is far, far lighter than the possibility was. Only thus can possibility educate; for finiteness and the finite relationships in which the individual is assigned a place, whether it be small and common-place or world-historical, educate only finitely, and one can always talk them around, always make something a little different out of them, always chaffer, always escape a little way from them, always keep a little apart, always prevent oneself from learning absolutely from them; and if one is to learn absolutely, the individual must in turn have the possibility in himself and himself fashion that from which he is to learn, even though the next instant it does not recognize that it was fashioned by him, but absolutely takes the power from him.

But in order that the individual may thus absolutely and in-finitely be educated by possibility, he must be honest towards possibility and must have faith. By faith I mean what Hegel in his fashion calls very rightly "the inward certainty which an-ticipates infinity." When the discoveries of possibility are hon-estly administered, possibility will then disclose all finitudes but idealize them in the form of infinity, and by dread overwhelm the individual, until he in turn conquers them by the anticipa-tion of faith.

What I say here appears perhaps to many an obscure and foolish saying, since they even boast of never having been in dread. To this I would reply that doubtless one should not be in dread of men, of finite things, but that only the man who has gone through the dread of possibility is educated to have no dread—not because he avoids the dreadful things of life, but because they always are weak in comparison with those of pos-sibility. If on the other hand the speaker means that the great thing about him is that he has never been in dread, then I shall gladly initiate him into my explanation, that this comes from the fact that he is spirit-less.

If the individual cheats the possibility by which he is to be educated, he never reaches faith; his faith remains the shrewd-ness of finitude, as his school was that of finitude. But men cheat possibility in every way—if they did not, one has only to stick one's head out of the window, and one would see enough for possibility to begin its exercises forthwith. There is an engraving by Chodowiecki[2] which represents the surrender of Calais as viewed by the four temperaments, and the theme of the artist was to let the various impressions appear mirrored in the faces which express the various temperaments. The most commonplace life has events enough, no doubt, but the question is about possibility in the individual who is honest with himself. It is recounted of an Indian hermit who for two years had lived upon dew, that he came once to the city, tasted wine, and then became addicted to drink. This story, like every other of the sort, can be understood in many ways, one can make it comic, one can make it tragic; but the man who is educated by possibility has more than enough to occupy him in such a story. Instantly he is absolutely identified with that unfortunate man, he knows no finite evasion by which he might escape. Now the dread of possibility holds him as its prey, until it can deliver him saved into the hands of faith. In no other place does he find repose, for every other point of rest is mere nonsense, even though in men's eyes it is shrewdness. This is the reason why possibility is so absolutely educative. No man has ever become so unfortunate in reality that there was not some little residue left to him, and, as common sense observes quite truly, if a man is canny, he will find a way. But he who went through the curriculum of misfortune offered by possibility lost everything, absolutely everything, in a way that no one has lost it in reality. If in this situation he did not behave falsely towards possibility, if he did not attempt to talk around the dread which would save him, then he received everything back again, as in reality

2 In 1762 a guiltless Jean Calas was executed. Presently Voltaire took a hand in the matter, and the judge was dismissed. In 1767 Chodowiecki made an engraving which profoundly caught the imagination of his contemporaries: "In Prison Calas takes leave of his Family before the Execution." Later Chodowiecki, in another drawing, portrayed four persons, symbolizing the four temperaments, beholding "Les Adieux de Calas." For reasons too involved and too unimportant to explain here, S. K. has confused the farewell of Calas with "the surrender of Calais."

no one ever did even if he received everything tenfold, for the pupil of possibility received infinity, whereas the soul of the other expired in the finite. No one ever sank so deep in reality that he could not sink deeper, or that there might not be one or another sunk deeper than he. But he who sank in the possibility has an eye too dizzy to see the measuring rod which Tom, Dick, and Harry hold out as a straw to the drowning man; his ear is closed so that he cannot hear what the market price for men is in his day, cannot hear that he is just as good as most of them. He sank absolutely, but then in turn he floated up from the depth of the abyss, lighter now than all that is oppressive and dreadful in life. Only I do not deny that he who is educated by possibility is exposed—not to the danger of bad company and dissoluteness of various sorts, as are those who are educated by the finite, but—to one danger of downfall, and that is self-slaughter. If at the beginning of his education he misunderstands the anguish of dread, so that it does not lead him to faith but away from faith, then he is lost. On the other hand, he who is educated by possibility remains with dread, does not allow himself to be deceived by its countless counterfeits, he recalls the past precisely; then at last the attacks of dread, though they are fearful, are not such that he flees from them. For him dread becomes a serviceable spirit which against its will leads him whither he would go. Then when it announces itself, when it craftily insinuates that it has invented a new instrument of torture far more terrible than anything employed before, he does not recoil, still less does he attempt to hold it off with clamor and noise, but he bids it welcome, he hails it solemnly, as Socrates solemnly flourished the poisoned goblet, he shuts himself up with it, he says, as a patient says to the surgeon when a painful operation is about to begin, "Now I am ready." Then dread enters into his soul and searches it thoroughly, constraining out of him all the finite and the petty, and leading him hence whither he would go.

When one or another extraordinary event occurs in life, when a world-historical hero gathers heroes about him and accomplishes heroic feats, when a crisis occurs and everything becomes significant, then men wish to be in it, for these are things which educate. Quite possibly. But there is a much simpler way of being educated much more fundamentally. Take the pupil of possibility, set him in the midst of the Jutland heath where nothing happens, where the greatest event is that a partridge flies up noisily, and he experiences everything more perfectly, more precisely, more profoundly, than the man who was applauded upon the stage of universal history, in case he was not educated by possibility.

Then when the individual is by possibility educated up to faith, dread will eradicate what it has itself produced. Dread discovers fate, but when the individual would put his confidence in fate, dread turns about and takes fate away; for fate is like dread, and dread is like possibility . . . a witch's letter.[3] If the individuality is not by itself transformed with relation to fate, it will always retain a dialectical remnant, which no finitude can eradicate, any more than a man will lose faith in the lottery who does not lose it by his own act but is supposed to lose it for the fact that he constantly loses what he gambles. Even in relation to the most trifling things dread is promptly at hand so soon as the individual would sneak away from something, would expect something by chance. In itself it is a trifle, and externally, the individual can learn nothing about it from the finite, but to cut the process short dread instantly plays the trump of infinity, that of the category, and the individuality cannot take the trick. Such an individual cannot possibly fear fate in an outward sense, its changeableness and its rebuffs, for in him dread has already fashioned fate and taken away from him everything that any fate could take away. Socrates says in the dialogue of *Cratylus*[4] that it is dreadful to be decieved by oneself, because one always has the deceiver with one. So one can say that it is good fortune to have with one such a deceiver as dread, which deceives piously and weans the child before finiteness begins to bungle it. Even if in our time an individuality is not thus educated by possibility, our age has after all a characteristic

[3] A witch's letter (*Heksebrev*) is a book containing a number of pictures, cut in two, of men or animals. The top halves and the bottom halves can be united in many different combinations to form all manner of strange figures.

[4] Cf. *Papers* IV A 124.

which is notably helpful to one who has a deeper nature and desires to learn the good. The more peaceful and quiet an age is, the more precisely everything follows its regular course, so that the good has its reward, all the more easily can an individual be deceived with regard to the question whether the goal of its striving, though it be a beautiful one, may not be a finite goal. In these times, on the contrary, one need not be more than sixteen years of age to perceive that he who now has to tread the stage of life is pretty much in the same fix as the man who went down to Jericho and fell among thieves. He then who does not wish to sink in the wretchedness of the finite is constrained, in the deepest sense, to assault the infinite. Such a preliminary orientation is analogous to education in possibility, and such an orientation cannot possibly come about except by the help of possibility. So when shrewdness has marshalled its innumerable calculations, upon the assumption of winning the game—then comes dread, even before the game was in reality lost or won, and against the devil dread makes the sign of the cross, then there is nothing shrewdness can do, and all its most sagacious combinations vanish like a ghost before that figure which dread fashions by the omnipotence of possibility. Even in relation to the most trifling matters, so soon as the individuality would make an artful turn which is only artful, would steal away from something, and there is every probability that it will succeed, for reality is not so sharp an examiner as dread—then dread is at hand. If it is sent away on the plea that this is a trifle, then dread makes this trifle as notable as the village of Marengo became in the history of Europe, because there the great Battle of Marengo was fought. In case an individuality is not thus weaned away from shrewdness by its own act, then this is never thoroughly accomplished, for finitude explains only piecemeal, never totally, and the man whose shrewdness was always at fault (and even this is inconceivable in reality) may seek the reason for his failure in a lack of shrewdness and strive to become all the shrewder. With the help of faith dread trains the individual to find repose in providence. So also it is with regard to guilt, which is the second thing dread discovers. The man who merely by finiteness learns to recognize his guilt is lost in finiteness, and in the end the question whether one is guilty or

not cannot be decided except in an external, juridical, exceed-
ingly imperfect way. He therefore who only learns to recognize
his guilt by analogy with the decisions of the police justice or
the supreme court never really comprehends that he is guilty;
for if a man is guilty, he is infinitely guilty. Therefore if such an
individual who is educated only by finiteness does not get a
verdict from the police or a verdict of public opinion that he is
guilty, he becomes about the most ludicrous and pitiable of all
men, a paragon of virtue who is a little better than people generally are, but not quite so good as the parson. What help does
such a man need in life? Why, even before he is dead he can
almost take his place in a gallery of wax figures. From finiteness
one can learn much, but one cannot learn dread, except in a
very mediocre and depraved sense. On the other hand, he who
truly has learned to be in dread will tread as in a dance when
the dreads of finiteness strike up their tune, and the disciples of
finiteness lose their wits and their courage. Thus it is life often
deceives. The hypochondriac is in dread of every unimportant
symptom, but when the important test comes he begins to draw
a full breath. And why is this? Because the important reality is
not so dreadful as the possibility he himself had fashioned and
employed his whole strength in fashioning, whereas now he can
employ all his strength against reality. The hypochondriac,
however, is only an imperfect autodidact in comparison with the
man who is educated by possibility, because hypochondria depends in part upon the bodily state and therefore is fortuitous.[5]

[5] It is therefore in a higher significance Hamann (Cf. *Papers* III
A 235.) employs the word "hypochondria" when he says: *Diese Angst
in der Welt ist aber der einzige Beweis unserer Heterogeneität. Denn
fehlte uns nichts, so würden wir es nicht besser machen als die Heiden
und Transcendental-Philosophen, die von Gott nichts wissen und in
die liebe Natur sich wie die Narren vergaffen; kein Heimweh würde
uns anwandeln. Diese impertinente Unruhe, diese heilige Hypochon-
drie, ist vielleicht das Feuer, womit wir Opferthiere gesalzen und vor
der Fäulniss des laufenden seculi bewahrt werden müssen.* Vol. 6,
p. 194.
  [Translation: "However, this dread which we experience in the
world is the only proof of our heterogeneity. For if we lacked nothing, we should do no better than the pagans and the transcendental

The true autodidact is precisely in the same degree a theodidact, as another author has said.[6] Or to avoid terms which stress so much the intellectual side, it may be said that he is αὐτουργός τις τῆς φιλοσοφίας[7] and in the same degree θεοῦργος. He who with respect to guilt is educated by dread will therefore repose only in atonement.

Here this deliberation ends where it began. So soon as psychology has finished with dread, it has nothing to do but to deliver it over to dogmatics.

Kierkegaard's Major Writings

(arranged chronologically)

A. Complete Works and Papers

Søren Kierkegaards Samlede Vaerker. Ed. A. B. Drachman, J. L. Heiberg & H. O. Lange. 2nd edition. 15 vols. Copenhagen: Gyldendalske Boghandel, Nordisk, 1920–1926.

Søren Kierkegaards Papirer. Ed. P. A. Heiberg, V. Kuhr & E. Torsting. 2nd edition. 11 vols. in 20 parts. Copenhagen: Gyldendalske Boghandel, Nordisk, 1909–1948.

B. English Translations

N.B. The year in brackets is the original year of publication.

The Concept of Irony [1841]. Tr. Lee Capel. New York: Harper, 1966.

Either/Or, A Fragment of Life [1843]. Vol. I. Tr. David & Lillian

---

philosophers who know nothing of God and like fools fall in love with this precious world; no homesickness would attack us. This impertinent uneasiness, this holy hypochondria, is perhaps the fire whereby we sacrificial animals must be salted and preserved from the decay of the passing age." Cf. the *Journal,* III A 235.]

[6] Cf. *Either/Or.* [II, p. 226]

[7] Cf. Xenophon's *Symposium* [1, 5], where Socrates applies this word to himself. (A "self-taught man in philosophy," in contrast to one who has learned it from others; αὐτουργός is properly used of a farmer who cultivates his own land himself. From the context, θεουργός must then mean one who works in the service of God.)

Swenson. Vol. II. Tr. Walter Lowrie. Princeton: Princeton University Press, 1944.

Fear and Trembling, A Dialectical Lyric [1843]. Tr. Walter Lowrie. Princeton: Princeton University Press, 1941.

Repetition. An Essay in Experimental Psychology [1843]. Tr. Walter Lowrie. Princeton: Princeton University Press, 1941.

Edifying Discourses [1843–1844]. Tr. David & Lillian Swenson. 4 vols. Minneapolis: Augsburg, 1943–1946.

Philosophical Fragments Or a Fragment of Philosophy [1844]. Tr. David Swenson. Revised tr. H. V. Hong. Princeton: Princeton University Press, 1962.

The Concept of Dread [1844]. Tr. Walter Lowrie. Princeton: Princeton University Press, 1944.

Stages on Life's Way [1845]. Tr. Walter Lowrie. Princeton: Princeton University Press, 1940.

Thoughts on Crucial Situations in Human Life. Three Discourses on Imagined Situations [1845]. Tr. David & Lillian Swenson. Minneapolis: Augsburg, 1941.

Concluding Unscientific Postscript to the Philosophical Fragments [1846]. Tr. David Swenson & Walter Lowrie. Princeton: Princeton University Press, 1941.

The Present Age & Two Ethico-Religious Discourses [1846–1859]. Tr. Alexander Dru & Walter Lowrie. London: Oxford University Press, 1940.

Works of Love [1847]. Tr. David & Lillian Swenson. Princeton: Princeton University Press, 1946. New translation by Howard & Edna Hong. New York: Harper, 1962.

Purity of Heart is to Will One Thing [1847]. Tr. Douglas Steere. New York: Harper, 1938.

The Gospel of Suffering & The Lilies of the Field [1847]. Tr. David & Lillian Swenson. Minneapolis: Augsburg, 1948.

Christian Discourses [1848]. Also included are: *The Lilies of the Field & The Birds of the Air* [1849]; *The High Priest; The Publican; The Woman that was a Sinner* [1849]. Tr. Walter Lowrie. New York: Oxford University Press, 1939.

The Sickness unto Death [1849]. Tr. Walter Lowrie. Princeton: Princeton University Press, 1941.

Training in Christianity [1850]. Also included is *An Edifying Discourse* [1850]. Tr. Walter Lowrie. New York: Oxford University Press, 1941.

For Self-Examination & Judge for Yourselves! [1851 & 1876]. Also included are: *Two Discourses at the Communion on Fridays*

[1851]; *The Unchangeableness of God* [1855]. Tr. Walter Lowrie. New York: Oxford University Press, 1941.

Attack upon "Christendom" [1854–1855]. Tr. Walter Lowrie: Princeton: Princeton University Press, 1944.

Crisis in the Life of an Actress [1855] and *Other Essays on the Drama.* Tr. Stephen Crites. New York: Harper, 1967.

The Point of View for My Work as an Author [1859]. Also included are: "The Individual," Two "Notes" concerning My Work as an Author [1859]; *On My Work as an Author* [1851]. Tr. Walter Lowrie. New York: Oxford University Press, 1939.

C. From Kierkegaard's Papers

On Authority and Revelation: The Book on Adler. Tr. Walter Lowrie. Princeton: Princeton University Press, 1955.

Johannes Climacus, or De Omnibus Dubitandum Est. Tr. T. H. Croxall. Stanford: Stanford University Press, 1958.

Armed Neutrality & an Open Letter. Tr. Howard & Edna Hong. Bloomington: Indiana University Press, 1968.

D. Journals and Prayers

The Journals of Kierkegaard. Ed. & tr. Alexander Dru. New York: Oxford University Press, 1938.

Kierkegaard's Diary. Ed. Peter Rohde. Tr. Gerda Andersen. New York: Philosophical Library, 1960.

The Prayers of Kierkegaard. Ed. Perry Le fevre. Chicago: University of Chicago Press, 1956.

The Last Years (Journal 1853–1855). Tr. Ronald Gregor Smith. New York: Harper, 1965.

Søren Kierkegaard's Journals and Papers. Ed. Howard & Edna Hong. Vol. I (A–E). Bloomington: Indiana University Press, 1967.

Selected Studies About Kierkegaard
(arranged alphabetically)

A. Bibliography

Himmelstrup, Jens. *Søren Kierkegaard: International Bibliography.* Copenhagen: Nyt Nordisk, 1962.

B. Monographs and Articles

Arbaugh, George E. & George B. *Kierkegaard's Authorship.* Rock Island: Augustana College Library, 1967.

Cantoni, Remo. *La coscienza inquieta*. Milan: Mondadori, 1949.

Collins, James. *The Mind of Kierkegaard*. Chicago: Regnery, 1953.

Croxall, T. H. *Kierkegaard Commentary*. New York: Harper, 1956.

———. *Kierkegaard Studies*. London: Lutterworth, 1948.

Diem, Hermann. *Kierkegaard's Dialectic of Existence*. Tr. H. Knight. London: Oliver & Boyd, 1959.

Dupré, Louis. *Kierkegaard as Theologian*. New York: Sheed & Ward, 1963.

Fabro, Cornelio (ed.). *Studi kierkegaardiani*. Brescia: Morcelliana, 1957.

Geismar, Eduard. *Søren Kierkegaard: Livsudvikling og Forfatter-virksomhed*. 6 vols. Copenhagen: Gads, 1926–1928.

Heywood, Thomas J. *Subjectivity and Paradox*. Oxford: Blackwell, 1957.

Høffding, Harald. *Søren Kierkegaard als Philosoph*. Stuttgart: Frommann, 1896.

Johnson, Howard, & Thulstrup, Niels (eds.). *A Kierkegaard Critique*. New York: Harper, 1962.

Lombardi, Franco. *Kierkegaard*. Florence: Nuova Italia, 1936.

Lowrie, Walter. *Kierkegaard*. 2 vols. New York: Oxford, 1938.

Pieper, Annemarie. *Geschichte und Ewigkeit bei Søren Kierkegaard; das Leitproblem der pseudonymen Schriften*. Meisenheim am Glan: Hain, 1968.

Price, George. *The Narrow Pass. A Study of Kierkegaard's Concept of Man*. London: Hutchinson, 1963.

Schmid, Johann. *Kritik der Existenz. Analysen zum Existenzdenken Søren Kierkegaard*. Zurich: EVZ, 1966.

Shestov, Lev. *Kierkegaard and the Existential Philosophy*. Tr. E. Hewitt. Athens: Ohio University Press, 1969.

Wahl, Jean. *Etudes kierkegaardiennes*. Paris: Aubier, 1938.

FRIEDRICH NIETZSCHE (1844–1900)

Nietzsche was born on October 15, 1844, in the town of Röcken which is in the Prussian province of Saxony. His father and both grandfathers were Lutheran ministers. When Nietzsche was four, his father seems to have suffered brain damage and consequently became mentally ill. Shortly thereafter his mother moved the family to Naumburg where Nietzsche spent the rest of his childhood together with his mother, sister, grandmother, and two maiden aunts.

In 1858 Nietzsche was admitted to Pforta, a renowned boarding school where he received a rigorous classical education. The medical records of the school indicate that his eyesight was poor, that he was subject to migraine headaches, and that the medical authorities were concerned about his mental health because of his father's history.

From Pforta, Nietzsche went to the University at Bonn where he studied theology and classical philology, but he transferred in 1865 to the University at Leipzig, concentrating on classical philology under the guidance of Friedrich Ritschl. At Leipzig, too, he read Schopenhauer's *World as Will and Representation* and was profoundly influenced by it as both his early and late writings suggest. His explicit disagreement with Schopenhauer is expressed by his rejection of resignation as the remedy for the bleakness of existence. Nietzsche began his military duty in 1867 but was injured while riding a horse and received his discharge late in 1868.

He returned to Leipzig and to his studies, only to be distressed at the barrenness of the work of classical philologists. Yet when the chair of classical philology at Basel was vacant, Ritschl recommended him despite the fact that he had not received his degree, had not written the dissertation to become a *Privatdozent*, and had not written the book required for the professorship. Leipzig conferred the degree without examination and Basel was persuaded by Ritschl, and thus Nietzsche became a professor in 1869 at the age of twenty-four. He taught there until 1879 when he had to retire because of poor health.

During Nietzsche's stay at Basel he became friendly with Richard Wagner and Cosima Bülow, Wagner's mistress, who was the illegitimate daughter of Franz Liszt and the wife of Hans von Bülow. Wagner's creative work was an epitome, for Nietzsche, of man's highest metaphysical activity, namely, dissimulation. Later, however, Nietzsche came to regard Wagner's music as an extreme example of romanticism, an abandonment of the values of classical antiquity.

When the Franco-Prussian War broke out, Nietzsche volunteered to serve as a medical orderly. In attending sick soldiers, he contracted dysentery and diphtheria. He returned to Basel to reassume his teaching duties and to publish his first book, *The Birth of Tragedy*.

The book was not well received by classical philologists, both because of Nietzsche's interpretation of Greek culture and because it lacked scholarly paraphernalia. But studies of the Greeks have been profoundly affected by it ever since.

Besides visiting the Wagners at Triebschen during this period, he also audited the lectures of the historian Jakob Burckhardt and struck up a friendship with his older colleague over their mutual interest in ancient Greece. Burckhardt, however, did not share Nietzsche's current admiration for Wagner.

After his resignation from his professorship in 1879, Nietzsche met a young Finnish woman, Lou Salomé, whose intelligence, vivacity, and attractiveness made her, he thought, a fitting disciple and companion. But this relationship proved to be tempestuous and unsatisfactory.

Nietzsche wandered, lonely and sickly, through Switzerland and Italy in search of a measure of decent health. In January 1889, he collapsed on a Turin street, embracing the neck of a horse that had just been beaten by a coachman. Insanity had overtaken him and he was subsequently committed to an asylum in Jena.

His sister, Elizabeth, who had married Bernhard Förster, a leader in German nationalist and anti-Semitic movements for which Nietzsche had nothing but contempt, played a persistently ambivalent role in her brother's life and after it. There was a suggestion of incest between them; there was her interference with his relationship to Lou Salomé; there was her tampering with some of his writings, the rights to which she gained after his death.

Nietzsche's mother took him home, but when she died in 1897 his sister removed him, now hopelessly insane and paralyzed, to Weimar, where he died on August 25, 1900.

On Truth and Falsity in Their Ultramoral Sense

Translated by M. A. Mügge

In some remote corner of the universe, effused into innumerable solar-systems, there was once a star upon which clever animals invented cognition. It was the haughtiest, most mendacious moment in the history of this world, but yet only a moment. After Nature had taken breath awhile the star congealed and the clever animals had to die.—Someone might write a fable after this style, and yet he would not have illustrated sufficiently, how wretched, shadow-like, transitory, purposeless and fanciful the human intellect appears in Nature. There were eternities during which this intellect did not exist, and when it has once more passed away there will be nothing to show that it has existed. For this intellect is not concerned with any further mission transcending the sphere of human life. No, it is purely human and none but its owner and procreator regards it so pathetically as to suppose that the world revolves around it. If, however, we and the gnat could understand each other we should learn that even the gnat swims through the air with the same pathos, and feels within itself the flying centre of the world. Nothing in

Nature is so bad or so insignificant that it will not, at the smallest puff of that force cognition, immediately swell up like a balloon, and just as a mere porter wants to have his admirer, so the very proudest man, the philosopher, imagines he sees from all sides the eyes of the universe telescopically directed upon his actions and thoughts.

It is remarkable that this is accomplished by the intellect, which after all has been given to the most unfortunate, the most delicate, the most transient beings only as an expedient, in order to detain them for a moment in existence, from which without that extra-gift they would have every cause to flee as swiftly as Lessing's son.[1] That haughtiness connected with cognition and sensation, spreading blinding fogs before the eyes and over the senses of men, deceives itself therefore as to the value of existence owing to the fact that it bears within itself the most flattering evaluation of cognition. Its most general effect is deception; but even its most particular effects have something of deception in their nature.

The intellect, as a means for the preservation of the individual, develops its chief power in dissimulation; for it is by dissimulation that the feebler, and less robust individuals preserve themselves, since it has been denied them to fight the battle of existence with horns or the sharp teeth of beasts of prey. In man this art of dissimulation reaches its acme of perfection: in him deception, flattery, falsehood and fraud, slander, display, pretentiousness, disguise, cloaking convention, and acting to others and to himself in short, the continual fluttering to and fro around the *one* flame—Vanity: all these things are so much the

---

[1] The German poet, Lessing, had been married for just a little over one year to Eva König. A son was born and died the same day, and the mother's life was despaired of. In a letter to his friend Eschenburg the poet wrote: ". . . and I lost him so unwillingly, this son! For he had so much understanding! so much understanding! Do not suppose that the few hours of fatherhood have made me an ape of a father! I know what I say. Was it not understanding, that they had to drag him into the world with a pair of forceps? that he so soon suspected the evil of this world? Was it not understanding, that he seized the first opportunity to get away from it? . . ."

Eva König died a week later.—Tr.

rule, and the law, that few things are more incomprehensible than the way in which an honest and pure impulse to truth could have arisen among men. They are deeply immersed in illusions and dream-fancies; their eyes glance only over the surface of things and see "forms"; their sensation nowhere leads to truth, but contents itself with receiving stimuli and, so to say, with playing hide-and-seek on the back of things.

In addition to that, at night man allows his dreams to lie to him a whole lifetime long, without his moral sense ever trying to prevent them; whereas men are said to exist who by the exercise of a strong will have overcome the habit of snoring. What indeed *does* man know about himself? Oh! that he could but once see himself complete, placed as it were in an illuminated glass-case! Does not nature keep secret from him most things, even about his body, *e.g.*, the convolutions of the intestines, the quick flow of the blood-currents, the intricate vibrations of the fibres, so as to banish and lock him up in proud, delusive knowledge? Nature threw away the key; and woe to the fateful curiosity which might be able for a moment to look out and down through a crevice in the chamber of consciousness, and discover that man, indifferent to his own ignorance, is resting on the pitiless, the greedy, the insatiable, the murderous, and, as it were, hanging in dreams on the back of a tiger. Whence, in the wide world, with this state of affairs, arises the impulse to truth?

As far as the individual tries to preserve himself against other individuals, in the natural state of things he uses the intellect in most cases only for dissimulation; since, however, man both from necessity and boredom wants to exist socially and gregariously, he must needs make peace and at least endeavour to cause the greatest *bellum omnium contra omnes* to disappear from his world. This first conclusion of peace brings with it a something which looks like the first step towards the attainment of that enigmatical bent for truth. For that which henceforth is to be "truth" is now fixed; that is to say, a uniformly valid and binding designation of things is invented and the legislature of language also gives the first laws of truth: since here, for the first time, originates the contrast between truth and falsity. The liar uses the valid designations, the words, in order to make the unreal appear as real; *e.g.*, he says, "I am rich," whereas the right designation for his state would be "poor." He abuses the fixed conventions by convenient substitution or even inversion of terms. If he does this in a selfish and moreover harmful fashion, society will no longer trust him but will even exclude him.

In this way men avoid not so much being defrauded, but being injured by fraud. At bottom, at this juncture too, they hate not deception, but the evil, hostile consequences of certain species of deception. And it is in a similarly limited sense only that man desires truth: he covets the agreeable, life-preserving consequences of truth; he is indifferent towards pure, ineffective knowledge; he is even inimical towards truths which possibly might prove harmful or destroying. And, moreover, what after all are those conventions of language? Are they possibly products of knowledge, of the love of truth; do the designations and the things coincide? Is language the adequate expression of all realities?

Only by means of forgetfulness can man ever arrive at imagining that he possesses "truth" in that degree just indicated. If he does not mean to content himself with truth in the shape of tautology, that is, with empty husks, he will always obtain illusions instead of truth. What is a word? The expression of a nerve-stimulus in sounds. But to infer a cause outside us from the nerve-stimulus is already the result of a wrong and unjustifiable application of the proposition of causality. How should we dare, if truth with the genesis of language, if the point of view of certainty with the designations had alone been decisive; how indeed should we dare to say: the stone is hard; as if "hard" was known to us otherwise; and not merely as an entirely subjective stimulus! We divide things according to genders; we designate the tree as masculine,[2] the plant as feminine:[3] what arbitrary metaphors! How far flown beyond the canon of certainty! We speak of a "serpent";[4] the designation fits nothing but the sinuosity, and could therefore also appertain to the worm. What arbitrary demarcations! what one-sided preferences given some-

[2] In German *the tree—der Baum*—is masculine.—Tʀ.

[3] In German *the plant—die Pflanze*—is feminine.—Tʀ.

[4] *Cf.* the German *die Schlange* and *schlingen*, the English *serpent* from the Latin *serpere.*—Tʀ.

times to this, sometimes to that quality of a thing! The different languages placed side by side show that with words truth or adequate expression matters little: for otherwise there would not be so many languages.

The "Thing-in-itself" (it is just this which would be the pure ineffective truth) is also quite incomprehensible to the creator of language and not worth making any great endeavour to obtain. He designates only the relations of things to men and for their expression he calls to his help the most daring metaphors. A nerve-stimulus, first transformed into a percept! First metaphor! The percept again copied into a sound! Second metaphor! And each time he leaps completely out of one sphere right into the midst of an entirely different one. One can imagine a man who is quite deaf and has never had a sensation of tone and of music; just as this man will possibly marvel at Chladni's sound figures in the sand, will discover their cause in the vibrations of the string, and will then proclaim that now he knows what man calls "tone"; even so does it happen to us all with language. When we talk about trees, colours, snow and flowers, we believe we know something about the things themselves, and yet we only possess metaphors of the things, and these metaphors do not in the least correspond to the original essentials. Just as the sound shows itself as a sand-figure, in the same way the enigmatical x of the Thing-in-itself is seen first as nerve-stimulus, then as percept, and finally as sound. At any rate the genesis of language did not therefore proceed on logical lines, and the whole material in which and with which the man of truth, the investigator, the philosopher works and builds, originates, if not from Nephelococcygia, cloud-land, at any rate not from the essence of things.

Let us especially think about the formation of ideas. Every word becomes at once an idea not by having, as one might presume, to serve as a reminder for the original experience happening but once and absolutely individualised, to which experience such word owes its origin, no, but by having simultaneously to fit innumerable, more or less similar (which really means never equal, therefore altogether unequal) cases. Every idea originates through equating the unequal. As certainly as no one leaf is exactly similar to any other, so certain is it that the idea "leaf" has been formed through an arbitrary omission of these individual differences, through a forgetting of the differentiating qualities, and this idea now awakens the notion that in nature there is, besides the leaves, a something called *the* "leaf," perhaps a primal form according to which all leaves were woven, drawn, accurately measured, coloured, crinkled, painted, but by unskilled hands, so that no copy had turned out correct and trustworthy as a true copy of the primal form. We call a man "honest"; we ask, why has he acted so honestly to-day? Our customary answer runs, "On account of his honesty." *The* Honesty! That means again: the "leaf" is the cause of the leaves. We really and truly do not know anything at all about an essential quality which might be called *the* honesty, but we do know about numerous individualised, and therefore unequal actions, which we equate by omission of the unequal, and now designate as honest actions; finally out of them we formulate a *qualitas occulta* with the name "Honesty."

The disregarding of the individual and real furnishes us with the idea, as it likewise also gives us the form; whereas nature knows of no forms and ideas, and therefore knows no species but only an *x*, to us inaccessible and indefinable. For our antithesis of individual and species is anthropomorphic too and does not come from the essence of things, although on the other hand we do not dare to say that it does not correspond to it; for that would be a dogmatic assertion and as such just as undemonstrable as its contrary.

What therefore is truth? A mobile army of metaphors, metonymies, anthropomorphisms: in short a sum of human relations which became poetically and rhetorically intensified, metamorphosed, adorned, and after long usage seem to a nation fixed, canonic and binding; truths are illusions of which one has forgotten that they *are* illusions; worn-out metaphors which have become powerless to affect the senses; coins which have their obverse effaced and now are no longer of account as coins but merely as metal.

Still we do not yet know whence the impulse to truth comes, for up to now we have heard only about the obligation which society imposes in order to exist: to be truthful, that is, to use the usual metaphors, therefore expressed morally: we have heard only about the obligation to lie according to a fixed convention, to lie gregariously in a style binding for all. Now man of course forgets that matters are going thus with him; he therefore lies in that fashion pointed out unconsciously and according to habits of centuries' standing—and by *this very unconsciousness*, by this very forgetting, he arrives at a sense for truth.

Through this feeling of being obliged to designate one thing as "red," another as "cold," a third one as "dumb," awakes a moral emotion relating to truth. Out of the antithesis "liar" whom nobody trusts, whom all exclude, man demonstrates to himself the venerableness, reliability, usefulness of truth. Now as a *"rational"* being he submits his actions to the sway of abstractions; he no longer suffers himself to be carried away by sudden impressions, by sensations, he first generalises all these impressions into paler cooler ideas, in order to attach to them the ship of his life and actions.

Everything which makes man stand out in bold relief against the animal depends on this faculty of volatilising the concrete metaphors into a schema, and therefore resolving a perception into an idea. For within the range of those schemata a something becomes possible that never could succeed under the first perceptual impressions: to build up a pyramidal order with castes and grades, to create a new world of laws, privileges, sub-orders, delimitations, which now stands opposite the other perceptual world of first impressions and assumes the appearance of being the more fixed, general, known, human of the two and therefore the regulating and imperative one. Whereas every metaphor of perception is individual and without its equal and therefore knows how to escape all attempts to classify it, the great edifice of ideas shows the rigid regularity of a Roman Columbarium and in logic breathes forth the sternness and coolness which we find in mathematics. He who has been breathed upon by this coolness will scarcely believe, that the idea too, bony and hexahedral, and permutable as a die, remains however only as the *residuum of a metaphor*, and that the illusion of the artistic metamorphosis of a nerve-stimulus into percepts is, if not the mother, then the grandmother of every idea.

Now in this game of dice, "Truth" means to use every die as it is designated, to count its points carefully, to form exact clas-

sifications, and never to violate the order of castes and the se-
quences of rank. Just as the Romans and Etruscans for their
benefit cut up the sky by means of strong mathematical lines
and banned a god as it were into a *templum*, into a space limited
in this fashion, so every nation has above its head such a sky of
ideas divided up mathematically, and it understands the demand
for truth to mean that every conceptual god is to be looked for
only in *his* own sphere. One may here well admire man, who
succeeded in piling up an infinitely complex dome of ideas on
a movable foundation and as it were on running water, as a
powerful genius of architecture.

Of course in order to obtain hold on such a foundation it must
be as an edifice piled up out of cobwebs, so fragile, as to be carried away by the waves: so firm, as not to be blown asunder by
every wind. In this way man as an architectural genius rises
high above the bee; she builds with wax, which she brings together out of nature; he with the much more delicate material
of ideas, which he must first manufacture within himself. He is
very much to be admired here—but not on account of his impulse for truth, his bent for pure cognition of things. If somebody hides a thing behind a bush, seeks it again and finds it in
the self-same place, then there is not much to boast of, respecting
this seeking and finding; thus, however, matters stand with the
seeking and finding of "truth" within the realm of reason. If I
make the definition of the mammal and then declare after in-
specting a camel, "Behold a mammal," then no doubt a truth is
brought to light thereby, but it is of very limited value, I mean
it is anthropomorphic through and through, and does not contain one single point which is "true-in-itself," real and universally valid, apart from man.

The seeker after such truths seeks at the bottom only the
metamorphosis of the world in man, he strives for an understanding of the world as a human-like thing and by his bat-
tling gains at best the feeling of an assimilation. Similarly,
as the astrologer contemplated the stars in the service of man
and in connection with their happiness and unhappiness,
such a seeker contemplates the whole world as related to man, as
the infinitely protracted echo of an original sound: man; as the
multiplied copy of the one arch-type: man. His procedure is to

apply man as the measure of all things, whereby he starts from the error of believing that he has these things immediately before him as pure objects. He therefore forgets that the original metaphors of perception *are* metaphors, and takes them for the things themselves.

Only by forgetting that primitive world of metaphors, only by the congelation and coagulation of an original mass of similes and percepts pouring forth as a fiery liquid out of the primal faculty of human fancy, only by the invincible faith, that *this* sun, *this* window, *this* table is a truth in itself: in short only by the fact that man forgets himself as subject, and what is more as an *artistically creating* subject: only by all this does he live with some repose, safety and consequence. If he were able to get out of the prison walls of this faith, even for an instant only, his "self-consciousness" would be destroyed at once. Already it costs him some trouble to admit to himself that the insect and the bird perceive a world different from his own, and that the question, which of the two world-perceptions is more accurate, is quite a senseless one, since to decide this question it would be necessary to apply the standard of *right perception*, i.e., to apply a standard which *does not exist*.

On the whole it seems to me that the "right perception"— which would mean the adequate expression of an object in the subject—is a nonentity full of contradictions: for between two utterly different spheres, as between subject and object, there is no causality, no accuracy, no expression, but at the utmost an *æsthetical* relation, I mean a suggestive metamorphosis, a stammering translation into quite a distinct foreign language, for which purpose however there is needed at any rate an intermediate sphere, an intermediate force, freely composing and freely inventing.

The word "phenomenon" contains many seductions, and on that account I avoid it as much as possible, for it is not true that the essence of things appears in the empiric world. A painter who had no hands and wanted to express the picture distinctly present to his mind by the agency of song, would still reveal much more with this permutation of spheres, than the empiric world reveals about the essence of things. The very relation of a nerve-stimulus to the produced percept is in itself no necessary one; but if the same percept has been reproduced millions of times and has been the inheritance of many successive generations of man, and in the end appears each time to all mankind as the result of the same cause, then it attains finally for man the same importance as if it were *the* unique, necessary percept and as if that relation between the original nerve-stimulus and the percept produced were a close relation of causality: just as a dream eternally repeated, would be perceived and judged as though real. But the congelation and coagulation of a metaphor does not at all guarantee the necessity and exclusive justification of that metaphor.

Surely every human being who is at home with such contemplations has felt a deep distrust against any idealism of that kind, as often as he has distinctly convinced himself of the eternal rigidity, omnipresence, and infallibility of nature's laws: he has arrived at the conclusion that as far as we can penetrate the heights of the telescopic and the depths of the microscopic world, everything is quite secure, complete, infinite, determined, and continuous. Science will have to dig in these shafts eternally and successfully and all things found are sure to have to harmonise and not to contradict one another. How little does this resemble a product of fancy, for if it were one it would necessarily betray somewhere its nature of appearance and unreality. Against this it may be objected in the first place that if each of us had for himself a different sensibility, if we ourselves were only able to perceive sometimes as a bird, sometimes as a worm, sometimes as a plant, or if one of us saw the same stimulus as red, another as blue, if a third person even perceived it as a tone, then nobody would talk of such an orderliness of nature, but would conceive of her only as an extremely subjective structure.

Secondly, what is, for us in general, a law of nature? It is not known in itself but only in its effects, that is to say in its relations to other laws of nature, which again are known to us only as sums of relations. Therefore all these relations refer only one to another and are absolutely incomprehensible to us in their essence; only that which we add: time, space, *i.e.*, relations of sequence and numbers, are really known to us in them. Everything wonderful however, that we marvel at in the laws of nature, everything that demands an explanation and might seduce us into distrusting idealism, lies really and solely in the mathematical rigour and inviolability of the conceptions of time and space. These however we produce within ourselves and throw them forth with that necessity with which the spider spins; since we are compelled to conceive all things under these forms only, then it is no longer wonderful that in all things we actually conceive none but these forms: for they all must bear within themselves the laws of number, and this very idea of number is the most marvellous in all things.

All obedience to law which impresses us so forcibly in the orbits of stars and in chemical processes coincides at the bottom with those qualities which we ourselves attach to those things, so that it is we who thereby make the impression upon ourselves. Whence it clearly follows that that artistic formation of metaphors, with which every sensation in us begins, already presupposes those forms, and is therefore only consummated within them; only out of the persistency of these primal forms the possibility explains itself, how afterwards out of the metaphors themselves a structure of ideas could again be compiled. For the latter is an imitation of the relations of time, space and number in the realm of metaphors.

2

As we saw, it is *language* which has worked originally at the construction of ideas; in later times it is *science*. Just as the bee works at the same time at the cells and fills them with honey, thus science works irresistibly at that great columbarium of ideas, the cemetery of perceptions, builds ever newer and higher storeys; supports, purifies, renews the old cells, and endeavours above all to fill that gigantic framework and to arrange within it the whole of the empiric world, *i.e.*, the anthropomorphic world. And as the man of action binds his life to reason and its ideas, in order to avoid being swept away and losing himself, so the seeker after truth builds his hut close to the towering edifice of science in order to collaborate with it and to find protection. And he needs protection. For there are awful powers which continually press upon him, and which hold out against the "truth" of science "truths" fashioned in quite another way, bearing devices of the most heterogeneous character.

That impulse towards the formation of metaphors, that fundamental impulse of man, which we cannot reason away for one moment—for thereby we should reason away man himself—is in truth not defeated nor even subdued by the fact that out of its evaporated products, the ideas, a regular and rigid new world has been built as a stronghold for it. This impulse seeks for itself a new realm of action and another river-bed, and finds it in *Mythos* and more generally in *Art*. This impulse constantly confuses the rubrics and cells of the ideas, by putting up new figures of speech, metaphors, metonymies; it constantly shows its passionate longing for shaping the existing world of waking man as motley, irregular, inconsequentially incoherent, attractive, and eternally new as the world of dreams is. For indeed, waking man *per se* is only clear about his being awake through the rigid and orderly woof of ideas, and it is for this very reason that he sometimes comes to believe that he was dreaming when that woof of ideas has for a moment been torn by Art. Pascal is quite right, when he asserts, that if the same dream came to us every night we should be just as much occupied by it as by the things which we see every day; to quote his words, "If an artisan were certain that he would dream every night for fully twelve hours that he was a king, I believe that he would be just as happy as a king who dreams every night for twelve hours that he is an artisan."

The wide-awake day of a people mystically excitable, let us say of the earlier Greeks, is in fact through the continually-working wonder, which the mythos presupposes, more akin to the dream than to the day of the thinker sobered by science. If every tree may at some time talk as a nymph, or a god under the disguise of a bull, carry away virgins, if the goddess Athene herself be suddenly seen as, with a beautiful team, she drives, accompanied by Pisistratus, through the markets of Athens—and every honest Athenian did believe this—at any moment, as in a dream, everything is possible; and all nature swarms around man as if she were nothing but the masquerade of the gods, who found it a huge joke to deceive man by assuming all possible forms.

Man himself, however, has an invincible tendency to let himself be deceived, and he is like one enchanted with happiness when the rhapsodist narrates to him epic romances in such a way that they appear real or when the actor on the stage makes the king appear more kingly than reality shows him. Intellect, that master of dissimulation, is free and dismissed from its service as slave, so long as It is able to deceive without *injuring*, and then It celebrates Its Saturnalia. Never is It richer, prouder, more luxuriant, more skilful and daring; with a creator's delight It throws metaphors into confusion, shifts the boundary-stones of the abstractions, so that for instance It designates the stream as the mobile way which carries man to that place whither he would otherwise go. Now It has thrown off Its shoulders the emblem of servitude. Usually with gloomy officiousness It endeavours to point out the way to a poor individual coveting existence, and It fares forth for plunder and booty like a servant for his master, but now It Itself has become a master and may wipe from Its countenance the expression of indigence. Whatever It now does, compared with Its former doings, bears within itself dissimulation, just as Its former doings bore the character of distortion. It copies human life, but takes it for a good thing and seems to rest quite satisfied with it.

That enormous framework and hoarding of ideas, by clinging to which needy man saves himself through life, is to the freed intellect only a scaffolding and a toy for Its most daring feats, and when It smashes it to pieces, throws it into confusion, and then puts it together ironically, pairing the strangest, separating the nearest items, then It manifests that It has no use for those makeshifts of misery, and that It is now no longer led by ideas but by intuitions. From these intuitions no regular road leads into the land of the spectral schemata, the abstractions; for them the word is not made, when man sees them he is dumb, or speaks in forbidden metaphors and in unheard-of combinations of ideas, in order to correspond creatively with the impression of the powerful present intuition at least by destroying and jeering at the old barriers of ideas.

There are ages, when the rational and the intuitive man stand side by side, the one full of fear of the intuition, the other full of scorn for the abstraction; the latter just as irrational as the

former is inartistic. Both desire to rule over life; the one by
knowing how to meet the most important needs with fore-
sight, prudence, regularity; the other as an "over-joyous" hero by
ignoring those needs and taking that life only as real which sim-
ulates appearance and beauty. Wherever intuitive man, as for
instance in the earlier history of Greece, brandishes his weapons
more powerfully and victoriously than his opponent, there under
favourable conditions, a culture can develop and art can establish her rule over life. That dissembling, that denying of needi-
ness, that splendour of metaphorical notions and especially that
directness of dissimulation accompany all utterances of such a
life. Neither the house of man, nor his way of walking, nor his
clothing, nor his earthen jug suggest that necessity invented
them; it seems as if they all were intended as the expressions of a
sublime happiness, an Olympic cloudlessness, and as it were a
playing at seriousness.

Whereas the man guided by ideas and abstractions only
wards off misfortune by means of them, without even enforc-
ing for himself happiness out of the abstractions; whereas
he strives after the greatest possible freedom from pains, the
intuitive man dwelling in the midst of culture has from his
intuitions a harvest: besides the warding off of evil, he attains a continuous in-pouring of enlightenment, enlivenment
and redemption. Of course when he *does* suffer, he suffers more:
and he even suffers more frequently since he cannot learn from
experience, but again and again falls into the same ditch into
which he has fallen before. In suffering he is just as irrational
as in happiness; he cries aloud and finds no consolation.

How different matters are in the same misfortune with the
Stoic, taught by experience and ruling himself by ideas! He
who otherwise only looks for uprightness, truth, freedom from
deceptions and shelter from ensnaring and sudden attack, in his
misfortune performs the masterpiece of dissimulation, just as the
other did in his happiness; he shows no twitching mobile human face but as it were a mask with dignified, harmonious
features; he does not cry out and does not even alter his voice;
when a heavy thundercloud bursts upon him, he wraps himself
up in his cloak and with slow and measured step walks away
from beneath it.

From *The Will to Power*

Translated by A. M. Ludovici

§ 516

We are not able to affirm and to deny one and the same thing: that is a principle of subjective experience—which is not in the least "necessary," *but only a sign of inability.*

If, according to Aristotle, the *principium contradictionis* is the most certain of all principles; if it is the most ultimate of all, and the basis of every demonstration; if the principle of every other axiom lie within it: then one should analyse it all the more severely, in order to discover how many assumptions *already lie* at its root. It either assumes something concerning reality and Being, as if these had become known in some other sphere—that is to say, as if it were *impossible* to ascribe the opposite attributes to it; or the proposition means: that the opposites *should* not be ascribed to it. In that case, logic would be an imperative, *not* directed at the knowledge of truth, but at the adjusting and fixing of a world *which must seem true to us.*

In short, the question is a debatable one: are the axioms of logic adequate to reality, or are they measures and means by which alone we can *create* realities, or the concept "reality"? . . . In order to affirm the first alternative, however, one would, as we have seen, require a previous knowledge of Being; which is certainly not the case. The proposition therefore contains no *criterion of truth,* but an *imperative* concerning that which *should* pass as true.

Supposing there were no such thing as A identical with itself, as every logical (and mathematical) proposition presupposes, and that A is in itself an *appearance,* then logic would have a mere world *of appearance* as its first condition. As a matter of fact, we believe in that proposition, under the influence of an endless empiricism which seems to *confirm* it every minute. The "thing"—that is the real substratum of A; *our belief in things* is the first condition of our faith in logic. The A

in logic is, like the atom, a reconstruction of the "thing." . . .
By not understanding this, and by making logic into a criterion
of *real being*, we are already on the road to the classification of
all those hypostases: substance, attribute, object, subject, action, etc., as realities—that is to say, the conception of a metaphysical world or a "real world" (—*this is, however, once more
the world of appearance* . . .).

The primitive acts of thought, affirmation, and negation, the
holding of a thing for true, and the holding of a thing for not
true,—in so far as they do not only presuppose a mere habit, but
the very *right* to postulate truth or untruth at all,—are already
dominated by a belief, *that there is such a thing as knowledge
for us,* and *that judgments can really hit the truth*: in short,
logic never doubts that it is able to pronounce something concerning truth in itself (—that is to say, that to the thing which is
in itself true, no opposite attributes *can* be ascribed).

In this belief there *reigns* the sensual and coarse prejudice
that our sensations teach us *truths* concerning things,—that I
cannot at the same moment of time say of one and the same
thing that it is *hard* and *soft*. (The instinctive proof, "I cannot
have two opposite sensations at once," is quite *coarse* and *false*.)

That all contradiction in concepts should be forbidden, is the
result of a belief, that we *are able* to form concepts, that a concept not only characterises but also *holds* the essence of a thing.
. . . As a matter of fact, logic (like geometry and arithmetic)
only holds good of *assumed existences which we have created.*
Logic is *the attempt on our part to understand the actual world
according to a scheme of Being devised by ourselves; or, more
exactly, it is our attempt at making the actual world more cal-
culable and more susceptible to formulation, for our own purposes.* . . .

A criticism of the concept "cause"

§ 551

We have absolutely no experience concerning *cause*; viewed
psychologically we derive the whole concept from the subjective conviction, that *we* ourselves are causes—that is to say,
that the arm moves. . . . *But that is an error.* We distinguish

ourselves, the agents, from the action, and everywhere we make use of this scheme—we try to discover an agent behind every phenomenon. What have we done? We have *misunderstood* a feeling of power, tension, resistance, a muscular feeling, which is already the beginning of the action, and posited it as a cause; or we have understood the will to do this or that, as a cause, because the action follows it. There is no such thing as "Cause," in those few cases in which it seemed to be given, and in which we projected it out of ourselves *in order to understand a phenomenon,* it has been shown to be an illusion. Our understanding of a phenomenon consisted in our inventing a subject who was responsible for something happening, and for the manner in which it happened. In our concept "cause" we have embraced our feeling of will, our feeling of "freedom," our feeling of responsibility and our design to do an action: *causa efficiens* and *causa finalis* are fundamentally one.

We believed that an effect was explained when we could point to a state in which it was inherent. As a matter of fact, we invent all causes according to the scheme of the effect: the latter is known to us. . . . On the other hand, we are not in a position to say of any particular thing how it will "act." The thing, the subject, the will, the design—all inherent in the conception "cause." We try to discover things in order to explain why something has changed. Even the "atom" is one of these fanciful inventions like the "thing" and the "primitive subject." . . .

At last we understand that things—consequently also atoms—effect nothing: *because they are non-existent;* and that the concept causality is quite useless. Out of a necessary sequence of states, the latter's causal relationship does *not* follow (that would be equivalent to extending their *active principle* from 1 to 2, to 3, to 4, to 5). *There is no such thing as a cause or an effect.* From the standpoint of language we do not know how to rid ourselves of them. But that does not matter. If I imagine *muscle* separated from its "effects," I have denied it. . . .

In short: *a phenomenon is neither effected nor capable of effecting. Causa is a faculty to effect something,* superadded fancifully to what happens. . . .

The interpretation of causality is an illusion. . . . A "thing" is the sum of its effects, synthetically united by means of a concept, an image. As a matter of fact, science has robbed the concept causality of all meaning, and has reserved it merely as an allegorical formula, which has made it a matter of indifference whether cause or effect be put on this side or on that. It is asserted that in two complex states (centres of force) the quantities of energy remain constant.

The calculability of a phenomenon does not lie in the fact that a rule is observed, or that a necessity is obeyed, or that we have projected a law of causality into every phenomenon: it lies in the *recurrence of "identical cases."*

There is no such thing as a *sense of causality*, as Kant would have us believe. We are aghast, we feel insecure, we will have something familiar, which can be relied upon. . . . As soon as we are shown the existence of something old in a new thing, we are pacified. The so-called instinct of causality is nothing more than the *fear of the unfamiliar*, and the attempt at finding something in it which is already *known*.—It is not a search for causes, but for the familiar. . . .

§ 554

It is obvious that neither things-in-themselves *nor* appearances can be related to each other in the form of cause and effect: and from this it follows that the concept "cause and effect" is *not applicable* in a philosophy which believes in things-in-themselves and in appearances. Kant's mistake— . . . As a matter of fact, from a psychological standpoint, the concept "cause and effect" is derived from an attitude of mind which believes it sees the action of will upon will everywhere,—which believes only in living things, and at bottom only in souls (not in things). Within the mechanical view of the world (which is logic and its application to space and time) that concept is reduced to the mathematical formula with which—and this is a fact which cannot be sufficiently emphasised—nothing is ever understood, but rather *defined*—deformed.

§ 555

The greatest of all fables is the one relating to knowledge. People would like to know how things-in-themselves are constituted: but behold, there are no things-in-themselves! But even supposing there *were* an "in-itself," an unconditional thing, it could on that very account *not be known*! Something unconditioned cannot be known: otherwise it would not be unconditioned! Knowing, however, is always a process of "coming into relation with something"; the knowledge-seeker, on this principle, wants the thing, which he would know, to be nothing to him, and to be nothing to anybody at all: and from this there results a contradiction,—in the first place, between this *will* to know, and this desire that the thing to be known *should* be nothing to him (wherefore know at all then?); and secondly, because something which is nothing to anybody, does not even *exist*, and therefore cannot be known. Knowing means: "to place one's self in relation with something," to feel one's self conditioned by something and one's self conditioning it—under all circumstances, then, it is a process of *making stable or fixed*, of *defining*, of *making conditions conscious* (not a process of *sounding* things, creatures, or objects "in-themselves").

NIETZSCHE'S MAJOR WRITINGS

(arranged chronologically)

A. Collected Works

There are several editions of the collected works. The following are two of them.

Gesammelte Werke, Musarionausgabe. 23 vols. Munich: Musarion, 1920–1929.

Werke in drei Bänden. Ed. Karl Schlechta. Munich: Hanser, 1954–1956.

There is also an English edition of the collected works.

The Complete Works. Ed. Oscar Levy. 18 vols. Edinburgh & London: Allen & Unwin, 1909–1913. Reprinted in New York: Russell & Russell, 1964. [The translations are not always reliable.]

B. The Individual Works and Translations

Die Geburt der Tragödie aus dem Geiste der Musik [1872].

The Birth of Tragedy. Tr. Wm. Haussmann in *The Complete Works.* Vol. 1.

"The Birth of Tragedy." Tr. W. Kaufmann in *The Birth of Tragedy* and *The Case of Wagner.* New York: Random House, 1967.

Unzeitgemässe Betrachtungen: David Strauss, Der Bekenner und der Schriftsteller [1873]; *Von Nutzen und Nachteil der Historie für das Leben* [1874]; *Schopenhauer als Erzieher* [1874]; *Richard Wagner in Bayreuth* [1876].

Thoughts out of Season, I—David Strauss, The Confessor and the Writer; Richard Wagner in Bayreuth. Tr. A. M. Ludovici. Complete *Works,* Vol. 4.

Thoughts out of Season, II—The Use and Abuse of History; Schopenhauer as Educator. Tr. Adrian Collins. *Complete Works,* Vol. 5.

Menschliches, Allzumenschliches. Ein Buch für freie Geister. Band I [1878]; Band II contains *Vermischte Meinungen und Sprüche* [1879] and *Der Wanderer und sein Schatten* [1880].

Human All-Too Human, I. Tr. Helen Zimmern. *Complete Works,* Vol. 6.

Human All-Too Human, II—*Mixed Opinions and Aphorisms; The Wanderer and His Shadow.* Tr. Paul Cohn. *Complete Works,* Vol. 7.

Morgenröte. Gedanken über die moralischen Vorurteile [1881].

The Dawn of Day: Reflections on Moral Prejudices. Tr. J. M. Kennedy. *Complete Works,* Vol. 9.

Die fröhliche Wissenschaft [1882].

The Joyful Wisdom. Tr. Thomas Common. *Complete Works,* Vol. 10.

Also sprach Zarathustra. Ein Buch für Alle und Keinen [1883–1885].

Thus Spake Zarathustra. Tr. Thomas Common. *Complete Works,* Vol. 11.

Thus Spoke Zarathustra. Tr. W. Kaufmann. New York: Viking, 1966.

Janseits von Gut und Böse. Vorspiel einer Philosophie der Zukunft [1886].

Beyond Good and Evil. Tr. Helen Zimmern. *Complete Works,* Vol. 12.

Beyond Good and Evil: Prelude to a Philosophy of the Future. Tr. W. Kaufmann. New York: Random House, 1966.

Zur Genealogie der Moral. Eine Streitschrift [1887].

The Genealogy of Morals. Tr. Horace Samuels. *Complete Works,* Vol. 13.

"On the Genealogy of Morals," Tr. W. Kaufmann & R. J. Hollingdale in *On the Genealogy of Morals and Ecce Homo*. New York: Random House, 1967.

Der Fall Wagner. Ein Musikanten Problem [1888].

The Case of Wagner. Tr. A. M. Ludovici. *Complete Works*, Vol. 8.

"The Case of Wagner." Tr. W. Kaufmann, in *The Birth of Tragedy and The Case of Wagner*. New York: Random House, 1967.

Götzen-Dämmerung, oder Wie man mit dem Hammer philosophiert [1889].

The Twilight of the Idols. Tr. A. M. Ludovici. *Complete Works*, Vol. 16.

"The Twilight of the Idols." Tr. W. Kaufmann. *The Portable Nietzsche*. New York: Viking, 1954.

Dionysos-Dithyramben [1892].

"*Dionysius Dithyrambs*." Tr. Paul V. Cohn et al. in *Ecce Homo, Complete Works*, Vol. 17.

Nietzsche Contra Wagner. Aktenstücke eines Psychologen [1895].

"Nietzsche contra Wagner." Tr. A. M. Ludovici in *The Case of Wagner. Complete Works*, Vol. 8.

"Nietzsche contra Wagner." Tr. W. Kaufmann in *The Portable Nietzsche*.

Der Antichrist [1895].

"The Antichrist." Tr. A. M. Ludovici in *The Twilight of the Idols. Complete Works*, Vol. 16.

"The Antichrist." Tr. W. Kaufmann in *The Portable Nietzsche*.

Ecce Homo. Wie man wird, was man ist [1908].

Ecce Homo. Tr. A. M. Ludovici. *Complete Works*, Vol. 17.

"Ecce Homo." Tr. W. Kaufmann in *On the Genealogy of Morals and Ecce Homo*.

Der Wille zur Macht [Constructed out of Nietzsche's literary remains and published in 1901 in an edition of his complete works supervised by his sister, Elizabeth Förster-Nietzsche, i.e., as Volume 15 in the so-called Grossotav edition of the *Werke*. There is considerable dispute among Nietzsche scholars about the status of these writings.]

The Will to Power, I & II. Tr. A. M. Ludovici. *Complete Works*, Vols. 14–15.

The Will to Power. Tr. W. Kaufmann & H. J. Hollingdale. New York: Random House, 1967.

C. Selected Posthumously Published Essays

"Über die Zukunft unserer Bildungs-Anstalen." [Lecture delivered in
      1872]
   The Future of our Educational Institutions. Tr. J. M. Kennedy.
   Complete Works, Vol. 3.
"Homer und die klassische Philologie." [Address delivered in 1869]
   "Homer and Classical Philology." Tr. J. M. Kennedy in *The Fu-
   ture of our Educational Institutions. Complete Works*, Vol. 3.
"Die Griechische Staat." [Written in 1871]
   "The Greek State." Tr. M. A. Mügge in *Early Greek Philosophy
   and Other Essays. Complete Works*, Vol. 2.
"Homers Wettkampf." [Written in 1872]
   "Homer's Contest." Tr. M. A. Mügge in *Early Greek Philosophy
   and Other Essays.*
"Das Verhältnis der Schopenhauerschen Philosophie zu einer
   deutschen Kultur." [Written in 1872]
   "The Relation of Schopenhauer's Philosophy to a German Cul-
   ture." Tr. M. A. Mügge in *Early Greek Philosophy and Other
   Essays.*
"Die Philosophie im tragischen Zeitalter der Griechen." [Written in
   1873]
   "Philosophy during the Tragic Age of the Greeks." Tr. M. A.
   Mügge in *Early Greek Philosophy and Other Essays.*
   Philosophy in the Tragic Age of the Greeks. Tr. Marianne Cowan.
   Chicago: Regnery, 1962.
"Über Wahrheit und Luge im aussermoralischen Sinn." [Written in
   1873]
   "Truth and Falsity in Their Ultramoral Sense." Tr. M. A. Mügge
   in *Early Greek Philosophy and Other Essays.*
"Wir Philogen." [Written in 1874]
   "We Philologists." Tr. J. M. Kennedy in *The Case of Wagner.
   Complete Works*, Vol. 8.

SELECTED STUDIES ABOUT NIETZSCHE
(arranged alphabetically)

A. Bibliography

Reichert, Herbert & Schlechta, Karl. *International Nietzsche Bibliography*. Chapel Hill: University of North Carolina Press, 1960.

B. Monographs and Articles

Andler, Charles. *Nietzsche, sa vie et sa pensée.* 6 vols. Paris: Gallimard, 1920–1931.

Brandes, Georg. *Friedrich Nietzsche.* Tr. A. G. Chates. London:
Heinemann, 1914.

Danto, Arthur. *Nietzsche as Philosopher.* New York: Macmillan,
1965.

Heidegger, Martin. *Nietzsche.* 2 vols. Pfüllingen: Neske, 1960.

———. "Nietzsche's Wort 'Gott ist tot,'" *Holzwege.* Frankfurt a.M.:
Klostermann, 1950.

Hollingdale, R. J. *Nietzsche: The Man and His Philosophy.* Baton
Rouge: Louisiana State University Press, 1965.

Jaspers, Karl. "Kierkegaard and Nietzsche," *Reason and Existenz.* Tr.
Wm. Earle. New York: Noonday, 1955.

———. *Nietzsche: An Introduction to the Understanding of His Philosophical Activity.* Tr. C. Wallraff & F. Schmitz. Tucson: University of Arizona Press, 1965.

Kaufmann, Walter. *Nietzsche: Philosopher, Psychologist, Antichrist.*
Princeton: Princeton University Press, 1950. Updated edition.
New York: Random House, 1968.

Löwith, Karl. *Nietzsches Philosophie der ewigen Wiederkehr des
Gleichen.* Stuttgart: Kohlhammer, 1956.

Morgan, George A. *What Nietzsche Means.* Cambridge: Harvard
University Press, 1941.

Mügge, M. A. *Friedrich Nietzsche.* London: T. F. Unwin, 1908.

Royce, Josiah. "Nietzsche," *Atlantic Monthly,* March 1917.

Simmel, Georg. *Schopenhauer und Nietzsche.* Berlin: Duncker &
Humblot, 1907.

Vaihinger, Hans. *Nietzsche als Philosoph.* Berlin: Reuther & Rei-
chard, 1902.

———. "Nietzsche and His Doctrine of Conscious Illusion (The Will
to Illusion)," *The Philosophy of As-If.* Tr. C. K. Ogden. New
York: Harcourt Brace, 1924.

WILHELM DILTHEY (1833–1911)

Dilthey was born at Biebrich am Rhein in the then independent duchy of Hesse-Nassau on November 19, 1833. His father was the pastor of the Reformed Church, and like many other German philosophers, Dilthey planned to pursue a theological or, at least, an ecclesiastical career.

He attended the *Gymnasium* at Wiesbaden where his intellectual curiosity was cultivated by his instructor and mentor, Carl Firnhaber. In 1852 he registered at the University of Heidelberg as a divinity student but was drawn to the study of philosophy by Kuno Fischer. Dilthey's study of the history of philosophy is suggestive of the influence of Fischer's writings on the great philosophers.

Dilthey followed the custom of many German students of the time by attending various universities. He went to Berlin in 1853 and received his degree in philosophy in 1864. While there he heard the lectures of some of the celebrated members of the German historical school such as the classical philologist Boeckh, the historian Ranke, and the geographer Ritter. He received, moreover, both philosophical and personal guidance from Adolf Trendelenburg. The discernibly clear formative influence on his thought are Kant's critical idealism, Hume's empiricism, and Comte's positivism. The less obvious influence is Hegel's conception of the historical character of consciousness. It is less obvious because of Dilthey's explicit opposition to Hegel's thought. Inseparable, of course, from Dilthey's philosophical formation is Schleiermacher's conception of the relation between the universal type and the individual instance as well as his hermeneutic, i.e., his method of analyzing the conditions that make literary or historical interpretations possible.

In 1865 he became a *Privatdozent* in philosophy at Berlin. Then a professor at Basel in 1867 where he came into contact with the historian Jakob Burckhardt, he went on to Kiel in 1868 and Breslau in 1871. Finally he was recalled to Berlin as professor of philosophy and remained there teaching and writing until 1906. His public life had been regular and unspectacular except for the influential character of his thought. He continued to write until his death on October 1, 1911, at Seis near Bolzano in the Tyrol.

From *The Essence of Philosophy*

Translated by Stephen A. and William T. Emery

Introduction

We customarily use the general idea, philosophy, to group certain products of mind which in the course of history have often arisen in various nations. If we then express in an abstract formula what is common to these particular products, usually called philosophy or philosophical, the concept of philosophy arises. This concept would reach its highest perfection in adequately presenting the essence of philosophy. Such a concept would express the formative law, operative in the origin of each individual philosophical system, and the genetic relations between the particular facts, falling under the law, would result from it.

A solution of this intellectual problem is possible only on the presupposition that what we call philosophy or philosophical really contains such a general property, so that one formative law operates in all these particular cases, and thus an inner unity embraces the whole philosophical field. And in every reference to the essence of philosophy this is the assumption. Here the term 'philosophy' means a general object. Behind the particular philosophical facts a systematic continuum of minds is presupposed as the unitary and necessary ground of these empirical facts, as the rule of their changes, and as the ordering principle which articulates their variety.

In this strict sense can one speak of an essence of philosophy? The possibility is by no means obvious. 'Philosophy' and 'philosophical' have so many meanings, differing with time and place, and the systems of thought to which their authors have applied these terms are so dissimilar, that different periods would seem to have attached to ever different systems the beautiful word 'philosophy,' coined by the Greeks. For some regard philosophy as laying the foundations of the particular sciences. Others extend the concept to include the task of deriving the system of these sciences from those foundations. Or philosophy is restricted to this system. Then again it is defined as the science of mind, the science of inner experience. Finally, it is regarded as wisdom concerning the conduct of life, or the science of the universally authentic values. Where is the inner bond, which ties together views so dissimilar, patterns so various—the unitary essence of philosophy? If such an essence cannot be found, then we are dealing merely with diverse activities which have appeared under changing historical conditions as cultural needs, and which bear a common designation only externally and through the historical accidents of terminology. There are philosophies, then; there is no philosophy. In that case the history of philosophy has no inner, necessary unity. It receives again and again different content and scope at the hands of the individual historians, always according to their conceptions of it in the contexts of their own systems. One historian may present this history as an advance to a deeper and deeper grounding of the particular sciences, another as the progressive reflection of the mind on itself, still another as the increasing knowledge concerning the experience or the values of life. In order to decide to what extent one may speak of an essence of philosophy, we must turn from the definitions, formulated by the individual philosophers, to the historical facts of philosophy itself. These facts provide the material for ascertaining what philosophy is. The result of this inductive procedure can then be understood more deeply in its conformity to law.

By what method can we solve the problem of determining the

essence of philosophy from the historical facts? The
here concerns a more general problem of method in the
studies. The subjects of all statements in these studies are socially interrelated, individual selves. These are, first of all, single
persons. Gestures, words, and acts are their manifestations. The
problem of the human studies is to relive these selves and to
grasp them in thought. The mental system expressed in these
manifestations makes it possible to disclose in them a typically
recurrent element, to bring the particular moments of life into
the system of life-phases and finally into that of the self. Individuals, however, are not isolated, but interrelated in families,
more complex groups, nations, eras, and finally humanity itself. The purposiveness in these several organizations makes possible the typical modes of approach in the human studies. Still,
no concept exhausts the contents of these individual selves.
Rather, the variety directly given in them can be only lived,
understood, and described. And even their interweaving in the
course of history is something unique, never wholly reducible to
concepts. But the formations and combinations of the unique are
not arbitrary. Each of them expresses the lived structural unity
of individual and community life. Every report of the facts of a
case, however simple, seeks at the same time to make them intelligible in the light of general ideas or concepts of mental activities. Every such report, on the basis of the general ideas or
concepts available, completes a separate percept in a context sup-
plied by one's own lived experience. Guided by the attainable
experiences of intrinsic values, instrumental values, and purposes, every such report selectively and connectively unites separate elements in something significant and meaningful. The
method of the human studies involves the perpetual reciprocity
of lived experience and concept. In the reliving of individual
and collective structural systems the concepts of the human
studies find their fulfillment, while conversely the immediate
reliving itself is raised to systematic knowledge by the universal
forms of thought. When these two functions of consciousness,
central in the human studies, finally coincide, then we grasp the
essence of human development. This consciousness shall contain no concept which has not been formed in the whole fullness
of historical reliving, nothing universal which does not express

the essence of an historical reality. Nations, eras, lines of historical development: in these formations we do not choose freely but, committed as we are to reliving, we seek in them to clarify the essence of men and of races. Accordingly, to regard constructive thought in the historical world as only an instrument to portray and present the particular as such is to misunderstand completely the interest which thinking man brings to this world. Beyond all portrayal and description of the factual and particular, thought aims to secure knowledge of the essential and the necessary. It seeks to understand the structural system of individual and of social life. We win power over this social life only in so far as we grasp and use its regularity and coherence. The logical form of expression for such regularities is the proposition whose subject is general like its predicate.

Among the various general subject-concepts which aid in this task of the human studies belong such concepts as those of philosophy, art, religion, law, and economy. Their character is determined by the fact that they express not only an attitude present in many persons, hence something uniform, general, repeating itself in them, but also an inner system, in which the various persons are joined by this attitude. So the expression 'religion' signifies not only a class of similar facts, a vital relation of the self to invisible forces; it signifies also a communal system in which persons are united for religious rites, and in which they have special rôles in religious performances. Accordingly, in those individuals to whom religion, philosophy, or art is ascribed, the facts show a double relation. These individuals stand as particulars under a universal, as cases under a rule, and they are also joined according to this rule as parts in a whole. The reason for this will emerge for us later from our insight into the two-fold tendency in the formation of psychological concepts.

The function of these general concepts is very important in the human studies. For in these studies, just as in the natural sciences, we can grasp regularities only by teasing particular systems out of the tangled tissue, which the human-social-historical world presents, and then being able to show uniformities, inner structure, and development in these systems. Analysis of the empirically given, complex reality is the initial step to great discoveries in the human studies also. In this task we first encounter general ideas in which such systems, whose appearance is always characterized by common features, are juxtaposed, already detached and withdrawn from the complex reality. Within limits, when the bounds are correctly set by these ideas, the general subjects of assertion arising in this way can support a self-contained body of fruitful truths. And already at this stage terms like 'religion,' 'art,' 'philosophy,' 'science,' 'economy,' and 'law' are fashioned for what is expressed in such ideas.

Scientific thought has now for its basis the schematism already contained in these general ideas. But it must first test the correctness of this schematism. For it is dangerous for the human studies to adopt these ideas, since the discovery of uniformities and articulation depends upon whether in addition a unitary content is really expressed in each of them. Accordingly, in the formation of concepts in this field we seek to find the objective essence which earlier determined the general idea and use of the term, and by this essence to clarify the indefinite idea, and, indeed, perhaps to correct it where faulty. So this is the task which is set for us also in regard to the concept and the essence of philosophy.

But how more exactly shall we determine the method of advancing safely from the general idea and use of the term to the concept of the thing? The formation of concepts seems to fall into a vicious cycle. The concept of philosophy or art or the religious attitude or law can be found only as we derive from the groups of facts, forming one of these fields, the relations of the characteristics constituting the concept. This already presupposes a decision as to which groups of mental facts are to be called philosophy. But, nevertheless, thought could make this decision only if it already possessed sufficient criteria to assign to the facts the character of philosophy. So it seems that one must already know what philosophy is, when he starts to form this concept from facts.

To be sure, the question of method would be answered at once, if these concepts could be deduced from more general truths. Then the conclusions from the particular examples would have to serve merely as a supplement. And this has been the opinion of many philosophers, especially in the German speculative school. But as long as this school cannot agree concerning a universally valid deduction or win universal recognition for an intuition, we shall have to rest content with reasoning which moves empirically from the examples and seeks to find the unitary content, the genetic laws expressed in the phenomena of philosophy. This procedure must presuppose that behind the discovered use of the term lies a unitary content, so that thinking, when it starts out from the group of phenomena called philosophy or philosophical, does not wander fruitlessly. And the validity of this presupposition must be proved by the investigation itself. It wins from the instances called philosophy or philosophical a concept of essence, which must then make it possible to explain the assignment of these words to the instances. Now, in the sphere of such concepts as those of philosophy, religion, art, and science two starting points are always given; the similarity of the particular instances and the system in which these are united. And however the special nature of each one of these general concepts helps to differentiate method, in our case we enjoy further the peculiar advantage that philosophy itself has early risen to consciousness of its activity. So we have at hand a great variety of attempts to define the concept, as our method strives to do. They show what individual philosophers, determined by given cultural conditions and guided by their own systems, have regarded as philosophy. Hence these definitions epitomize its historical forms. They reveal the inner dialectic, in which philosophy has run through its possible positions in the system of culture. We must be able to make each of these possibilities fruitful for our definition.

The circularity, involved in the procedure of defining philosophy, is inevitable. In fact, a great uncertainty persists as to the bounds within which systems are called philosophy and works philosophical. This uncertainty can be overcome only by first establishing sound, even if inadequate, definitions and then moving on from these in other ways to further definitions which gradually exhaust the content of the concept. Therefore the method can be only this: through particular procedures, each of which in itself still fails to guarantee a universally valid and complete solution of the problem, step by step to mark off more precisely the essential features of philosophy and the extent of the instances possessing these features, and finally from the vitality of philosophy to explain why border fields remain, which prevent a clear demarcation of its scope. We must first try to ascertain a common property in those systems to which the general idea, philosophy, refers. Then the other side of the concept, the interconnection of the systems in a larger context, can be used to test the result and to complete it through a deeper insight. So here the basis is given for investigating the relation of the essential features of philosophy, thus discovered, to the structural system of the individual and of society, and for grasping philosophy as a vital individual and social function. We can thus combine these features into a concept of essence, from which we can understand the relations of the particular systems to the function of philosophy, put its systematic concepts into their places, and sharpen the blurred boundary of its scope. This is the way for our cursory survey.

[The Historicity of Consciousness]

When viewed historically, every solution of a philosophical problem belongs to a situation present at that time. Man, this temporal creature, maintains the security of his existence, as long as he works in time, by lifting his creations out of the temporal flux as enduring objects. While under this illusion he creates with greater joy and power. Herein lies the eternal contradiction between the creative and the historical consciousness. The former naturally tries to forget the past and to ignore the better in the future. But the latter lives in the synthesis of all times, and it perceives in all individual creation the accompanying relativity and transience. This contradiction is the silently born affliction most characteristic of philosophy today. For in the contemporary philosopher his own creative activity is co-present with the historical consciousness, since at present his philosophy without this would embrace only a fragment of reality. He must recognize his creative activity as a part of the historical continuum, in which he consciously produces something dependent. Then a resolution of this contradiction becomes possible for him, as will later appear. Now he can calmly submit to the authority of the historical consciousness, and he can view even his own daily work from the historical system, in which the essence of philosophy is realized in the variety of its appearances.

In this historical view every particular concept of philosophy becomes an instance, referring to the formative law which the essence of philosophy contains. And however untenable in itself each of the definitions may be, when formulated from the systematic standpoint, yet now they are all important for answering the question as to the essence of philosophy. Indeed, they are an essential part of the historical facts from which we are now to reason.

For this conclusion we gather up all the empirical data of our survey. We found the term 'philosophy' assigned to situations of very different kinds. We saw that philosophy is extraordinarily mobile, always setting itself new tasks and adjusting itself to the conditions of culture. It takes up problems as worth while and then discards them. At one stage of knowledge it regards questions as answerable, and then drops them later on as unanswerable. But we always saw working in it the same tendency toward universality and logical grounding, the same direction of the mind toward the whole of the given world. And the metaphysical urge to penetrate into the heart of this whole constantly struggles with the positivistic demand of philosophy for universally valid knowledge. Those are the two sides of its essence which distinguish it from even the most closely related fields of culture. Unlike the particular sciences philosophy seeks to solve the very riddle of the world and of life; unlike art and religion it tries to present this solution in universally valid form. For that is the chief result emerging from the historical evidence discussed: an insulated logical and historical continuum leads from the metaphysics of the Greeks, who undertook to solve the great riddle of the world and of life with universal validity, to the most radical positivists or sceptics of the present. The fortunes of philosophy are all determined somehow by this starting point and the basic philosophical problem. All possible attitudes of the human mind to the riddle are surveyed. In this historical continuum the contribution of each particular position of philosophy is the realization of one possibility under the given conditions. Each expresses an essential feature of philosophy, while its limitations point to the teleological system on which it depends as part of a whole, which alone contains the whole truth.

[The Decline of the Power of Metaphysics]

But although no metaphysics can satisfy the demands for scientific proof, philosophy still has a sound position in studying the relation of the mind to the world, each general attitude expressing an aspect of this world. Philosophy is not able to grasp the world in its essence through a metaphysical system, demonstrated with universal validity. But every serious poem discloses a feature of life, never before seen in this light, and poetry thus reveals to us the various sides of life in ever new products. No work of art contains the whole view, and yet we approach it by means of them all. Likewise in the typical *Weltanschauungen* of philosophy a world confronts us, as it appears when a powerful philosophical personality makes one of the general attitudes toward the world dominant over the others, and its categories over theirs. So from the vast labor of the metaphysical mind the historical consciousness remains, repeating this labor in itself and thus coming to know the unfathomable depth of the world. The last word of the mind which has surveyed all these *Weltanschauungen* is not the relativity of each but the sovereignty of the mind over against every single one of them, and also the positive consciousness of how in the various attitudes of the mind the one reality of the world exists for us.

It is the task of the theory of *Weltanschauungen* so to analyze the historical development of the religious attitude, poetry, and metaphysics, in opposition to relativism, as to present systematically the relation of the human mind to the riddle of the world and of life.

The Concept of the Essence of Philosophy. A View of Its History and Structure

Philosophy has proved to be a group of very diverse functions, which, through insight into their regular connection, are collectively regarded as the essence of philosophy. A function always refers to a purposive system, and consists of a group of related activities which occur within this systematic whole. The concept is not derived from the analogy of organic life, nor does it refer to a faculty or an original ability. The functions of philosophy are related to the purposive structure both of the philosopher and of society. They are activities in which the person turns in upon himself and at the same time produces outward effects. In this they are akin to the activities of religion and of poetry. So philosophy is an activity which springs from the need of the individual mind for reflection on its behavior, for inner pattern and security of action, for a fixed form of its relation to the whole of human society. And philosophy is at the same time a function rooted in the structure of society and requisite for the completeness of social life. Accordingly, philosophy is a function which occurs uniformly in many persons and unites them in a social and historical continuum. In this latter sense it is a cultural system. For the characteristics of such a system are: uniformity of the activity in each individual member of the system, and solidarity of the individuals in whom this activity takes place. If this solidarity assumes fixed forms, organizations arise in the cultural system. Among all purposive systems those of art and of philosophy bind the individuals together least, for the function which the artist or the philosopher performs is dependent on no institutional forms of life. In this realm there is the highest freedom of the mind. The membership of the philosopher in such organizations as a university or an academy may increase his contribution to society. Nevertheless his permanent principle of life is the freedom of his thought, which must never be infringed, and which is indispensable not only for his philosophical character but also for the confidence in his absolute sincerity, and thus for his influence.

The most general characteristic, which belongs to all functions of philosophy, is rooted in the nature of objective awareness and conceptual thought. So regarded, philosophy appears as only the most consistent, vigorous, and comprehensive thinking, and it is separated from the empirical consciousness by no fixed boundary. From the form of conceptual thinking it follows that judging advances to highest generalizations, the forming and classifying of concepts to a conceptual architectonic with a highest apex; relating proceeds to an all-comprehensive system, and grounding to an ultimate principle. In this activity thinking refers to the common object of all the thinking acts of various persons, the systematic unity of sense-perception: the world. To form this world the plurality of things is ordered in space, and the variety of their changes and movements in time. All feelings and volitional acts of this world are arranged through the definite location of the bodies belonging to them and the perceptual elements woven into them. All values, purposes, and goods, posited in these feelings or volitional acts, are fitted into it. Human life is embraced by it. And now thinking strives to express and to unite the whole content of perceptions, lived experiences, values, and purposes, as it is lived and given in the empirical consciousness (experience and the sciences of experience). In so doing thinking moves from the concatenation of things and of changes in the world toward a world-concept. For a ground it regresses to a world-principle, a world-cause. It seeks to determine the value, sense, and meaning of the world, and it asks for a world-purpose. Wherever this procedure of generalizing, of integrating, and of logical grounding is borne on by the cognitive drive and frees itself from the particular need and the limited interest, it passes over into philosophy. And wherever the subject, who relates himself to this world in his activity, rises in the same way to reflection on this activity of his, the reflection is philosophical. Accordingly, the fundamental characteristic in all functions of philosophy is the drive of the mind which transcends attachment to the determinate, finite, limited interest and strives to fit into some inclusive, definitive idea every theory which has arisen from a restricted need. This drive of thought springs from its rationality, and meets needs of human nature which well nigh defy reliable analysis: the joy in knowledge, ultimate security in relation to the world, the endeavor to release life from its restricted conditions. Every mental attitude seeks a fixed point, free from relativity.

This general function of philosophy is expressed, under the various conditions of historical life, in all the philosophical activities which we have surveyed. Particular functions of great vitality arise from these differing conditions: the development of a *Weltanschauung* to universal validity; the reflection of knowing on itself; the relation of theories, formed in the particular purposive systems, to the system of all knowledge; a culturally pervasive spirit of criticism, of universal synthesis, and of grounding in principle. They all prove to be particular activities which are rooted in the unitary essence of philosophy. For philosophy adapts itself to every stage in the development of culture and to all conditions determining its historical situation. And so we understand the continual change of its activities, the flexibility and mobility with which it now unfolds to the breadth of a system, now focuses its whole force effectively on a single problem, and is ever shifting its working energy to new tasks.

We have reached the point at which the presentation of the essence of philosophy illuminates its history in retrospect and clarifies its systematic unity as we look ahead. This history would be understood: (1) if the coherence of the functions of philosophy were to explain the order in which, under the conditions of culture, the problems appear, together and successively, and their possible solutions are considered in turn; (2) if the progressive reflection of knowing upon itself were described in its chief stages; (3) if the history studied how the theories, arising in the purposive systems of culture, are related by the comprehensive philosophical spirit to the systematic unity of knowledge, and hence further developed; how philosophy creates new disciplines in the human studies and then transfers these disciplines to the particular sciences; and (4) if it showed how from the state of consciousness of an era and from national traits one can gain insight into the particular forms which the philosophical *Weltanschauungen* assume, and yet at the same time into the steady advance of the great types of these *Weltanschauungen*. So then, the history of philosophy leaves a legacy to systematic philosophical labor: the three problems of laying a foundation for the particular sciences, establishing them on this foundation, and bringing them together; and the task of coming to final terms with the incessant need for ultimate reflection on being, ground, value, purpose, and their interconnection in the *Weltanschauung,* no matter in what form and direction this settlement takes place.

DILTHEY'S MAJOR WRITINGS
(arranged chronologically)

There is an edition of the collected writings.

Gesammelte Schriften. 12 vols. Leipzig and Berlin: Teubner, 1914–1936; 2nd ed., Stuttgart and Göttingen: Teubner; Vandenhoeck & Ruprecht, 1957–1960.

N.B. Not all of Dilthey's work is found in these collected writings.

"Die dichterische und philosophische Bewegung in Deutschland 1770–1800" [1867], in *G.S.*, Vol. V.

Das Lebens Schleiermachers. Berlin: G. Reimer, 1870.

"Uber das Studium der Geschichte der Wissenschaften vom Menschen, der Gesellschaft und dem Staat" [1875], in *G.S.*, Vol. V.

Einleitung in die Geisteswissenschaften [1883], in *G.S.*, Vol. I.

"Auffassung und Analyse des Menschen im 15 und 16 Jahrhundert" [1893], in *G.S.*, Vol. II.

"Ideen über eine beschreibende und zergliedernde Psychologie" [1894], in *G.S.*, Vol. V.

"Über vergleichende Psychologie" [1895], in *G.S.*, Vol. V.

"Beiträge zum Studium der Individualität" [1896], in *G.S.*, Vol. V.

"Die Entstehung der Hermeneutik" [1900], in *G.S.*, Vol. V.

Das Erlebnis und die Dichtung. Leipzig: Teubner, 1905.

"Die Jugendgeschichte Hegels" [1906], in *G.S.*, Vol. IV.

"Das Wesen der Philosophie" [1907], in *G.S.*, Vol. V.

   The Essence of Philosophy. Tr. S. A. & W. T. Emery. Chapel Hill: University of North Carolina Press, 1954.

"Der Aufbau der geschichtlichen Welt in den Geisteswissenschaften" [1910], in *G.S.*, Vol. VII. Portions of the foregoing are found in:

   Pattern and Meaning in History. Tr. & ed. H. P. Rickman. London: Allen & Unwin, 1961.

"Plan der Fortsetzung" [1911], in *G.S.*, Vol. VII. Portions of the foregoing are found in *Pattern and Meaning in History.*

"Das geschichtliche Bewusstsein und die Weltanschauungen" [1911], in *G.S.*, Vol. VIII.

"Die Typen der Weltanschauung und ihre Ausbildung in den metaphysischen Systemen" [1911], in *G.S.*, Vol. VIII.

Philosophy of Existence. Tr. W. Kluback & M. Weinbaum. New York: Bookman Associates, 1957.

Selected Studies About Dilthey
(arranged alphabetically)

Bischoff, D. *Wilhelm Diltheys geschichtliche Lebensphilosophie.* Leipzig und Berlin: Teubner, 1935.

Bollnow, O. F. *Dilthey: eine Einführung in seine Philosophie.* Leipzig und Berlin: Teubner, 1936.

Diaz de Cerio Ruiz, F. *W. Dilthey y el problema del mundo storico.* Barcelona: J. Flors, 1959.

Hodges, H. A. *The Philosophy of Wilhelm Dilthey.* London: Routledge & Kegan Paul, 1952.

———. *Wilhelm Dilthey: An Introduction.* London: Routledge & Kegan Paul, 1944.

Holborn, Hajo. "Dilthey and the Critique of Historical Reason," *Journal of the History of Ideas,* XI [1950], 93–118.

Kluback, William. *Wilhelm Dilthey's Philosophy of History.* New York: Columbia University Press, 1956.

Landgrebe, L. *Wilhelm Dilthey's Theorie der Geisteswissenschaften.* Halle: 1928.

Misch, Georg. *Lebensphilosophie und Phänomenologie: Eine Auseinandersetzung der Diltheyschen Richtung mit Heidegger und Husserl.* Bonn: Cohen, 1930.

Morgan, G. A. "Wilhelm Dilthey," *Philosophical Review,* XLII [July 1933], 351–380.

Rickman, H. P. "Wilhelm Dilthey," *Encyclopedia of Philosophy.* Ed. P. Edwards. New York: Macmillan, 1967, Vol. 2.

Rossi, Pietro. *Lo Storicismo Contemporaneo.* Turin: Loescher, 1968.

———. *Storia e storicismo nella filosofia contemporanea.* Milan: Lerici, 1960.

Suter, J. F. *Philosophie et histoire chez Wilhelm Dilthey.* Basel: Verlag für Recht und Gesellschaft, 1960.

Edmund Husserl (1859–1938)

Husserl was born in Prossnitz, a town in Czechoslovakian Moravia, on April 8, 1859. His family was Jewish but did not have a strong religious tradition. He went to elementary school there and then to the *Gymnasia* in Vienna and Olmütz where his academic record was not unusual.

Between the years 1876 and 1878 he attended the University at Leipzig to study astronomy, mathematics, and physics. He also availed himself of the philosophy lectures of Wilhelm Wundt. At Leipzig, Husserl became friendly with the future founder and first president of Czechoslovakia, Thomas Masaryk, who introduced him to the Bible. Masaryk was a nonpracticing Catholic who respected religion but was not religiously committed. Husserl, however, on the basis of his reading of the Bible, wished to be baptized and was so a few years later at the age of twenty-seven in the Lutheran Church of Vienna. Late in his life he seemed impressed by Catholicism, but it was not he but his wife who, shortly after his death, became a Catholic.

In 1878 Husserl moved to the University of Berlin to pursue mathematics under Leopold Kronecker, Ernst Kummer, and especially Karl Weierstrass. There it was Friedrich Paulsen who kept his interest in philosophy alive. He transferred to Vienna in 1881 to continue his studies in mathematics, completing his degree in 1883 with a thesis on the theory of the calculus of variations.

Weierstrass invited him to become his assistant at Berlin. Weierstrass, however, became ill and could not carry out his duties; Husserl returned to Vienna to study philosophy with

Franz Brentano. As a former Dominican priest, Brentano had received training in medieval scholastic accounts of knowledge. The view that concepts are intentions, i.e., that they refer to objects, was passed on to Husserl and became an important part of the Phenomenological method and theory of consciousness. Brentano also brought to Husserl's attention the work of Hume and Mill and especially the work of the logician Bernard Bolzano (also previously a priest), who had argued the objective and non-psychologistic character of logical and mathematical relations—a view that Husserl was later to adopt.

Husserl, on Brentano's advice, went to the University of Halle in 1886 to be an assistant under Carl Stumpf, from whom he received a background in psychology. He published the *Philosophie der Arithmetik* in 1891, his *Habilitationsschrift* which had a decided psychologistic cast to it, and on that account received the criticism of Gottlob Frege among others. By the time he wrote his *Logische Untersuchungen* in 1900, he had abandoned the psychologistic conception of logic and mathematics. By 1900 he also joined the faculty of philosophy at Göttingen and there wrote many of the works that indicate both the powerful influence of Descartes and Kant upon his thinking and the originality of his own efforts, henceforward referred to as Phenomenology.

A professorship opened up for him in 1916 at Freiburg-im-Breisgau and he taught there until his retirement in 1928. Among his younger colleagues between the years 1916 and 1923 was a young *Privatdozent*, Martin Heidegger, whom Husserl recognized as an original and forceful thinker. Heidegger's interest in Phenomenology gave Husserl cause to believe that he had a successor and continuator of his work. But it was precisely Heidegger's originality that made this impossible. The relationship between the two men cooled to such a degree that after Heidegger published *Being and Time,* Husserl referred to Heidegger's thought as poles apart from his own. Despite his misgivings, however, he did submit Heidegger's name to be his successor to the chair of philosophy at Freiburg.

Between the time of his retirement and the time of his death, Husserl wrote an enormous amount of material and continued to lecture despite the harassment he received from the Nazis as an ethnically Jewish member of the Freiburg faculty. In 1937 he fell ill with pleurisy, and was cared for until his death on April 27, 1938, by nuns of the Benedictine priory of St. Lioba.

Author's Preface to the English Edition of *Ideas*

Translated by W. R. Boyce-Gibson

May the author of this work, which first appeared in the year 1913, be permitted to contribute to the English Edition certain explanations that may prove of use to the reader, both before and as he reads?

Under the title "A Pure or Transcendental Phenomenology", the work here presented seeks to found a new science—though, indeed, the whole course of philosophical development since *Descartes* has been preparing the way for it—a science covering a new field of experience, exclusively its own, that of "Transcendental Subjectivity". Thus Transcendental Subjectivity does not signify the outcome of any speculative synthesis, but with its transcendental experiences, capacities, doings, is an absolutely independent realm of direct experience, although for reasons of an essential kind it has so far remained inaccessible. Transcendental experience in its theoretical and, at first, descriptive bearing, becomes available only through a radical alteration of that same dispensation under which an experience of the natural world runs its course, a readjustment of viewpoint which, as the method of approach to the sphere of transcendental phenomenology, is called "phenomenological reduction".

In the work before us transcendental phenomenology is not founded as the empirical science of the empirical facts of this field of experience. Whatever facts present themselves serve only as examples similar in their most general aspect to the empirical illustrations used by mathematicians; much, in fact, as the actual intuitable dispositions of numbers on the abacus assist us, in their merely exemplary capacity, to grasp with insight, and in their pure generality the series 2, 3, 4 . . . as such, pure numbers as such, and the propositions of pure mathematics relative to these, the essential generalities of a mathematical kind. In this book, then, we treat of an *a priori* science ("eidetic", directed upon the universal in its original intuitability), which appropriates, though as pure possibility only, the empirical field of fact of transcendental subjectivity with its factual (*faktischen*) experiences, equating these with pure intuitable possibilities that can be modified at will, and sets out as its *a priori* the indissoluble essential structures of transcendental subjectivity, which persist in and through all imaginable modifications. Since the reduction to the transcendental and, with it, this further reduction to the Eidos is the method of approach to the field of work of the new science, it follows (and we stress the point in advance) that the proper starting-point for the systematic unravelling of this science lies in the chapters which treat of the reductions we have indicated. Only from this position can the reader, who follows with inner sympathy the indications proffered step by step, judge whether something characteristically new has really been worked out here—worked out, we say, and not constructed, drawn from real, general intuition of essential Being, and described accordingly.

Eidetic phenomenology is restricted in this book to the realm of pure eidetic "description", that is to the realm of essential structures of transcendental subjectivity immediately transparent to the mind. For this constitutes in itself already a systematically self-contained infinitude of essential characteristics. Thus no attempt is made to carry out systematically the transcendental knowledge that can be obtained through logical deduction. Here we have one difference (though not the only one) between the whole manner of this new *a priori* science and that of the mathematical disciplines. These are "deductive" sciences, and that means that in their scientifically theoretical mode of development mediate deductive knowledge plays an incomparably greater part than the immediate axiomatic knowledge upon which all the deductions are based. An infinitude of deductions rests on a very few axioms.

But in the transcendental sphere we have an infinitude of knowledge previous to all deduction, knowledge whose mediated connexions (those of intentional implication) have nothing to do with deduction, and being entirely intuitive prove refractory to every methodically devised scheme of constructive symbolism.

A note of warning may be uttered here against a misunderstanding that has frequently arisen. When, in an anticipatory vein, it is stated right from the start that, according to the author's views (to be established in those further portions of the whole work which are still to be published), all radically scientific philosophy rests on the basis of phenomenology, that in a further sense it is phenomenological philosophy right through, this does not mean to say that philosophy itself is an *a priori* science throughout. The task which this book was planned to carry out, that of establishing a science of the eidetic essence of a transcendental subjectivity, is as far as it can be from carrying the conviction with it that philosophy itself is entirely a science *a priori*. A glance at the mathematical sciences, these great logical instruments for corresponding sciences of fact, would already lead us to anticipate the contrary. The science of fact in the strict sense, the genuinely rational science of nature, has first become possible through the independent elaboration of a "pure" mathematics of nature. The science of pure possibilities must everywhere precede the science of real facts, and give it the guidance of its concrete logic. So is it also in the case of transcendental philosophy, even though the dignity of the service rendered here by a system of the transcendental *a priori* is far more exalted.

The understanding, or at any rate the sure grasp, of the distinction between *transcendental phenomenology* and *"descriptive"*, or, as it is often called nowadays, *"phenomenological" psychology*, is a problem that as a rule brings great difficulties with it, which indeed are grounded in the very nature of the case. It has led to misunderstandings, to which even thinkers who subscribe to the phenomenological line of thought are subject. Some attempt to clarify the situation should prove useful.

The change of standpoint which in this work bears the name phenomenological reduction (transcendental-phenomenological we now say, to be more definite) is effected by me, as the actually philosophizing subject, from the natural standpoint as a basis, and I experience myself here in the first instance as "I" in the ordinary sense of the term, as this human person living among others in the world. As a psychologist, I take as my theme this I-type of being and life, in its general aspect, the human being as "psychical". Turning inwards in pure reflexion, following exclusively "inner experience" (self-experience and "empathy", to be more precise), and setting aside all the psychophysical questions which relate to man as a corporeal being, I obtain an original and pure descriptive knowledge of the psychical life as it is in itself, the most original information being obtained from myself, because here alone is perception the medium. If, as is often done, descriptions of all sorts, which attach themselves purely and truly to the data of intuition, are referred to as phenomenological, there here grows up, on the pure basis of inner intuition, of the intuition of the soul's own essence, a phenomenological psychology. A right form of method (on this point we shall have something further to say) gives us in point of fact not only scanty, superficially classificatory descriptions, but a great self-supporting science; the latter, however, properly speaking, only when, as is possible also here, one first sets before oneself as goal a science which deals not with the factual data of this inner sphere of intuition, but with the essence, inquiring, that is, after the invariant, essentially characteristic structures of a soul, of a psychical life in general.

If we now perform this transcendental-phenomenological reduction, this transformation of the natural and psychologically inward standpoint whereby it is transcendentalized, the psychological subjectivity loses just that which makes it something real in the world that lies before us; it loses the meaning of the soul as belonging to a body that exists in an objective, spatio-temporal Nature. This transformation of meaning concerns myself, above all, the "I" of the psychological and subsequently transcendental inquirer for the time being. Posited as real (*wirklich*), I am now no longer a human Ego *in* the universal, existentially posited world, but exclusively a subject *for* which this world has being, and purely, indeed, *as* that which appears to me, is presented to me, and of which I am conscious in some way or other, so that the real being of the world thereby remains unconsidered, unquestioned, and its validity left out of account.

Now if transcendental description passes no judgment whatsoever upon the world, and upon my human Ego as belonging to the world, and if, in this description, the transcendental Ego exists (*ist*) absolutely in and for itself prior to all cosmic being (which first wins in and through it existential validity), it is still at the same time evident that, at every conversion of meaning which concerns the phenomenological-psychological content of the soul as a whole, this very content by simply putting on another existential meaning (*Seinssinn*) becomes transcendental-phenomenological, just as conversely the latter, on reverting to the natural psychological standpoint, becomes once again psychological. Naturally this correspondence must still hold good if, prior to all interest in the development of psychological science, and of a "descriptive" or "phenomenological psychology" in particular, a transcendental phenomenology is set up under the leading of a philosophical idea, so that through phenomenological reduction the transcendental Ego is directly set up at the focus of reflexion, and made the theme of a transcendental description.

We have thus a remarkable thoroughgoing parallelism between a (properly elaborated) phenomenological psychology and a transcendental phenomenology. To each eidetic or empirical determination on the one side there must correspond a parallel feature on the other. And yet this whole content as psychology, considered from the natural standpoint as a positive science, therefore, and related to the world as spread before us, is entirely non-philosophical, whereas "the same" content from the transcendental standpoint, and therefore as transcendental phenomenology, is a philosophical science—indeed, on closer view, *the* basic philosophical science, preparing on descriptive lines the transcendental ground which remains henceforth the exclusive ground for all philosophical knowledge.

Here in fact lie the chief difficulties in the way of an understanding, since it must be felt at first as a most unreasonable demand that such a "nuance" springing from a mere change of standpoint should possess such great, and indeed, for all genuine philosophy, such decisive significance. The wholly unique meaning of this "nuance" can be clearly appreciated only when he who philosophizes has reached a radical understanding with himself as to what he proposes to bring under the title "philosophy", and only in so far as he is constrained to look for something differing in principle from positive science: the theoretic control, that is, of something other than the world ostensibly given to us through experience. From such understanding with one's own self, carried out in a really radical and consistent way, there springs up of necessity a motivation which compels the philosophizing Ego to reflect back on that very subjectivity of his, which in all his experience and knowledge of the natural world, both real and possible, is in the last resort the Ego that experiences and knows, and is thus already presupposed in all the natural self-knowledge of the "human Ego who experiences, thinks, and acts naturally in the world".

In other words: from this source springs the phenomenological transposition as an absolute requirement, if philosophy generally is to work out its distinctive purposes upon a basis of original experience, and so contrive to begin at all. It can make a beginning, and generally speaking develop all its further philosophical resources, only as a science working from the transcendental-philosophical standpoint. For this very reason the immediate *a priori* phenomenology (portrayed in this work in its actual functioning as that which directly prepares the transcendental basis) is the "first philosophy" in itself, the philosophy of the Beginning. Only when this motivation (which stands in need of a very minute and comprehensive analysis) has become a vital and compelling insight, does it become clear that the "change in the shading", which at first appears so strange, transforming as it does a pure psychology of the inner life into a self-styled transcendental phenomenology, determines the being and non-being of philosophy—of a philosophy which knows with thoroughgoing scientific assurance what its own distinctive meaning calls for as the basis and the method of its inquiry.

In the light of such self-comprehension, we understand for the first time that deepest and truly radical meaning of "psychologism" (that is, of transcendental psychologism) as the error that perverts the pure meaning of philosophy, proposing as it does to found philosophy on psychology, on the positive science of the life of the soul. This perversion persists unmodified when, in sympathy with our own procedure, the pure psychology of the inner life is set up also as an *a priori* science; even then it remains a positive science, and can provide a basis for positive science only, never for philosophy.

In the course of many years of brooding over these matters, the author has followed up different lines of inquiry, all equally possible, in the attempt to exhibit in an absolutely transparent and compelling way the nature of such motivation as propels beyond the natural positive realism of life and science, and necessitates the transcendental transposition, the "phenomenological Reduction". They are the ways of reaching the starting-point of a serious philosophy, and as they must be thought out in conscious reflexion, they themselves belong properly to the Beginning, as is possible, indeed, only within the beginner as he reflects upon himself. For each of these ways the point of departure is, of course, the natural unsophisticated standpoint of positive reality (*Positivität*) which the world of experience has as the basis of its being, and is confessedly "taken for granted" (the nature of such Being never having been questioned). In the work here presented (Second Section, second chapter, § 33 f.), the author selected that way of approach, which then appeared to him the most effective. It develops as a course of self-reflexion taking place in the region of the pure psychological intuition of the inner life, or, as we might also say, as a "phenomenological" reflexion in the ordinary psychological sense. It leads eventually to the point that I, who am here reflecting upon myself, become conscious that under a consistent and exclusive focusing of experience upon that which is purely inward, upon what is "phenomenologically" accessible to me, I possess in myself an essential individuality, self-contained, and holding well together in itself, to which all real and objectively possible experience and knowledge belongs, through whose agency the objective world is there for me with all its empirically confirmed facts, in and through which it has for me at any rate trustworthy (even if never scientifically authorized) essential validity. This also includes the more special apperceptions through which I take myself to be a man with body and soul, who lives in the world with other men, lives the life of the world, and so forth.

Continuing this self-reflexion, I now also become aware that my own phenomenologically self-contained essence can be posited in an *absolute* sense, as I am the Ego who invests the being of the world which I so constantly speak about with existential validity, as an existence (*Sein*) which wins for me from my own life's pure essence meaning and substantiated validity. I myself as this individual essence, posited absolutely, as the open infinite field of pure phenomenological data and their inseparable unity, am the "transcendental Ego"; the absolute positing means that the world is no longer "given" to me in advance, its validity that of a simple existent, but that henceforth it is exclusively my Ego that is given (given from my new standpoint), given purely as that which has being in itself, in itself experiences a world, confirms the same, and so forth.

Within this view of things there grows up, provided the consequences are fearlessly followed up (and this is not everybody's business), *a transcendental-phenomenological Idealism* in opposition to every form of psychologistic Idealism. The account given in the chapter indicated suffers, as the author confesses, from lack of completeness. Although it is in all real essentials unassailable, it lacks what is certainly important to the foundation of this Idealism, the proper consideration of the problem of transcendental solipsism or of transcendental intersubjectivity, of the essential relationship of the objective world, that is valid for me, to others which are valid for me and with me. The completing developments should have been furnished in a Second Volume which the author had hoped to be able to supply very soon after the first, as a sequel that had been planned at the same time with it.

The objections raised against this Idealism and its alleged Solipsism seriously impeded the reception of the work, as though its essential significance lay in any way in this sketch of its philosophical import: whereas this was no more than a means devised in the interest of the problem of a possible objective knowledge, for winning this necessary insight: that the very meaning of that problem refers us back to the Ego that is in and for itself; and that this Ego, as the presupposition of the knowledge of the world, cannot be and remain presupposed as having the existence of a world, and must therefore, in respect of the world's being, be brought to its pure state through phenomenological reduction, that is, through "Epoché". I might have been better advised if, without altering the essential connexions of the exposition, I had left open the final decision in favour of transcendental Idealism, and contented myself with making clear that trains of thought of crucial philosophical significance with a trend that is towards Idealism necessarily arise here, and must by all means be thought out; so that to this end one needs in any case to make sure of the ground of transcendental subjectivity.

I must not hesitate, however, to state quite explicitly that in regard to transcendental-phenomenological Idealism, I have nothing whatsoever to take back, that now as ever I hold every form of current philosophical realism to be in principle absurd, as no less every idealism to which in its own arguments that realism stands contrasted, and which in fact it refutes. Given a deeper understanding of my exposition, the solipsistic objection should never have been raised as an objection against phenomenological idealism, but only as an objection to the incompleteness of my exposition. Still, one should not overlook what is the radical essential in all philosophizing to which, in this book, a path will be opened. Over against the thinking, rich in presuppositions, which has as its premises the world, science, and sundry understandings bearing on method, and rooted in the scientific tradition as a whole, a radical form of the autonomy of knowledge is here active, in which every form of datum given in advance, and all Being taken for granted, is set out as invalid, and there is a reversion to that which is already presupposed *implicite* in all presupposing and in all questioning and answering, and herewith of necessity exists already, immediate and persistent. This is the first to be freely and expressly posited, and with a self-evidence which precedes all conceivable instances of self-evidence, and is contained implicitly in them all.

Although it is only with the phenomenological reduction which would convert this radicalism into conscious work, that

genuine work-performing philosophizing begins, the whole pre-
paratory reflexion has already been carried through, and precisely in this spirit. It is phenomenological, though still unconsciously so. It follows, therefore, that it is a piece of pure
self-reflexion revealing original self-evident facts; and, moreover,
when it exhibits in these facts (though incompletely) the outlines of Idealism, it is as far as can be from being one of the
usual balancings between Idealism and Realism, and cannot be
affected by the arguments involved in any of their objections.
Such essential connexions of a phenomenological kind, and
such motivations in an "idealistic" direction as are in fact revealed, hold firm under all the improvements and completions
that may eventually prove necessary, even as the reality of rivers
and mountain ranges, which the first explorer has really seen
and described, remains standing despite the improvements and
additions to which his descriptions are subjected by later ex-
plorers.

The first preliminary steps towards a fresh formulation
of the transcendental problem (to subserve mere purposes of
motivation) must then be taken in accord with its phenomenological content, and in accord with what from this point of
departure forecasts with objective necessity the true meaning
of an objective being that is subjectively knowable. Moreover,
transcendental phenomenology is not a theory, devised merely
as a reply to the historic problem of Idealism, it is a science
founded in itself, and standing absolutely on its own basis; it
is indeed the one science that stands absolutely on its own
ground. Only in such wise, however, that when consistently
carried forward, it leads, as is already apparent in the important
concluding portions of the book, to the "constitutive" problems,
which take in all the conceivable objects we could ever meet
with in experience, briefly the whole real world spread out before us together with all its categories of the object, and likewise
all "ideal" worlds, and makes these all intelligible as transcendental correlates. Whence it clearly follows that transcendental
phenomenological Idealism is not a special philosophical thesis,
a theory among others; that transcendental phenomenology,
rather, as concrete science, is, in itself, even when no word is
spoken concerning Idealism, universal Idealism worked out as a

science. And it proves it through its own meaning as transcendental science in each of its special constitutive domains. But we also need to make clearly explicit the fundamental and essential difference between transcendental-phenomenological Idealism and that form of Idealism which in popular realism is opposed to it as its incompatible opposite.

And in the very first place let this be said: Our phenomenological idealism does not deny the positive existence of the real (*realen*) world and of Nature—in the first place as though it held it to be an illusion. Its sole task and service is to clarify the meaning of this world, the precise sense in which everyone accepts it, and with undeniable right, as really existing (*wirklich seiende*). That it exists—given as it is as a universe out there (*daseiendes*)[1] in an experience that is continuous, and held persistently together through a thread of widespread unanimity—that is quite indubitable. It is quite another consideration, although in the light of the discussions in the text of this work one of great philosophical importance, that the continuance of experience in the future under such form of universal agreement is a mere (although reasonable) presumption, and that accordingly the non-existence of the world, although, and whilst it [the world] is in point of fact the object of a unanimous experience, always remains *thinkable*.

The result of the phenomenological clarification of the meaning of the manner of existence of the real world (and, eidetically, of a real world generally) is that only transcendental subjectivity has ontologically the meaning of Absolute Being, that it only is non-relative, that is relative only to itself; whereas the real world indeed exists, but in respect of essence is relative to transcendental subjectivity, and in such a way that it can have its meaning as existing (*seiende*) reality only as the intentional meaning-product of transcendental subjectivity. But that first attains its full meaning when the phenomenological disclosure of the transcendental Ego is so far advanced that the experience of fellow-subjects implicit in it has won its reduction to transcendental experience; in other words, when the self-

[1] The term *daseiendes* is more accurately rendered as "existing" rather than as "out there" (Editor's note).

interpretation carried out purely on the basis of transcendental experience has led to the knowledge of the real and whole meaning of the transcendental subjectivity, which, for the Ego reflecting at the time means this: "I, the transcendental, absolute I, as I am in my own life of transcendental consciousness; but besides myself, the fellow-subjects who in this life of mine reveal themselves as co-transcendental, within the transcendental society of 'Ourselves', which simultaneously reveals itself." It is thus within the intersubjectivity, which in the phenomenological reduction has reached empirical givenness on a transcendental level, and is thus itself transcendental, that the real (*reale*) world is constituted as "objective", as being there for everyone.

The world has this meaning, whether we are aware of it or not. But how could we ever be aware of it prior to the phenomenological reduction which first brings the transcendental subjectivity as our absolute Being into the focus of experience? So long as it was only the psychological subjectivity that was recognized, and one sought to posit it as absolute, and to understand the world as its correlate, the result could only be an absurd Idealism, a psychological Idealism—the very type which the equally absurd realism has as its counterpart. Now by such as have won their way to the genuine transcendental subjectivity it can assuredly be seen that the great idealists of the eighteenth century, Berkeley and Hume on the one side, Leibniz on the other, had, properly speaking, already reached beyond psychological subjectivity in the sense it bears within the natural world. But since the contrast between psychological and transcendental subjectivity remained unexplained, and the all-dominant sensationalism of the school of Locke could not render intelligible the constituting of what is real as a performance giving to subjectivity meaning and true being, the unfruitful and unphilosophical conflict fought out on the field of nature remained in vogue for the times that followed, and there prevailed a perverse interpretation of the meaning which the great idealists had really intended, yet to be sure without making that meaning scientifically clear.

The new publications which the author began to issue in 1929 (the first since the *Ideen*) will contribute far-reaching advances, clarifications, and completions of what, for the rest, had already been begun in the *Logische Untersuchungen* (1900–1901), and then in the *Ideen*, so that the claim to have set going the necessary beginnings of a philosophy, "which can present itself as a science", cannot well be regarded as self-deception. In any case, he who for decades instead of speculating concerning a New Atlantis has really wandered in the trackless wilds of a new continent and undertaken bits of virgin cultivation, will not allow himself to be diverted by the refusals of geographers who judge the reports in the light of their own experiences and habits of thought, and on the strength of this exempt themselves from all the trouble of making a journey into the land proclaimed to be new.

There is still one point that calls for a remark. In the eyes of those[2] who set aside the phenomenological reduction as a philosophically irrelevant eccentricity (whereby, to be sure, they destroy the whole meaning of the work and of my phenomenology), and leave nothing remaining but an *a priori* psychology, it often happens that this residual psychology is identified as to its main import with Franz Brentano's psychology of intentionality. Great indeed as is the respect and gratitude with which the author remembers this gifted thinker as his teacher, and strongly convinced as he is that his conversion of the scholastic concept of intentionality into a descriptive root-concept of psychology constitutes a great discovery, apart from which phenomenology could not have come into being at all; none the less we must distinguish as essentially different the author's pure psychology implicitly contained in this transcendental phenomenology and the psychology of Brentano. This holds good also of his "psychognosis" limited to pure description in the region of inner experience. It is indeed "phenomenological" psychology if, as has often happened at the present time, we are to give the title "phenomenological" to every psychological inquiry conducted purely within the framework of "inner experience", and, grouping all such studies together, to speak further of a phenomenological psychology.

[2] This is an oblique reference to Scheler and Heidegger (Editor's note).

For this latter discipline, quite apart from its name, takes us back, naturally, to John Locke and to his school, including John Stuart Mill. One can then say that David Hume's *Treatise* gives the first systematic sketch of a pure phenomenology, which, though under the name of psychology, attempts to supply a philosophical transcendental philosophy. Like his great predecessor, Berkeley, it is as a psychologist that he is regarded and has exercised his influence. Thus, excluding all transcendental questions, it is this whole "phenomenological" school which alone calls here for our consideration. Characteristic of it and of its psychology is the conception set forth in Locke's "white paper"[3] simile of the pure soul as a complex or heap of temporally co-existing and successive data, which run their course under rules partly their own, partly psychophysical. It would thus be the function of descriptive psychology to distinguish and classify the main types of these "sense-data", data of the "inner sense", of inner experience, and likewise the elementary basic forms of the psychical complex; that of explanatory psychology to seek out the rules of genetic formations and transformations, much as in the case of natural science, and on similar lines of method. And quite naturally so, since the pure psychical being or the psychical life is regarded as a nature-resembling flow of events in a quasi-space of consciousness.

On grounds of principle, we may say that it obviously makes no difference whether we let the psychic "data" be blown along in a collective whole "atomistically", though in accordance with empirical laws, like heaps of sand, or regard them as parts of wholes which by necessity, whether empirical or *a priori*, can alone operate as such parts, and principally perhaps within the whole of consciousness fettered as that is to a rigid form of wholeness. In other words, atomistic and Gestalt-psychology alike participate in that intrinsic meaning of psychological "naturalism", as defined in terms of what we have stated above, which, having regard to the expression "inner sense", may also be termed "sensationalism"

[3] The expression meant here is the Latin *"tabula rasa"* which is more accurately translated as "blank slate" (Editor's note).

(*Sensualismus*). Clearly Brentano's psychology of intentionality also remains fettered to this inherited naturalism, though in virtue of its having introduced into psychology as a main concept, descriptive in type and universal in scope, that of Intentionality, it has worked therein as a reforming factor.

The essentially new influence which in transcendentally directed phenomenology becomes active for descriptive psychology, and is now completely changing the whole aspect of this psychology, its whole method, the setting of its concrete aims, is the insight that a concrete description of the sphere of consciousness as a self-contained sphere of intentionality (it is never otherwise concretely given), a concrete description, for instance, of perceptions or recollections, and so forth, also calls, of necessity, for a description of the object as such, referred to in intentional experiences, as such, we say, indicating thereby that they belong inseparably to the current experience itself as its objectively intended or "objective meaning". Furthermore, that one and the same intentional object as such, from the viewpoint of descriptive psychology, is an ideal indicator of a group of ways of being conscious that are proper to it, whose system of typical differences tallies essentially with the typical articulation of the intentional object.

It does not suffice to say that every consciousness is a consciousness-of on the lines, perhaps, of Brentano's classification (to which I cannot subscribe) into "presentations", "judgments", "phenomena of love and of hate"; but one must question the different categories of objects in their pure objectivity as objects of possible consciousness, and question back to the essential configurations of possible "manifolds" to be synthetically connected, through which an object of the relevant category can alone be known as the same, that is, as that which can be known through experiences of very differing description, differing and always differing still again, but always restricted to the descriptive types of such ways of consciousness as belong to it essentially and *a priori*. The reference to the fact that every object is either experienced or thought or sought after as an end, and so forth, is only a first step, and still tells us very little. The task of a phenomenological "constitution" of objects referred to at the close of this book, in a transcendental setting, it is true, finds its place here, only that now it is conceived as projected back upon the natural psychological standpoint.

Unfortunately, the necessary stressing of the difference between transcendental and psychological subjectivity, the repeated declaration that transcendental phenomenology is not in any sense psychology, not even phenomenological psychology has had this effect upon the majority of professional psychologists (who are wont to be very frugal, moreover, in all that concerns philosophy), that they failed to notice at all the radical psychological reform which was involved in the transcendental; they interpreted my utterances as an intimation that as psychologists they were not concerned in any way with phenomenology, or with any part of it. Even the few who noticed here that it was very relevant to psychology, and sought to make it accessible, have not grasped the whole meaning and scope of an intentional and constitutive phenomenology, and have not seen that here for the first time, in contrast with naturalistic psychology from an outer standpoint, a psychology comes to words and deeds, a psychology in which the life of the soul is made intelligible in its most intimate and originally intuitional essence, and that this original intuitional essence lies in a "constituting" of meaning-formations in modes of existential validity, which is perpetually new and incessantly organizing itself afresh— briefly, in the system of intentional actions, whereby existential (*seiende*) objects of the most varied grades right up to the level of an objective world are there for the Ego as occasion demands.

It was, moreover, not without reason that the psychological reform made its first entry as the concealed implication of a transcendental reform. For only a compulsion grounded on the philosophically transcendental problem, an urge towards extreme radicalism in the clearing up of the modes in which knowledge and object stand to each other in the conscious life itself, necessarily led to a universal and concrete phenomenology of consciousness, which received its primary orientation from the intentional object. In the transition to the psychology of the natural standpoint, it is then obvious that an intentional psychology has a quite different meaning from that of the traditions of the school of Locke or of that of Brentano. A. von Meinong also, although, in writings that appeared subsequently to my *Logical Studies*, his teaching comes here and there into touch with my own, is in no way to be regarded here as an exception: he remains bound to Brentano's leading conceptions, or to psychological sensationalism, as does the entire psychology of the modern tradition and the whole psychology of the present day.

The present work, however, as a philosophical treatise does not include psychological reform among its themes, although it should not be wholly lacking in indications bearing on a genuine intentional psychology. Even as philosophical, moreover, its task is limited. It does not claim to be anything more than an attempt that has been growing through decades of meditation exclusively directed to this one end: to discover a *radical beginning* of a philosophy which, to repeat the Kantian phrase, "will be able to present itself as science". The ideal of a philosopher, to think out sooner or later a logic, an ethic, a metaphysic, and so forth, which he can at all times justify to himself and others with an insight that is absolutely cogent—this ideal the author had early to abandon, and has not resumed it to this day. And for no reason other than the following, seeing that at any rate this insight was and remained for him indubitable, that a philosophy cannot start in a naïve straightforward fashion—not then as do the positive sciences which take their stand on the previously given ground of our experience of a world, presupposed as something that exists as a matter of course. That they do it causes them all to have problems in respect of their foundations, and paradoxes of their own, a condition which a subsequent and belated theory of knowledge first seeks to remedy.

For this very reason the positive sciences are unphilosophical, they are not ultimate, absolute sciences. A philosophy with problematic foundations, with paradoxes which arise from the obscurity of the fundamental concepts, is no philosophy, it contradicts its very meaning *as* philosophy. Philosophy can take root only in radical reflexion upon the meaning and possibility of its own scheme. Through such reflexion it must in the very first place and through its own activity take possession of the absolute ground of pure pre-conceptual experience, which is its own proper preserve; then, self-active again, it must create original concepts, adequately adjusted to this ground, and so generally utilize for its advance an absolutely transparent method.

There can then be no unclear, problematic concepts, and no paradoxes. The entire absence of this procedure, the overlooking of the immense difficulties attaching to a correct beginning, or the covering up of the same through the haste to have done with them, had this for its consequence, that we had and have many and ever new philosophical "systems" or "directions", but not the *one* philosophy which as Idea underlies all the philosophies that can be imagined. Philosophy, as it moves towards its realization, is not a relatively incomplete science improving as it goes naturally forward. There lies embedded in its meaning as philosophy a radicalism in the matter of foundations, an absolute freedom from all presuppositions, a securing for itself an absolute basis: the totality of presuppositions that can be "taken for granted". But that too must itself be first clarified through corresponding reflexions, and the absolutely binding quality of its requirements laid bare.

That these reflexions become more and more interwoven as thought advances, and lead eventually to a whole science, to a science of Beginnings, a "first" philosophy; that all philosophical disciplines, the very foundations of all sciences whatsoever, spring from its matrix—all this must needs have remained implicit since the radicalism was lacking without which philosophy generally could not be, could not even make a start. The true philosophical beginning must have been irretrievably lost in beginning with presuppositions of a positive kind. Lacking as did the traditional schemes of philosophy the enthusiasm of a first beginning, they also lacked what is first and most important: a specifically philosophical groundwork acquired through original self-activity, and therewith that firmness of basis, that genuineness of root, which alone makes real philosophy possible.

The author's convictions on such lines have become increasingly self-evident as his work progressed. If he has been obliged, on practical grounds, to lower the ideal of the philosopher to that of a downright beginner, he has at least in his old age reached for himself the complete certainty that he should thus call himself a beginner. He could almost hope, were Methuselah's span of days allotted him, to be still able to become a philosopher. He has always been able to follow up the problems that issue from the Beginning, and primarily from what is first for a descriptive phenomenology, the beginning of the beginning, and to develop it concretely in what to him have been instructive pieces of work. The far horizons of a phenomenological philosophy, the chief structural formations, to speak geographically, have disclosed themselves; the essential groups of problems and the methods of approach on essential lines have been made clear. The author sees the infinite open country of the true philosophy, the "promised land" on which he himself will never set foot. This confidence may wake a smile, but let each see for himself whether it has not some ground in the fragments laid before him as phenomenology in its beginnings. Gladly would he hope that those who come after will take up these first ventures, carry them steadily forward, yes, and improve also their great deficiencies, defects of incompleteness which cannot indeed be avoided in the beginnings of scientific work.

But when all is said, this work of mine can help no one who has already fixed his philosophy and his philosophical method, who has thus never learnt to know the despair of one who has the misfortune to be in love with philosophy, and who at the very outset of his studies, placed amid the chaos of philosophies, with his choice to make, realizes that he has really no choice at all, since no one of these has taken care to free itself from presuppositions, and none has sprung from the radical attitude of autonomous self-responsibility which the meaning of a philosophy demands. He who believes that he can appeal to the "fruitful βάθος" of experience in the current sense of that term, or to the "assured results" of the exact sciences, or to experimental or physiological psychology, or to a constantly improved logic and mathematics, and so forth, and therein find premises for his philosophy, cannot have much susceptibility for the contents of this book. He is unable to bring to his reading an intensive interest, nor can he hold that the time and effort have been well spent which the sympathetic understanding of such a way of beginning demands. Only he who is himself striving to reach a beginning will herein behave otherwise, since he must say to himself: *tua res agitur*.

Those who are interested in the author's continued work and progress since 1913 may be referred to the recently published writing entitled "Formale und transzendentale Logik, Versuch einer Kritik der logischen Vernunft" (in the *Jahrbuch f. Phänomenologie und phänomenologische Forschung*, Bd. X, 1929). Also to his *Cartesianischen Meditationen*, an extended elaboration of the four lectures which he had the pleasure of giving first in the spring of 1922 at the University of London, and in this last year in an essentially maturer form at the Sorbonne in Paris. They furnish once again, though merely in outline an Introduction to phenomenological philosophy, but contain an essential supplement in the detailed treatment of the fundamental problem of transcendental intersubjectivity, wherewith the solipsistic objection completely collapses. They will presumably appear simultaneously with this English edition of the *Ideen* in a French rendering in the *Bulletin de la Société de Philosophie*. In the same year a German edition should be appearing, published by Niemeyer of Halle a.d.S, containing as additional matter a second Introduction, in which the clarification of the idea of a personal (on the lines of a mental science) and natural anthropology and psychology, and lastly of a pure intuitional psychology, is undertaken as an initial problem. At a later stage only is it shown how, starting from this discussion, which, like all that has preceded, remains on natural ground, the Copernican reversal to the transcendental standpoint finds its motive. At the same time a series of publications is being started in my *Jahrbuch*: the concrete phenomenological studies which I have drafted as the years went by, to clear up my own mind, and for the safeguarding of the structure of phenomenology.

Husserl's Major Writings
(arranged chronologically)

There is a complete works in progress.

Gesammelte Werke (Husserliana). Auf Grund des Nachlasses Veröffenheit vom Husserl-Archiv (Louvain) Unter Leitung von

H. L. van Breda. Band I–XI. The Hague: Nijhoff, 1950–1966.

Band I—*Cartesianische Meditationen und Pariser Vorträge.* Ed. S. Strasser, 1950.

Cartesian Meditations. An Introduction to Phenomenology. Tr. Dorion Cairns. The Hague: Nijhoff, 1960.

The Paris Lectures. Tr. P. Koestenbaum. The Hague: Nijhoff, 1964.

Band II—*Die Idee der Phänomenologie. Fünf Vorlesungen* [1907]. Ed. Walter Biemel, 1950.

The Idea of Phenomenology. Tr. W. Alston & G. Nakhnikian. The Hague: Nijhoff, 1964.

Band III—*Ideen zu einer reinen Phänomenologie und phänomenologischen Philosophie.* Erstes Buch: *Allgemeine Einführung in die reine Phänomenologie.* Ed. Walter Biemel, 1950.

Band IV—*Ideen zu einer reinen Phänomenologie.* Zweites Buch: *Phänomenologische Untersuchungen zu Konstitution.* Ed. Marly Biemel, 1952.

Band V—*Ideen zu einer reinen Phänomenologie.* Drittes Buch: *Die Phänomenologie und die Fundamente der Wissenschaften.* Ed. Marly Biemel, 1952.

Band VI—*Die Krisis der europäischen Wissenschaften und die transzendentale Phänomenologie.* Eine Einleitung in die phänomenologische Philosophie. Ed. Walter Biemel, 1954.

The Crisis of European Sciences and Transcendental Phenomenology. An Introduction to Phenomenological Philosophy. Tr. D. Carr. Evanston: Northwestern University Press, 1970.

Band VII—*Erste Philosophie* [1923/24]. Erster Teil: *Kritische Ideengeschichte.* Ed. Rudolf Boehm, 1956.

Band VIII—*Erste Philosophie* [1923/24]. Zweiter Teil: *Theorie der phänomenologischen Reduktion.* Ed. Rudolf Boehm, 1959.

Band IX—*Phänomenologische Psychologie.* Ed. Walter Biemel, 1962.

Band X—*Zur Phänomenologie des Inneren Zeitbewusstseins.* Ed. Rudolf Boehm, 1966.

The Phenomenology of Internal Time-Consciousness. Ed. Martin Heidegger. Tr. J. Churchill. Bloomington: University of Indiana Press, 1964.

Band XI—*Analysen zur Passiven Synthesis.* Ed. Margot Fleischer, 1966.

Philosophie der Arithmetik. Psychologische und logische Unter-suchungen. Erster Band. Halle: Pfeffer, 1891.

Logische Untersuchungen. Vol. I [1900], Vol. II [1901]; second re-vised edition in 3 vols. Halle: Niemeyer, 1913.

Logical Investigations. Tr. J. N. Findlay. 2 vols. New York: Humani-ties, 1970.

"Philosophie als strenge Wissenschaft," *Logos,* I [1910], 289–341. "Philosophy as Rigorous Science" in *Phenomenology and the Crisis of Philosophy.* Tr. Quentin Lauer. New York: Harper, 1965.

Ideen zu einer reinen Phänomenologie und phänomenologischen Philosophie. Vol. I. Halle: Niemeyer, 1913. Also *Husserliana,* Band III.

  Ideas: General Introduction to Pure Phenomenology. Tr. W. R. Boyce Gibson. New York: Macmillan, 1931.

"Phenomenology," *Encyclopedia Britannica,* 14th ed., 1927, vol. 17, 699–702. There are three German versions of this article as well as Heidegger's marginal notes to it in *Husserliana,* Band IX.

  The English version was reprinted in *Realism and the Background of Phenomenology.* Ed. R. M. Chisholm. Illinois: Free Press of Glencoe, 1960.

Vorlesungen zur Phänomenologie des inneren Zeitbewusstseins. Ed. Martin Heidegger. Halle: Niemeyer, 1928. Also *Husserliana,* Band X.

Formale und transcendentale Logik. Versuch einer Kritik der logischen Vernunft. Halle: Niemeyer, 1929.

  Formal and Transcendental Logic. Tr. Dorion Cairns. The Hague: Nijhoff, 1969.

Nachwort zu meinen Ideen zu einer reinen Phänomenologie. Halle: Niemeyer, 1930.

  "Author's Preface to the English Edition," *Ideas: General Intro-duction to Pure Phenomenology.*

Méditations cartésiennes. Tr. J. Peiffer and E. Levinas. Paris: Colin, 1931. The original German version was published posthumously in *Husserliana,* Band I.

Die Krisis der europäischen Wissenschaften und die transcendentale Phänomenologie. Part I, *Philosophia,* 1936. All parts were pub-lished in *Husserliana,* Band VI.

Erfahrung und Urteil, Untersuchungen zur Genealogie der Logik. Ed. Ludwig Landgrebe. Hamburg: Classen, 1939.

Selected Studies About Husserl
(arranged alphabetically)

Bachelard, Suzanne. *La Logique de Husserl*. Paris: Presses Universitaires, 1957.

Berger, Gaston. *Le Cogito dans la philosophie de Husserl*. Paris: Aubier, 1941.

Brand, Gerd. *Welt, Ich, und Zeit*. The Hague: Nijhoff, 1955.

Chiodi, Pietro. *Esistenzialismo e Fenomenologia*. Milano: Edizioni di Communità, 1963.

Chisholm, R. M. *Realism and the Background of Phenomenology*. Illinois: Free Press of Glencoe, 1960.

Diemer, Alwin. *Edmund Husserl. Versuch einer systematischen Darstellung seiner Phänomenologie*. Meisenheim am Glan: Hain, 1956.

Farber, Marvin. *The Aims of Phenomenology: The Motives, Methods and Impact of Husserl's Thought*. New York: Harper, 1966.

——. *The Foundation of Phenomenology. Edmund Husserl and the Quest for a Rigorous Science of Philosophy*. Cambridge: Harvard University Press, 1943.

——, (ed.). *Philosophical Essays in Memory of Edmund Husserl*. Cambridge: Harvard University Press, 1940.

Fink, Eugen. "Die Phänomenologische Philosophie Edmund Husserls in der gegenwärtigen Kritik," *Kantstudien* XXXVIII [1933], 319–383.

Kocklemans, Joseph. *A First Introduction to Husserl's Phenomenology*. Pittsburgh: Duquesne University Press, 1967.

——, (ed.). *Phenomenology: The Philosophy of Edmund Husserl and Its Interpretation*. New York: Doubleday, 1967.

Landgrebe, Ludwig. *Phänomenologie und Metaphysik*. Hamburg: Schröder, 1949.

Lauer, Quentin. *The Triumph of Subjectivity. An Introduction to Transcendental Phenomenology*. New York: Fordham University Press, 1958.

Paci, Enzo. *Tempo e verità nella fenomenologia di Husserl*. Bari: Laterza, 1961.

Ricoeur, Paul. *Husserl: An Analysis of His Phenomenology*. Tr. E. Ballard & L. Embree. Evanston: Northwestern University Press, 1967.

Sokolowski, Robert. *The Formation of Husserl's Concept of Constitution.* The Hague: Nijhoff, 1964.
Various Authors. *Edmund Husserl 1859–1959. Recueil commemoratif.* The Hague: Nijhoff, 1959.

Max Scheler (1874–1928)

Scheler was born in Munich on August 22, 1874, of a Protestant father and a Jewish mother. But he received no religious formation. His mother was a dissatisfied temperamental woman who nagged her husband and favored Max over his sister. The mother persistently contrasted the life style of her wealthy brother to the modest one her retired husband was able to provide. Max later recalled the mood of resentment that hung about his mother's presence.

Scheler had been impressed by the spirit of community in the Catholic population of Munich so that shortly after he entered the *Gymnasium,* he converted to Catholicism under the guidance of the chaplain. His academic work at the *Gymnasium* was weak in languages and mathematics and he received private tutoring in these areas. He was interested, however, in the natural sciences, especially biology, and decided to pursue a medical career.

After graduating from the *Gymnasium,* Scheler had an affair with a married woman who was eight years his senior and had a young child. Throughout his life, apparently, Scheler remained within the grip of a powerful sexual drive.

In 1893 he enrolled in the medical faculty at the University of Munich but did not attend classes and transferred to Berlin the next year in order to study philosophy and sociology. His mistress divorced her husband and Scheler married her in a civil ceremony and adopted her child. One child was born to them in 1900, but the marriage was unhappy and ended after fifteen years.

Dilthey and Georg Simmel were setting the tone in philosophy and sociology at Berlin, but apparently they did not impress Scheler since he moved to Jena the following semester and studied under Rudolf Eucken and Otto Leibmann, a neo-Kantian. He wrote his dissertation in 1897 on the relationship between logic and ethics and his *Habilitationsschrift* on philosophical method in 1899 which earned him an assistant professorship at Jena.

A critical turn in Scheler's intellectual career occurred when he met Husserl at a party given by Hans Vaihinger in 1901 at Halle. The direction his thought took was what he later termed Phenomenology, "a surrender of self to the intuitional content of things, a movement of profound trust in the unshakableness of all that is simply *given,* a courageous letting-oneself-go in intuition and in the loving movement toward the world in its capacity for being intuited." The relationship between Husserl and Scheler cooled as Scheler realized that Husserl was moving in the opposite direction toward Cartesianism and Kantianism while Husserl referred to Scheler's Phenomenology as "fool's gold," grouping him later with Heidegger as one of his two "antipodes."

Scheler moved back to his home town of Munich in 1907 and taught there until 1910 when he was forced to resign because of the scandal over the affairs which his wife reported to the newspapers as being the cause of his debts and of his neglect of her children and herself.

During the next nine years he lived as a private scholar in Göttingen and Berlin. He used a cafe as his lecture hall in Göttingen in 1911 and captivated his audiences with the excitement he generated. He seems also to have done some of his research in restaurants and cafes, preferring their atmosphere to that of the library or study. It was at this time that he wrote his major works, i.e., his *Formalism in Ethics* and *Ressentiment,* a work that bore a Nietzschean influence. He received a divorce in 1912, married again, was reconciled to the Catholic Church, and found a position in journalism.

The period during the First World War was important to Scheler in various ways. He wrote a work which praised the "civilizing" agency of war and as a result became a popular public figure. He tried to enlist in the army in 1914 but was rejected because of his age. When, however, he was drafted in 1915 as manpower in Germany decreased, he was discharged because of bad eyesight, but served as a propaganda lecturer in Austria, Holland, and Switzerland for the German Foreign Office. After 1915 and until his death he produced a sizable literature on the destiny of Germany.

After the war, the rector of the University of Cologne overlooked the occasion of Scheler's dismissal from Munich and in 1919 offered him an appointment to a special chair of philosophy and sociology.

In 1921 he became romantically involved with one of his students and wished to marry her. He divorced his second wife and married the student in 1924. He had left the Catholic Church in 1922, it seems, both because of personal difficulties surrounding his inability to have his second marriage annulled and because of philosophical incompatibility engendered by what he believed was the stultifying dogmatism of the Church.

The last period of Scheler's thought, concerned as it is with the concept of man, strongly suggests the influence of Nietzsche. He planned to write a book on Nietzsche, in fact, as a result of a lecture he was invited to give to the Nietzsche Society in Weimar by Elizabeth Förster-Nietzsche. Scheler's personal problems, however, constantly required his attention. His son from his first marriage, Wolf, had turned out to be a delinquent who plagued his father with debts and difficulties and eventually became a Brownshirt, only to be killed in a street brawl.

In his last year at Cologne with the prospects of a move to the University of Frankfurt, his health failed. He died on May 19, 1928.

"Philosopher's Outlook" from *Philosophical Perspectives*

Translated by Oscar A. Haac

"The masses will never be philosophers." These words of Plato are also valid today. Most men derive their view of the world from a religious or some other *tradition* which they imbibe with their mother's milk. However, the man who strives for an outlook founded on philosophy must dare to stand on his *own* reason. He must tentatively doubt all inherited opinions and must accept nothing which he himself cannot *clearly see* and prove. Although philosophy belongs and always did belong to an *elite* centered around the outstanding personality of a thinker, an outlook founded on philosophy is by no means without influence on the course of history. For all history is essentially the work of elites and of those who imitate them. To find an example of the influence of a philosophical elite, one need but think of the influence of Plato and Aristotle on church doctrine, or of the powerful, moving, and inspiring effect of Immanuel Kant, Johann Gottlieb Fichte, Schelling, and Hegel on the Germany of the wars of liberation and on its political and military leaders, poets, and educators.

It is true that, until recently, German philosophy itself, especially its academic branch, did not try to develop a truly *philosophical outlook*. For decades, it exhausted itself trying to serve the experimental sciences as it tested their assumptions, methods, and aims. Thus, the philosophy of the last third of the nineteenth century dissolved almost exclusively into theories of knowledge and experience; yet, philosophy must no more be the mere servant of the sciences than the servant of religious faith.

In recent decades, philosophy has realized this and has fundamentally changed its nature and objectives. After long struggles it has again developed thorough and rigorous methods in order to bring even so-called *"metaphysical"* problems closer to a solution, *in collaboration* with experimental science, but not under its patronage. Today, only a few stragglers continue the three major trends of thought, so-called positivism, Neo-Kantianism, and historicism, which declared that *all* forms of metaphysics were impossible. *Positivism* (e.g., Ernst Mach and Richard Avenarius) derived conceptions of being and knowledge from the evidence of sensory perception. It had to conclude that not only metaphysical solutions but even *investigations* of this kind were meaningless and based on false thinking "habits." So-called *Neo-Kantianism*, which, according to modern Kant studies, almost completely misunderstood the great thinker, did recognize metaphysical questions as eternal problems of reason, but considered them theoretically insoluble. *Historicism* (Karl Marx, Wilhelm Dilthey, Ernst Troeltsch, Oswald Spengler) saw in all views of the world, religious as well as philosophical, only changeable expressions of varying historical and social conditions. We can say today that philosophers have completely and fully refuted the reasons which these three groups of thinkers gave for their negative attitude toward metaphysics.[1]

It was necessary, however, not only to refute but to reconstruct in a positive spirit, and this was done. Man is not free to choose whether or not he wants to develop a metaphysical idea and a metaphysical awareness, i.e., an idea of the basis of man himself and of the world, of ontological reality which is only through itself (*ens per se*) and from which all other reality depends. Man, *necessarily* and always, consciously or unconsciously, *has* such an idea, such a feeling acquired by himself or inherited from tradition. All he can choose for himself is a good and reasonable or a poor and unreasonable idea of the absolute. Intellectual consciousness of absolute being is a part of man's *nature* and forms *a single* indestructible unit with consciousness of self, consciousness of the world, language, and conscience. Man can, of course, artificially exclude a clear consciousness of this realm by adhering to the sensory shell of the world. In such a case, the striving for the realm of the absolute persists, but the realm itself remains *empty* and without specific content. The place of the spiritual part of man also remains empty, and empty his heart. Even without being quite aware of it, man can fill this sphere of absolute being and of highest good with a *finite* content and good which, in his life, he treats "as if" it were absolute. Money, country, a loved one can be so treated. This is fetishism and idol worship. If man is to transcend this spiritual position, he must learn two things. First, through self-analysis, he must become conscious of the "idol" which, for him, has replaced absolute being and good. In the second place, he must smash this idol, i.e., put the overly loved object back into its

[1] Cf. "Probleme einer Soziologie des Wissens," in Scheler, *Die Wissensformen und die Gesellschaft* (Leipzig, 1926), critical comments on historicism and positivism.

relative position in the finite world. Then the sphere of the absolute will reappear, and only then will man be spiritually prepared to philosophize independently about the absolute.

Metaphysics is always *real*. This fact is only one reason why free philosophical investigation of the absolute is possible. Man, by right, also possesses the *means to know* and perceive the source of all things, cautiously and thoroughly, within limits that can be clearly determined, always imperfectly, but with truth and insight. He possesses, in the kernel of his individuality, the ability to win a *living share* in the source of all things. We shall show how he does this.

Man is capable of *threefold knowledge*—knowledge of *control* and achievement, knowledge of *essence* or culture, knowledge of *metaphysical reality* or salvation. None of these three kinds of knowledge exists for its own sake. Each kind serves to reshape a *realm of being*[2]—that of things, that of the culture pattern of *man* himself, or that of the *absolute*.

1

The first type of knowledge, that of achievement and control, serves our ability to exercise *power* over nature, society, and history. It is the knowledge of the *experimental specialized sciences* which support our entire occidental civilization. The supreme objective of this knowledge is to discover, wherever and in as far as possible, the *laws* regulating space and time relationships between environmental phenomena which can be definitely classified, the laws of their fortuitous circumstance here and now. We certainly do not seek such laws because we derive a special pleasure from laws, but for the sake of our *control* over the world and ourselves. Only what recurs according to laws can be predicted; only the predictable can be controlled. It is difficult to find such laws. Each day science discovers new ones and modifies old ones. In principle, however, it is always possible to find such laws. This is because sensory functions of all kinds (seeing, hearing, smelling, etc.), which we use for all possible *observations* and measurements, have been perfected by man, and by each animal, under the impetus and direction of their *drives* and *needs*. The lizard hears the softest rustle, but not the shot of the pistol. The control exercised by an organism can regulate only those elements and aspects of the actual world which recur in identical patterns according to the rule, "similar causes, similar effects." Therefore, our own and any *possible* sensory experience of animals is itself subject to an inner law. It tends to register *identical* rather than irregular segments of experience.

By analogy, physicists today wonder whether the ultimate and most fundamental laws of nature may not be just laws of a purely *statistical* type, laws of the "greatest number," and whether the principles involving *necessity*, in traditional physics, may not be solely the work of man. Space and time concepts, as Immanuel Kant correctly believed, do not stem from the content of our sensations but precede all sensory experience, like a plan and a diagram of all its potential individual patterns of content. Thus, even before space and time are conceptualized, e.g., visually or mentally represented, they are already inclusive terms for our capability to move spontaneously, inclusive terms for our capability to change spontaneously while doing and acting (time of eating, sleeping, space for motion). Only later on do we attribute to things *our* organic ability to move as *their* ability to move around each other. The same applies to time. The inclusive terms for all potential movement and change, which space and time actually are, in the last analysis, serve only our desire to control reality. A purely intellectual being would have no reality, and *reality* is here the inclusive concept of *what resists our desires*.[2] Thus, one can imagine the magnitude of the error which, inherent in the natural outlook of man, held sciences under its spell for so long. This error consists in the assumption that space and time are infinite "empty forms" and that these would remain as inactive forms, by themselves, and, whether we existed or not, if things, matter, and energy were destroyed, that they are empty forms within which the finite world and the historical process are merely a strange "island." In a similar way, *all* the basic forms of being in our natural and experimental scientific conceptions of the world are *determined* not only by

[2] Cf. "Erkenntnis und Arbeit," in Scheler, *op. cit.*, p. 455 f on reality, p. 278 f on the idea of knowledge.

the nature of our reason, as Kant thought, but also and in addition by our active *drive for control over nature.*

2

The second type of possible knowledge is that of *the* fundamental philosophy which Aristotle called *"first philosophy,"* i.e., the knowledge of all forms of being and of the essential structure of all that is. It was not until relatively recently that Edmund Husserl and his school rediscovered that this *knowledge of essence* is a way of knowing sharply opposed to knowledge of control and to the realm of existence which corresponds to it. Knowledge of essence involves a tremendous field of philosophical investigation with its particular methods. Knowledge of control seeks, as we have seen, the laws of coincidence in space and time, laws of fortuitous realities in the world and of their circumstance. Conversely, the second direction of investigation rigorously and methodically *disregards* fortuitous place in space and time and what happens to be this way or some other way. Instead, it asks: *"What* is the world, what is, e.g., each so-called 'body,' each 'living being'; what is the *essence* of plant, animal, man, etc., in its invariable structure and essential qualities?" In a similar way it asks: "What is 'thought,' what is it to feel 'love' or 'beauty' quite independent from the fortuitous temporal stream of consciousness of this or that man in whom these activities *de facto* appear?"

What are the *main characteristics* of this kind of knowledge and investigation? First of all, the orientation toward controlling the world is replaced by the attempt to *exclude,* as far as possible, all attitudes based on the senses and *drives* since, as we saw, an attitude based on drives is prerequisite to all impressions of reality and also prerequisite to the formation of all sense perception of fortuitous *circumstance* here and now; prerequisite, also, to the preconception of space and time. Stated in positive terms, the orientation toward control, set on determining the laws of nature, consciously reflecting the *essence* of *what* is involved in the relationships subject to the laws of nature, is replaced by a *loving* attitude which seeks out the basic phenomena and ideas of the world.

In the second place, this orientation expressly disregards the real existence of things, i.e., their possible resistance to our desire and action, and thus disregards all simple fortuitous circumstance here and now such as that which sensory perception furnishes. We can, therefore, in principle, also gain knowledge of essence from things imagined. I am able, for instance, to see beyond movements on a movie screen or a good painting of a dog and to grasp, in addition, the ultimate components which pertain to the essence (*essentia*) of motion and to every "living being," etc.

In the third place, while knowledge of essence is not independent of all experience, it is independent of the *quantum* of experience or of so-called "induction." It precedes all induction just as it precedes all observation and measurement of reality. Such knowledge of essence can be derived from *each individual* case and example. *Once* such knowledge of essence, e.g., of the essence of life, has been acquired, it is valid "a priori," as schoolmen put it, i.e., "from the start," infinitely and generally valid, for all fortuitous observable facts concerning the particular essence, much as are principles of pure mathematics which render the multiple aspects of all *possible* natural phenomena and their inherent and necessary ideal relationships *before* real nature is explored by observation and measurement.

In the fourth place, it is precisely in this way that knowledge of essence and of essential relationships is valid, *above and beyond* that diminutive realm of the real world which is accessible to us through sensory experience and through any instrumental measurement which might support it. This knowledge is valid also for being *by itself and in itself*. It has a "transcendental" dimension, and thus becomes the jumping-off point for all "critical metaphysics."

Furthermore (in the fifth place), knowledge of essence in "first philosophy" is the true knowledge of *"reason,"* to be sharply distinguished from those extensions of our knowledge beyond sensory experience which rest solely on the mediate conclusions of the *"mind."* "Mind" or "intellect" enables an organism to adapt meaningfully to new situations for which the inborn instinct and associative memory have not prepared it. This happens suddenly and without reference to the number of previous trial attempts to solve the task.[3] This ability belongs not only to man but, to a lesser extent, also to animals, e.g., to the monkey who suddenly uses a stick to extend his reach in order to pull a fruit toward him. However, as long as the logical mind serves exclusively vital drives—the drives of food, sex, and power—and merely directs practical adjustment to stimuli of the environment, it is not yet specifically *human*. It becomes something specifically human only when the intellect (in animals there is only cleverness and cunning) begins to serve *reason*, i.e., applies formerly acquired, a priori knowledge of *essence* to the fortuitous circumstances of experience, when it, furthermore, begins to serve the highest insights into the relationships of the objective order of *values*, i.e., begins to serve *wisdom* and a moral idea.

Finally, knowledge of essence *can be applied in two ways*. It circumscribes the ultimate assumptions of the particular research of each field of experimental science (mathematics, physics, biology, psychology, etc.). Knowledge of essence furnishes each field the "axioms of its essential nature." In *metaphysics,* this knowledge of essence is what Hegel once very graphically called "the window into the absolute." For everything of *essential* nature, i.e., every truly basic phenomenon and idea, in the world and in the operations through which man plans and grasps his world, all that remains constant if one disregards the fortuitous distribution of things and acts in space and time—all this sets an insuperable limit for experimental science. Neither true essence nor the existence of something containing true essence can ever be explained or made intelligible by experimental science. The success of the task of experimental science depends precisely on strictly intentional exclusion of questions concerning the essence of things (e.g., *what* is life?). Therefore, both the essential structure and the existence of the world must, in the last analysis, be derived from *absolute reality,* i.e., from the common and supreme source of the world and of man's self.

The supreme aim in forming a metaphysical outlook through philosophy is, therefore, to conceive and consider absolute being through itself *in such a way* that it corresponds and is appro-

[3] Cf. Scheler, *Die Stellung des Menschen im Kosmos* (1928) [(5th ed.; Munich, 1949), p. 26 f].

priate to the *essential* structure of the world as discovered in "first philosophy," to the real *existence* of the world as it appears to us in its resistance to our drives, and to all fortuitous circumstance.

From what we have already said we can establish *two fundamental attributes* of ultimate being. Ultimate being must contain an infinite, ideating *spirit* and a *rational power* which causes the essential structures of the world and of man himself to emanate jointly from itself. In the second place, it must contain an irrational driving force which posits equally irrational existence and fortuitous circumstance (the "images" we see), a dynamic, imaginative potency, the common root for centers and fields of force of organic nature and for the *one life* which rhythmically appears in the birth and death of all individuals and species. The philosophy devoted to inorganic and organic nature must show more precisely how this takes place. An increasing *understanding* of these two attributes of the activity of ultimate being thus forms the *meaning* of that historical phenomenon in time which we call "the world." The understanding is twofold. It is a *growing spiritualization* of the creative *driving force* which had originally been blind to ideas and ultimate values. From the other point of view, it is the *progressive acquisition of power and strength* by the infinite *spirit* which originally was powerless and could not formulate ideas. This process is most apparent in human history, where ideas and moral values slowly acquire a certain amount of effective "power" as they amalgamate more and more with interests and passions and with all the institutions resting on them.[4]

3

With these considerations, we have already reached the nucleus of the *third* type of knowledge accessible to man, the knowledge of *metaphysical reality* and *salvation*. "First philosophy," i.e., the ontology of the nature of the world and the self, is a springboard to this knowledge, but it is not yet metaphysics.

[4] *Ibid.* [p. 65 f], and "Probleme einer Soziologie des Wissens," section I.

We obtain *metaphysics* only when we tie *together* the findings of reality-conscious, experimental sciences and the results of ontological first philosophy and then relate both of these to the conclusions of the disciplines which involve judgment (general theory of values, esthetics, ethics, philosophy of civilization). This process leads us first to metaphysical "problems on the frontiers" of the experimental sciences, i.e., to metaphysics of the first order (what is "life," what is "matter"?) and, through it, to metaphysics of the absolute, metaphysics of the second order.

Between the metaphysical problems along the frontiers of mathematics, physics, biology, psychology, law, history, etc., and metaphysics of the absolute, there lies, however, one more important discipline which is now attracting interest and gaining significance, *"philosophical anthropology."* It asks *the* question in which Immanuel Kant (*Logic*) once said *all* philosophical problems meet: *"What is man?"* All Western metaphysics before Kant had attempted to proceed from the being of the *cosmos,* or, in any case, from *concrete* being, to absolute, ontological being. This is what Kant, in his critique of reason (transcendental dialectics) proved to be *impossible.* Quite correctly, he stated that *all* concrete being, of the inner as well as of the outer world, must first be related to *man.* All forms of being depend on man's being. The concrete world and its modes of being are not "being in itself" but only an appropriate counterbalance to the entire spiritual and physical order of man and a "segment" of being in itself. A *conclusion* as to the true attributes of the *ultimate source* of all things can only be drawn by *starting from* the picture of the essence of *man* explored by "philosophical anthropology." This conclusion is an inverse prolongation of the spiritual acts which originally sprang from the center of man.

This way of reasoning and concluding is as important a (second) springboard toward modern metaphysics as "knowledge of essence." We call it the *"transcendental argument."* Its principle is: It is certain that the being of the world itself depends neither on the fortuitous existence of man on earth nor on his empirical consciousness. However, there are strong *essential analogies* between certain categories of spiritual *acts* and certain realms of *being* to which these categories give us access. For these two reasons, *all* acts and operations that grant this access to us transitory creatures *must* be ascribed to the source of all things. In other words, what shall we do if we can, e.g., prove that what space is accessible to us depends on certain motives of human action, but, nevertheless, must admit that a world of organized space was already present before the appearance of diluvial man? What are we to do if we must distinguish the absolute order of values itself from the changeable human view of the order of values, even though we must admit that an absolute order of values without a loving spirit realized in man is a contradiction in itself? By analogy, is not an order of ideas independent from us, without a thinker, as absurd as a reality without a "drive" to posit it? We can only relate the realms of being, which are and persist independently of short-lived man, to the acts of a single supra-individual spirit which must be an attribute of original being, is active in man, and *grows* through him. The same considerations apply wherever we find this *simultaneous* dependence and independence of things from earthly man. We can also say man is a microcosm, i.e., "a miniature world," because all essential aspects of being—physical, chemical, living, spiritual—are found in and intersect in man. Thus, the ultimate source of the "great world," the macrocosm, can also be studied in man. And for this reason the *being of man as microtheos is also the primary access to God.*

This modern metaphysics is no longer cosmology and metaphysics of concrete objects, but *metanthropology* and metaphysics of *action.* Its guiding principle is that the ultimate source of all which can concretely exist *cannot* itself be concrete but is, rather, a purely potential *actuality,* as the attribute of being which perpetually re-creates itself. The only access to God is, therefore, not theoretical contemplation which tends to represent God as a concrete being, but personal and active *commitment* of man to God and to *progressive* self-realization. It is a *collaboration* in the two attributes of the eternal act, in its spiritual power to create ideas as well as in its momentous force which we can feel present in our drives. The purest and supreme finite representation of both attributes is "man" himself. This kind of metaphysics considers it idolatry to make God into an object, a thing. Participation in the divine is possible only if one lives, plans, wills, thinks, and loves "in him" and through him and, so to say, *out of him*. Saint Augustine called it *cognoscere in lumine Dei, velle in Deo* [to know in the light of God, to want in God]. This completely excludes the material orientation which we usually find wherever the world, the self, and others are observed.

The spiritual *"person"* of man is neither a substantial thing nor a form of concrete entity. Man can rejoin his spiritual person only by acting. For this person is a hierarchical organic unit of spiritual acts which, at any moment, represents the unique and individual self-concentration of an infinite *spirit, one* and always the same, the root of the essential structure of the *objective world*. However, as a creature of drives and life, man is, by analogy, just as fundamentally rooted in the divine drive of *"nature,"* in the other attribute of God. This common root of all men and all life in the divine drive is sensed in the great movement of sympathy and love and whenever we feel one with the universe. This is the "Dionysian" way to God.

Man is thus not the imitator of a "world of ideas" or "providence" which arose spontaneously, or was already present in God before the creation, but he is *co*-creator, *co*-founder, *co*-executor of a stream of ideas which *develop* throughout world history and with man. Man is the only locus in which and through which original being grasps and recognizes itself, but man is also the being in whose free *decision* God can *realize* and sanctify his pure essence. It is man's destiny to be more than a "serf" and obedient servant, more also than merely the "child" of a ready-made and completed God. In his being as man, a condition involving *decisions,* man bears the higher dignity of an ally and even collaborator of God. Amid the storms of the world, man must carry before everything the flag of divinity, the flag of the *"Deitas"* [divinity] which realizes itself only *in the course of* world history.

Since the individual person of each man is *immediately* rooted in eternal being and spirit, no philosophical outlook is universally true, but, in each case, its "content" is valid only for one individual and history then determines its measure of perfection and appropriateness. There is, however, a universally valid *method* by which each person, whoever he may be, can find "*his*" metaphysical truth.

We have attempted, in these reflections, to indicate this method.[5]

SCHELER'S MAJOR WRITINGS
(arranged chronologically)

An edition of Scheler's complete works is in progress. It has been scheduled to appear in thirteen volumes but only six volumes have been published to date.

Gesammelte Werke. Bern: Francke, 1954 ff.

Band II— *Der Formalismus in der Ethik und die Materiale Wertethik,* 1954.

Band III— *Vom Umsturz der Werte,* 1955.

Band V— *Vom Ewigen im Menschen, Religiöse Erneuerung,* 1954.

Band VI— *Schriften zur Soziologie und Weltanschauungslehre,* 1963.

Band VIII—*Die Wissensformen und die Gesellschaft,* 1960.

Band X— *Schriften aus dem Nachlass,* 1957.

Beiträge zur Feststellung der Beziehungen zwischen den logischen und ethischen Prinzipien. Jena: Vopelius, 1899.

[5] Further discussions of these issues: (i) Concerning the nature of philosophy: E. Husserl, "Philosophie als strenge Wissenschaft," *Logos* I (1910). Scheler, "Vom Wesen der Philosophie," *Vom Ewigen im Menschen* (1921) [4th ed.; Bern, 1954]; also, "The Forms of Knowledge and Culture" in this collection, Essay II. (ii) Concerning metaphysical knowledge: N. Hartmann, *Metaphysik der Erkenntnis.* Scheler, "Erkenntnis und Arbeit"; and "Idealismus-Realismus," *Philosophischer Anzeiger* II, 3 (Bonn, 1927). (iii) Concerning philosophical anthropology: Scheler, *Die Stellung des Menschen im Kosmos.* (iv) Concerning ethics: Scheler, *Der Formalismus in der Ethik und die materiale Wertethik* (1913–16) [4th ed.; Bern, 1954]. N. Hartmann, *Ethik* (Berlin, 1926). (v) Concerning the philosophy of nature: H. Weyl in *Handbuch der Philosophie* (Munich, 1927), fasc. 5. H. Driesch, *Philosophie des Organischen.*

Cf. also the vols. of *Jahrbuch für Philosophie und phänomenologische Forschung* (Halle, 1913 sq.), ed. E. Husserl.

Die transcendentale und die psychologische Methode: Eine grund-
sätzliche Erörterung zur philosophischen Methodik. Leipzig:
Durr, 1900.

Über Ressentiment und Moralisches Werturteil: Ein Beitrag zur
Pathologie der Kultur. Leipzig: Engelmann, 1912. Also in *G.W.,*
III.

Ressentiment. Tr. W. Holdheim. New York: Free Press of Glencoe, 1961.

Zur Phänomenologie und Theorie der Sympathiegefühle und von
Liebe und Hass. Mit einem anhang über den Grund zur
Annahme der Existenz des fremden Ich. Halle: Niemeyer, 1913.

Der Genius des Krieges und der deutsche Krieg. Leipzig: Weissen
Bücher, 1915.

Abhandlungen und Aufsätze (2 vols.). Leipzig: Wissen Bücher,
1915. The second edition was published under the title *Vom*
Umsturz der Werte, 1919. Also in *G.W.,* III.

Der Formalismus in der Ethik und die materiale Wertethik. Mit
besonderer Berucksichtigung der Ethik I. Kants. Halle: Niemeyer, 1916. Also in *G.W.,* II.

Krieg und Aufbau. Leipzig: Wissen Bücher, 1916. Also in *G.W.,* VI.

Die Ursachen des Deutschenhasses. Eine national pädagogische
Erörterung. Leipzig: Wolf, 1917.

Vom Ewigen im Menschen, Religiöse Erneuerung. Leipzig: Neue
Geist, 1921. Also in *G.W.,* V.

On the Eternal in Man. Tr. G. Noble. London: SCM, 1958.

Wesen und Formen der Sympathie. Bonn: Cohen, 1923.

The Nature of Sympathy. Tr. P. Heath. London: Routledge &
Kegan Paul, 1958.

Schriften zur Soziologie und Weltanschauungslehre. 4 vols. Leipzig:
Neue Geist, 1923–1924. Also *G.W.,* VI.

Die Formen des Wissens und die Bildung. Bonn: Cohen, 1925.

Die Wissensformen und die Gesellschaft. Leipzig: Neue Geist, 1926.
Also *G.W.,* VIII.

Die Stellung des Menschen im Kosmos. Darmstadt: Reichl, 1928.

Man's Place in Nature. Tr. H. Meyerhoff. Boston: Beacon Press,
1961.

Der Mensche im Weltalter des Ausgleichs. Berlin: Rothschild, 1929.

Philosophische Weltanschauung. Bonn: Cohen, 1929.

Philosophical Perspectives. Tr. O. Haac. Boston: Beacon Press,
1958.

Die Idee des Friedens und der Pazifismus. Berlin: Neue Geist, 1931.

Schriften aus dem Nachlass, Band I: Zur Ethik und Erkenntnislehre.

Ed. Maria Scheler. Berlin: Neue Geist, 1933. Also in *G.W.*, X. *Liebe und Erkenntnis*. Bern: Francke, 1955.

SELECTED STUDIES ABOUT SCHELER
(arranged alphabetically)

Buber, Martin. "The Philosophical Anthropology of Max Scheler," *Philosophy and Phenomenological Research*, VI [1946], 307–321.

Dupuy, Maurice. *La philosophie de Max Scheler. Son évolution et son unité*. 2 vols. Paris: Presses Universitaires de France, 1959.

Farber, Marvin. "Max Scheler on the Place of Man in the Cosmos," *Philosophy and Phenomenological Research*, XIV [1954], 393–400.

Frings, Manfred. *Max Scheler. A Concise Introduction into the World of a Great Thinker*. Pittsburgh: Duquesne University Press, 1965.

Hartmann, Nicholai. "Max Scheler," *Kantstudien*, XXXIII [1926], IX–XVI.

Landsberg, Paul. "L'acte philosophique de Max Scheler," *Recherches Philosophiques*, VI [Sept. 6, 1936], 299–312.

Löwith, Karl. "Max Scheler und das Problem einer philosophischen Anthropologie," *Theologische Rundschau*. Neue Folge, VII, No. 6 [1935], 349–372.

Merleau-Ponty, Maurice. "Christianisme et ressentiment," *La vie intellectuelle*, VII [June 1935], 278–306.

Ortega y Gasset, José. "Max Scheler," *Neue Schweizer Rundschau*, XXXIV [October 1928], 725–729.

Schuetz, Alfred. "Max Scheler's Epistemology and Ethics," *Review of Metaphysics*, XI [1957], 304–314; 486–501.

Staude, John R. *Max Scheler: An Intellectual Portrait*. New York: Free Press of Glencoe, 1967.

Karl Jaspers (1883–1969)

Jaspers was born at Oldenburg, Germany, on February 23, 1883. His parents were descended from a family of merchants and farmers. His father, however, became a jurist, high constable of the district of Jever, and director of a bank. The religious background of the family was Protestant, but Jaspers himself seems not to have practiced Christianity in any formal way.

In his "Philosophical Autobiography," Jaspers states that all of the decisions of his life were partially conditioned by the fact that from childhood he had been organically ill with bronchiectasis with cardiac decompensation. In order to stay alive, he worked out a regimen which profoundly restricted his work, recreation, and social life.

At the *Gymnasium* he had trouble with the authorities over his refusal to follow regulations blindly which seemed to him unreasonable. The conflict reached a climax when he refused to join one of the student fraternities which he claimed were based on social status rather than friendship.

Upon his graduation from the *Gymnasium*, Jaspers studied law and medicine at the universities of Heidelberg, Munich, Berlin, and Göttingen before he became, after receiving his medical degree in 1909, an assistant in the psychiatric hospital of the University of Heidelberg. In 1913 he wrote his *Habilitationsscrift, Allegmeine Psychopathologie* under Wilhelm Windelband, thus becoming a *Privatdozent* in psychology within the philosophy faculty at Heidelberg.

Three years earlier, Jaspers married a woman of Jewish extraction, Gertrud Mayer. Several years later his refusal to part from her was among the items of complaint that the Nazis had with him. The couple was childless. His wife's brother, Ernst, had been a close friend and, although he too was a physician, made a profound contribution to Jaspers' philosophical work by critically reading and correcting the manuscripts of *Philosophie*.

Jaspers' principal formation in philosophy came through a reading of Kierkegaard and Nietzsche whom he had been studying since 1914. From them he takes the emphasis on the contingent existence of the individual and the conviction that philosophy is the expression of the individual's quest for the meaning of existence. Kant, too, is a formative influence which is evident from Jaspers' concept of "the encompassing" and his stress on the limits of experience. But it is of Max Weber who died in 1920 that Jaspers himself claims to have spent a life understanding "his reality." For Jaspers, Weber was like Socrates, a demonic figure through whom the character of individual existence is illuminated and by whom the freedom and irreducibility of the individual is maintained in pointing out the limits of empirical science.

After Windelband's death, Heinrich Rickert was called to Heidelberg in 1916 as head of the department of philosophy. Jaspers taught with him for many years until 1936, first as a *Privatdozent,* then as a colleague from 1921 when he took a full professional chair in philosophy at Heidelberg. A profound disagreement and enmity took place between them. Jaspers extended his general view that philosophy is not a science to Rickert's writings. Rickert, on the other hand, rejected the idea that philosophy was a set of logical analyses independent of reference to the world. They also disagreed on the character and stature of Weber's work. In addition to this, Rickert objected to Jaspers' not receiving a proper and traditional philosophical education, so that he tried to prevent him from receiving his 1922 appointment. But the faculty and appointment committee confirmed Jaspers.

The book, *Psychologie der Weltanschauungen,* written by Jaspers in 1919 is regarded by some historians of philosophy (e.g., Abbagnano) and Jaspers himself as the earliest document of the twentieth-century Existentialism.

From 1933 to 1937 the National Socialists excluded Jaspers

from any part in the administration of the university; in 1937 they took his professorship from him; and in 1938 they forbade him to publish. When the Americans had occupied Heidelberg on April 1, 1945, they reinstated him, whereupon he organized a commission of thirteen professors in order to prepare for the reopening of the university.

Jaspers ended his association with Heidelberg in 1949 when he assumed the chair of philosophy at the University of Basel in Switzerland. He died on February 26, 1969, in that city a year after suffering a stroke.

"Philosophizing Starts with Our Situation" from *Philosophy*

Translated by E. B. Ashton

I do not begin at the beginning when I ask questions such as "What is being?" or "Why is anything at all? Why not nothing?" or "Who am I?" or "What do I really want?" These questions arise from a *situation* in which, coming from a past, I find myself.

When I become aware of myself I see that I am in a world in which I take my bearings. Previously I had taken things up and dropped them again; everything had been a matter of course, unquestioned, and purely present; but now I wonder and ask myself what really is. For all things pass away, and I was not at the beginning, nor am I at the end. Even between beginning and end I ask about the beginning and the end.

I would like an answer that will give me *support*. For though I can neither fully grasp my situation nor see through its origin, the sense of it oppresses me with a vague fear. I can see the situation only as a motion that keeps transforming me along with itself, a motion that carries me from a darkness in which I did not exist to a darkness in which I shall not exist. I concern myself with things and doubt if they matter. The motion takes its course and frightens me with the idea that something will be lost forever if I do not seize it now—yet I do not know what it is. I look for a being that will not just vanish.

I should, it seems, be able to get *generally valid* answers to my questions that will tell me what is and will make me understand how I come to find myself in this situation and what matters in it, to the whole and to me. I am offered such answers. They would make "being" an object for me and would tell me about it, as about the arrangement of the universe. But any such doctrine is only something that appears to me, along with other objects, in an irresistibly fluid situation. The only way in which I might hold on to some allegedly objective, teachable "being" would be to forget myself, to turn myself into an object among others. My situation would no longer be the way whose perils are unknown, besetting me, at first, only as fear; it would be something deducible in which I can act correctly because I know whence it comes and whither it goes.

But there is no achieving the self-obliviousness in this deceptive escape from my situation. I might indeed let myself drift awhile, tied to the supposedly known, the supposedly objective, which is and happens without me. But I no sooner start questioning this objectivity than I feel lost again and keep facing myself in the situation along which I change. I remain between beginning and end, fearful of nonexistence, unless I take hold, decide, and thus *dare to be myself*. For in awakening to myself I have a twofold experience: in my situation "the other"—all that is not I, all that is given and happens without me—is as real and resistant as I myself, in choosing and taking hold, am real and free.

Rather than know the being from which all things come, my objective cognition in this experience is confined to *things in being,* things that occur to me in my situation. The things in the *world* in which I take my bearings can be known and, hopefully, mastered. My orientation in the world proves to be the endlessly advancing illumination of my situation in the direction of an objective being.

But what I know of the world is not to be rounded out into a knowledge of being as such. I may think I grasp the whole situation along with myself, but I never get to the bottom of anything. For the situation is not the beginning of being; it is only the beginning of world orientation and philosophizing. The situation comes out of the past and has historic depth; it is never finished, harboring within itself the possibilities and inevitabilities of the future. There is no other form of reality for me, as I exist in it. It is what I start thinking from and what I return to. Here, at each moment, lies the immediacy of the present, the only thing I am sure of.

When I conceive my situation as such, directly, I am drafting patterns only; as a real situation it is always different. There is always more to it. It is *never something purely immediate*. As something that has come to be, it contains past realities and free decisions. As something that is now, it lets me breathe the possible future. It is never *merely general*—though we can draft general structures of it, as the network of an analysis of existence. In essence, the situation is the historically conveyed, momentarily complete appearance of being.

My chance to see through the situation, to visualize its origins and possible futures, would come only at the end of time. Being, then, would mean a terminated world whose beginning and end I might survey. Until then, however, I still find myself in quest of being. I search for it by my own actions within events outside. From the standpoint of my situation I view other situations, and past situations. But my view always ends in obscurity.

The world, with its knowable premises and historic realities, cannot help me understand my situation; but neither can my situation enable me to understand the world. A philosophizing that begins by casting light on the situation remains in flux because the situation is nothing but a ceaseless flow of mundane events and free choices. For all the determinacy of detail, therefore, philosophizing as a whole remains as *incomplete* as the situation itself. If I take the illumination of the situation for the starting point of philosophizing, I renounce objective explanations that would deduce existence from principles as one whole being. Instead, each objective thought structure merely has its own function.

Awakening to myself, in my situation, I raised the question of being. Finding myself in the situation as an indeterminate possibility, I must *search for being* if I want to find my real self. But it is not till I fail in this search for intrinsic being that I begin to philosophize. This is what we call *philosophizing on the ground of possible Existenz,* and the method used is *transcending.*

"The Search for Being" from *Philosophy*

General, Formal Concepts of Being:
Objective Being, Subjective Being, Being-in-Itself

To think of being is to make it a distinct being. If we ask what being is, we have many answers to choose from: empirical reality in space and time; dead and living matter; persons and things; tools and material; ideas that apply to reality; cogent constructions of ideal objects, as in mathematics; contents of the imagination—in a word, objectiveness. Whatever being I find in my situation is to me an object.

I am different. I do not confront myself as I confront things. I am the questioner; I know that I do the asking and that those modes of objective being are offered to me as replies. Whichever way I turn, trying to make an object of myself, there is always the "I" for which my self becomes an object. There remains a being that is I.

Objective being and *subjective being* are the two modes that strike us first of all, as most different in essence. Objects include persons, of course, who are their own subjects just as I can be their object—and I, as I exist, can even become my own object. But there remains a point where the objective and subjective I are one, despite the dichotomy.

The being of things is unaware of itself; but I, the thinking subject, know about it. When I conceive of this being in the abstract, the way it is independently of its being an object for a subject—that is to say, not as a phenomenon for something else —I call it *being in itself.* This being-in-itself is not accessible to me, however, for the mere thought of it will turn it into an object and thus into something that appears to me as being. It is in myself alone that I know a being that not merely appears to, but is for, itself—one in which being and being known go together. My own being differs radically from any being of things because I can say, "I am." But if I objectify my empirical existence, this is not the same as the I-in-itself. I do not know what I am in myself if I am my own object; to find out, I would have to become aware of myself in some way other than cognitive knowledge. And even then the being-in-itself of other things would remain alien to me.

The division of being into objective being, being-in-itself, and subjective being does not give me three kinds of being that exist side by side. It does give me three inseparable poles of the being I find myself in. I may tend to *take one of the three for being as such*. Then I either construe the one and only being as being-in-itself, without noticing that I am making it an object for myself in the process—or I construe it as this object of mine, forgetting in this phenomenal transformation of all being that in objectiveness there must be something which appears, and something it appears to—or I construe it as subjective being, with myself as ultimate reality, without realizing that I can never be otherwise than in a situation, conscious of objects and searching for being-in-itself. Objective being pours out to me in endless variety and infinite abundance; it means the world I can get to know. Subjective being is to me as certain as it is incomprehensible; it can come to be known only to the extent to which it has been objectified as empirical existence and is no longer truly subjective. Being-in-itself defies cognition. It is a boundary concept we cannot help thinking, one that serves to question everything I know objectively—for whenever some objective being should be taken for being proper, in the absolute sense, it will be relativized into a phenomenon by the mere idea of being-in-itself.

Thus we fail to hold fast any being as intrinsic. None of them is being pure and simple, and none can do without the other; each one is a being within being. *The whole eludes us.* There is nothing like a common genus of which the three modes—objective, subjective, and in-itself—might be species; nor is there one source to which they can be traced. They are heterogeneous and repel each other as much as they need each other to be at all— to be, that is, for our consciousness. They almost seem to have dropped out of the unfathomable, three mutual strangers who belong together even though there is no link between them and none of them will help us comprehend another. None may claim precedence, except in some particular perspective. For naïve metaphysics, seeking direct possession of intrinsic being, being-in-itself comes first; but it can only be populated with conceptions from the objective world, which in such metaphysics is supposed to be underlying all existence. Objective being has precedence for all cognition, because objects alone are knowable, and also because in cognition we take being for the sum of knowledge—not including the knower, who is merely added to this being. In illustrative philosophizing, on the other hand, subjective being will come briefly to the fore; from this standpoint of self-comprehension, the questioning and knowing subject tends to accord precedence to itself.

Existence Analysis as an Analysis of Consciousness

We have found being distinctly conceived in objects, directly grasped in self-reflection and evanescently touched—and recognized as inconceivable—in the boundary idea of being-in-itself.

All of these thoughts spring from *the thinker's existence*. From this common ground, to which the search for being takes me, the modes of being appear as perspectives for my thought. The thought itself comprises all perspectives; what it means by being is simply all there is at a time, comprising whatever may occur to me as being. It is my consciousness of temporal existence in the situation I find myself in.

Since existence is consciousness and I exist as consciousness, things are for me only as objects of consciousness. For me, nothing can be without entering into my consciousness. Consciousness as existence is the medium of all things—although we shall see that it is the mere fluid of being.

To analyze existence is to analyze consciousness.

1. Consciousness of Objects and of Self; Existing Consciousness

To be conscious is not to be the way a thing is. It is a peculiar kind of being, the essence of which is to *be directed at objects we mean*. This basic phenomenon—as self-evident as it is marvelous—has been called intentionality. Consciousness is intentional consciousness, which means that its relation to its object is not the relation of a thing that strikes another, or is struck by another. There is no causal relation, and indeed no interrelation at all, as between two of a kind or two on one level. In consciousness, rather, I have an object before me. The way I have it does not matter. It may be perception, which is biologically based on causal relations between physical phenomena, though the phenomena as such can never cause intentionality but require intentional acts to animate perception. It may be imagination, or recollection. Or it may be thinking, which can be visual or abstract, aimed at real objects or at imaginary ones. One thing always remains: my consciousness is aimed at what I mean.

Consciousness is self-reflexive. It not only aims at objects, but turns back upon itself—that is to say, it is not only conscious but self-conscious at the same time. The reflection of consciousness upon itself is as self-evident and marvelous as is its intentionality. I aim at myself; I am both one and twofold. I do not exist as a thing exists, but in an inner split, as my own object, and thus in motion and inner unrest. No consciousness can be understood as stable, as merely extant. Because it is not like the being of spatial and ideal things—things I can walk around, things I can hold fast, things I can visualize so that they stand before me—consciousness evaporates when I would take it for being. While I am conscious of objects as of something else, I am also conscious of myself as an object, but so as to coincide with this object that is myself. It is true that what happens in this confrontation when I observe myself psychologically is that the experience I know and my knowledge of this experience will be so aimed at each other as to make me conscious of two different things at once: what I know, and my knowing it. Yet at the core of the process stands my subjective consciousness, with the one identical "I" actually doubled by the thought that "I am conscious of myself." The coincidence of "I think" and "I think that I think" permits neither one to be without the other. A seeming logical absurdity becomes a reality: one is not one but two—and yet it does not become two, but remains precisely this unique one. It is the general, formal concept of the I.

The omnipresent and not otherwise deducible basic phenomenon of consciousness as the split into subject and object means that *self-consciousness and consciousness of objects go together*. True, I become so absorbed in things that I forget myself. But there always remains a last subjective point, an impersonal and purely formal I-point which a thing will confront by existing— that is to say, for which the thing will be an object. Conversely, I cannot so isolate my self-consciousness that I know myself alone: I exist only by confronting other things. There is no subjective consciousness without an objective one, however slight.

Finally there is a consciousness that is neither like the external being of things nor an objectless intentionality. This is the experience of mere inward motion that can light up in sudden intentionality and be known in retrospect, although the lack of any split keeps it dormant and its existence can only be remembered —of experiences had while awakening, for example, and of undefinable sensations. Viewed from the split consciousness, this *merely existing* one is a *limit* that can be empirically illuminated as a start and a transition, and as the encompassing ground; from the viewpoint of things outwardly extant, it is inwardness. Without any splits into subjective and objective consciousness, the merely existing one would be a fulfillment distinguished from an objective, concrete process by the fact that I can recall this experience as existing at a time when I was not myself, and that I can but retrospectively visualize it, that is, make it conscious, objective, and plain.

If existence is consciousness, it is still not just one or all of the definite concepts of consciousness. Opposed to them is *the unconscious*. But if this is to have any being for us, we must either make it conscious or we must be conscious of it as "the unconscious"—in other words, as a phenomenon, an object of consciousness—and thus, for our consciousness, enable it to be.

The several meanings in which we conceive the unconscious correspond to the concepts of consciousness. The unconscious equivalent of intentional, objective consciousness is nonobjectiveness. The unconscious equivalent of self-consciousness is what we have experienced and objectively sensed but not expressly reflected upon and rated as known. The unconscious equivalent of merely existing consciousness is what we have not inwardly experienced in any sense, what lies entirely outside the realms of our consciousness.

The statement that all existence is consciousness does not mean that consciousness is all. It does mean that for us there is only what enters into the consciousness to which it appears. For us the unconscious is as we become conscious of it.

2. *Possibilities of Analyzing Consciousness*

Real consciousness is always the existence of an individual with other things that exist in time; it has a beginning and an end. As such, consciousness is an object of empirical observation and study. It contains the fullness of the world if the world is only the temporal world of real consciousness.

Our *conscious existence as a temporal reality* is a ceaseless urge to satisfy many desires. Raised from a state of nature by knowledge and the faculty of choice, we consciously envision death and seek to avoid it at all costs. The instinct of self-preservation makes us fear perils and distinguish them so as to meet them. We seek pleasure in the enjoyment of existence and in the sense of its expansion, for which we toil each day. In anticipation of things to come we think of distant possibilities and goals and dangers. Worry, born of this reflection on what lies ahead, forces us to provide for the future. To satisfy the boundless will to live and the power drives of existence, we conquer others and delight in seeing our status reflected in our environment; indeed, it is this mirror that seems to give us our real sense of existence. Yet all this will satisfy our consciousness only for moments. It keeps driving us on. Never really bringing content, it achieves no goal and ceases only when we die.

Such are the descriptions of consciousness as the empirically real existence of an instinctual life. It can also be described as formal *consciousness at large*. In self-consciousness, distinct from other selves and from the objects I mean, I know myself as acting, then, and as identical with myself as time passes; I know I remain the one I. In objective consciousness I have the modes of objective being in the categories; I understand what definite being I encounter, and I know that cognition of all mundane existence is possible in generally valid form. My consciousness at large is interchangeable with that of anyone else who is my kind, even though not numerically identical.

Insofar as consciousness with its world—whether existing reality or consciousness at large—is an object and may thus come to be known, it becomes a topic either of psychology, if it is empirical existence, or of logic, if possessed of generally valid knowledge.

But there is a third way to analyze consciousness: not as naturally given the way it is, but as a fulfilled real consciousness which never remains the same, which undergoes transformations and is thus historic. *Historically changing consciousness* not only happens, as does a natural process; it remembers, it affects itself, it engenders itself in its history. Man actively lives the life of his successive generations, instead of merely suffering it in a repetition of the same.

An *objective study* of these metamorphoses constitutes world orientation—as anthropology and analytical psychology and intellectual history. Beginning with the dull mind of primitive man, such study allows us to glimpse the leaps in human history from one form to the other, to see now how germs unfold slowly, and then again the sudden flash of new origins of consciousness. In the individual we trace the inner changes and analyze them up to the limit where the processes defy analysis. We seek to penetrate the worlds and self-illuminations of the personally and historically strangest and most remote forms of consciousness.

The study of changeable consciousness teaches us that we cannot set up any substantial real consciousness as the "natural consciousness," or its substance as the "natural view of the world." This would be a reduction to the slicked-down form of a distinct phenomenal consciousness—as a society of historically linked individuals will take it for granted—or to the psychological pattern of the drives of living existence in its environment. There is no immediate existence that might be scientifically analyzed, in one exclusively correct way, as the natural one. Objectively, any attempt to construe and characterize such an existence has only relative significance. The man who takes it for a radical cognition of being determines only what his narrow mind will make him think of himself. We can, of course, try to go back beyond all historicity and all concreteness in pursuit of what we might call "bare existence"—but this will only impoverish us. We may claim that what we know at the end will fit the universal immediacy of existence, but in fact we shall have stated only a very meager and formally empty consciousness of being that will be historically particular and fixed in time. And if we approach the supposedly immediate by construing the seeming genetic priority of primitive tribes as "natural," we find that once we know more about their existence it proves to be not at all natural but specifically artificial and strange.

There is no radical departure for the awaking of consciousness. Nobody begins afresh. I do not step into a primal situation. So, as there is no generally determinable, natural, unveiled existence to be discovered by removing fallacies, what really lies at the root of it cannot be sought by abstracting from acquired traits. It can be sought only by questioning what these traits have led to. An understanding of all that has been acquired and evolved remains the ground on which we understand existence. The utmost clarity about existence that we can achieve comes to depend upon what scientific intellectual history has achieved already. I cannot see through existence if I merely know general structures, but only if I take a concrete part in the historic process of factual, active, and cognitive world orientation.

Thus the existence analysis conceived as preceding any research operation in the world—though actually performed only after the completed operation—will be either a schema for consciousness at large, showing the network of the modes of being and the sense of validity, or it will be a diagram of conscious existence in reality, isolating the psychological forces at work as libido, fear, worry, will to power, fear of death, or death wish; or it will be the historic self-understanding of consciousness as it has evolved.

No way of making existence conscious gets me to the bottom of it. Instead, unless I confine myself artificially and try to use a supposed knowledge as an anchor in existence where it cannot take hold, any existence analysis will leave me suspended in my situation. The fact that efforts to get underneath it all—as if there were an existing ground to penetrate—seem to plunge me into a void indicates that existence is not what counts if I want to get at being. What counts is myself. Constructions of existence will not take me to being. They can only help me get there by a leap; and the approach that may enable me to take this leap is not existence analysis any more; it is elucidation of Existenz.

3. Consciousness as a Boundary

In analyzing consciousness we work out constructive schemata for logic (the formal visualization of what is valid for consciousness at large), for psychology (the study of empirically existing consciousness), and for the history of consciousness (the reproduction of the mental process).

In part, these objectifying analyses are available in magnificent drafts, but they can never be conclusive. They keep encountering limits that make us feel what is beyond the analyses. Logic, then, will turn about into a formal metaphysical transcending (as in the case of Plotinus); psychology, into elucidation of Existenz (as in Kierkegaard's); and the history of consciousness, into consummate metaphysics (as in Hegel's). Philosophizing cannot be consummated in the self-observation of an empirically existing consciousness, nor in the construction of the ever-present consciousness at large, nor in historical knowledge.

Consciousness is a boundary. It is an object of observation, and yet it already defies objective observation. The statement that in philosophizing we start out from consciousness is untrue insofar as it would seem to confirm that the general—logical, psychological, or historical—analyses of the kind of consciousness that anyone can have at any time amount to philosophical thinking. The statement truly refers to the elucidations that begin and end with *existential consciousness*.

Distinguishing Existenz

We saw being as kept in suspension by the inconceivable being-in-itself. We sensed it as a boundary in existence analysis. But while being-in-itself was the utterly other, completely inaccessible to me as nonexistent for thought, I myself, as I exist, am the limit to analyzing existence. Herein lies the next step we must take in our search for being.

1. Empirical Existence; Consciousness at Large; Possible Existenz

What do I mean when I say "I"?

The first answer is that in thinking about myself I have made myself an object. I am this body, this individual, with an indefinite self-consciousness reflected in my impact upon my environment—I am *empirical existence*.

Second, I am a subject essentially identical with every other subject. I am interchangeable. This interchangeability is not the identity of average qualities among empirical individuals; it is subjective being as such, the subjectiveness that is the premise of all objectiveness—I am *consciousness at large*.

Third, I experience myself in potential unconditionality. I not only want to know what exists, reasoning pro and con; I want to know from a source beyond reasoning, and there are moments of action when I feel certain that what I want now, what I am now doing, is what I really want myself. I want to be so that this will and this action are mine. My very essence—which I do not know even though I am sure of it—comes over me in the way I want to know and to act. In this potential freedom of knowledge and action I am *"possible Existenz."*

Thus, instead of an unequivocally determined I, we have several meanings. As consciousness at large I am the subject whose objects are the things of reality and general validity. Every individual shares in this conceptual general consciousness if objectified being appears to him as it does to all men. Next, I am empirical individuality as objectified subjectiveness; as such I am a special and, in this form, singular occurrence in the endless diversity of individuals. Then, again as empirical existence, I am this individual for consciousness at large, which makes me an object for psychology, and an inexhaustible one at that—an object of observation and research, but not of total cognition. Finally, as possible Existenz, I am a being related to its potential and, as such, nonexistent for any consciousness at large. To conceive the meaning of possible Existenz is to break through the circle of all modes of objective and subjective being.

In philosophizing we admit each of the modes of subjective

being. We do not lump them together as identical; and in a limited sense we accord a primacy to each one, though reserving the absolute primacy for possible Existenz.

We recognize the primacy of the empirical I as compelled by the needs of existence, but we recognize it relatively, and not for philosophizing itself.

Consciousness at large will be paramount as a requisite of any being for me as the subject. The following two trains of thought may illustrate the meaning of this formal paramountcy that covers all subjectiveness and objectiveness. First, I not only exist like any living thing; I also know that I exist. I can conceive the possibility of my nonexistence. If I try to think of myself as not being at all, however, I notice that in allowing the rest of the world to stand I am involuntarily letting myself stand as well, as a point in consciousness at large for which the world would be. Then I go on to think of the possibility that there were no being at all. But while I can say this, I cannot really think it either, because I still keep thinking as this "I"—as if I had being even though the world had not. Each time, the questioner remains extant as consciousness at large, while it seems that all other being can really be thought out of existence. The thinker's consciousness at large is entitled to its specific primacy in the limited sense that we can temporarily conceive it as the ultimate being without which there is no other.

In philosophizing, the I of possible Existenz has the decidedly dominant function of breaking through the circle of objective and subjective being, toward the being-in-itself which in that circle can be only negatively defined. Possible Existenz may perhaps open the positive way that is closed to consciousness at large in the world of objects. This kind of philosophizing is as nothing for empirical existence, and a groundless figment of the imagination for consciousness at large. But for possible Existenz it is the way to itself, and to being.

2. Existenz

Existenz is the never objectified source of my thoughts and actions. It is that whereof I speak in trains of thought that involve no cognition. It is what relates to itself, and thus to its transcendence.[1]

Can something be, and yet not be a real object among objects? Obviously it cannot be the "I am" we conceive as empirical existence or consciousness at large, as comprehensible and deducible. The question is whether all the objective and subjective conceptions of being have brought me to the end, or whether my self can be manifested to me in yet another fashion. We are touching what seems to me the pivotal point of the sense of philosophizing.

To be means to decide about being. It is true that, as I observe myself, I am the way I am; although an individual, I am a case of something general, subject to causality or responding to the valid challenge of objectively fixed commandments. But where I am my own origin, everything has not yet been settled in principle, in accordance with general laws. It is not only due to the infinity of conditions that I do not know how it might be, had it been settled. On quite a different plane it is still my own self that decides what it is.

This thought—impossible to conceive objectively—is the sense of *freedom*, of possible Existenz. In this sense I cannot think that, after all, everything takes its course, and that I might therefore do just as I please and vindicate my action by whatever general arguments come to hand. Instead, for all the dependence and determinacy of my existence, I feel sure that ultimately something rests with me alone. What I do or forego, what I want first and foremost, where I cling to options and where I proceed to realizations—all this results neither from general rules I act upon, as right, nor from psychological laws to which I am subject. It does spring, in the restlessness of my existence and by the certainty of self-being, from freedom. Where I stop observing myself psychologically and still do not act with unconscious naïveté; where I act positively, rather, soaring with a bright as-

[1] No definable concept—which would presuppose some kind of objective being—can express the being of Existenz. The very word is just one of the German synonyms for "being." The philosophical idea began obscurely, as a mere inkling of what Kierkegaard's use of the word has since made historically binding upon us.

surance that gives me nothing to know but sustains my own being—there I decide what I am.

I know a kind of appeal to which my true self inwardly responds by the realization of my being. But it is not as an isolated being that I come to sense what I am. Against my self-will, against the accident of my empirical existence, I experience myself in *communication*. I am never more sure of being myself than at times of total readiness for another, when I come to myself because the other too comes to himself in our revealing struggle.

As possible Existenz I seize upon the *historicity* of my existence. From the mere diversity of knowable realities it will expand to an existential depth. What is outwardly definite and delimiting is inwardly the appearance of true being. The man who loves mankind only, does not love at all, but one who loves a particular human being does. We are not yet faithful if we are rationally consistent and will keep agreements; we are faithful if we accept as our own, and know ourselves bound to, what we have done and loved. A will to reorganize the world properly and permanently is no will at all; a proper will is to seize as my own whatever chances my historic situation offers.

If I am rooted in historicity, my temporal existence carries no weight in and by itself; but it does carry weight in the sense that *in time I decide for eternity*. What is time, then? As the future, it is possibility; as the past, it is the bond of fidelity; as the present, it is decision. Time, then, is not something that merely passes; it is the *phenomenality of Existenz*. Existenz is gained in time, by our own decisions. Once temporality has this weight and I know it, I have overcome temporality—not by replacing it with an abstract timelessness, not by putting myself outside of time, but by the fact that in time I stand above time. In my conscious life, governed by vital urges and the finite will to be happy, I want time to last as though deliverance from the anxieties of existence were found in blind permanence. I can no more eliminate this will from my living consciousness than I can void the sorrows of mortality. They are part of my existence as such. But if, in time, I act and love absolutely, time is eternal. This is something my intellect cannot grasp, something that will light up only at the moment, and afterwards only in doubtful remembrance. It is no outward possession, to have and to hold.

There is a distinguishing formula, meaningless to intellectual consciousness at large, but an appeal to possible Existenz. It goes as follows: real being loses its reality in all objective cognition, turning into endless duration, into laws of nature, or into the nonbeing of mere transience; but Existenz is realized in choices made in temporal historicity. Thus, despite its objective disappearance, Existenz achieves reality as fulfilled time. Eternity is neither timelessness nor duration for all time; it is the depth of time as the historic appearance of Existenz.

3. World and Existenz

Existenz will find itself with other Existenz in the mundane situation, without coming to be recognizable as mundane being. What is in the world appears as being to my consciousness at large, but only a transcending possible Existenz can be sure of Existenz.

Being that compels recognition exists directly. I can take hold of it, can make something of it, and with it—technically with things, or in arguing with myself and with other consciousness. In it lies the *resistance* of anything given, whether the real resistance of empirical reality or the resistance of logical necessities or impossibilities. It is always objective being, an original object or an adequate objectification like the models or types that serve as research tools, for instance.

Existenz, which in itself does not exist, *appears* to possible Existenz as existence. In our minds, of course, we cannot close the gap between world and Existenz, between things we can know and things we can elucidate, between objective being and the free being of Existenz. In fact, however, the two modes of being are so close together that a consciousness which is also possible Existenz will find the distinction an infinite task whose performance combines the cognition of mundane being with the elucidation of Existenz.

It is only abstractly that we can formulate the distinction of objective being and the free being of Existenz. We can say, for instance, that objective being is given as mechanism, life, and

consciousness, while I as Existenz am original—not original being, but my own origin in existence. Measured by the being of
things, there is no freedom; measured by freedom, the being of
things is not true being. Or we can say that extant being and free
being are not two antithetical kinds of being which might be
coordinated. They are interrelated but flatly incomparable; being
in the sense of objectivity and being in the sense of freedom exclude one another. The one steps from time into timelessness or
endless duration; the other steps from time into eternity. What is
for all time, or valid, is objectiveness; what is evanescent and
yet eternal is Existenz. We can say that one is for a thinking
subject only, while the other, though never without an object,
is real only for communicating Existenz.

From the point of view of the world, any appearance of Existenz is merely objective being. From that viewpoint we see consciousness and the subjective I, but not Existenz; from there we
cannot even understand what is meant by Existenz. *From the
point of view of Existenz,* its own being is merely something
that appears in existence, an existence that is not an appearance
of Existenz, and is not its true self, but is recreant. It is as
though originally all existence should be Existenz, and as though
whatever part of it is nothing but existence could be understood
as depleted, entangled, bereft of Existenz.

There is no pointer to lead us from objective being to another
kind of being, unless it be done indirectly, by the disjointness
and inconclusiveness of objective being. But Existenz does permeate the forms of that being as media of its realization, and as
possibilities of its appearance. Standing *on the borderline of
world and Existenz,* possible Existenz views all existence as more
than existence. Proceeding from the most remote, from the mechanism, being will approach itself, so to speak, via life and
consciousness, seeking to find itself in Existenz as what it is.
Or—while consciousness at large conceives existence from this
borderline as pure existence—it may be the character of all existence to be potentially relevant for Existenz by providing the impulse for it or serving as its medium.

There can be no Existenz without other Existenz, and yet
objectively it makes no sense to speak of it as manifold. For
whenever Existenz and Existenz communicate historically in

the dark of mundane being, they are one for the other only, invalid for any watching consciousness at large. What is invisible from outside is not surveyable as a being of many.

On the one side, possible Existenz can see the being of the world, split into modes of being, in the medium of consciousness at large; on the other side is every Existenz. *On no side is there a conclusive being,* neither objectively as the one mundane existence nor existentially as a conceivable and surveyable world of all Existenz. If I think of being, it will always be a distinct being, not *the* being. In the ascertainment of possible Existenz I do not have an Existenz for an object, nor do I make sure of an Existenz at all. I only make sure of myself and of the Existenz I communicate with; we are what simply admits of no substitution; we are not cases of a species. Existenz is a sign pointing toward this self-ascertainment of a being that is objectively neither conceivable nor valid—a being that no man knows or can meaningfully claim, either in himself or in others.

Being

We have found no one answer to the question we raised at the start: what is being? An answer to this question satisfies the questioner if it allows him to recognize his own being. But the question of being itself is not unequivocal; it depends upon who asks it. It has no original meaning for our existing consciousness at large, which we can break up into the multiplicity of distinct being. It is only with possible Existenz, in transcending all existence and all objective being, that the impassioned search for being-in-itself begins—only to fall short of the goal of definite knowledge. Whatever exists is phenomenal; it is *appearance,* not being. And yet it is not nothing.

1. *Appearance and Being*

The sense of "appearance" in such statements has its categorial derivation in a particular, objective relationship: between the way something appears from a standpoint, as a phenomenon, and the way it is in-itself, regardless of the standpoint. In an objectifying sense, then, phenomenality is the aspect of a mental addendum, of something we have to think as objectively underlying but not yet objective itself—something I conceive as an object only because, in principle, I might come to know it as such (as the atom, for instance).

It is in the category of appearance—using it to transcend this definite objectifying relation of phenomenal and underlying elements—that we conceive all being when we seek being as such.

Even so, the being that appears will remain twofold. In temporal existence we cannot overcome the duality of the inaccessible being-in-itself of *transcendence*—which we cannot conceive as the objectively underlying addendum—and the self-being manifest to Existenz, which is not existing consciousness. Existenz and transcendence are heterogeneous, but interrelated. Their relationship appears in existence.

As an object of science, existence is the appearance of something *theoretically* underlying. Science has no access to Existenz, nor to transcendence. But in a philosophical sense the appearance of being-in-itself results from the scientific cognition of a phenomenon *plus* the conception of the underlying addendum. In the scientific study of phenomena we think up the underlying addendum; in philosophizing we use the phenomena to touch being in our interpretation of *ciphers of transcendence,* and in the thinking that *appeals to Existenz.*

Nor is the consciousness we study the same consciousness in which I am sure of self-being and aware of transcendence. There is no unconscious Existenz, but consciousness as an object of scientific cognition is never that existential consciousness. This is why I, the single living individual existing for objective research, can turn, for myself, into the encompassing medium of all being when my consciousness is the psychologically inaccessible absolute assurance of Existenz. For the same reason, the statement that nothing lies outside consciousness is untrue if I understand consciousness as a mere research object. The statement is true in the sense that for me there is only what becomes phenomenal and thus enters into my consciousness. It is in going beyond its own explorable existence that consciousness begins and ends its contact with the unexplorable. For science this is the unconscious with its many meanings; for Existenz, it is transcendence. Yet this supplement to consciousness will of necessity be conscious again—for science as a theory of the unconscious, and for Existenz as the cipher of being in a self-contradictory and thus evanescent form.

The phrase "appearance of being" must be understood as ambiguous if we are to grasp the thesis that *Existenz appears in its own consciousness*. It means neither the appearance of an underlying objectivity nor of a transcendent being-in-itself.

On the one hand, Existenz cannot be psychologically understood as a conscious phenomenon. Only the forms of the existence of consciousness can be objects of psychology—its causally conditioned and intelligibly motivated experiences, but not its existential ground. Instead, in psychological research we think up an underlying unconscious, which we consider the reality of consciousness. In an objectifying sense, consciousness is the phenomenon of this underlying addendum, the way in which it appears. In an existential sense, however, appearance means a way of becoming conscious, a way of having been objectified, in which a simultaneously and wholly present being understands itself. I know eternally what in this way is never known objectively. I am what appears in this way—not as something underlying, but as myself. We group the appearance of consciousness as a research object with the underlying, which to us is outright alien. And we group the appearance of Existenz with what we are originally, what we will answer for. The appearance of the underlying objectivity is generally valid for cognition; the appearance of Existenz is manifest in existential communication.

On the other hand, as the appearance in consciousness of its *subjective* being, Existenz can be sure of itself only in relation to transcendent being-in-itself. This it can feel but cannot be. What manifests itself to Existenz is not plain, straightforward being; it is being that addresses Existenz—itself no more than a subjective appearance—as a possibility.

Appearance is heterogeneous. The underlying objectivity appears in phenomena, transcendent being-in-itself in ciphers, Existenz in the assurance of absolute consciousness. In each direction, this heterogeneousness voids the stability of being. In its entirety it will keep being definitively *disjoint for the questioner as possible Existenz in temporal existence,* even at the root of his search.

2. *Being and the Many Modes of Being*

In thinking about our question, what is being, we may try to *take one thing for being as such* and all other being for derivative. There are many possible ways to try this, but none to carry it through. Suppose, for instance, I were to equate intrinsic being with objective knowability and to regard myself as derived from the objects, thus making a thing of myself and denying all freedom. Or suppose I were to turn the freedom of the subject into original being, and to derive things from that. Each time, the derivation of one from the other would be a fantastic leap. I can neither comprehend myself by the being of things, nor can I take all things to be myself. Instead, I am in the world; there are things that exist for me; I do make original decisions as a possible Existenz that appears to itself in the world. No rudiment of being enables me to comprehend all the being I find myself in. This is my situation, which I must not forget as I philosophize.

Our search for being started out from manifold being and led back to it, as to the modes of being. If we did not find being, there is still the question *why everything is called being* even though it cannot be brought under one principle or derived from one origin.

The fact we face here is that any statement is made in the form of language. Whatever we may be discussing will take the form of a definite sentence with the predicate "is"—even if the sentence refers to no being at all, even if it is an indirect suggestion or if it connects a train of thought that may be illustrative as a whole but that does not define an object as the one referred to.

Language is the phenomenal form of all thought. Whether in objective cognition or in nonobjective elucidation—in either case I am thinking. And what I think I have to think in *categories*. These are basic definitions of all thought; there is no superior category of which the rest might be species or derivations; but what they have in common, what defines them, is that they will always state a being. It is thought itself which in some sense is one and will accordingly call heterogeneous being—though no common concept of it is discoverable—by the one name of being.

As we think in categories, the question is whether our thoughts are adequately or inadequately categorized. We have to distinguish between, on the one hand, what is directly what it is, what is to be discovered and then to be straightforwardly discussed in categories—and on the other hand, what is not such an object but will be discussed just the same, in an indirect way, open to misunderstanding, and necessarily also in categories. Schematically we can formulate the distinction as follows: The *discovery of being* is scientific cognition; it gives us our bearings in the world and will always more or less adequately grasp a definite being. The *ascertainment of being* is philosophizing as the transcending of objectivity; in the medium of categories it grasps inadequately, in substituted objectivities, what can never become objective.

Methodologically, therefore, the genuine philosophical steps are to be grasped as modes of transcending. What they express regarding content, from the existential source of an absolute consciousness, is a being that employs such thought for its self-ascertainment as intrinsic being.

As possible Existenz comes to itself by way of philosophizing, it cannot exchange its freedom for the stifling narrowness of a being known as intrinsic. It will always be freedom, not cognition, that lets us experience what proper being is. The impulse behind our dissection of the concepts of being is to loosen our consciousness, to experiment with possibilities so as to get at the root of true philosophizing and there to *search* for the one being, as being proper.

We can approach being either by its *dilution* into everything of which we can indefinitely say it "is," or by its *fixation* into a categorially *defined* being that is known, or by the accentuation of *true* being, which is ascertained in thought. We differentiate, accordingly, between definite and indefinite being, between the various definitions, and between the true and the trivial.

True being cannot be found in a sense that we might know. It is to be sought in its *transcendence*, to which only Existenz, not consciousness at large, can ever relate.

One might suppose that any meaningful thinking must indirectly aim at this transcendence if it is not to deteriorate into vacuous intellectual gamesmanship and indifferent factuality. It could be that the designation of all being as being, with no noticeable common denominator save the form of language—that this most tenuous appearance of being in our speech indicates how deeply rooted all of it is in the one being. But these are indefinite thoughts, unless they already signify a transcending. For all categories can be used as means to transcend themselves, to dissolve their particularity in a unity that has neither an existence in the world nor a meaning in logic—namely, in the one being of transcendence which enters only the soul of a historic Existenz, if anything. From there it pervades meaning and existence, seeming to confirm them both, and then again to fracture and dissolve them both.

Ontology as a doctrine of being can achieve only one result nowadays: to make us conscious of being by the modes of being that occur to our thought. In the performance of this task it never touches the one being; it only clears the way for its ascertainment. Today's ontology will not be metaphysics any more; it will be a doctrine of categories. Whatever I may be thinking can only make room for the "I" as possible Existenz—which is outside my every thought at the same time. To possible Existenz, thoughts mean relative knowabilities, possibilities, appeals, but no more. In the same way, my partner in communicative thinking will stay outside his thoughts, for himself and for me, in order to move with me in possible thoughts and not to be subjected to absolute ones. To meet in communication is to break through the thought that made the breakthrough possible.

JASPERS' MAJOR WRITINGS
(arranged chronologically)

Heimweh und Verbrechen. (Inaugural Dissertation, Heidelberg) Leipzig: Vogel, 1909.

Allgemeine Psychopathologie. Berlin: Springer, 1913. Completely revised 4th ed., 1946.

  General Psychopathology. Tr. J. Hoening & M. Hamilton. Chicago: University of Chicago Press, 1963.

Psychologie der Weltanschauungen. Berlin: Springer, 1919.

Max Weber. Tubingen: Mohr, 1921.

Strindbergh und van Gogh. Bern: Bircher, 1922. 2nd revised ed. Berlin: Springer, 1926.

Die Idee der Universität. Berlin: Springer, 1923.

Die Geistige Situation der Zeit. Berlin: de Gruyter, 1931. Revised ed. 1933.

  Man in the Modern Age. Tr. E. & C. Paul. London: Routledge & Kegan Paul, 1933.

Max Weber; Deutsches Wesen im politischen Denken, im Forschen und Philosophieren. Oldenburg: Stallung, 1932.

Philosophie. 3 vols. Berlin: Springer, 1932.

  Philosophy. Vol. I. Tr. E. B. Ashton. Chicago: University of Chicago Press, 1969. Vol. II, 1970. Vol. III is forthcoming.

Vernunft und Existenz. Gronigen: Wolters, 1935.

  Reason and Existenz. Tr. W. Earle. New York: Noonday, 1955.

Nietzsche: Einführung in das Verständnis seines Philosophierens. Berlin: de Gruyten, 1936.

  Nietzsche: An Introduction to the Understanding of His Philosophical Activity. Tr. C. Wallraff & F. Schmitz. Tucson: University of Arizona Press, 1965.

Descartes und die Philosophie. Berlin: de Gruyter, 1937.

  In *Three Essays: Leonardo, Descartes, Max Weber.* Tr. R. Manheim. New York: Harcourt Brace, 1964.

Existenzphilosophie. Berlin: de Gruyter, 1938.

Nietzsche und das Christentum. Hamelin: Seifert, 1946.

  Nietzsche and Christianity. Tr. E. B. Ashton. Chicago: Regnery, 1961.

Die Schuldfrage. Heidelberg: L. Schneider, 1946.

  The Question of German Guilt. Tr. E. B. Ashton. New York: Dial Press, 1947.

Vom lebendigen Geist der Universität. Heidelberg: L. Schneider, 1946.

Die Idee der Universität. Berlin: Springer, 1946. (This is a different book from the publication of the same title issued in 1923.)

  The Idea of the University. Tr. K. W. Deutsch. Boston: Beacon Press, 1959.

Vom europäischen Geist. Munich: Piper, 1947.

  The European Spirit. Tr. R. G. Smith. New York: Macmillan, 1949.

Philosophische Logik, Band I: *Von der Wahrheit.* Munich: Piper, 1947.

Tragedy is not Enough. Tr. of pp. 915–961 by H. Reich, H. Moore & K. Deutsch. Boston: Beacon Press, 1952.

Truth and Symbol. Tr. of pp. 1022–1054 by J. Wilde, W. Kluback & W. Kimmel. New York: Twayne, 1959.

Der Philosophische Glaube. Zürich: Artemis, 1948.

The Perennial Scope of Philosophy. Tr. R. Manheim. New York: Philosophical Library, 1949.

Unsere Zukunft und Goethe. Bremen: J. Storm, 1949.

In *Existentialism and Humanism.* Tr. E. B. Ashton. New York: Russell Moore, 1952.

Philosophie und Wissenschaft. Zürich: Artemis, 1949.

"Philosophy and Science." Tr. R. Manheim. *Partisan Review.* New York, Vol. XVI, No. 9.

Vom Ursprung und Ziel der Geschichte. Zürich: Artemis, 1949.

The Origin and Goal of History. Tr. M. Bullock. New Haven: Yale University Press, 1953.

Einführung in die Philosophie. Zürich: Artemis, 1950.

Way to Wisdom. Tr. R. Manheim. Yale University Press, 1951.

Vernunft und Widervernunft in Unserer Zeit. Munich: Piper, 1950.

Reason and Anti-Reason in our Time. Tr. S. Godman. New Haven: Yale University Press, 1952.

Rechenschaft und Ausblick. Munich: Piper, 1951.

Lionardo als Philosoph. Bern: Francke, 1953.

In *Three Essays: Leonardo, Descartes, Max Weber.*

Die Frage der Entmythologisierung (with Rudolf Bultmann). Munich: Piper, 1954.

Myth and Christianity. Tr. H. Wolff. New York: Noonday Press, 1958.

Schelling: Grösse und Verhägnis. Munich: Piper, 1955.

Die Grossen Philosophen. Vol. I. Munich: Piper, 1957. Vols. II & III were scheduled to be published.

The Great Philosophers. Vol. I. Ed. Hannah Arendt. Tr. R. Manheim. New York: Harcourt Brace, 1962.

"Philosophical Autobiography" and "Reply to My Critics," in Schilpp, P. (ed.) *The Philosophy of Karl Jaspers.* New York: Tudor, 1957. (German originals in *Karl Jaspers' Philosophie.* Stuttgart: Kohlhammer, 1956.)

Philosophie und Welt. Munich: Piper, 1958.

Philosophy and the World. Tr. E. B. Ashton. Chicago: Regnery, 1963.

Max Weber: Politiker, Forscher, Philosoph. Munich: Piper, 1958.

In *Three Essays: Leonardo, Descartes, Max Weber.*

Wahrheit, Freiheit, und Friede. Munich: Piper, 1958.

Die Atombombe und die zukunft des Menschen. Munich: Piper, 1958.

  The Future of Mankind. Tr. E. B. Ashton. Chicago: University of Chicago Press, 1961.

Freiheit und Wiedervereinigung: Über Aufgaben deutscher Politik. Munich: Piper, 1960.

Die Philosophische Glaube angesichts der Offenbarung. Munich: Piper, 1962.

  Philosophical Faith and Revelation. Tr. E. B. Ashton. New York: Harper, 1967.

Gesammelte Schriften zur Psychopathologie. Berlin: Springer, 1963.

Nikolaus Cusanus. Munich: Piper, 1964.

Hoffnung und Sorge; Schriften zur deutschen Politik 1945–1965. Munich: Piper, 1965.

Kleine Schule des Philosophischen Denkens. Munich: Piper, 1965.

  Philosophy is for Everyone. A Short Course in Philosophical Thinking. Tr. R. Hull & G. Wels. New York: Harcourt Brace, 1967.

Wohin Treibt die Bundesrepublik? Stuttgart: Deutscher Bücherland, 1966.

  Partly translated in *The Future of Germany.* Tr. E. B. Ashton. Chicago: University of Chicago Press, 1967.

Philosophische Aufsätze. Frankfurt a.M.: Fischer, 1967.

Aneignung und Polemik: Gesammelte Reden und Aufsätze zur Geschichte der Philosophie. Ed. Hans Saner. Munich: Piper, 1968.

Selected Studies About Jaspers

(arranged alphabetically)

Allen, E. L. *The Self and Its Hazards: A Guide to the Thought of Karl Jaspers.* New York: Philosophical Library, 1951.

Dufrenne, M. & Ricoeur, P. *Karl Jaspers et la philosophie de l'existence.* Paris: Seuil, 1947.

Fries, H. *Ist der Glaube ein Verrat am Menschen? Eine Begegnung mit Karl Jaspers.* Stuttgart: Schwaben, 1948.

Knudsen, Robert. *The Idea of Transcendence in the Philosophy of Karl Jaspers.* Kampen: J. H. Kok, 1958.

Lichtigfeld, Adolph. *Aspects of Jaspers' Philosophy.* Pretoria: Universiteit von Suid-Afrika, 1963.

———. *Jaspers' Metaphysics.* London: Colibri, 1954.

Masi, Giuseppe. *La ricerca della verità in Karl Jaspers.* Bologna: Zuffi, 1953.

Pareyson, Luigi. *La filosofia dell'esistenza e Carlo Jaspers*. Napoli: Loffredo, 1940.

———. *Esistenza e persona*. Turin: Taylor, 1950.

Paumen, Jean. *Raison et existence chez Karl Jaspers*. Brussels: Parthénon, 1958.

Piper, Klaus (ed.). *Offener Horizont; Festschrift für Karl Jaspers*. Munich: Piper, 1953.

Ricoeur, Paul. *Gabriel Marcel et Karl Jaspers: Philosophie du mystère et philosophie du paradoxe*. Paris: Temps présent, 1947.

Schilpp, Paul (ed.). *The Philosophy of Karl Jaspers*. New York: Tudor, 1957.

Tonquedoc, Joseph de. *Une philosophie existentielle. L'existence d'après Karl Jaspers*. Paris: Beauchesne, 1945.

Wahl, Jean. *La pensée de l'existence*. Paris: Flammarion, 1951.

Wallraff, Charles. *Karl Jaspers: An Introduction to His Philosophy*. Princeton: Princeton University Press, 1970.

MARTIN HEIDEGGER (1889–   )

Heidegger was born at Messkirch in Baden, Germany, on September 26, 1889. He was the eldest son of Johanna Kempf and Friedrich Heidegger, the sexton of St. Martin's Catholic Church in Messkirch. After completing his studies at the *Gymnasium*, he became a Jesuit postulant for ten days but left for unknown reasons to enter the diocesan seminary of Freiburg. At one point during his two years there he was introduced to Franz Brentano's doctoral dissertation on the many senses of "being" in Aristotle. Interestingly enough, it is the problem of the meaning of "being" that has been the principal concern of Heidegger's philosophical career.

Apparently Heidegger received a solid foundation in Greek and medieval philosophy at the *Gymnasium* and seminary; his mature work bears the marks of these two epochs of philosophical inquiry. It seems, however, that he had trouble with the seminary authorities when he tried to organize seminars in modern philosophy.

In 1909 he entered the University of Freiburg where he studied philosophy under Heinrich Rickert. Before completing his dissertation he published in 1912 a critical survey of current logical studies for a Catholic journal. The survey showed familiarity with Russell and Whitehead's *Principia Mathematica* as well as Husserl's *Logische Untersuchungen*. The article notes and approves of Husserl's attack on the psychologistic interpretation of the foundations of logic. Another article written in the same year on the problem of reality in modern philosophy for another Catholic journal indicates Heidegger's preference for the Aristotelian and scholastic analyses of the "problem of reality" over those of Hume, Kant, and Mach.

In 1914 Heidegger submitted his dissertation *Die Lehre vom Urteil im Psychologismus* (The Theory of Judgment in Psychologism) and in 1916 published his *Habilitationsscrift* entitled *Die Kategorien und Bedeutungslehre des Duns Scotus* (Duns Scotus' Doctrine of Categories and Meanings). The same year Husserl arrived at Freiburg, and in 1920 Heidegger became his assistant. This association between the full professor and the *Privatdozent* is an important one in the history of twentieth-century philosophy, as much for the disagreements between the two as for their agreements.

Heidegger did his turn of military service during World War I between 1917 and 1919. In the same year that he entered the service, he married Elfride Petrie. Three children were born to them, two sons and a daughter.

In 1923 Heidegger was called to Marburg as a full professor. He became friendly with Rudolf Bultmann, who suggested that he look at Karl Barth's analysis of St. Paul's *Epistle to the Romans*. Kierkegaard's influence on that work led Heidegger to make a study of the Danish thinker.

Heidegger's lectures made a profound impression on those who heard them. He taught simply, patiently, clearly, and deliberately. His teaching has been the source of praise from philosophers as diverse as Ralph Barton Perry and Hannah Arendt. Leo Strauss also alludes to it in commenting on the Davos discussion between Heidegger and Cassirer. There have been remarks to the effect that his teaching was in marked contrast to the bombastic and abstruse character of his writing. These remarks betray a misunderstanding of his fundamental philosophical aim—the raising of the most ordinary characteristics of reality, by means of ordinary German expressions, to the level of theoretical inquiry.

In 1927 Heidegger published *Being and Time* which was dedicated to Husserl, as was the essay of 1929, *Vom Wesen des Grundes*. The relationship between the two cooled, as joint ventures such as the article on phenomenology for the Encyclopaedia Britannica failed or Heidegger's editing of Husserl's *The Phenomenology of Internal Time-Consciousness* proved unsatisfactory to the latter. But the real source of the estrangement was a difference between their conceptions of philosophical inquiry—Husserl maintaining that its task is the analysis of the structures of consciousness; Heidegger the analysis of the structures of being. Husserl became convinced that Heidegger had fallen into the error of anthropologism, another guise of the error of psychologism against which Husserl had directed so much of his energy. Despite his reservations about him, Husserl, at the point of retirement in 1928, nominated Heidegger as his successor for the chair of philosophy at Freiburg.

Then in 1933 there occurred an incident in Heidegger's career that bears the mark of tragedy. He had been elected *Rector Magnificus* of the University of Freiburg by his colleagues. On May 27 he delivered his inaugural address entitled *Die Selbstbehauptung der deutschen Universität* (The Self-Affirmation of the German University), endorsing the National Socialist government which had come to power that year. His brief flirtation with politics was described recently by Hannah Arendt in *Merkur* as a misadventure comparable to that of Plato with the tyrant Dionysius in Syracuse. Heidegger saw through his error quickly and resigned from the Rectorship early in 1934, apparently for political reasons. As a matter of fact, although he had been elected by the faculty, he never received the necessary confirmation of the Nazi government. Heidegger did not publish frequently during these years. It seems that he was forbidden to do so because of his lack of cooperation with the government.

The accounts of what occurred during the occupation at the end of the Second World War differ to some extent. One report states that from 1944 to 1951 he was forbidden to teach. Another report claims that although he was forbidden to teach in 1944, the French Occupation reinstated him in 1945. In this report he refused the reinstatement and withdrew from public academic life. In 1952 he became emeritus. He did, however, continue to lecture and give addresses during the Occupation with relative frequency. Since 1957 he has appeared rarely on the public scene, living a fairly isolated life in Todtnauberg near Freiburg.

The belief that Heidegger was an out and out Nazi and that

the philosophical inquiry served as a propaedeutic for Nazism is fairly widespread. As recently as July 12, 1970, a book review in the New York *Times* repeated the claim that tied Heidegger to the Nazi intellectual establishment. The persistence of this claim requires an explanation of some of the facts that have become available since it was originally made. The claim stems from the events surrounding his becoming the rector at Freiburg.

In an article entitled "Trois attaques contre Heidegger," published in the French journal *Critique* (November 1966), François Fedier conscientiously lays bare both the facts and the fictions of Heidegger's association with Nazism.

First of all, Fedier says that Heidegger did not belong to any political party and avoided political activity. But in the "new" Germany of 1933, holding a position of responsibility was almost automatically accompanied by registration in the Nazi party. Thus when Heidegger was persuaded and then elected by his colleagues to be the rector of the university, Nazi officials made it clear to him that enrollment in the party would facilitate dealing with the ministry of education. Heidegger consequently enrolled but only on the condition that he neither attend meetings nor participate in activities of the party. This condition probably led to the government's not confirming his rectorship.

This, of course, does not excuse the fact that on at least two occasions Heidegger publicly endorsed certain positions of the Nazi party. His inaugural lecture, moreover, not only endorsed certain of the party's positions but the party itself, inasmuch as Nazism had brought national stature to the university and awareness of national destiny to the students. Heidegger argued that university training had been haphazard and without relation to concrete social and political needs, that vague ideals of scientific progress and academic freedom should be rooted and strengthened in German tradition as it struggled to achieve its destiny of self-determination. Commitment to this struggle on the part of the students and professors in union with the labor force, said Heidegger, was the initial grasp of the glory and greatness of Hitler's revolution.

The strength of his endorsement may be gauged by these

words which appear on page 22 of the published version of the speech: "It is not theses and ideas that are the laws of your being! The Führer himself, and he alone, is Germany's reality and law today and in the future."

Another occasion on which Heidegger's political views coincided with those of the Nazis occurred in the fall of 1933 when he publicly encouraged his fellow Germans to vote affirmatively in the plebescite on whether or not to withdraw from the League of Nations.

Yet in February 1934, after Heidegger refused government orders to discharge two anti-Nazi deans, von Mollendorf and Wolf, and when he realized that the government was not going to confirm his rectorship, he resigned from the position. The ministry of education chose his successor, who was congratulated in the Nazi press as "the first National Socialist rector of Freiburg University." Heidegger was conspicuously absent from the new rector's investiture.

From 1934 to 1944, those students of Heidegger who attended his lectures claim that his public posture was one of obstinate disapproval of the Nazi regime, with the result that the lectures received surveillance from the secret police. Furthermore, in 1944 when labor conscription was begun in order to construct entrenchments along the Rhine, the current rector, with the party's approval, "volunteered" Heidegger and designated him "the least indispensable of the university's professors."

The claims that Heidegger lectured in an S.A. uniform as reported in *France-Observateur* (December 19, 1964), and that he refused Husserl access to the university or to its library as reported in *Der Neue Zürcher Zeitung* (January 5, 1961) and repeated in *Der Spiegel* (February 7, 1966), are false. Heidegger, in fact, has made a public denial of these claims (*Der Spiegel*, March 7, 1966).

Finally we must deal with the allegation that Heidegger tended toward anti-Semitism. The only ascertainable source for this is a remark made by Frau Toni Cassirer in memoirs (*Aus meinem Leben mit Ernst Cassirer*) published in 1950. On pages 165–67, she refers to the occasion of the 1929 Davos discussion between her husband and Heidegger. Besides finding his presence discomforting, she makes the following assertion:

"His inclination toward anti-Semitism was not strange to us." Fedier questions the objectivity and validity of that assertion and calls attention to the fact that Heidegger's first disciplinary act as Freiburg's rector was to forbid anti-Semitic propaganda at the university by the Nazi students.

Sometimes the claim that Heidegger was a committed Nazi is repeated innocently and out of ignorance; at other times the malice and shamelessness seem obvious. An instance of the latter is a book brought out in 1965 by a New York publisher with the title *German Existentialism* enclosed in a jacket carrying a white swastika against a black and red background. Though Heidegger is named as the author, the book contains only snatches of some of Heidegger's speeches, and it is composed mostly of newspaper reports from 1933 with none later than February 1, 1934. Another example of this mischievous detraction can be found in *The Philosophy of Ernst Cassirer*. One of the contributors, in referring to the Davos discussion on Kant between Cassirer and Heidegger in 1929, compares the two philosophers in a reckless display of misrepresentation. Cassirer is the "heir of Kant," "tall, powerful and serene," his effect upon the audience "Apollonian." He is the product of liberal culture of Central Europe. Heidegger, on the other hand, despite his "gigantic intellect," is "of *petit bourgeois* descent from Southwest Germany" who "had never lost his accent." The writer then forgives him this and takes it as a "mark a firm-rootedness and peasant genuineness." He is, however, "a renegade" from the seminary; his "gloomy, somewhat whining and apprehensive tone of voice" expressed his "feeling of loneliness, of oppression and of frustration." He is a "little man with sinister willful speech . . . who loved to say that philosophy is no fun . . . over against the representative of Enlightenment, basking in spiritual fortune, for whom the philosopher's life was joy and inspiration. . . ." This remark, of course, illustrates the depth of the writer's understanding of philosophy and neatly complements his report of the debate. But he is not yet finished with Heidegger, for he adds that subsequently the philosopher "professed himself unreservedly for National Socialism" and that he "placed his philosophy at the service of the self-destruction of the German intelligentsia."

Such remarks could very well be dismissed were it not for the wide measure of acceptance they have received.

A Discussion Between Ernst Cassirer and Martin Heidegger[1]

Translated by Francis Slade

[P. 17.] CASSIRER: What does Heidegger understand by Neo-Kantianism? Who is the opponent whom Heidegger has in mind? The concept "Neo-Kantianism" must not be defined substantially, but functionally. What is at issue is not the character of that philosophy as a dogmatic doctrinal system, but a way of formulating the question.

HEIDEGGER: If I am to begin by naming names, I will men-

[1] The following piece is a translation of "Arbeitsgemeinschaft Cassirer-Heidegger" (printed in Guido Schneeberger, *Ergänzungen zu einer Heidegger-Bibliographie*, Bern, 1960, pp. 17–27) and is a record of the discussion between Cassirer and Heidegger which took place at Davos, Switzerland, in March 1929 during the second Davoser Hochschulkurse. Since this record was made by two auditors of the discussion, the statements contained in what is here translated under the title "A Discussion Between Ernst Cassirer and Martin Heidegger" do not represent the written statements either of Cassirer or of Heidegger. However, they do not contradict the known and acknowledged views of either of these philosophers. Contrasting accounts of this encounter between Cassirer and Heidegger can be found in Hendrick J. Pos, "Recollections of Ernst Cassirer" in *The Philosophy of Ernst Cassirer*, edited by Paul A. Schilpp, New York, 1949, pp. 67–69 and in Leo Strauss, "Kurt Riezler: In Memoriam" in *What Is Political Philosophy*, Glencoe (Illinois), 1960, pp. 245–246. Also of interest is the account given in T. Cassirer, *Aus meinem Leben mit Ernst Cassirer*, New York, 1950, pp. 165–167.

The translator wishes to thank Joseph Carpino and Thomas Prufer for their many comments and suggestions during the course of the preparation of this translation. He would also like to acknowledge the generosity of Willi Schmidt who read parts of this translation and made suggestions for its improvement.

tion Cohen, Windelband, Rickert, Erdmann, Riehl. What is common to every form of Neo-Kantianism can only be understood in terms of its origin. This is the embarrassing dilemma of philosophy before the question of what still really remains to it [as a field of inquiry][2] within the totality of knowledge. There appeared to remain only the knowledge about science, not of "that-which-is" [das Seiende]. It was this point of view that defined the movement back to Kant. Kant was seen as the theoretician of the mathematico-physical theory of knowledge. Kant, however, did not wish to provide a theory of natural science, but to show the problematic of metaphysics, more specifically of ontology. My intention is to work this essential content of the positive basis of the *Critique of Pure Reason* into ontology. By reason of my interpretation of the Dialectic as ontology, I believe that the problem of Being [Sein] in the Transcendental Logic, seemingly only negative in Kant, is really a positive problem.

CASSIRER: Cohen is only understood correctly if he is understood historically, not simply as an epistemologist. I do not conceive of my own development as a defection from Cohen. The positioning of the mathematical sciences of nature is for me only a paradigm, not the whole of the problem.—Heidegger and I are in agreement on one point: for Kant the productive imagination is of central significance. I have been led to this through my work on the symbolic. The imagination is the relation of all thinking to intuition, *synthesis speciosa*. The synthesis is the fundamental power of pure thought. What matters for Kant is the synthesis which makes use of the species. [P. 18.] And this leads to the heart of the image-concept,[3] of the symbol-concept. —Kant's major problem is how is freedom possible. Kant says that we conceive only that freedom is inconceivable. And yet there is the Kantian ethics. The categorical imperative ought to be such that the moral law holds not only for men, but for all rational beings in general. The moral as such leads beyond the

[2] Material enclosed within brackets [ ] has been inserted by the translator. Material enclosed within parentheses ( ) appears in parentheses in the German text. Page numbers in brackets are the page numbers of the German text.

[3] Reading "Bildbegriffes" for "Bildungbegriffes" as emended by Guido Schneeberger in a letter to the editor of this anthology.

world of appearances. What is at stake here is the break-through to the *mundus intelligibilis*. In the ethical realm a point is reached which is no longer relative to the finitude of the cognizing being.—And this ties in with what Heidegger has done. The extraordinary importance of the schematism cannot be overestimated. Yet in the ethical realm Kant suppresses the schematism. For he says our concepts are "senses of . . ." [Einsichten] (not cognitions), "senses of . . ." which can no longer be schematized. There is at most a typology, not a schematism, of Practical Reason. For Kant the schematism is a *terminus a quo,* not a *terminus ad quem.* Kant's point of departure is the problem posed by Heidegger. However, this circle widened for Kant. Heidegger has made the point that our cognitive power is finite. It is relative and confined. But how does such a finite being attain knowledge, reason, truth?—Heidegger formulates the problem of truth and says there cannot be any truths in themselves, or eternal truths, but truths are always relative to *Dasein.* For Kant, on the other hand, this was exactly the problem. Granted this finitude, how can there be necessary and universal truths? How are synthetic judgments *a priori* possible? That is the problem which Kant exemplifies with mathematics. Finite cognition involves itself with truth, but this relationship again works into a "merely" [i.e., is qualified] (?) Heidegger has said that Kant has given no demonstration of the possibility of mathematics. But this problem is posed in the *Prolegomena.* Once more, then, this pure theoretical question, how does a finite being come to a determination of objects which as such are not limited by finitude, must first of all be clarified.—My question now is this: Does Heidegger wish to renounce this complete objectivity, this form of absoluteness, which Kant has stood for in the realms of the ethical and the theoretical and in the *Critique of Judgment?*

HEIDEGGER: To begin with the question of the mathematical sciences of nature. [P. 19.] In Kant nature does not mean an object of the mathematical science of nature, but rather the totality of "that-which-is" in the sense of the present-at-hand [*das Ganze des Seienden im Sinne des Vorhandenen*]. Kant means "that-which-is" as such without limitation to a determinate area of "that-which-is." What I want to show is that the Analytic is not an ontology of nature as object of natural science, but a general ontology, that is, a critically based *metaphysica generalis*. Kant himself says that the problematic of the *Prolegomena* is not the central theme. This is, rather, the question concerning the possibility of a *metaphysica generalis,* more exactly, of its realization.—Cassirer wants to show further that finitude is transcended in the ethical writings. There is something in the categorical imperative which exceeds the finite being. Yet precisely the concept of the imperative displays in itself the inner relation to a finite being. Even this transcendence still remains within finitude. For Kant human reason is completely dependent upon itself and cannot escape from itself into an eternal and absolute nor into the world of things. This "In-between" is the essence of practical reason. One goes astray in the interpretation of the Kantian ethics if one does not see the inner function of the Law for *Dasein*. Certainly there is something in the moral law which goes beyond sensibility. However, the question is, what is the character of the inner structure of *Dasein* itself? Is this structure finite or infinite? There lies in this question a really central problem. Just in that which one puts forward as constitutive infinity, the character of the finite comes to light. Kant designates the imagination of the schematism as *exhibitio originaria*. This power of origination is, it is true, in a certain way, a creative power there, but as *exhibitio* it cannot dispense with receptivity. Man is never infinite and absolute in the creation of "that-which-is" itself [*des Seienden selbst*], but he is infinite in the sense of the understanding of Being [*des Seins*]. This infinity of the ontological is by its very nature bound to ontic experience, so that one must say just the opposite: this infinity which breaks forth in the imagination is precisely the most acute argument for finitude. Ontology is an index of finitude. God does not have it. [i.e., ontology]—Thereupon Cassirer's next question with reference to the concept of truth arises. At the most profound level truth itself is at one with the structure of transcendence through the fact that *Dasein* is "something-which-is" which is open to other "things-which-are" and to itself. We are "something-which-is" that keeps itself in the unhiddenness of "that-which-is." [P. 20.] To keep oneself in this way in the openness of "that-which-is" is what I call Being-in-the-truth

[*In-der-Wahrheit-sein*]. And I go further. Because of its finitude man's Being-in-the-truth is at the same time a Being-in-the-untruth. Untruth belongs to the inmost core of *Dasein*. I believe that I have found only here the root which establishes a metaphysical explanation for what Kant called "metaphysical illusion."—To take Cassirer's question concerning universally valid eternal truths. When I say truth is relative to *Dasein*, that is no ontic statement in the sense that what is true is always only what the individual man thinks. The proposition is metaphysical. Truth as such can only be as truth if *Dasein* exists. Only with the existence of something such as *Dasein* does truth first come about. But now to the question: What about the validity, the eternity of truth? One commonly formulates this question in terms of the problem of validity, i.e., in terms of the asserted proposition. The problem must be broached differently. Truth is relative to *Dasein*. The transsubjectivity of truth, this breaking-out of truth beyond the individual, signifies that Being-in-the-truth means to be given over to and to be taken up with "that-which-is." What can here be separated as objective knowledge, taking into account the particular matter-of-fact individual existence, has a truth content which says something about "that-which-is." This is, however, badly interpreted if it is said that over against the flow of experience there is something permanent, the eternal, the meaning and concept. At this point, then, I pose the question: What does eternal really mean here? Is this eternity not merely permanence in the sense of the *aei* [the "forever"] of time? Is it possible only by reason of an inner transcendence of time itself? What do all those expressions of transcendental metaphysics, *a priori, aei on, ousia,* mean? They are only to be understood and are only possible through the fact that time itself has the character of horizon, so that I have always conjointly in an anticipatory remembering stance, a horizon of present, futurity, and pastness, and, consequently, there is given a transcendental-ontological time determination within which alone something such as the permanence of substance is constituted.—My entire interpretation of temporality is to be understood from this point of view. The whole problematic in *Sein und Zeit,* which treats of the *Dasein* of man, is no philosophical anthropology. It is much too limited and much too sketchy for that. Here there is a problematic which has not as such hitherto been broached. The question [of *Sein und Zeit*] is this: if the possibility of the understanding of "that-which-is" is based on an understanding of Being, and if this ontological understanding is in some sense in terms of time [P. 21], then the task is to expose the temporality of *Dasein* in terms of the possibility of the understanding of Being. And all problems [in *Sein und Zeit*] are in terms of this. The analysis of death is intended to expose in *one* direction *Dasein's* radical futurity, and not to furnish a final and metaphysical teaching concerning the essence of death. The analysis of dread [*Angst*] has the sole function of preparing the question: On the basis of what metaphysical meaning of *Dasein* itself is it possible that man as such can be put before such a thing as Nothing [*das Nichts*]? Only if I understand Nothing or Dread do I have the possibility of understanding Being. Only in the unity of the understanding of Being and Nothing does the question of the origin of the "Why" suddenly arise. This central problem of Being, of Nothing, and of the Why, is the most elementary, the most concrete problem. The entire Analytic of *Dasein* is directed toward this. At the same time I pose a further question of method. In what way must a metaphysics of *Dasein* be initiated? Is there not a definite over-all view of life [*Weltanschauung*] at its basis? It is not the task of philosophy to provide such an over-all view of life, though certainly such a view is already the presupposition of the activity of philosophizing. The over-all view of life which the philosopher provides is not a direct one in the sense of a doctrine, but rests in this, that in the act of philosophizing it comes about that the transcendence of *Dasein* itself, i.e., the inner possibility possessed by this finite being to be in relation to "that-which-is" in its totality, is made radical. The question, how is freedom possible, does not make sense because freedom is not an object of theoretical comprehension, but an object of the act of philosophizing. That can mean nothing else than that freedom is, and can only be, in the act of freeing. The sole adequate relation which man has to freedom is [in terms of] the act by which freedom sets itself free in man.

Questions Addressed to Cassirer (by a student of philosophy):

1. What way can man find to infinity? In what fashion can man participate in infinity?
2. Is infinity to be achieved as a privative determination of finitude, or is it a domain in its own right?
   [P. 22.]
3. To what extent should it be the task of philosophy to effect a liberation from dread, or is it its task to hand man over quite radically to dread?

CASSIRER: Ad 1. In no other way than through the medium of Form. The function of Form is such that man, while he changes his existence [*Dasein*] into Form, i.e., while he has to transform everything which is in him as experience into some kind of objective structure, does not, it is true, thereby become radically freed from the finitude of the point of departure (for this is still definitely related to his finitude), but in so far as his existence develops out of finitude, his existence leads finitude out of itself into something new, immanent infinity. Man cannot make the jump out of his own finitude into a realistically understood infinity. However, he can have, and must have, a *metabasis* which leads him from the immediacy of his own existence into the region of pure Form. He possesses his infinity exclusively in this Form. "From the chalice of this realm of spirits, infinity pours forth for him."[4] The realm of spirits is not a metaphysical realm of spirits. The realm of spirits is just that spiritual world which he himself has created. That he could create it is the seal of his infinity.—Ad 2. It is not only a privative determination, but is a domain in its own right. Not, however, a domain that is won only in conflict with finitude, but rather infinity is precisely the totality, the perfect fulfillment of finitude itself. And this fulfillment of finitude is just what constitutes infinity. Thus Goethe's "Wouldst thou stride into the

[4] The German text reads: "Aus dem Kelche dieses Geisterreiches strömt ihm die Unendlichkeit." Cf. Schiller's poem "Die Freundschaft," lines 59–60; and Hegel's *Phänomenologie des Geistes,* concluding lines.

infinite, thou hast but to go in the finite in every direction."[5]
Ad 3. That is a question which goes right to the roots, and one
can answer it only with a kind of profession of faith. Philosophy
has allowed man to become free just so far as he can become
free. Thereby it frees him radically, to be sure, from dread as a
pure state of feeling. The aim is liberation in this sense: "Cast
the anxiety of the terrestrial from yourselves." That is the position of Idealism which I have myself always professed.

HEIDEGGER: In his first lecture Cassirer has used the expressions *terminus a quo* and *terminus ad quem*. One could say
that the *terminus ad quem* is a complete Philosophy of Culture
in the sense of a clarification of the wholeness of the Form of a
structure-creating consciousness. The *terminus a quo* in Cassirer
is completely problematical. [P. 23.] My position is the opposite: the *terminus a quo* is my central problematic. The question is whether the *terminus ad quem* is just as clear for me.
This, I hold, consists not in a complete Philosophy of Culture,
but in the question: *ti to on?* The problematic of a metaphysics
of *Dasein,* for me, grows out of this question. Or, to come once
again to the heart of the Kant interpretation, I attempted to
show that to start from a concept of the *logos* is not quite such
an obvious procedure, but, on the contrary, that the question of
the possibility of metaphysics requires a metaphysics of *Dasein*
itself, in such a way that the question, what man is, doesn't
have to be answered so much in the sense of an anthropological
system, but that this question must first of all be really clarified
with respect to the perspective in which it will be posed. Are the
concepts *terminus a quo* and *terminus ad quem* only a heuristic
formulation of the question or are they based in the essence of
philosophy itself? This problematic does not seem to me to be
clearly worked out in Cassirer's philosophy up till now. What
matters first of all for Cassirer is to expose the different Forms of
the form-giving activity and then, subsequently, to push forward
from there into a certain dimension of the form-creating powers
themselves. Now one could say it follows that this dimension is still basically the same as that which I call *Dasein.*

[5] "Gott, Gemüt und Welt," *Sprüche im Reimen.*

This would be wrong, however. The difference appears most clearly in the concept of freedom. I have spoken of an act of freeing in the sense that the setting free of the inner transcendence of *Dasein* is the very character of the act of philosophizing. And here the real meaning of this act of freeing consists in becoming free for the finitude of *Dasein,* entering directly into the thrownness [*Geworfenheit*] of *Dasein.* I have not given freedom to myself although I can be the self that I am only through being free. The self that I am, however, now not in the sense of an undifferentiated ground of explanation, but in the sense that *Dasein* is the really fundamental event in which the act of existing of man, and with that, every problematic of existence as such essentially comes about.—I believe that what I designate with the term *Dasein* cannot be translated by one of Cassirer's concepts. What I call *Dasein* is essentially characterized not only through that which is designated as "spirit," or as "life," but rather it is the original unity and the immanent structure of the relatedness of a man who, in his shackledness to the body, stands in a special boundness with "that-which-is" [P. 24], in the sense that *Dasein* as free, thrown in the midst of "that-which-is," effects a breaking-into "that-which-is," a breaking-into which is always historically in the final sense fortuitous; so fortuitous that man exists at the highest point of his own possibility only in a very few moments of *Dasein's* duration between life and death.—In all my philosophical work I have completely left out of consideration the traditional form and division of the philosophical disciplines, because I believe that orienting oneself in terms of these constitutes the greatest snare in the way of getting back to the inner problematic of philosophy. Neither Plato nor Aristotle knew anything about such a division in philosophy. This was an affair of the Schools. Effort is required to break through these disciplines and to come back again to the specifically metaphysical mode of Being of the respective areas [underlying these disciplines]. Art is not merely a Form of the form-creating consciousness, rather art has itself a metaphysical sense within the fundamental event that *Dasein* itself is.—I have intentionally stressed these differences. The work that really has to be done is not helped by smoothing them over. For the sake of clarity I would like to place our entire discussion once more under the sign of Kant's *Critique of Pure Reason,* and once more to fix upon the question, what man is, as the central question. This question need not be put anthropocentrically, but it must be shown, through the fact that man is the being who transcends, i.e., is open to "that-which-is" in its totality and to himself, that by means of this eccentric character man is also at the same time put into the totality of "that-which-is" as such. The question and the idea of a philosophical anthropology has this meaning, not that of investigating man empirically as a given object. Rather it has to be motivated out of the central problematic of philosophy itself which must lead man back beyond himself into the whole of "that-which-is," in order to make manifest to him, for all his freedom, the nothingness of his *Dasein.* This nothingness is not an inducement to pessimism and dejection, but to the understanding of this, namely, that there is genuine activity only where there is opposition and that philosophy has the task of throwing man back into the hardness of his fate from out of the softness of one who merely lives off the work of the spirit.

[P. 25.] CASSIRER: I believe it has already become clearer in what the opposition consists. It is, however, not fruitful to stress this opposition repeatedly. We are at a point where little is to be gained through purely logical arguments. It seems, then, we are condemned here to some sort of relativity. However, we may not persist in this relativity which would place empirical man in the center. What Heidegger said at the end was most important. His position cannot be anthropocentric either. And then, I ask, where now lies the common center in our opposition? We do not need to look for this. For we have this center, and we have it indeed because there is one common objective human world in which, although the differences of individuals are in no way cancelled, a bridge is built from individual to individual. That I find again and again in the primal phenomenon of language. Everyone speaks his own language, and yet we understand one another through the medium of language. There is something such as *the* language, something such as a unity over and above the endlessly different ways of speaking. Therein lies the decisive point for me. And therefore I start from the objectivity of the symbolic Form because here "the inconceivable is achieved."⁶ That is what I should like to call the world of objective spirit. There is no other way from one existence [*Dasein*] to another existence [*Dasein*] than through this world of Form. If it did not exist, then I would not know how such a thing as a common understanding could be. Cognition, too, is therefore simply only a basic instance of this position, because an objective assertion is formulated which no longer takes into consideration the subjectivity of the particular individual.—Heidegger has correctly said that the fundamental question of his metaphysics is the same one which formed Plato and Aristotle: What is "that-which-is"? And he has said further that Kant once again took up with this question. However, here an essential difference seems to me to obtain, which is in fact what Kant called the Copernican revolution. The question of being seems to me, I admit, to be in no way eliminated as a result of this revolution. However, the question of being acquires a much more complicated form. In what does that revolution consist? The question of how objects are determined is preceded by a question about the constitution of the being of an objectivity as such. What is new in this revolution seems to me to lie in this, that there is now no longer a single such structure of being, but rather that we have completely different structures of being. [P. 26.] Each new structure of being has new *a priori* presuppositions. Kant shows how every kind of new Form always bears upon a new world of objectivities. In that way a whole new multiplicity enters into the problem of the object as such. By that means the old dogmatic metaphysics becomes the new Kantian metaphysics. The being of the old metaphysics was substance, that *one* which underlies. In the new metaphysics being is in my language no longer the being of a substance, but the being that proceeds from a manifold of functional determinations and meanings. And here appears to me to lie the essential point of distinction of my position in opposition to Heidegger.—I hold to the Kantian formulation of the question of the transcendental. The essential of the transcendental

---

⁶ The German text, in quotation marks here, reads: *Weil hier "das Unbegreifliche getan" ist.* It seems intended to recall *"Das Unbeschreibliche, Hier ist es getan"* in *Faust*, Part II.

method lies in this, that it begins with a given. Thus I inquire into the possibility of the given called "language." How is it conceivable that we as one existence [*Dasein*] to another can understand each other in this medium? Or, how is it possible that we are able to see at all a work of art as an objective determinate thing? This question must be solved. Perhaps not all questions in philosophy are to be solved on this basis. I believe that only if one has posed this question does he gain access to Heidegger's formulation of the question.

HEIDEGGER: To repeat Plato's question cannot mean that we fall back upon the answer of the Greeks. Being itself is splintered into a multiplicity, and a central problem consists in gaining a position from which to understand the inner diversity of the ways of Being out of the idea of Being.—Just reconciling differences will never be really productive. It is the essence of philosophy, as a finite affair of man, that it is limited within the finitude of man. Since philosophy is concerned with the whole of man and the highest in man, this finitude must show itself in philosophy in a completely radical manner.—What matters to me is that you retain this one thing from our confrontation: don't fasten on our differences as the disagreements of individuals engaged in philosophy, but rather come to feel that we are once again on the way towards taking seriously the central question of metaphysics. What you see here on a small scale, the difference of individuals engaged in philosophy within the unity of the problematic, is also to be found, though quite differently, on a large scale [P. 27]; and that is just the essential thing in confronting the history of philosophy, to see how it is precisely the differentiating of standpoints which is the root of philosophical work.

Letter on Humanism[1]

Translated by Edgar Lohner

Our thinking about the essence of action is still far from resolute
enough. Action is known only as the bringing about of an effect;
it is assessed by its utility. But the essence of action is fulfillment.
To fulfill is to unfold something in the fullness of its essence,
to usher it forward into that fullness: *producere*. Hence only
that can be truly fulfilled which is already in existence. Yet that
which, above all, "is," is Being. Thought brings to fulfillment
the relation of Being to the essence of man, it does not make or
produce this relation. Thought merely offers it to Being as that
which has been delivered to itself by Being. This offering consists in this: that in thought Being is taken up in language.
Language is the house of Being. In its home man dwells. Whoever thinks or creates in words is a guardian of this dwelling. As
guardian, he brings to fulfillment the unhiddenness of Being
insofar as he, by his speaking, takes up this unhiddenness in
language and preserves it in language. Thought does not become
action because an effect issues from it, or because it is applied.
Thought acts in that it thinks. This is presumably the simplest
and, at the same time, the highest form of action: it concerns
man's relation to what is. All effecting, in the end, rests upon
Being, is bent upon what is. Thought, on the other hand, lets
itself be called into service by Being in order to speak the truth
of Being. It is thought which accomplishes this letting be
(*Lassen*). Thought is *l'engagement par l'Etre pour l'Etre*. I do
not know if it is linguistically possible to express both (*"par"* et
"pour") as one, i.e. by *penser, c'est l'engagement de l'Etre*. Here
the possessive form *"de l' . . ."* is meant simultaneously to express the genitive as *genitivus subiectivus* and *obiectivus*. In this,

[1] *Platons Lehre von der Wahrheit. Mit einen Brief uber den "Humanismus,"* pp. 53–119. A. Francke, Bern, 1947. [The letter is addressed to a French student of Heidegger's, Jean Beaufret.]

"subject" and "object" are inadequate terms of the metaphysics which, in the form of Western "logic" and "grammar," early took possession of the interpretation of language. Today we can but begin to surmise what lies hidden in this process. The freeing of language from grammar, and placing it in a more original and essential framework, is reserved for thought and poetry. Thought is not merely *l'engagement dans l'action* for and by "what is" in the sense of the actual and present situation. Thought is *l'engagement* by and for the truth of Being. Its history is never past, it is always imminent. The history of Being sustains and determines every *condition et situation humaine*. In order that we may first learn how to perceive the aforesaid essence of thinking in its pure form—and that means to fulfill it as well—we must free ourselves from the technical interpretation of thought. Its beginnings reach back to Plato and Aristotle. With them thought is valued as τέχνη, the procedure of reflection in the service of doing and making. The reflection here is already seen from the viewpoint of πρᾶξις and ποίησις. Hence thought, when taken by itself, is not "practical." The characterization of thought as θεωρία and the determination of cognition as "theoretical" behavior occur already within the "technical" interpretation of thought. They constitute a reactive attempt of saving for thought an independence in the face of doing and acting. Ever since, "philosophy" has faced the constant distress of justifying its existence against "science." It believes it accomplishes this most securely by elevating itself to the rank of science. Yet this effort is the surrender of the essence of thought. Philosophy is haunted by the fear of losing prestige and validity, unless it becomes science. It is considered a failure equated with unscientific rigor. Being as the element of thought has been abandoned in the technical interpretation of thought. "Logic," since sophistry and Plato, is the initial sanction of this interpretation. Thought is judged by a measure inadequate to it. This judgment is like the procedure of trying to evaluate the nature and the capability of a fish by how long it is able to live on dry land. Too long, all too long, thought has been lying on dry land. Can the effort to bring thought back to its element be called "irrationalism" now?

The questions your letter raises would undoubtedly be more

easily clarified in personal conversation. In writing thought tends
to lose its flexibility. Above all, however, it can hardly preserve
the multidimensional quality peculiar to its realm. Strictness of
thought consists, in contradistinction to science, not merely in
the artificial, i.e. the technico-theoretical exactitude of terms. It
rests on the fact that speaking remains purely in the element of
Being and lets the simplicity of the manifold dimensions of
Being rule. But the written, on the other hand, offers the salu-
tary compulsion toward thought-out composition of the spoken
word. Today I should like to select only one of your questions,
the discussion of which may cast light on the others too.

You ask: *Comment dedonner un sens au mot "Humanisme"*?
This question is asked with the intention of retaining the word
"humanism." I wonder if it is necessary. Or is the harm wrought
by all such terms not obvious enough yet? Of course, for some
time now, "isms" have been suspect. But the market of public
opinion always demands new ones. Again and again this demand
is readily answered. And terms like "logic," "ethics," "physics"
occur only when original thinking has stopped. The Greeks, in
their great age, did their thinking without such terms. They did
not even call it "philosophy." Thinking ceases when it withdraws
from its element. The element is that by means of which thinking can be thinking. It is the element which is potent, which is
potency.[2] It concerns itself with thought and so brings thought
into its essence. Thought is, more simply, thought of Being. The
genitive has two meanings. Thought is of Being, insofar as
thought, eventuated by Being, belongs to Being. Thought is at
the same time thought of Being insofar as thought listens to,
heeds, Being. Listening to and belonging to Being, thought constitutes what it is in its essential origin. Thought is—this means,
Being has always, in the manner of destiny, concerned itself

---

[2] This and the following passage depends essentially on a play on
words though it is not just that. The verb "vermögen" means "to be
able to," "to have the power to do . . ." The noun "Vermögen"
means "potency," also "wealth," "resources," "means." "Vermögend"
means accordingly "potent" and also "propertied." The play lies in this
that, without the prefix "ver" there is a word "mögen" meaning "to
like." "Mögen" is then used here in a fusion of the two strains of
meaning, potency and liking.

about its essence, embraced it. To concern oneself about a "thing" or a "person" means, to love, to like him or it. Such "liking," understood in a more original way, means: to confer essence. Such "liking origin" is the proper nature of potency (*Vermögen*), which not only can perform this or that, but which can let something be what it is as it stems from its true origin. It is the potency of this loving on the "strength of which something is in fact capable of being." This potency is the truly "possible," that whose essence rests on "Mögen." Being is capable of thought. The one makes the other possible. Being as the element is the "quiet power" of the loving potency, i.e. of the possible. Our words "possible" and "possibility," however, are, under the domination of "logic" and "metaphysics," taken only in contrast to "actuality," i.e. they are conceived with reference to a determined—viz. the metaphysical—interpretation of Being as *actus* and *potentia* the distinction of which is identified with that of *existentia* and *essentia*. When I speak of the "quiet power of the possible," I do not mean the possible of a merely represented *possibilitas*, nor the *potentia* as *essentia* of an *actus* of the *existentia*, but Being itself, which in its loving potency commands thought and thus also the essence of man, which means in turn his relationship to Being. To command something is to sustain it in its essence, to retain it in its element.

When thought comes to an end of withdrawing from its element, it replaces the loss by making its validity felt as τέχνη, as an educational instrument and therefore as a scholarly matter and later as a cultural matter. Philosophy gradually becomes a technique of explanation drawn from ultimate causes. One no longer thinks, but one occupies oneself with "philosophy." In competition such occupations publicly present themselves as "isms" and try to outdo each other. The domination achieved through such terminology does not just happen. It rests, especially in modern times, on the peculiar dictatorship of the public. So-called private existence does not mean yet, however, essentially and freely being human. It merely adheres obstinately to a negation of the public. It remains an offshoot dependent on the public and nourishes itself on its mere retreat from the public. So it is witness, against its own will, of its subjection to the public. The public itself, however, is the metaphysically conditioned—as it is derived from the domination of subjectivity —establishment and authorization of the overtness of the existent in the absolute objectivization of everything. Therefore, language falls into the service of arranging the lines of communication, on which objectification as the uniform accessibility of everything for everybody expands, disregarding all limits. So language comes under the dictatorship of the public. This public predetermines what is intelligible and what must be rejected as unintelligible. What has been said in *Sein und Zeit* (1927), §27 and §35, about the word *"man"* (the impersonal one) is not simply meant to furnish, in passing, a contribution to sociology. In the same way the word *man* does not simply mean the counterpart—in an ethical existential way—to a person's self-Being. What has been said contains rather an indication— thought of from the question of the truth of Being—of the original pertinence of the word Being. This relationship remains concealed under the domination of subjectivity, which is represented as the public. When, however, the truth of Being has become memorable to thought, then reflection on the essence of language must obtain a new rank. It can no longer be mere philosophy of language. And for just this reason *Sein und Zeit* (§34) contains an indication of the essential dimension of language and broaches the simple question of what mode of Being the language as language from time to time is in. The ubiquitous and fast-spreading impoverishment of language does not gnaw only at aesthetic and moral responsibility in all use of language. It rises from an endangering of man's essence. A merely cultured use of language still does not demonstrate that we have as yet escaped this essential danger. Today it may rather signify that we have not yet seen the danger and cannot see it, because we have never exposed ourselves to its gaze. The decadence of language, quite recently considered though very late, is, however, not the cause but rather a consequence of the process that language under the domination of the modern metaphysics of subjectivity almost always falls out of its element. Language still denies us its essence: that it is the house of the truth of Being. Language, moreover, leaves itself to our mere willing and cultivating as an instrument of domination over beings. This itself appears as the actual in the concatenation of cause and effect.

Calculating and acting we encounter beings as the actual, but also scientifically and in philosophizing with explanations and arguments. To these also belongs the assurance that something is inexplicable. Through such assertions we believe we confront the mystery. As if it were taken for granted that the truth of Being could be set up over causes and basic explanations or, what is the same, over their incomprehensibility.

If man, however, is once again to find himself in the nearness of Being, he must first learn to exist in the nameless. He must recognize the seduction of the public, as well as the impotence of the private. Man must, before he speaks, let himself first be claimed again by Being at the risk of having under this claim little or almost nothing to say. Only in this way will the preciousness of its essence be returned to the word, and to man the dwelling where he can live in the truth of Being.

But is there not now in this claim upon man, is there not in the attempt to make man ready for this claim, an effort in behalf of man? Where else does "Care" (*Sorge*) go, if not in the direction of bringing man back to his essence again? What else does this mean, but that man (*homo*) should become human (*humanus*)? Thus *humanitas* remains the concern of such thought; for this is humanism: to reflect and to care that man be human and not un-human, "inhuman," i.e. outside of his essence. Yet, of what does the humanity of man consist? It rests in his essence.

But whence and how is the essence of man determined? Marx demands that the "human man" be known and acknowledged. He finds this man in society. The "social" man is for him the "natural" man. In "society" the "nature" of man, which means all of his "natural needs" (food, clothing, reproduction, economic sufficiency), is equally secured. The Christian sees the humanity of man, the *humanitas* of the *homo,* as the delimitation of *deitas.* He is, in the history of Grace, man as the "child of God," who hears in Christ the claim of the Father and accepts it. Man is not of this world, insofar as the "world," theoretically and Platonically understood, is nothing but a transitory passage into the other world.

Expressly in its own name, *humanitas* is first considered and striven for at the time of the Roman republic. The *homo humanus* is opposed to the *homo barbarus.* The *homo humanus* is here the Roman who exalts and ennobles the Roman *virtus* by the "incorporation" of the *paideia,* taken over from the Greeks. The Greeks are the Greeks of Hellenism, whose culture was taught in the philosophical schools. It is the *eruditio et institutio in bonas artes. Paideia* so understood, is translated by *humanitas.* The authentic *romanitas* of the *homo humanus* consists of such *humanitas.* In Rome we encounter the first humanism. It, thus, remains in its essence a specific Roman phenomenon, born of the encounter between the Roman and Hellenistic cultures. The so-called Renaissance of the fourteenth and fifteenth centuries in Italy is a *renascentia romanitatis.* Since the *romanitas* is what matters, all we are concerned with is *humanitas* and for that reason, the Greek *paideia.* The Greek world, however, is always seen in its late form and this, in turn, is seen as Roman. In addition the *homo romanus* of the Renaissance is seen in opposition to the *homo barbarus.* But the inhuman is now the pretended barbarism of the Gothic scholasticism of the Middle Ages. To humanism, historically understood, therefore, always belongs a *studium humanitatis,* which reaches back to antiquity and so always also becomes a revival of the Greek world. This is shown in our humanism of eighteenth century, which is sustained by Winckelmann, Goethe, and Schiller. Hölderlin, however, does not belong to "humanism" and thinks of the destiny of the essence of man in a more original way than this "humanism" is capable of doing.

But when one understands by humanism, in general, the effort of man to become free for his humanity and to find therein his dignity rather than some conceptual understanding of the "freedom" and the "nature" of man, the humanism is in each instance different. Likewise its modes of realization differ. Marx's humanism requires no return to antiquity, nor does the humanism which Sartre conceives existentialism to be. In this broad sense Christianity is also a humanism, insofar as, according to its doctrine, everything comes down to the salvation of the soul (*salus aeterna*) of man and the history of mankind appears in the frame of the history of salvation. However different these kinds of humanism may be, in regard to their aims and basis, in regard to the ways and means of their respective realizations, in regard to the form of their doctrine, all of them coin-

cide in that the *humanitas* of the homo humanus is determined
from the view of an already-established interpretation of nature,
of history, of world, of the basis of the world (*Weltgrund*), i.e.
of beings in their totality.

Every humanism is either founded in a metaphysics or is converted into the basis for a metaphysics. Every determination of
the essence of man that presupposes the interpretation of beings
without asking the question of the truth of Being, be it wittingly
or not, is metaphysical. Therefore, and precisely in view of the
way in which the essence of man is determined, the characteristic of all metaphysics shows itself in the fact that it is "humanistic." For this reason every humanism remains metaphysical.
Humanism not only does not ask, in determining the humanity
of man, for the relation of Being to the essence of man, but humanism even impedes this question, since, by virtue of its derivation from metaphysics it neither knows nor understands it.
Inversely, the necessary and the proper way of asking the question of the truth of Being, in metaphysics but forgotten by it,
can only come to light, if amidst the domination of metaphysics
the question is asked: "What is metaphysics?" First of all each
question of "Being," even that of the truth of Being, must be
presented as a "metaphysical" question.

The first humanism, the Roman, and all the humanisms that
have since appeared, presupposes as self-evident the most general
"essence" of man. Man is considered as the *animal rationale*.
This determination is not only the Latin translation of the
Greek ζῷον λόγον ἔχον but a metaphysical interpretation. This
essential determination of man is not wrong, but it is conditioned by metaphysics. Its essential extraction and not merely
its limit has, however, become questionable in *Sein und Zeit*.
This questionableness is first of all given to thought as what has
to be thought, but not in such a way as to be devoured by an
empty skepticism.

Certainly metaphysics posits beings in their Being and so
thinks of the Being of beings. But it does not discriminate between the two (cf. "Vom Wesen des Grundes" 1929, p. 8; *Kant
und das Problem der Metaphysik, 1929,* p. 225; *Sein und Zeit,*
p. 230). Metaphysics does not ask for the truth of Being itself.
Nor does it ever ask, therefore, in what way the essence of man

belongs to the truth of Being. This question metaphysics has not only not asked up to now, but this question cannot be treated by metaphysics as metaphysics. Being still waits for Itself to become memorable to man. However one may—in regard to the determination of the essence of man—determine the *ratio* of the animal and the reason of the living being, whether as "capacity for principles," or as "capacity for categories," or otherwise, everywhere and always the essence of reason is based upon the fact that for each perceiving of beings in their Being, Being itself is discovered and realized in its truth. In the same way, an interpretation of "life" is given in the term "animal," ζῷον, which necessarily rests on an interpretation of beings as ζωή and φύσις, within which what is living appears. Besides this, however, the question finally remains whether, originating and predetermining everything, the essence of man lies in the dimension of the *animalitas*. Are we on the right track at all to reach the essence of man, if and as long as we delimit man as a living-being amongst others, against plant, animal and God? One can so proceed, one can in such a way put man within beings as a being amongst others. Thereby one will always be able to assert what is correct about man. But one must also be clear in this regard that by this man remains cast off in the essential realm of *animalitas,* even when one does not put him on the same level as the animal, but attributes a specific difference to him. In principle one always thinks of the *homo animalis,* even when one puts *anima* as *animus sive mens* and later as subject, as person, as spirit. To put it so is the way of metaphysics. But by this the essence of man is too lightly considered and is not thought of in the light of its source, that essential source which always remains for historical humanity the essential future. Metaphysics thinks of man as arising from *animalitas* and does not think of him as pointing toward *humanitas.*

Metaphysics shuts itself off from the simple essential certitude that man is essentially only in his essence, in which he is claimed by Being. Only from this claim "has" he found wherein his essence dwells. Only from this dwelling "has" he "language" as the home which preserves the ecstatic for his essence. The standing in the clearing of Being I call the ex-sistence of man. Only man has this way to be. Ex-sistence, so understood, is not only the basis of the possibility of reason, *ratio,* but ex-sistence is that, wherein the essence of man preserves the source that determines him.

Ex-sistence can only be said of the essence of man, i.e. only of the human way "to be"; for only man, as far as we know, is admitted into the destiny of ex-sistence. Thus ex-sistence can never be thought of as a specific way, amongst other ways, of a living being, so long as man is destined to think of the essence of his Being and not merely to report theories of nature and history about his composition and activity. Thus all that we attribute to man as *animalitas* in comparing him to the "animal" is grounded in the essence of ex-sistence. The body of man is something essentially different from the animal organism. The error of biologism has not yet been overcome by the fact that one affixes the soul to corporeal man and the mind to the soul and the existential to the mind, and more strongly than ever before preaches the appreciation of the mind, in order that everything may then fall back into the experience of life, with the admonitory assurance that thought will destroy by its rigid concepts the stream of life and the thought of Being will deform existence. That physiology and physiological chemistry can scientifically examine man as an organism, does not prove that in this "organic" disposition, i.e. in the body scientifically explained, the essence of man rests. This has as little value as the opinion that the essence of nature is contained in atomic energy. It may very well be that nature hides its essence in that aspect of which human technology has taken possession. As little as the essence of man consists of being an animal organism, so little can this insufficient determination of the essence of man be eliminated and compensated for by the fact that man is equipped with an immortal soul or with the capability of reason or with the character of a person. Each time the essence is overlooked and, no doubt, on the basis of the same metaphysical design.

All that man is, i.e. in the traditional language of metaphysics the "essence" of man, rests in his ex-sistence. But ex-sistence, so thought of, is not identical with the traditional concept of *existentia,* which signifies actuality in contrast to essentia as possibility. In *Sein und Zeit* (p. 42) is the sentence, italicized: "The 'essence' of being-there (*Dasein*) lies in its existence."

Here, however, this is not a matter of opposing *existentia* and *essentia*, because these two metaphysical determinations of Being have not yet been placed in question, let alone their relationship. The sentence contains even less a general statement about "being-there," insofar as this term (brought into usage in the eighteenth century for the word "object") is to express the metaphysical concept of the actuality of the actual. The sentence says rather: man is essentially such that he is "Here" (*Da*), i.e. within the clearing of Being. This "Being" of the Here, and only this, has the basic trait of ex-sistence: i.e. it stands outside itself within the truth of Being. The ecstatic essence of man rests in the ex-sistence that remains different from the metaphysically conceived *existentia*. Medieval philosophy conceived this *existentia* as *actualitas*. Kant presents *existentia* as actuality in the sense of the objectivity of experience. Hegel determines *existentia* as the self-knowing idea of the absolute subjectivity. Nietzsche understands *existentia* as the eternal return of the same. Whether, however, through *existentia*, in its various interpretations as actuality, different only at first glance, the Being of the stone, or even life as the Being of plants and animals, has been sufficiently thought about, remains an open question here. In each case animals are as they are, without their standing—from their Being as such—in the truth of Being and preserving in such standing what is essentially their Being. Presumably, animals are the most difficult of all entities for us to think of, because we are, on the one hand, most akin to them and, on the other hand, they are, at the same time separated from our existential essence by an abyss. And against this it might seem that the essence of the divine is much nearer us than the strangeness of animals, nearer in an essential distance, which as distance is much more familiar to our existential essence than the barely conceivable abysmal corporeal kinship to the animal. Such reflections cast a strange light on the current and therefore still premature designation of man as an *animal rationale*. Because plants and animals, although bound to their environment, are never freely placed in the clearing of Being—and only this clearing is "world"—they have no language. But it is not because they are without language that they find themselves hanging worldless in their environment. Yet in the word "environment" is concentrated all the enigma of the animal. Language is in its essence not utterance of an organism nor is it expression of an animal. Thus it is never thought of with exactness in its symbolical or semantic character. Language is the clearing-and-concealing advent of Being itself.

Ex-sistence, ecstatically thought of, does not coincide with *existentia* either in regard to content or form. Ex-sistence means substantially the emerging into the truth of Being. *Existentia* (existence) means, however, *actualitas,* actuality in contrast to mere possibility as idea. Ex-sistence states the characteristic of man as he is in the destiny of truth. *Existentia* remains the name for the actualization of something-that-is, as an instance of its idea. The phrase, "man exists," does not answer the question of whether there are actually men or not; it answers the question of the "essence" of man. We usually put this question in an equally unsuitable way, whether we ask what man is or who he is. For, in the Who or What we are already on the lookout for something like a person or an object. Yet the personal, no less than the objective, misses and obstructs at the same time all that is essentially ex-sistence in its historical Being. Therefore, the quoted phrase in *Sein und Zeit* (p. 52) deliberately puts the word "essence" in quotation marks. This indicates that the "essence" is not now determined either from the *esse essentiae* or from the *esse existentiae,* but from the ec-static nature of "being-there." Insofar as he ex-sists, man endures the "being-there" by taking the There as the clearing of Being within his "care." The *Dasein* itself, however, is essentially the "thrown" (*geworfene*). It is essentially in the cast (*Wurf*) of Being, a destiny that destines, projects a destiny.

It would undoubtedly be the greatest error, if one were to explain the existent essence of man, as though it were the secularized translation of a thought about man by Christian theology via God (*Deus est suum esse*); for ex-sistence is neither the actualization of an essence, nor does ex-sistence itself realize and constitute the essential. If one understands the "project" (*Entwurf*), alluded to in *Sein und Zeit* as a representative concept [an idea in the mind of an agent] then one considers it as an act of subjectivity and does not think of it as one should within the realm of the "existential analysis" of the "Being-in-the-world" (*In-der-Welt-Seins*), i.e. as the ecstatic relation to the clearing of Being. The necessary and sufficiently verified comprehension of this other way of thought—the thought that abandons subjectivity—is, however, made more difficult by the fact that at the publication of *Sein und Zeit* the third section of the first part, i.e. "Time and Being," was suppressed (cf. *Sein und Zeit*, p. 39). Here the whole thing is reversed. The section in question was suppressed because the thinking failed to find language adequate to this reversal and did not succeed through the aid of the language of metaphysics. The lecture "On the Essence of Truth," which was composed and delivered in 1930, but was first printed in 1943, gives some insight into the thought of the reversal from "Being and Time" to "Time and Being". This reversal is not a change from the standpoint of *Sein und Zeit*, but in it the intended thought for the first time attains the place of the dimension from which "Being and Time" is experienced; and, indeed, experienced from the basic experience of Being.

Sartre formulates, on the other hand, the basic principle of existentialism as this: existence precedes essence, whereby he understands *existentia* and *essentia* in the sense of metaphysics, which since Plato has said *essentia* precedes *existentia*. Sartre reverses this phrasing. But the reversal of a metaphysical phrase remains a metaphysical phrase. As such it remains with metaphysics in the oblivion of the truth of Being. For though philosophy may determine the relationship between *essentia* and *existentia* in the sense of the controversy of the Middle Ages or in the sense of Leibniz or others, one must first of all ask, through what destiny of Being this difference in Being as *esse essentiae* and *esse existentiae* precedes thought. It remains to be considered why this question about the destiny of Being has never been asked and why it could never be thought. Or isn't this a sign of the oblivion of Being that there is this difference between *essentia* and *existentia*? We may suppose that this destiny does not lie in a mere neglect by human thought, let alone in an inferior capacity of earlier western thought. The difference —hidden in its essential source—between *essentia* (essentiality) and *existentia* (actuality) dominates the destiny of Western history and of all the history determined by Europe.

Sartre's key phrase on the superiority of *existentia* over *essentia* undoubtedly justifies the name "existentialism" as a suitable title for this philosophy. But the key phrase of "existentialism" has not the least thing in common with the same phrase in *Sein und Zeit;* apart from the fact that in *Sein und Zeit* a phrase about the relationship between *essentia* and *existentia* cannot yet be expressed, for there we are concerned with settling something preliminary. This, as can be seen from what has been said, is done there rather clumsily. What is yet to be said today might, perhaps, become an impulse to guide the essence of man to attend in thought to the dimension of the truth of Being, which pervades it. Yet even this can only happen for the dignity of Being and for the benefit of *Dasein* which man endures in existing; not for the sake of man, but that through his works civilization and culture may be vindicated.

In order that we today, however, may arrive at the dimension of the truth of Being, we have first of all to make clear how Being concerns man and how it claims him. Such an essential experience happens to us when it dawns upon us that man is, as long as he exists. Let us say this first in the language of tradition, which says: the ex-sistence of man is his substance. For this reason in *Sein und Zeit* the following phrase often recurs: "the 'substance' of man is ex-sistence" (pp. 117, 212, 314). But "substance" is already understood according to the history of Being, the blanket translation of οὐσία, a word which designates the presence of one present and at the same time very often signifies with a mysterious ambiguity what is present (*das Anwesende*). If we think of the metaphysical term "substance" in this sense, which in *Sein und Zeit* is already suggested because of the "phenomenological destruction" realized there (cf. p. 25), then the phrase "the 'substance' of man is ex-sistence" does not say anything other than that the way in which man is essentially in his own essence moving toward Being, is that he stands outside himself within the truth of Being. Through this essential determination of man the humanistic interpretations of man as *animal rationale,* as "person," or as an intellectual, spiritual, corporeal, being, are not declared wrong, nor rejected. The only thought is rather that the highest humanistic determinations of the essence of man do not yet come to know the authentic dignity of man. In this the thinking in *Sein und Zeit* runs counter to humanism. But this opposition does not mean that such thinking would make common cause with the opposite of the human and espouse the inhuman, defend inhumanity and degrade the dignity of man. Humanism is opposed because it does not set the *humanitas* of man high enough. However, the essential dignity of man does not lie in the fact that he is as the "subject" of beings, their substance, so that as the despot of Being he may let the character of beings dissolve into an "objectivity" that is much too loudly praised.

Man is rather "cast" by Being itself into the truth of Being, in order that he, ex-sisting thus, may guard the truth of Being; in order that in the light of Being, beings as beings may appear as what it is. Whether and how it appears, whether and how God and the gods, history and nature, enter, presenting and absenting themselves in the clearing of Being, is not determined by man. The advent of beings rests in the destiny of Being. For man, however, the question remains whether he finds what is appropriate to his essence to correspond to his destiny; according to this, as an ex-sisting person, he has to guard the truth of Being. Man is the guardian of Being. The thinking in *Sein und Zeit* proceeds towards this, when ecstatic existence only is experienced as "care" (cf. §44a, p. 226 ff.).

Yet Being—what is Being? It is Itself. Future thought must learn to experience and to express this. "Being" is neither God nor the basis of the world. Being is further from all that is being and yet closer to man than every being, be it a rock, an animal, a work of art, a machine, be it an angel or God. Being is the closest. Yet its closeness remains farthest from man. Man first clings always and only to beings. But when thought represents beings as beings it no doubt refers to Being. Yet, in fact, it always thinks only of beings as such and never of Being as such. The "question of Being" always remains the question of beings. The question of Being still does not get at what this captious term means: the question seeking for Being. Philosophy, even when critical, as in Descartes and Kant, always follows the procedure of metaphysical representation. It thinks from beings to beings with a glance in passing at Being. For the light of Being already implies each departure from beings and each return to them.

Metaphysics, however, knows the clearing of Being as the looking toward what is present in its appearance (ἰδέα), or critically as what is seen of the external aspect of the categorical representation from the side of subjectivity. This means: the truth of Being as the clearing itself remains concealed from metaphysics. This concealment, however, is not a defect of metaphysics, but the treasure of its own richness, which is withheld and yet held up to it. The clearing itself, however, is Being. Within the destiny of Being the clearing grants a view to metaphysics, a view from which all that is present is attained by man as he presents himself to it, so that man himself can only attain Being (θιγεῖν, Aristotle, *Metaphysics*, theta, 10) through intellection (νοεῖν). The outward view only draws upon itself. Man yields to this, when intellection has become the projection in the *perceptio* of the *res cogitans* taken as the *subiectum* of the *certitudo*.

Or to proceed in more straightforward fashion perhaps: What relation has Being to ex-sistence? Being itself is the relationship, insofar as It retains and reunites ex-sistence in its existential (i.e. ecstatic) essence—as the place of the truth of Being amidst the beings. Since man as an existing one comes to stand in this relationship which Being itself professes to be, insofar as he, man, ecstatically stands (*aussteht*) it, i.e. insofar as he, caring, takes over, he fails to recognize at first the closest and clings to the next closest. He even believes that this is the closest. Yet closer than the closest and at the same time, for ordinary thought, farther than his farthest is closeness itself: the truth of Being.

The oblivion of the truth of Being under the impact of beings, which is not considered in its essence, is the sense of "decadence" in *Sein und Zeit*. This word does not signify the fall of man, understood as in a "moral philosophy" that has been secularized; this word states an essential relationship between man and Being within the relation of Being to man's essence. In view of this, the terms "authenticity" and "un-authenticity" (*Eigentlichkeit und Uneigentlichkeit*) do not signify a moral-existential or an "anthropological" distinction, but the "ecstatic" relation of man's essence to the truth of Being, which is still to be realized and up to now has remained concealed from philosophy. But this relation, such as it is, does not derive from ex-sistence, but the essence of ex-sistence derives existential-ecstatically from the essence of the truth of Being.

The unique thought that *Sein und Zeit* attempts to express, wants to achieve, is something simple. As such, Being remains mysterious, the plain closeness of an unobtrusive rule. This closeness is essentially language itself. Yet the language is not merely language, insofar as we imagine it at the most as the unity of sound-form (script), melody and rhythm and meaning. We think of sound-form and script as the body of the word; of melody and rhythm as the soul and of meaning as the mind of language. We generally think of language as corresponding to the essence of man, insofar as this essence is represented as *animal rationale,* i.e. as the unity of body-soul-mind. But as in the *humanitas* of the *homo animalis* ex-sistence remains concealed and through this the relation of the truth of Being to man, so does the metaphysical-animal interpretation of language conceal its essence from the point of view of the history of Being. According to this, language is the house of Being, owned and pervaded by Being. Therefore, the point is to think of the essence of language in its correspondence to Being and, what is more, as this very correspondence, i.e., the dwelling of man's essence.

Man, however, is not only a living being, who besides other faculties possesses language. Language is rather the house of Being, wherein living, man ex-sists, while he, guarding it, belongs to the truth of Being.

Thus, what matters in the determination of the humanity of man as ex-sistence is not that man is the essential, but that Being is the essential as the dimension of the ecstatic of ex-sistence. This, however, is not the spatial dimension. All that is spatial and all time-space is essentially dimensional, which is what Being itself is.

Thought heeds these simple relationships. It seeks the appropriate word for them amidst the traditional language and grammar of metaphysics. Can such thought, if terminology is important at all, still be denominated as humanism? Certainly not, insofar as humanism thinks metaphysically. Certainly not, when it is existentialism and bears out the idea expressed by

Sartre: *précisement nous sommes sur un plan où il y a seulement des hommes* (*L'Existentialisme est un humanisme,* p. 36). Instead of this, if we think as in *Sein und Zeit,* we should say: *précisement nous sommes sur un plan où il y a principialement l'Être.* But whence does *le plan* come and what is it? *L'Être et le plan* are the same. In *Sein und Zeit* (p. 212) it is said intentionally and cautiously: *il y a l'Être:* "it gives" (there is) Being. The *il y a* translates the "it gives" inexactly. For the "it," which here "gives," is Being itself. The "gives" names, however, the essence of Being; the giving itself and the imparting of its truth. The giving itself into the open with this self, is Being itself.

At the same time "it gives" is used in order to avoid at once the locution: "Being is;" for usually the "is" is said of what-is. This we call "the being." Being "is," however, precisely not "the being." Were the "is" said without closer interpretation of Being, then Being would all too easily be represented as a "being" in the manner of the known being, which as cause effects and as effect is effectuated. Nevertheless, Parmenides had already said in the early days of thought: ἔστιν γὰρ εἶναι, "Being is." In this utterance the original mystery of all thought is concealed. Perhaps this "is" is not and could only be appropriately said of Being, so that no being ever properly "is." But because thought should first manage to express Being in its truth, instead of explaining it as a trait of the being, it must be open to the attention of thought whether and how Being is.

The ἔστιν γὰρ εἶναι of Parmenides has as yet been given no thought. From this we can realize the state of progress in philosophy. If it considers its essence, it never progresses at all. It marks time by continually thinking the same thing. The progressing, i.e., away from this spot, is an error that follows thought as the shadow it casts. Since Being is as yet unthought of, it is said of Being in *Sein und Zeit,* "it gives." Yet one cannot speculate directly and without help upon this *il y a.* The "it gives" rules as the destiny of Being. Its history finds expression in the words of the essential thinkers. So the thought that thinks of the truth of Being thinks historically. There is no "systematic" thinking, nor is there a history of past opinions as illustration. Nor is there even, as Hegel believed, a systematics, which could deduce from the laws of its thought a law of history and at the same time reduce it to the system. There is, it was originally believed, the history of Being, to which thought belongs as the remembrance of this history, realized by itself. This remembrance is to be distinguished essentially from the posterior representation of history in the sense of the past passing. History does not at first occur as occurrence. And it is not the passing. The occurrence of history lives as the destiny of the truth of Being, and derives from it (cf. The essay on Hölderlin's Hymn *"Wie wenn am Feiertage,"* 1941, p. 31). Being comes to destiny, as It, Being, gives itself. This, however, means from the point of view of destiny that it gives itself and negates itself at the same time. Nonetheless, Hegel's determination of history as the development of the "mind" is not wrong. Nor is it neither partly right, nor partly wrong. It is as true as metaphysics is, which through Hegel for the first time absolutely expresses its essence systematically. Absolute metaphysics belongs with its inversions via Marx and Nietzsche to the history of the truth of Being. Whatever stems from it cannot be affected or done away with by refutation. It can only be appraised, as its truth is reintegrated more incipiently into Being itself and removed from the sphere of mere human opinion. To refute everything in the field of essential thought is ridiculous. A quarrel amongst thinkers is a "lovers' quarrel" for the thing itself. It helps them mutually in their belonging to that one and the same sphere, in which they find what is appropriate in the destiny of Being.

Granted that man is capable of thinking of the truth of Being in the future, he will think from his ex-sistence. Ex-sisting, he stands in the destiny of Being. The ex-sistence of man as ex-sistence is historical, but not primarily for that reason, or simply for that reason, because many a thing may occur with man and human affairs in the course of time. Because it is important to think of the ex-sistence of *Da-sein*, it is quite essential to the thinking in *Sein und Zeit* that the historicity of *Dasein* be grasped.

But is it not said in *Sein und Zeit* (p. 212), where the "it gives" finds expression that "only as long as Dasein is, is there Being?" Indeed, it is. This means that only as long as the clearing of Being is realized, is Being itself conveyed to man. That the

"Da" (Here), however, the clearing of Being itself, is realized, is the destination of Being itself. This is the destiny of the clearing. The sentence, however, does not mean that the Dasein of man in the traditional sense of *existentia*, understood more recently as the actuality of the *ego cogito*, would be the existent through which alone Being is created. The sentence does not say that Being is a product of man. The introduction to *Sein und Zeit* (p. 38) states simply and clearly and even in italics that "Being is the *transcendens* as such." Just as the openness of spatial nearness surpasses everything near and far, so Being is essentially broader than all the beings, because it is the clearing itself. Thus, in accordance with the next inevitable attack of the still dominant metaphysics, Being will be thought of as deriving from beings. Only from such an outlook does Being show itself in such a surpassing.

The preliminary definition of "Being as the *transcendens* as such" expresses simply the way in which the essence of Being has so far been cleared for man. This retrospective definition of the essence of Being out of the clearing of beings is and remains indispensable for further thinking of the question of the truth of Being. So thought attests to its historical essence. It is far from the pretension of wishing to begin from the beginning and to declare all previous philosophy wrong. Whether, however, the definition of Being as the simple *transcendens* yet expresses the simple essence of the truth of Being, this and this alone is the immediate question for the thinking that tries to think of the truth of Being. For this reason you find (on page 230) that only from "meaning," that is from the truth of Being, can one understand how Being is. Being clears itself for man in ecstatic projection. But this projection does not create Being.

Moreover, the projection is essentially a matter of being cast. What projects in the project is not man, but Being itself, which destines man to the ex-sistence which is the essence of *Dasein*. This destiny is realized as the clearing of Being. The clearing imparts the closeness to Being. In this closeness, in the clearing of the "Da" (Here), man dwells as one ex-sisting, without being capable now of properly experiencing and taking over this dwelling. The closeness of Being, which is the "Da" of Dasein, is thought of (from the point of view of *Sein und Zeit*) in my essay on Hölderlin's elegy *"Heimkunft"* (1943) as the "Home-land" (*Heimat*), as understood by the poet from the experi-ence of the oblivion of Being. The word is here thought of in an essential sense, neither patriotic, nor nationalistic, but ac-cording to the history of Being. The essence of the homeland, however, is at the same time expressed with the intention of thinking of the homelessness of modern man as seen from the essence of the history of Being. The last one to experience this homelessness was Nietzsche. He was incapable of finding any other way out of metaphysics than by the reversal of meta-physics. This, however, is the height of being lost. Hölderlin, in contrast, when he writes *"Heimkunft"* is concerned that his "countrymen" find their essential home. He by no means seeks this in an egoism of his people. He sees it rather in their be-longing to the destiny of the Western world. But even the Western world is not thought of regionally as the Occident in contrast to the Orient, nor merely as Europe, but in the frame of world history from the closeness to its origin. We have hardly begun to think of the mysterious relations to the East, which find expression in Hölderlin's poetry (cf. *"Der Ister"* as well as *"Die Wanderung,"* 3rd. stanza and ff.). The "German" is not said to the world so that the world may be healed thanks to the German essence, but it is said to the Germans so that they from their fateful membership amongst the nations may become with them world-historical (cf. Hölderlin's poem *"Andenken,"* *Tübinger Gedenkschrift*, 1943, v. 322). The homeland of this historical dwelling is the closeness to Being.

In this closeness the decision, if any, is reached as to whether and how God and the gods deny themselves and the night re-mains, whether and how the day of the Holy dawns, whether and how in the rise of the Holy an appearance of God and the gods can start anew. The Holy, however, which is only the es-sential space of divinity, for its part yields; but the dimension for the gods and God only comes into appearance when, first and after a long preparation, Being itself has been cleared and been experienced in its truth. Only in this way does the overcoming of homelessness start from Being, where not only man, but the essence of man, wanders about.

Homelessness, so understood, lies in beings' abandonment of

Being. It is the sign of the oblivion of Being. Consequently, the truth of Being remains unthought of. The oblivion of Being is indirectly evidenced in the fact that man only considers and cultivates beings. Since he cannot help having a conception of Being it is explained as the "most general" and for that reason as what embraces beings; or as the universe of an infinite being or as the handiwork of a finite subject. At the same time "Being" stands of old for "beings" and vice-versa, both are tossed about in a strange and still thoughtless confusion.

Being as the destiny that destines truth remains concealed. But the world's destiny is proclaimed in poetry without its becoming apparent at once as the history of Being. Hölderlin's world-historical thought, which finds expression in the poem *"Andenken,"* is therefore essentially much more original and so much more appropriate to the future than the mere cosmopolitanism of Goethe. For the same reason Hölderlin's relation to the Greek world is an essentially different thing from humanism. Therefore, young Germans who knew of Hölderlin have thought and lived (in the face of death) other than what publicity proclaimed as the German attitude.

Homelessness becomes a world destiny. It is, therefore, necessary to think of this destiny from the point of view of the history of Being. What Marx, deriving from Hegel, recognized in an essential and significant sense as the alienation of man, reaches roots back into the homelessness of modern man. This is evoked —from the destiny of Being—in the form of metaphysics, strengthened by it and at the same time covered by it in its character as homelessness. Because Marx, in discovering this alienation, reaches into an essential dimension of history, the Marxist view of history excels all other history. Because, however, neither Husserl nor, as far as I can see, Sartre recognizes the essentially historical character of Being, neither phenomenology nor existentialism can penetrate that dimension within which alone a productive discussion with Marxism is possible.

For this it is necessary to liberate oneself from the naive conceptions of materialism and from the cheap, supposedly effective, refutations of it. The essence of materialism does not consist of the assertion that everything is merely matter, but rather of a metaphysical determination, according to which everything being appears as the material of labor. The modern metaphysical essence of labor is anticipated in Hegel's *Phenomenology of the Spirit* as the self-establishing process of unconditional production; i.e., the objectivization of the actual through man experienced as subjectivity. The essence of materialism is concealed in the essence of technics, about which, indeed, a great deal is written, but little is thought. Technics in its essence is a destiny (in the history of Being) of the truth of Being resting in oblivion. It not only goes back in its name to the Greek τέχνη, but it historically stems from τέχνη as a way of the ἀληθεύειν, i.e. the making open of beings. As a form of truth technics is grounded in the history of metaphysics. This is itself an exceptional phase of the history of Being. One can take various positions in regard to the theories (and arguments) of communism, but from the point of view of the history of Being, it is indisputable that in it an elementary experience has been made manifest of what is world-historical. He who takes "communism" only as a "party" or as *"Weltanschauung,"* is thinking just as narrowly as those who by the term "Americanism" mean—and what is more in a depreciatory way—a particular mode of life. The danger into which Europe up to now has been more and more clearly pushed, probably consists of the fact that its thought, which was once its greatness, lags behind the destiny that opens for the world, a destiny which undoubtedly in the basic traits of its essential origin remains European in its determination. No metaphysics, be it idealistic, materialistic, or Christian, considering its essence and not its sporadic efforts, can, to develop itself overtake this destiny, i.e. reach it by thought and bring together what, in a complete sense of Being, now is.

In view of the essential homelessness of man the thought of the history of Being demonstrates the future destiny of man in that he investigates the truth of Being and sets out toward its discovery. Each nationalism is metaphysically an anthropologism and as such subjectivism. Nationalism is not overcome by mere internationalism, but only expanded and elevated to a system. Nationalism is far from being annulled by it or brought to *humanitas,* as individualism is by historical collectivism. This is the subjectivity of man in totality. He realizes its absolute self-assertion. This cannot be canceled. It cannot even be sufficiently experienced by one-sided thinking that tries to mediate. Everywhere man, thrust out from the truth of Being, runs around in a circle as the *animal rationale*.

The essence of man, however, consists of being more than mere man, insofar as this mere man is represented as a rational animal. "More" must not be understood here in an additive sense, as if the traditional definition of man were to remain as the basic definition, in order to undergo an expansion through an addition of the existential. The "more" means: more original and, therefore, in essence more essential. But here the mysterious is manifest: man is in his thrownness (*Geworfenheit*). This means that man is as the ex-sisting counter-throw (*Gegenwurf*) of Being even more than the *animal rationale*, insofar as he is less related to the man who is conceived from subjectivity. Man is not the master of beings. Man is the shepherd of Being. In this "less" man does not suffer any loss, but gains, because he comes into the truth of Being. He gains the essential poverty of the shepherd whose dignity rests in the fact that he was called by Being itself into the trueness of his truth. This call comes as the throw, from which stems the thrownness of the *Da-sein*. Man is in his essence (from the point of view of the history of Being) that being whose Being as ex-sistence consists of dwelling in the nearness of Being. Man is the neighbor of Being.

But no doubt, you have wanted to reply for some time now, does not such thinking think precisely of the *humanitas* of the *homo humanus*? Does it not think of this *humanitas* in such a decisive meaning as no metaphysics has thought or even can think of it? Is not this "humanism" in an extreme sense? Certainly. It is the humanism that thinks of the humanity of man from the nearness to Being. But it is at the same time the humanism for which not man, but the historical essence of man in his derivation from the truth of Being, is playing. But does not the ex-sistence of man then stand and fall in this game at the same time? Indeed, it does.

In *Sein und Zeit* (p. 38) it is said that all questioning of philosophy "strikes back into existence." But existence is here not the actuality of the *ego cogito*. Nor is it the actuality of subjects that act with and for each other and in this way come into their own. "Ex-sistence" is basically different from all *existentia* and "existence," the ec-static dwelling in the nearness of Being. It is the guardianship, i.e. the concern of Being. Since in this thinking something simple is to be thought, it is very difficult to represent it by traditional philosophy. Yet the difficulty does not consist of indulging in a particular profundity and of forming complex conceptions, but it conceals itself in stepping back and letting thought take up a skilful inquiry and abandon the trained opinions of philosophy.

It is everywhere believed that the effort in *Sein und Zeit* has ended up a blind alley. We won't discuss this opinion here. The thought, which in the above mentioned essay attempted a few steps, has not yet passed beyond *Sein und Zeit*. But perhaps it has in the meantime come a little bit more into its own. As long as philosophy, however, occupies itself only with constantly obstructing possibilities, with engaging in matters of thought—i.e. the truth of Being—, so long is it perfectly secure from the danger of ever breaking down at the hardness of its matter. So the "philosophizing" about the failure is separated by an abyss from a failing thought. If a man should be fortunate in this, no misfortunes would occur. For him it would be the only gift that thought could receive from Being.

Yet this too is important: the matter of thinking is not reached by talking about "the truth of Being" and of "the history of Being." Everything depends upon bringing into language the truth of Being and letting thought penetrate this language. Perhaps then language requires far less precipitate utterance than correct silence. Yet who amongst us today would like to imagine that his attempts at thought were at home on the path of silence? If it goes far enough, our thought might perhaps point to the truth of Being and to it as what is to be thought. In this way it would be more than anything else removed from mere suspicion and opinion and be allotted to the already rare handiwork of script. The matters, in which something is, even if they are not determined for eternity, come in due time.

Whether the realm of the truth of Being is a blind alley or whether it is the free dimension in which freedom saves its essence, each one may judge for himself after having tried to go his appointed way or blaze a better; that is, one in more accord with the question. On the next to the last page of *Sein und*

Zeit (p. 437) are the words "the *dispute* in regard to the inter-pretation of Being (i.e. not of the existent, nor of the Being of man) cannot be straightened out, *because it has not even been begun*. And in the end one cannot 'pick a quarrel,' for the be-ginning of a dispute requires some equipment. Only towards that is the investigation aimed." These words retain their validity even after two decades. Let us also in the coming days be voy-agers to the neighborhood of Being. The question which you put helps to clarify the way.

You ask: *Comment redonner un sens au mot "Humanisme"?* "How can one restore meaning to the word humanism?" Your question not only presupposes that you want to retain the word "humanism," but it also contains the admission that the word has lost its meaning.

It has lost it through the realization that the essence of hu-manism is metaphysical and this now means that metaphysics not only does not ask the question of the truth of Being, but even abstracts asking it, insofar as metaphysics persists in its oblivion of Being. The thought, however, that leads to this reali-zation of the questionable essence of humanism has at the same time brought us to think of the essence of man more originally. In view of this more essential *humanitas* of the *homo humanus*, the possibility follows of restoring to the word humanism an historical meaning that is older than what "history" considers the oldest. This restoration is not to be understood as though the word humanism were without meaning at all and a mere *flatus bocis*. The *"humanum"* in the word points to the *humanitas,* the essence of man. The "ism" indicates that the essence of man would like to be understood essentially. The word "humanism" has this meaning as a word. This requires first that we experience the essence of man more originally; and then show in what de-gree this essence becomes in its own way a destiny. The essence of man rests in ex-sistence. This essence desires from Being it-self, insofar as Being raises man as the ex-sisting one for the guardianship of the truth of Being. "Humanism" means now, should we decide to retain the word: the essence of man is essen-tial for the truth of Being, and apart from this truth of Being man himself does not matter. So we think of a "humanism" of a strange sort. The word offers a term which is a *lucus a non lucendo*.

Should one still call "humanism" this view which speaks out against all earlier humanism, but which does not at all advocate the in-human? And this only in order to swim perhaps in the dominant currents, which are stifled in a metaphysical subjectivism and find themselves drowned in the oblivion of Being? Or should thought, resisting the word "humanism," make an effort to become more attentive to the *humanitas* of the *homo humanus* and what grounds this *humanitas*? So, if the world-historical moment has not already gone that far itself, a reflection might be awakened that would not only think of man, but of the "nature" of man, and even more than this of his nature, the original dimension in which the essence of man, determined as coming from Being itself, is at home. But perhaps we should rather suffer for a while the inevitable misinterpretations to which the way of thought that centers on Being and time has so far been exposed and let them gradually be worn out? These misinterpretations are the natural reinterpretations of what people had read or rather, what they later thought they had read, but which, in fact, was preconception. They all show the same structure and the same basis.

Because "humanism" is argued against, one fears a defense of the inhuman and a glorification of barbaric cruelty. For what is more "logical" than that for one who negates humanism only the affirmation of inhumanity can remain?

Because "logic" is argued against, one believes that we renounce the rigor of thinking and in its place enthrone the despotism of instincts and emotions, and so proclaim "irrationalism" as the truth. For what is more "logical" than that one who argues against the logical defends the a-logical?

Because "values" are argued against, one is shocked by a philosophy that allegedly dares to neglect the highest goods of humankind. For what is more "logical" than that thinking which negates values must necessarily declare everything valueless?

Because it is said that the Being of man consists of "Being-in-the-World" (*In-der-Welt-sein*), one considers man to have been degraded to the level of a mere this-worldly being, and that philosophy thereby sinks into positivism. For what is more "logical" than that one who maintains the worldliness of man only admits the this-worldly, thereby negating the other-worldly and renouncing all "transcendency"?

Because reference is made to Nietzsche's expression of "God's death," one declares such a procedure to be atheism. For what is more "logical" than that one who has experienced "God's death" is a godless person?

Because in all that has been said I have argued everywhere against what mankind values as high and holy, this philosophy therefore teaches an irresponsible and destructive "nihilism." For what is more "logical" than that one who negates everywhere what is truly being, places himself on the side of the nonbeing and with that advocates mere nothingness as the meaning of reality?

What is happening here? One hears talk of "humanism," of "logic," of "values," of "world," of "God." One hears talk of an opposition to these. One knows and takes these things as positive. What is expressed against them, one immediately takes as their negation and thus "negative" in a sense of the destructive. This is a question of what, in a certain part of *Sein und Zeit*, we called "the phenomenological destruction." One believes that with the help of logic and *ratio* [Reason] that all that is not positive is negative and so would reject reason; and therefore, deserves to be branded as an infamy. One is so full of "logic," that everything which is repugnant to the usual somnolence of opinion is immediately charged to a censurable contrariness. One casts all that does not remain in the well-known beloved positive into the prearranged pit of bare negation that negates everything and therefore ends in nothingness and so achieves nihilism. In this logical way one lets everything succumb to a nihilism that one has fabricated with the help of logic.

But is it certain that the apparition that thought brings up against common opinion necessarily points to mere negation and to the negative? This occurs only when (but then so inevitably and so definitively, that is, without a free view of other directions) one fixes beforehand what is meant by "the positive" and from this decides absolutely and negatively against the sphere of possible oppositions to it. Such a procedure hides the refusal to expose to scrutiny the preconceived "positive," together with the black and white opposition, in which it believes that it has preserved itself. Through the constant appeal to logic one produces the illusion that one has yielded to thought, while one has abjured it.

That the opposition to "humanism" by no means implies the defence of the inhuman, but opens other prospectives must have become clearer to some extent now.

"Logic" understands thought as the representation of beings in their Being, and this Being as producing this representation as a universal concept. But how is it with the consideration of Being itself, i.e., with thought that thinks of the truth of Being? Such thought reaches the original essence of the λόγος, which in Plato and Aristotle, the founder of "logic," had already been dead and buried. To think "counter to logic" does not mean to stick up for the illogical, but only means to think the *logos*, and its essence as it appeared in the early days of thought; i.e. to make an effort first of all to prepare such an act of re-flecting (*Nach-denkens*). Of what use are all such prolix systems of logic to us, when even without knowing what they are doing they immediately avoid the task of asking after the essence of the λόγος? If one wanted to retaliate with objections, which is frankly fruitless, then one could more rightly say that irrationalism, as a renunciation of *ratio*, rules as unrecognized and undisputed master of that "logic" which believes it can avoid a consideration of the *logos* and of the essence of *ratio*, which is founded on the *logos*.

The thinking that runs counter to "values" does not state that all that one declares "values"—"culture," "art," "science," "human dignity," "world," and "God"—is worthless. One should rather come to understand that it is exactly through the characterization of something as "value," that it loses its dignity. This is to say that through the estimation of something as a value, one accepts what is evaluated only as a mere object for the appreciation of man. But what a thing is in its Being is not exhausted by its being an object, much less when the objectivity has the character of value. All valuing, even when it values positively, subjectivizes the thing. It does not let beings be, but makes them valuable as the object of its action. The extravagant effort to demonstrate the objectivity of values does not know what it is doing. When one proclaims "God" as altogether "the highest value," this is a degradation of the essence of God. Thinking in values here and in general is the greatest blasphemy that can be thought of in the face of Being. To think counter to values, therefore, does not mean to beat the drum for the worthlessness and nullity of the existent, but means to bring—against the subjectivization of the existent as mere object—the clearing of the truth of Being before thought.

To refer to "Being-in-the-World" as the basic trait of the *humanitas* of the *homo humanus* is not to claim that man is simply a secular being, in the Christian sense, and so turned away from God and devoid of "transcendency." What is meant by this last word might be more clearly called: the Transcendent. The Transcendent is the super-sensual being. This is valued as the supreme being in the sense of the first cause of every being. God is thought of as this first cause. "World," however, does not in any way signify, in the term "Being-in-the-World," the earthly being in contrast to the heavenly, nor does it mean the "secular" in contrast to the "spiritual." "World" does not signify in this determination a being at all and no realm of beings, but the openness of Being. Man is and is man insofar as he is the existing. He stands exposed to the openness of Being, an openness which is Being itself, that has projected the essence of man into "care." So thrown, man stands "in" the openness of Being. "World" is the clearing of Being, wherein man stands out from his thrown essence. "Being-in-the-World" names the essence of ex-sistence in relation to the cleared dimension out of which the "ex" of the ex-sistence essentially arises. Thought of from the point of view of ex-sistence, "world" is in a way transcendence within and for existence. Man is never this-worldly and of the world as a "subject," whether this "subject" be understood as "I" or as "We." He is also not essentially a subject who is also always in reference to an object, so that his essence lies in the subject-object relation. Man is rather in his essence ex-sistent in the openness of Being; this Open only clears the "between," within which the "relation" between subject and object can "be."

The statement that the essence of man rests in Being-in-the-World contains no resolution about whether man is in the theological-metaphysical sense a mere this-worldly creature or an other-worldly one.

Therefore, with the existential determination of the essence of man nothing has yet been decided about the "existence" or "non-existence" of God, not about the possibility or impossibility of God. It is thus not only precipitate but erroneous to assert that the interpretation of the essence of man in its relation to the truth of Being is atheism. This arbitrary classification, besides everything else, lacks carefulness in reading. One ignores the fact that since 1929 the following statement could be found in the work *Vom Wesen des Grundes* (p. 28, fn. 1): "Through the ontological interpretation of *Dasein* as Being-in-the-World, there is neither a positive nor a negative resolution of a possible Being-towards-God. However, through the elucidation of the transcendency there is first obtained *an adequate concept of Dasein*, in consideration of which one may now ask what exactly is, ontologically, the relationship between God and *Dasein*." Now when this observation, too, is, as usual, taken too narrowly, one is likely to say that this philosophy makes no decision either for or against the existence of God. It remains indifferent. Thus, the religious question does not concern it. Such "indifferentism" must surely turn into nihilism.

But does the quoted remark really teach indifferentism? Why, then, are some words, and not others, printed in italics in the footnotes? Only to indicate, surely, that thought that thinks from the question of the truth of Being questions more originally than metaphysics can. Only from the truth of Being can the essence of the holy be thought. Only from the essence of the holy can the essence of divinity be thought. Only in the light of the essence of divinity can it be thought and said what the word "God" is to signify. Or must we not first be able to understand and hear these words carefully if we as men, i.e., as existing beings, are to have the privilege of experiencing a relation of God to man? How, then, is the man of the present epoch even to be able to ask seriously and firmly whether God approaches or withdraws when man omits the primary step of thinking deeply in the one dimension where this question can be asked: that is, the dimension of the holy, which, even as dimension, remains closed unless the openness of Being is cleared and in its clearing is close to man. Perhaps the distinction of this age consists in the fact that the dimension of grace has been closed. Perhaps this is its unique dis-grace.

But with this indication, which points to the truth of Being as what-has-to-be-thought, this thought would in no way wish to have declared itself for theism. It can no more be theistic than it can be atheistic. This, however, is not because of any indifferent attitude but out of respect for the limits which have been set upon thought as thought, and precisely through which it is understood as that which has-to-be-thought, through the truth of Being. In so far as thought does not exceed the limits of its task, at the moment of present world destiny it gives man an indication of the original dimension of his historical abode. In so far as thought expresses in this way the truth of Being, it has entrusted itself to what is more essential than all values and all beings. Thought does not overcome metaphysics by surpassing and cancelling it in some direction or other and ascending even higher: it descends into the nearness of the nearest. The descent, especially where man has ascended too far into subjectivity, is more difficult and more dangerous than the ascent. The descent leads to the poverty of the ex-sistence of the *homo humanus*. In ex-sistence, the sphere of the *homo animalis* of metaphysics is abandoned. The domination of this sphere is the indirect and very old reason for the delusion and arbitrariness of what is denominated as biologism, but also for what is known as pragmatism. To think of the truth of Being means at the same time to think of the *humanitas* of the *homo humanus*. What is at stake is *humanitas*, in the service of the truth of Being but without humanism in the metaphysical sense.

But if the thought of Being is so essentially focused on humanitas, must ontology then not be completed by "ethics"? Is not that effort essential which you express in the sentence, *"Ce que je cherche à faire, depuis longtemps déjà, c'est préciser le rapport de l'ontologie avec une éthique possible"*?

Shortly after *Sein und Zeit* appeared, a young friend asked me, "When are you going to write an ethics?" Where the essence of man is thought of so essentially, i.e., only from the question of the truth of Being, but without raising man to the center of beings, there the desire must arise for personally relevant directives and rules that tell how man, having gathered from his ex-sistence experience for Being, is to live "fatefully." The wish for an ethics needs to be fulfilled, all the more urgently, because the overt no less than the concealed, perplexity of man increases to immeasurable dimensions. Every care must be given to ties to ethics, in an age of technology when the individual, subject to the nature of a mass society, can be brought to a dependable steadfastness only by means of ordering and gathering his plans and actions as a whole in a way that corresponds to a technological age.

Who can ignore this crisis? Should we not preserve and secure the ties we now have, even if they only hold human beings together precariously and in mere immediacy? Certainly. But does this crisis ever absolve thought of the responsibility of thinking of that which primarily remains to-be-thought and, as Being, remains the guarantee and truth prior to every being? Can thought continue to retreat from the thought of Being after this has lain so long hidden in oblivion and at the same time announces itself at this very moment of world history through the uprooting of every being?

Before we attempt to determine more precisely the relationship between "ontology" and "ethics," we must ask what "ontology" and "ethics" themselves are. It is necessary to consider whether what can be designated by these terms still remains adequate and close to what has been assigned to thought, which as thought has to think before all else of the truth of Being.

Should, however, "ontology" as well as "ethics" and all thinking in disciplines become untenable and our thinking thereby become more disciplined, what happens then to the question of the relationship between these two disciplines of philosophy?

Ethics appeared for the first time, along with logic and physics in the school of Plato. These disciplines were born at a time that converted thought into "philosophy," but philosophy into *episteme* (science) and science itself into a matter for schools and school administrations. In passing through philosophy, so understood, science was born and thought [*Denken*] vanished. Thinkers up to then had known neither a "logic," nor an "ethics," nor a "physics." Yet their thinking is neither illogical nor immoral. But their conception of *physis* had a profundity and breadth which all the later "physics" was never again able to attain. The tragedies of Sophocles, if such a comparison can be made at all, hold the ethics more originally concealed in their telling than Aristotle's lecture on "ethics." A saying of Heraclitus that only consists of three words says something so simple that from it the essence of the *ethos* immediately comes to light.

The saying of Heraclitus goes (fragment 119): ἦθος ἀνθρώπῳ δαίμων. This is usually translated as: "A man's character is his daimon." This translation is modern but not Greek thinking. ἦθος means abode, place of dwelling. The word designates the open sphere in which man dwells. The openness of his abode allows that to appear which approaches toward the essence of man and so arriving abides near him. The abode of man contains and maintains the advent of that to which man in essence belongs. This, according to Heraclitus' saying, is δαίμων, God. The fragment says: Man, insofar as he is man, dwells in the nearness of God. A story that Aristotle relates (de part. anim. A 5, 645 a 17) coincides with this saying of Heraclitus. It runs:

"An anecdote tells of an explanation that Heraclitus is said to have given strangers who wanted to approach him. Upon approaching they found him warming himself at a stove. They stopped surprised and all the more so because as they hesitated he encouraged them and bade them come in with the words: 'For here too there are Gods present.'"

The story speaks for itself, yet some aspects should be stressed. The group of unknown visitors in its inquisitive curiosity about the thinker is disappointed and puzzled at first by his abode. It believes that it must find the thinker in conditions which, contrary to man's usual way of living, show everywhere traits of the exceptional and the rare, and, therefore, the sensational. The group hopes to find through its visit with the thinker things which, at least for a time, will provide material for entertaining small talk. The strangers who wish to visit the thinker hope to see him perhaps precisely at the moment when, sunk in profound meditation, he is thinking. The visitors wish to experience this, not in order to be affected by his thinking, but merely so that they will be able to say that they have seen and heard one who is reputed to be a thinker.

Instead, the inquisitive ones find Heraclitus at a stove. This is a pretty ordinary and insignificant place. True enough, bread is baked there. But Heraclitus is not even busy with baking at the stove. He is there only to warm himself, and so he betrays the whole poverty of his life at this spot which is in itself prosaic. The glimpse of a freezing thinker offers little of interest. And so the inquisitive ones at this disappointing sight immediately lose their desire to come any closer. What are they to do there? This ordinary dull event of someone cold and standing by the stove one can find any time in his own home. Then, why look up a thinker? The visitors are about to leave again. Heraclitus reads the disappointed curiosity in their faces. He realizes that with the crowd the mere absence of an expected sensation is enough to make those who have just come leave. Therefore, he heartens them. He especially urges them to enter with the words εἶναι γὰρ καὶ ἐνταῦθα θέους. "There are Gods present even here."

This statement puts the abode (ἦθος) of the thinker and his doing in a different light. Whether the visitors have understood the statement immediately or at all and then seen everything in this different light, the story does not tell. But that the story was told and transmitted to us today, is due to the fact that what it reports is of the bearing of this thinker and characterizes it. καὶ ἐνταῦθα. "Even here," at the baking oven, at this common place, where all things and every condition, each act and thought, are familiar and current, i.e., securer, "even there" in the sphere of the secure εἶναι θεούς, it is so "that even there there are gods present."

ἦθος ἀνθρώπῳ δαίμων as Heraclitus says: "The (secure) abode for man is the open quality of the presence (Anwesung) of God" (of the insecure, the strange) (des Un-geheuren).

If now, in accord with the basic meaning of the word ἦθος, ethics dwells in the abode of man, then that thought which thinks the truth of Being as the original element of man as existing is already in itself at the source of ethics. But then this kind of thinking is not ethics, either, because it is ontology. For ontology always thinks only the being (ὄν) in its Being. As long as the truth of Being, however, is not thought, all ontology remains without its base. Hence the thought, which with Sein und Zeit tried to think forward into the truth of Being, called itself fundamental ontology. It attempts to go back to the basic essence, from which the thought of the truth of Being derives. The formulation of different questions removes this thinking from the "ontology" of metaphysics (including that of Kant). The reason, however, why "ontology," be it transcendental or precritical, is not subject to criticism is not that it thinks the Being of beings and thereby forces Being into a concept, but that it does not think the truth of Being and so fails to realize the fact that there is a mode of thinking more rigorous than the conceptual. Thinking which tries to think forward into the truth of Being in the struggle of the first breakthrough expresses only a small part of this entirely different dimension. And the latter is further distorted in that it no longer retains the essential health of phenomenological vision and has not yet abandoned its inadequate pretensions toward "science" and "research." In order to make this attempt of thinking recognizable and understandable within philosophy, it was possible at first to speak only within the horizon of the existing philosophy and within the usage of the terms familiar to it.

In the meantime I have come to be convinced that even these terms must immediately and inevitably lead astray. For the terms and their corresponding conceptual language were not rethought by the readers from the thing which had-to-be-thought first; instead, this thing was imagined through terms maintained in their usual signification. Thinking that seeks for the truth of Being and thereby determines the essential abode of man from Being is neither ethics nor ontology. Therefore, the question of the relationship of the two to each other has no longer any basis in this sphere. Nevertheless your question, if it be thought more originally, continues to make sense and be of essential importance.

One must, of course, ask: If thought, considering the truth of Being, determines the essence of the *humanitas* as ex-sistence from its pertinence to Being, does this thought only remain a theoretical imagining of Being and of man, or is it possible to extract from knowledge directives for action and put them to use for life?

The answer is that such thinking is neither theoretical nor practical. It occurs before such a differentiation. This thinking is, insofar as it is, the recollection of Being and nothing else. Belonging to Being, because it is thrown by being into the true-ness of its truth and claims for it, it thinks Being. Such thinking results in nothing. It has no effect. It suffices its own essence, in that it is. But it is, in that it expresses its matter. At each epoch of history one thing only is important to it: that it be in accord with its matter. Its material relevance is essentially superior to the validity of science, because it is freer. For it lets Being—be.

Thinking works at building the house of Being; in which house Being joins and as such the joining of Being enjoins that man, according to destiny, dwell in the truth of Being. This dwelling is the essence of "Being-in-the-World" (cf. *Sein und Zeit*). The reference there to the "in-Being" (*In-Sein*) as "dwell-ing" is no etymological game. The reference in the essay of 1936 to Hölderlin's phrase, "Laboring, yet poetically man dwells on this earth" is no mere gilding of a thought that abandoning science, takes refuge in poetry. To talk of the house of Being is not to transfer the image of "house" to Being, but from the ma-terially understood essence of Being we shall some day be more easily able to think what "house" and "dwelling" are.

Nonetheless, thought never creates the house of Being. Thought accompanies historical existence, i.e., the *humanitas* of the *homo humanus,* to the domain where grace arises.

With grace, evil appears in the clearing of Being. The essence of evil does not consist in pure wickedness of human action, but in the malice of anger. Both grace and anger can, however, essentially only be in Being, insofar as Being itself is what is disputed. In it is hidden the essential source of nihilation (*das Nichten*). What nihilates, is manifest as the nothing-like (*das Nichthafte*). This can be approached in the "No." The "Not" does not arise from the Nay-saying of negation. Each "No" which is not misinterpreted as a self-willed insistence on the positing power of subjectivity (but remains letting-be of ex-sistence) answers the claim of the manifest nihilation. Every "No" is only the affirmation of the "Not." Every affirmation rests in recognition. This lets that towards which it goes ap-proach it. It is believed that nihilation cannot be found any-where in beings themselves. This is true as long as one seeks for nihilation as something that is being, as an existing quality of the existent. But that is not the place to seek for nihilation. Being is no existing quality which characterizes the being. Nevertheless, Being is being more than any actual being. Because nihilation is essentially in Being itself, we can never become aware of it as something that is being in the existent. But this impossibility does not prove that the source of the Not is from Nay-saying. This proof only seems conclusive if one posits the existent as the object of subjectivity. From this alternative it then follows that each Not, since it never appears as something objective, must inevitably be the product of a subjective act. Whether, however, the Nay-saying constitutes the Not as something merely thought, or whether the nihilation only demands the "No" as what-is-to-be-said in the letting-be of beings, certainly can never be distinguished from the subjective reflection of thinking, which has already been posited as subjectivity. In such a reflection, the dimension for the formulation of the questions adequate to the matter has not yet been reached. It remains to be asked, granted that thought belongs to ex-sistence, whether all "Yes" and "No" is not already existent in the truth of Being. If so, then "Yes" and "No" are already in themselves bound to Being. As bondsmen, they can never first posit that to which they themselves belong.

Nihilation is essentially in Being itself and by no means in the *Dasein* of man, insofar as this is thought as subjectivity of the *ego cogito*. The Dasein by no means nihilates, insofar as man as subject performs the nihilation in the sense of rejection, but the Da-sein nihilates, insofar as, as essence, wherein man ex-sists, it itself belongs to the essence of Being. Being nihilates —as Being. Therefore, in the absolute idealism of Hegel and Schelling, the Not appears as the negativity of the negative in the essence of Being. This, however, is thought there in the essence of absolute actuality as the unconditioned will, which wills itself and, indeed, as the will of knowledge and love. In this will, Being is still concealed as the will to power. Why, however, the negativity of the absolute subjectivity is the "dialectical" and why, through the dialectic, the nihilation is discovered, but at the same time is concealed in its essence cannot here be discussed.

The nihilating (*das Nichtende*) in Being is the essence of

what I call the Nothing. Because it thinks Being, thought thinks the Nothing.

Only Being lends to grace the ascent to graciousness and to anger the push toward disgrace.

Only so far as man, ex-sisting in the truth of Being, belongs to it, can the assigning of all the directions which must become for man law and rule, come from Being itself. The verb "assign" in Greek is νέμειν. The νόμος is not only law, but more originally the assigning concealed in the destiny of Being. Only this is capable of ordering man in Being. Only such ordering is capable of bearing up and binding. Otherwise, all law remains but the handiwork of human reason. More essential than any establishment of rule is the abode in the truth of Being. Only this abode yields the experience of the tenable (*das Haltbare*). The hold (*Halt*) for all behavior (*Verhalten*) is given by the truth of Being. "Hold" in our language means "shelter." Being is the shelter that in view of its own truth shelters man in his ex-sisting essence in such a way that it lodges ex-sistence in language. Thus language is at once the house of Being and the dwelling of human beings. Only because language is the dwelling of the essence of man, can the historical ways of mankind and men not be at home in their language, so that for them it becomes the shell of their machinations.

In what relationship now does the thought of Being stand to theoretical and practical behavior? It is superior to all contemplation, because it cares for the light in which only a seeing as theory can abide and move. Thought attends to the clearing of Being by putting its speaking of Being into language as the dwelling of existence. Thus thought is an action. But an action that is superior at the same time to all practice. Thinking surpasses doing and producing, not through the magnitude of its performance, nor through the consequences of its activity, but through the humbleness of the achievement that it accomplishes without result.

Thinking, as you know, brings into language in its saying only the unspoken word of Being.

The expression used here, "to bring into language," is now to be taken quite literally. Being, clearing itself, comes into language. It is always on its way towards it. As it arrives, it in its turn brings ex-sisting thought to language in its telling, which is thus elevated into the clearing of Being. Only thus, language *is* in its mysterious and yet humanly pervasive way. Insofar as language, thus brought fully into its essence, is historical, Being is preserved in remembering. Ex-sistence inhabits as it thinks the house of Being. In all this, it is as if nothing had happened at all through the utterance of thought.

But we have just seen an example of this insignificant act of thinking. For while we specifically think the expression "to bring to language," which was given to language, only this and nothing else, and while we retain in the observance of speaking what we have thought as something that always has-to-be-thought in the future, we have ourselves brought something essential of Being into language.

The strange thing in this thought of Being is its simplicity. This is precisely what keeps us from it. For we seek for the thought that in the name of "philosophy" has its world-historical prestige in the form of the unusual, which is only accessible to the initiate. At the same time we represent thought to ourselves in the manner of scientific knowledge and research. We measure the act against the impressive and successful achievements of practice. But the act of thinking is neither theoretical nor practical, nor is it the coupling together of both ways of behavior.

Through its simple essence the thought of Being is disguised for us. But when we become friends with the unusualness of the simple, another affliction befalls us at once. The suspicion arises that this thought of Being may lapse into the arbitrary; for it cannot cling to beings. From whence does thought derive its rule? What is the law of its action?

Here the third question of your letter must be heard: *Comment sauver l'élément d'aventure que comporte toute recherche sans faire de la philosophie une simple aventurière?* I shall mention poetry only in passing at this point. It confronts the same question in the same way as thought. But Aristotle's point in his *Poetics,* scarcely considered today, is still of value— that the making of poetry is truer than the exploration of beings.

But thought is *une aventure* not only as seeking and asking into the realm of the unthought. Thought, in its essence as thought of Being, is claimed by it. Thought is related to Being as the arriving (*l'avenant*). Thought is as thought in the advent of Being, is bound to Being as arrival. Being has already destined itself to thought. Being *is* as the destiny of thought. The destiny, however, is in itself historical. Its history has already arrived at language in the speaking of thinkers.

To express over and over again the advent of Being, permanent and in its permanence waiting for man, is the only matter for thought. That is why the essential thinkers always say the same thing. But that does not mean: the like. Yet they say this only to the one who undertakes to follow their thought. While thought, remembering historically, attends to the destiny of Being, it has already bound itself to what is according to destiny. To escape into the like is not dangerous. To venture into discord in order to say the same thing, that is the danger. Ambiguity and mere quibbling threaten.

That the speaking of Being can become the destiny of truth is the first law of thought and not the rules of logic, which can become rules only through the law of Being. To attend to the destiny of the thinking-speaking does not only include our recollecting each time *what* is to be said about Being and *how* it is to be said. It remains equally essential to consider *whether* that which has-to-be-thought may be said, to what extent, at what moment in the history of Being, in what dialogue with it, and with what claim. That threefold thing, mentioned in a previous letter, is determined in the interdependence of its parts by the law of the destiny or historical thought of Being: the rigor of reflection, the carefulness of speaking, the economy of the word.

It is about time to get rid of the habit of overestimating philosophy and thereby asking too much of it. It is necessary in the present plight of the world that there be less philosophy, but more attention to thought; less literature, but more cultivation of the letter.

Future thought is no longer philosophy, because it thinks more originally than metaphysics. But neither can future thought, as Hegel demanded, lay aside the name "love of wisdom" and become wisdom itself in the form of absolute knowledge. Thought is on its descent to the poverty of its provisional essence. Thought gathers language in simple speech. Language is thus the language of Being, as the clouds are the clouds of the sky. Thought by its speaking traces insignificant furrows in language. They seem even more insignificant than the furrows the peasant with deliberate steps traces in the field.

HEIDEGGER'S MAJOR WRITINGS
(arranged chronologically)

Die Lehre vom Urteil im Psychologismus: Ein Kritisch-positiver Beitrag zur Logik. Leipzig: J. A. Barth, 1914.

Die Kategorien- und Bedeutungslehre des Duns Scotus. Tübingen: Mohr, 1916.

Sein und Zeit. Halle: Niemeyer, 1927.

   Being and Time. Tr. J. Macquarrie and E. Robinson. New York: Harper, 1962.

Kant und das Problem der Metaphysik. Bonn: Cohen, 1929.

   Kant and the Problem of Metaphysics. Tr. James Churchill. Bloomington: Indiana University Press, 1962.

Vom Wesen des Grundes. Halle: Niemeyer, 1929. Foreword added to third edition; Frankfurt a. M.: Klostermann, 1949.

   The Essence of Reasons. Tr. Terrence Malick. Evanston: Northwestern University Press, 1969.

Was ist Metaphysik? Bonn: Cohen, 1929. Postscript added to fourth edition and introduction added to fifth edition. Frankfurt a. M.: Klostermann, 1949.

   What is Metaphysics? Tr. R. Hull and A. Crick, in *Existence and Being,* ed. W. Brock. Chicago: Regnery, 1949.

Die Selbstbehauptung der deutschen Universität. Breslau: Korn, 1933.

Hölderlin und das Wesen der Dichtung. Munich: Albert Langen, 1937.

   Hölderlin and the Essence of Poetry. Tr. Douglas Scott, in *Existence and Being.*

Vom Wesen der Wahrheit. Frankfurt a. M.: Klostermann, 1943.

   On the Essence of Truth. Tr. R. Hull and A. Crick, in *Existence and Being.*

Erläuterungen zu Hölderlins Dichtung. Frankfurt a. M.: Klostermann, 1944.

Platons Lehre von der Wahrheit. Mit einem Brief über den "Humanismus." Bern: Francke, 1947.

   "Plato's Doctrine of Truth." Tr. J. Barlow; "Letter on Humanism." Tr. E. Lohner in Barrett, W. & Aiken, H. (eds.). *Philosophy in the Twentieth Century.* 4 vols. New York: Random House, 1962. Vol. 3.

"Einleitung," *Was ist Metaphysik,* 5th printing. Frankfurt a. M.: Klostermann, 1949.

"The Way Back into the Ground of Metaphysics." Tr. W. Kaufmann in *Existentialism from Dostoevsky to Sartre.* Ed. W. Kaufmann. New York: Meridian, 1956.

Holzwege. Frankfurt a. M.: Klostermann, 1953.

An essay from *Holzwege* was recently translated as *Hegel's Concept of Experience.* Ed. J. Glenn Gray. New York: Harper, 1970.

Der Feldweg. Frankfurt a. M.: Klostermann, 1953.

Einführung in die Metaphysik. Tübingen: Niemeyer, 1953.

Introduction to Metaphysics. Tr. Ralph Manheim. New Haven: Yale University Press, 1958.

Was heisst Denken? Tübingen: Niemeyer, 1954.

What is Called Thinking? Tr. J. Glenn Gray. New York: Harper, 1968.

Aus der Erfahrung des Denkens. Pfullingen: Neske, 1954.

Vorträge und Aufsätze. Pfullingen: Neske, 1954.

Hebel—Der Hausfreund. Pfullingen: Neske, 1956.

Was ist das—die Philosophie? Pfullingen: Neske, 1956.

What is Philosophy? Tr. W. Kluback and J. T. Wilde. New York: Twayne, 1958.

Zur Seinsfrage. Frankfurt a. M.: Klostermann, 1956.

The Question of Being. Tr. W. Kluback and J. Wilde. New York: Twayne, 1958.

Der Satz vom Grund. Pfullingen: Neske, 1957.

Identität und Differenz. Pfullingen: Neske, 1957.

Essays in Metaphysics: Identity and Difference. Tr. K. Leidecker. New York: Philosophical Library, 1960.

Unterwegs zur Sprache. Pfullingen: Neske, 1958.

Gelassenheit. Pfullingen: Neske, 1959.

Discourse on Thinking. Tr. J. Anderson and H. Freund. New York: Harper, 1966.

Nietzsche. 2 vols. Pfullingen: Neske, 1960.

Die Frage nach dem Ding. Tübingen: Niemeyer, 1962.

What is a Thing. Tr. W. Barton/V. Deutsch. Chicago: Regnery, 1967.

Wegmarken. Frankfurt a. M.: Klostermann, 1967.

Zur Sache des Denkens. Tübingen: Niemeyer, 1969.

Phänomenologie und Theologie. Frankfurt a. M.: Klostermann, 1970.

SELECTED STUDIES ABOUT HEIDEGGER
(arranged alphabetically)

A. Bibliography

Lübbe, Hermann. *Bibliographie der Heidegger-Literatur, 1917–1955.* Meisenheim a. Glan: Hain, 1957.

Sass, Hans-Martin-*Heidegger-Bibliographie.* Meisenheim a. Glan: Hain, 1968.

B. Monographs and Articles

Astrada, Carlos. *Idealismo fenomenologico y metafisica existencial.* Buenos Aires: Facultad de Filosofia y Letras, 1936.

Barrett, William. *What is Existentialism?* New York: Grove Press, 1964.

Biemel, Walter. *Le concept de monde chez Heidegger.* Louvain: Nauwelaerts, 1951.

Chiodi, Pietro. *L'esistenzialismo di Heidegger.* Turin: Taylor, 1947.

———. *L'ultimo Heidegger.* Turin: Taylor, 2nd ed., 1960.

De Waelhens, Alphonse. *La philosophie de Martin Heidegger.* Louvain: Institut Supérieur de Philosophie, 1942.

———. *Chemins et impasses de l'ontologie heideggériene.* Louvain: Nauwelaerts, 1953.

Farber, Marvin. "Heidegger on the Essence of Truth," *Philosophy and Phenomenological Research,* XVIII [1958], 523–532.

Gray, J. Glenn. "Heidegger's 'Being,' " *Journal of Philosophy,* XLIX [1952], 415–422.

Grene, Marjorie. *Martin Heidegger.* New York: Hillary House, 1957.

King, Magda. *Heidegger's Philosophy.* New York: Macmillan, 1964.

Kocklemans, Joseph. *Martin Heidegger. A First Introduction to His Philosophy.* Pittsburgh: Duquesne University Press, 1965.

Langan, Thomas. *The Meaning of Heidegger.* New York: Columbia University Press, 1959.

Levinas, Emmanuel. *En découvrant l'existence avec Husserl et Heidegger.* Paris: Vrin, 1949.

Löwith, Karl. *Heidegger, Denker in dürftiger Zeit.* Frankfurt a. M.: Fischer, 1953.

Marx, Werner. "Heidegger's New Concept of Philosophy. The Second Phase of Existentialism," *Social Research,* XXII [1953], 451–474.

Misch, Georg. *Lebensphilosophie und Phänomenologie: Eine Ausein-*

andersetzung der Diltheyschen Richtung mit Heidegger und Husserl. Bonn: Cohen, 1930.

Pöggeler, Otto (ed.). *Heidegger.* Köln: Kiepenheuer & Witsch, 1969.

Prufer, Thomas. "Dasein and the Ontological Status of the Speaker of Philosophical Discourse" in *Twentieth Century Thinkers.* Ed. J. K. Ryan. New York: Alba House, 1965, pp. 159–173.

Richardson, William. *Heidegger: Through Phenomenology to Thought.* The Hague: Nijhoff, 1963.

Schmitt, Richard. *Martin Heidegger on Being Human: An Introduction to Sein und Zeit.* New York: Random House, 1969.

Schrader, George. "Heidegger's Ontology of Human Existence," *Review of Metaphysics,* X [1956], 35–56.

Schrag, Calvin. "Phenomenology, Ontology, and History in the Philosophy of Heidegger," *Revue internationale de philosophie,* XII [1958], 117–132.

Seidel, George. *Martin Heidegger and the Pre-Socratics.* Lincoln: University of Nebraska Press, 1964.

Versényi, Lazlo. *Heidegger, Being and Truth.* New Haven: Yale University Press, 1965.

Vycinas, Vincent. *Earth and Gods: An Introduction to the Philosophy of Martin Heidegger.* The Hague: Nijhoff, 1961.

Wahl, Jean. *Sur l'interprétation de l'histoire de la métaphysique d'après Heidegger.* Paris: Tournier et Constans, 1953.

José Ortega y Gasset (1883–1955)

Ortega was born in Madrid on May 9, 1883, of a well-to-do aristocratic family. His father who was the editor of an influential Madrid newspaper sent him to receive his secondary education from the Jesuits at Miraflores del Palo near Malaga. From 1898 to 1902 he studied at the Universidad Central in Madrid and took his degree in philosophy in 1904. His departure from Madrid for Leipzig was, according to him, an escape from the intellectual desert of his native land for the oasis of the German universities and a response to the secret voice, as he put it, "of the fair German, pensive and romantic" that dwelt subconsciously in his soul.

Ortega made several comparisons between what he called "Latin" (or "Mediterranean") and Germanic cultures, much to the disfavor of the former. He regarded Latin clarity a myth and its culture a gilded illusion; he believed that German culture was Greece's legitimate heir.

From Leipzig, Ortega moved to Berlin where Dilthey was just about to retire but whose influence at Berlin was in full force. Ortega's mature work manifests a rediscovery of Dilthey. The theme, for example, "Man does not have a nature, but a history . . . ," found in Ortega's *Historia como sistema* bears the Diltheyian stamp upon it.

Ortega studied next at Marburg under the neo-Kantians Hermann Cohen and Paul Natorp. While the former gave him inspiration for his philosophy of "existence," the latter seems to have introduced him to the writings of Husserl. But Ortega found Husserl's arguments on the priority of consciousness deficient (as do all of the Existentialists). "Real human life," ac-

cording to Ortega, does not give priority to consciousness but
manifests the coincidence of consciousness and its circumstances
or situation.

But the philosopher that Ortega seems most to have admired
was Max Scheler, whom he thought was Europe's best mind.
But his admiration was not uncritical. Although Ortega believed
that Scheler's *Formalismus in der Ethik* was one of the most
formidable philosophical documents written in the twentieth
century, he was deeply opposed to Scheler's conclusions in *The
Genius of War and the German War*. Moreover, the lack of
order, system, and argument in Scheler's work was as distressing
to Ortega as the wealth of brilliance and subtlety was admi-
rable. Curiously enough, similar criticisms are made of the work
of Ortega.

The relationship between the work of Ortega and that of
Heidegger is worth comment. There may have been some bitterness on the part of Ortega for not receiving due credit for
formulations somewhat similar to Heidegger's some twenty
years before *Being and Time*. Even the concept of ontological
difference (i.e., the distinction between things possessing being
and being itself) seems to have received Ortega's attention before
Heidegger dealt with it in *Being and Time*. Ortega, moreover,
unjustifiably held Heidegger responsible for what he believed
were the romantic excesses of Sartrian Existentialism.

In 1910 he received an appointment to the chair of metaphysics at the University of Madrid and taught there until the
outbreak of the Spanish Civil War in 1936. During the same
period he worked as a journalist and a politician. In 1923 he
founded the *Revista de Occidente,* a review intended to terminate Spain's isolation from the trends in philosophy and science
and especially its isolation from German culture. During the
dictatorship of Primo de Rivera (1923–1930), Ortega was a
prominent figure among the intellectuals of the republican opposition. He also had a role in ousting King Alfonso XIII in
1931. Upon his election as deputy for the province of León in
the constituent assembly of the Second Spanish Republic, he
led a parliamentary group of intellectuals called *La Agrupación
al servicio de la república.* He was appointed, moreover, to the
post of civil governor of Madrid.

His political involvement obliged him to leave Spain at the inception of the Civil War and he spent the next few years in Argentina as well as in several European countries. In 1945 he settled in Portugal, making some forays into Spain. He returned to Madrid in 1948 where, together with Julián Marías, he established the Institute of Humanities where he lectured frequently. Ortega did not limit himself to lecturing in Spain. Between 1949 and 1951, he gave lectures in the United States, Germany, and Switzerland and received an honorary doctorate from the University of Glasgow in Scotland.

Ortega was married to a woman of Italian background. They had two children, a daughter and a son, José Ortega Spotorno, the present editor of the *Revista de Occidente*. Ortega fell ill with cancer and died in Madrid on October 18, 1955.

From *What Is Philosophy?*

The Basic Reality Is Our Life.
The Categories of Life. Theoretic Life. Destiny and Freedom.

Translated by Mildred Adams

Whenever I have said that we were seeing ourselves forced to move beyond the boundaries of antiquity and modernity, I have added that we go beyond them only insofar as we conserve them. The spirit, by its very essence, is at once most cruel, most tender, and most generous. In order to live, the spirit must murder its own past, thus denying it, but this it cannot do without at the same time reviving the thing it kills and keeping it alive within itself. If it kills once and for all, it could not go on denying that past, and because it denies it, superseding it. If our thought did not re-think the thought of Descartes, and if Descartes did not re-think the thought of Aristotle, ours would be primitive; we would no longer be the heirs of what has gone before, but would have to go back and begin again. To surpass is to inherit and to add to.

When I say that we need new concepts I refer to all that

we must add to what already exists—the old concepts endure, but they become subordinate. If we discover a new manner of being which is more fundamental than the old, it is evident that we need a concept of being which was previously unknown —but at the same time our newest concept has the obligation to explain the old ones, it must demonstrate that portion of truth which they contained. Thus we suggested some days ago (there was no time to do more than hint) how the old idea of cosmic being and the substantive self had value for a reality in which the most basic fact of consciousness had not yet been discovered, and later we showed how the concept of the subjective being would be valid if there were not a previous reality which is life itself.

Well then, antiquity and modernity coincide in seeking, under the name of philosophy, a knowledge of the Universe, or whatever there is. But on taking the first step, on seeking the first truth about the Universe, the two of them begin to draw apart. The ancient starts off in search of primary reality, understanding by primary that reality which is most important in the structure of the Universe. If this reality is theist, this means that the most important reality, the one which explains the rest, is God: if it is materialist, the most important will be matter; if pantheist, it will be an undifferentiated entity, at once God and matter—*natura sive Deus*. But the modern will hold up all this searching and will dispute it, saying, "It is possible that this reality or that may, in fact, be the most important in the Universe, but even after we have demonstrated this we will be not one step further ahead because you have forgotten to ask yourselves whether that reality which explains all the rest is a reality with full evidence; and more, whether those other less important realities which it explains are realities that exist beyond the shadow of a doubt."

The first problem of philosophy is not one of finding out which reality in the Universe is the most important, but which is the most sure, the one beyond any trace of doubt, even though it be perhaps the least important, the most humble and insignificant. In short, the primary philosophic problem consists in determining what of the Universe is given to us, the problem of fundamental data. The ancients never posed this problem formally; hence, whatever their skill in regard to the other questions, their level is below the level of modernity. So we install ourselves on this level, and the only thing we do is to dispute with the moderns about which reality is fundamental and indubitable. We find that it is not the conscious self, the subject, but life which includes both the subject and the world. In this way we escape from idealism and win to a new level.

But note that we do all this without departing from philosophy's first problem, that we move exclusively on the plane of what, among all there is, has been given to us. If we believe that this datum is our own life, that of all the Universe what is given to each of us is only his own life, we do not allow ourselves the slightest opinion on the question as to whether, in addition to what is given us, there are not other realities which, though not given us, are much more important. The problem of that which is given or indubitable is not philosophy but only its doorstep, its preliminary chapter. I want to remind you that this was said in the beginning.

But I do not know whether you have all noted the consequence that this statement carries with it; this is an elemental consequence, so elemental that, strictly speaking, I ought not to voice it, but I fear it should be stated. It is this: if we have recognized that the only indubitable reality is as we have already defined it, nothing else that we may say will ever be able to contradict the attributes which, with all evidence, make up that basic reality. Because all the other things of which we speak, different from that primordial thing, are doubtful and secondary, and firm only insofar as they rest on that reality which is beyond doubt.

Suppose, for example, that someone starts from the modern principle and says that the only thing which is beyond doubt is the existence of thought—with this statement he takes his stand on the level that we call modernity. But then he adds: of course in addition there is matter, the matter which physics knows, composed of atoms ruled by certain laws. If by that "in addition there is" he means that what physics says has the same operative rank as the principle of subjectivism, the statement is utterly absurd. This principle says that the indubitable real is nonmaterial and that for it the rules of physics (a science which, like every individual science, occupies itself with secondary and quasi-realities) have no force. This is not to deny the truth of physical laws, but to relegate their operative force to the secondary order of phenomena which they concern; the order of phenomena which do not pretend to be basic. The idealist physicist, that is to say, the modern one, like the idealist philosopher, will have to explain how, if there is no other indubitable reality than thought, which is nonmaterial, one can talk with good sense and truth about material things, about physical laws and so on—but what he cannot do sensibly is to let physics exercise retroactive effects on the definition of that reality which is beyond doubt.

This definition is something not to be touched, and not to be destroyed by what, using it as a point of departure, we will add later. This is the elemental thing which I suspect it would be not inopportune to emphasize.

The new fact, the new fundamental reality, is "our life," the life of every one of us. Let anyone try to talk of any other reality as being freer from doubt, more primary than this, and you will see that such a thing is impossible. Even thinking is not anterior to living—because thinking is found to be a piece of my life, a particular act in that life. This seeking for an indubitable reality is something that I do because I live and inasmuch as I live—that is to say, it is not isolated and done for its own sake. I seek reality because I am now busying myself with philosophy, and I do this as a first act in philosophizing. And philosophizing is, in turn, a particular form of living which assumes this living—for if I work with philosophy it is because of an earlier desire to know what the Universe is, and this curiosity, in turn, exists because of what I feel as a desire of my life which is restless about itself, and perhaps finds itself lost in itself. In short, whatever reality we set up as primary, we find that it assumes our life to be a fact; the act of giving it place is in itself a vital act, is "living."

It may seem very surprising that the only indubitable reality should be "living" and not thinking—the idealist "*cogito*" (which in turn was very surprising in its day), or Aristotle's "form," or Plato's "idea," each of which in its own moment seemed an intolerable paradox. But what can we do? This is the way it is.

But if it is thus, there is no remedy but to fix the attributes of that new fundamental reality, and no remedy but to accept them even though they may seem to give the lie to all our pre-existent theories and to all the other science we follow, while recognizing them as true at certain points. In a system of philosophy, we would, then, have to show how, taking the reality of our life as a point of departure, and without contradicting our concept of living at a single point, there are also organic bodies, moral and physical laws, and even theology. But what I say does not include any statement that in addition to that indubitable life of ours—that life which is given to us—there may not perhaps exist the "other life." What is certain is that that "other life" is, from the point of view of science, problematical, as are organic reality and physical reality—and that, on the other hand, this life of ours, this life of every one of us, is not problematical but indubitable.

Earlier, we began the definition of life in the rapid form which haste demands. You may feel disturbed because what we were saying was something of a platitude. But this means that it was evident, and we are clinging to evidence. Life is not a mystery, but quite the opposite; it is the clearest and most present thing there is, and being so, being purely transparent, we find difficulty in studying it closely. The eye goes beyond it, toward wisdoms that are still problematical, and it is an effort for us to stop it at these immediate evidences.

Thus it is obvious that to live is to find myself in the world. If I should suddenly find myself alone with myself, I would be existing, but that existing would not be living—it would be merely the subjective existence of idealism. But the fact is that I should not find myself alone with myself, for when I explore that self I find it to consist of a person who is occupied with something which is not the self, with other things that show themselves united as if articulated among themselves; these face me in the shape of my surroundings as an enveloping unity of a world where I exist—and I am here not passively, not prone and inert, but under pressure by that world or exalted by it.

The world is what I find confronting and surrounding me when I find myself, the thing that clearly exists for me and acts upon me. The world is not the same as nature, not the same as that cosmos familiar to the ancients, which was an underlying reality subsisting by itself, a reality of which its subjects may know this bit or that, but which reserves to itself its own mystery. The vital, living world has no mystery at all for me, because it consists exclusively of what I observe in it and just as I observe it. Nothing intervenes in my life except what presents itself to me. In short, the world is what is lived, as it is lived. Let us suppose that my world were composed of pure mysteries, of things that were masked and enigmatic, like the world in certain American films. Well then, that fact that they were mysteries, were enigmas, would be evident and transparent to me, would act on me in the shape of mystery and enigma; I would then have to say that the world in which I live is an evident and in-dubitable mystery, its self is clearly composed of the mysterious; and all this would be as simple as though I said that the world is blue or is yellow.

The primary attribute of this basic reality which we call "our life" is the fact of existing on one's own account, of entering into an understanding of oneself, of being transparent to one-self. Only thus is it, and whatever forms part of it, indubitable —and only because it is the uniquely indubitable is it the fun-damental reality.

This "finding oneself," this "understanding oneself," this "be-ing transparent," is the first category of living. Some of you do not know what a category is. Do not be ashamed. A category is an elemental thing in philosophic science. Do not be ashamed at ignorance of a thing that is elemental. All of us are ignorant of elemental things which our neighbors know all too well. The shameful thing is not ignorance—on the contrary, that is the natural thing. The really shameful thing is to not want to know, to resist finding out when the occasion offers. It is never the ignorant who offer that resistance, but the ones who think they know. That is the shameful thing—to think you know. He who thinks he knows something, but is in fact ignorant of it, closes the door of his mind through which authentic truth could enter. His own dull idea, held proudly or stubbornly, acts as does the guard among the termites—a type with an enormous head, var-nished and very hard, dedicated to the duty of standing in the entrance to the nest, blocking the orifice with its own head so that nothing can enter. In the same way he who believes that he knows something uses his own head to close the mental trap door through which true knowledge might enter.

Anyone who has carried on an active and public intellectual life, within Spain and without, will automatically make comparisons; he is forced to the conviction that this mental attitude of being hermetically sealed is in the Spaniard a permanent and endemic vice. And this is not chance. If the Spaniard shows very little intellectual porosity, it is because he also is a hermit in zones of his soul which go much deeper than intellect. But perhaps even graver than this lack of porosity on the part of the Spanish man is that same weakness in the soul of the Spanish woman. To say this is to commit an atrocity, but I do not do it carelessly. As soon as words can circulate freely, I shall begin a campaign against the Spanish woman's way of living. It will not be flattering, and for me it will be very painful.

I have always been repelled by the person who is continually saying that he believes that this, that, or the other thing ought to be done. During my lifetime I have thought of myself very seldom in terms of duty. I have lived my life, and I continue to live it, pushed almost entirely not by duties, but by illusions. More than that; the ethics which I may be able to set before you in the coming year differs from traditional ethics in that it considers the primary idea in morality to be not duty but illusion. Duty is important, but it is a secondary thing—it is the substitute for, the *ersatz* of illusion. What we cannot manage to achieve out of illusion we must at least do out of a sense of duty.

Well, then, this campaign, on the theme of the Spanish woman, is too harsh to be an illusion; on the contrary, it will be a sacrifice. For many years of meditation I have believed it to be a duty. Of all the things in our Spanish life which need basic reform I think the one most fundamentally in need of it is the feminine soul. And for one who believes, as I do, that woman intervenes in history infinitely more than is generally believed or suspected, and that she does this in continuous, irresistible and most subtle ways, it is clear as crystal that no small number of capital defects, persistent throughout Spanish existence, of which the origin is sought in the most abstruse causes, arise simply out of the inadequacy of Spanish femininity. Difficult and dangerous though it may be, and although I can foresee the uncomfortable consequences which it will bring for me, I feel obliged to take this task upon myself.

As you see, at this point, too, I depart absolutely from the official stereotypes. I am hardly gallant, but one must lay all gallantry aside, must overcome it along with the modernity and idealism which made up its climate—one must move ahead to forms of enthusiasm about women which are much more difficult, energetic and ardent. Nothing today seems more untimely than the devoted and curving gesture with which the lordly gentleman of 1890 approached a woman to address her with a phrase that was as gallant and curled as a shaving. Young girls are losing the habit of being addressed with gallantry, and that gesture which thirty years ago oozed virility in every pore would today seem to them a bit effeminate.

But let us go back to our subject, which was the matter of categories. We were saying that some of you neither had, nor had any reason for having, a clear idea of what categories are. The idea of the category is the simplest in the world. A horse and a star differ in many of their elements and in the major part of their ingredients. But however different they are, they have something in common when we say of them that they are both corporeal things. The horse and the star are both real things; moreover they both occupy space, they exist in time, they suffer changes in the course of moving about, and in turn they produce changes in other things on colliding with them; each has its own color, form and density, that is to say, its own qualities. Thus we find that over and above their innumerable differences they coincide in a small number of elements and attributes—being real, occupying space and time, having qualities, acting and suffering. Like them, everything which pretends to be a corporeal thing will possess that minimal group of conditions or properties, that essential skeleton of the corporeal being. Well then, these are the categories as Aristotle defined them. The properties which every real being, simply by the fact of being real, carries with it and contains, quite apart from other elements which differentiate it.

As our reality, "living," is very different from the ancient cosmic reality, it will be made up of a group of categories or components, all of them essential, equally original and inseparable among themselves. It is these categories of "our life" that we seek. Our life is the life of "each one of us"; therefore mine is different from yours, but both of them are "my living," and both of them will have a series of common ingredients—the categories of "my life." Nevertheless, there is a radical difference between the reality called "my life" and the reality which the older philosophy called "being." "Being" is a general thing which does not pretend in itself to be the character of the individual. The Aristotelian categories are categories of being in general— őν ἡ őν. But "my life" is different; whether this name is applied in my case, or to any one of you, it is a concept which then involves the individual; hence we have found one of those very rare ideas which is equally "general" and "individual." Up to now, logic has ignored the possibility of a concept which in appearance is so contradictory. Hegel himself, who wanted to search for something similar, did not succeed; his "concrete universal" is in the last analysis universal, but not truly and fundamentally concrete; it is not individual. But I cannot even start now to go into this theme. Let us move ahead, leaving the windward beat as it was.

The first category of our lives is "to find oneself," "to understand oneself," "to be transparent," and once more I want to warn you not to forget that here it is not merely the self which is the subject, but also the world. I take account of myself in the world, of myself and the world, that is to say, I live.

But this "to find oneself" is, after all, to find oneself occupied with something in the world. I consist in an occupying of myself with what there is in the world, and the world consists of everything with which I occupy myself, and of nothing else. To occupy oneself is to do this or that—it is, for example, to think. Thinking is living because it is occupying myself with objects in that peculiar dealing with them which is thinking them. To think is to make; for example, to create truths, to make a philosophy. To occupy oneself is to make a philosophy, or to make a revolution, to make a cigarette, to make a footing, to make time. This is what I am during my lifetime.

As for things, what are they? In this basic perspective and primary mode of thinking which is their being lived by me, what are they? I am he who makes—who thinks, runs, rebels, or hopes—and what is the thing that is made?

Curious! That which is made is also my life. When what I do is to wait, the thing which is done is the act of having waited; when what I make is the cigarette, the thing done is not, properly speaking, the cigarette, but my action in rolling it. In itself and apart from my activity, the cigarette has no primary being; this was the ancient error. The cigarette is what I manipulate in making it, and when I have finished my activity and the object of my rolling has ceased to be, it is converted into another object —it is that which someone must light and must then smoke. Its true being is reduced to what it represents as the object of my occupation. It has no being in itself, subsistent, χωριστόν, apart from my living it, my action with it. Its being is functional, its function in my life: it is a being *so that,* a being toward an end —so that I may do this or that with it. Nevertheless, as in traditional philosophy, I talk of the being of things as something which these things have by themselves and apart from their manipulation and their service in my life—I use the ancient meaning of the concept "to be"; the result is apparent when I abstract from a thing its primary being, which is the usual, serviceable, and lived being; then I find that the thing has not disappeared because I am not occupied with it, but that it remains apart, outside my life, perhaps in the hope that it may be of some service to me another time.

But then that thing which is in being on *its own account,* and not for reasons of my life, surges forth in virtue of my abstracting it from my life—and abstracting is also a doing, a making and an occupying oneself, it is occupying myself in pretending that I do not live, or at least that I do not live this thing or that, it is *putting* this apart from me. Therefore the manner in which things exist for themselves, their cosmic and subsistent being, is also a being *for* me; it is what they are when I leave off living them, when I pretend not to live them. This attitude of pretense (which is not to say that it is insincere or false, but only possessed of certain attributes of its own) in which I assume that I do not exist, and therefore that I do not see things as they are for me, and ask myself how they will then be, this attitude of virtual nonliving is the theoretic attitude.

Do you see how Fichte continues to be right, and theorizing, philosophizing are, properly speaking, not living—precisely because they are a form of living; *the theoretic life, the contemplative life?* Theory, and its extreme form, philosophy, are the attempt which life makes to transcend itself; it is to de-occupy oneself, to de-live, to cease to be interested in things. But this dis-interesting of oneself is not a passive process. On the contrary, it is a form of being interested: for instance, to be interested in something while cutting the intro-vital threads which link it to me—saving it from its immersion in my life, leaving it alone, in pure reference to its own self, seeking in it its very being. To be dis-interested is, then, to be interested in the inner self of each individual thing, to dower it with independence, with substance, one might almost say with personality—putting myself in a position to look at it from within its own point of view, not from mine. Contemplation is an attempt at transmigration. But that—to seek in a thing what it has of the absolute and to cut off all other partial interest of my own toward it, to cease to make use of it, to cease to wish that it serves me, but to serve it myself as an impartial eye so that it may see itself and find itself and be its very own self and for itself—this—this—is this not love? Then is contemplation, at root, an act of love, in that in loving, as differentiated from desiring, we are trying to live from within the other and we un-live ourselves for the sake of the other? The old and divine Plato, whom we deny, continues generously to encourage and cheer us in our denial, nourishing it, inspiring it and giving it flavor. Thus we find his idea about the erotic origin of knowledge in a form which is certainly new and different.

I have touched this point headlong, without purifying or analyzing any of the expressions employed, so that in this short and crude form you may glimpse where the traditional meaning of being will appear in this new philosophy; and incidentally, so that you may see what our path would have been if time had not been lacking. To the question, "What is philosophy?" we would have responded more from the root up than has ever been done up to now. Earlier we defined what philosophic doctrine is and we have progressed to the point where we met life—but now we have reached the point where we are really going to answer our question. Because the philosophic doctrine, as it is or can be in books, is only the abstraction of the authentic reality which is philosophy—is only its precipitate, its semi-moribund body. As the concrete, not the abstract, reality of the cigarette is what the smoker will go on rolling, so philosophy's self is what the philosopher makes it; philosophizing is a form of living. And this is what I would like to have investigated most carefully in your company. What is philosophizing as a form of living? We have seen vaguely that it is a de-living, a de-living for whatever there is, for the Universe—a making of oneself a place where the Universe is known and recognized. But it is useless, without long analysis, to try to give those words all their strict and fruitful meaning. Let me rest content with remembering that the Greeks, having no books which could properly be called philosophic, when asked by someone like Plato, "What is philosophy?"—thought of man, of the philosopher, of life. For them, philosophizing was first of all βίος δεωρητιχός, a theory of life. Strictly speaking, the first philosophic books which they had were books of the lives of the seven sages, biographies. All that which does not define philosophy as philosophizing, and philosophizing as an essential type of life, is neither sufficient nor basic.

But before concluding, I would like to carry the definition of "our life" a bit further. We have seen that it is finding oneself occupied with this or that, a form of doing or making. But all doing is a process of occupying oneself with something and for something. The occupation which is now an expression of ourselves is rooted in and directed toward what is commonly called an end. That "toward" in view of which I now do this, and in so doing live and have my being, I chose because among the possibilities which lay before me I believed that my life would be better if I occupied myself this way.

Each of these words is a category, and as such, an analysis of it would be inexhaustible. Out of them comes my actual life, the life I make, or what I actually do, the life that I decided upon: that is to say, before my life as I make it comes a process of deciding to make it—of deciding my life. Our life decides itself, anticipating itself. It is not given to us ready-made—not like the trajectory of the bullet to which I referred earlier. But it consists in deciding, because living is finding oneself in a world which, by no means hermetically sealed, is always offering opportunities. For me the vital world, every instant of it, is composed of being able to do this or that, not of having perforce to do this and only this.

On the other hand, these possibilities are not unlimited—if they were, they would not be concrete possibilities but a purely indeterminate collection, and in a world of absolute indetermination, in which everything is equally possible, it is not possible to decide on anything. In order that there may be decision there must be both space and limitation, relative determination. This I express in the category called "circumstances." Life always finds itself amid certain circumstances, in an arrangement surrounding it, filled with things and other people. One does not live in a world which is vague; constitutionally the vital world is circumstance, the things and the people about one, this world, here and now. And circumstance is something determined, closed, but at the same time open and with internal latitude, with space or emptiness in which to move about and to make one's decisions; circumstance is a riverbed which life goes on cutting within a valley from which it cannot escape. To live is to live here, now; the here and the now are specific, not to be exchanged for others, but they are ample.

All life is a constant process of deciding between various possibilities. *Astra inclinant, non trahunt*—the stars impel, but they do not compel. Life is at the same time freedom and fatality; it is being free within a given destiny. This fate offers us a determined and inexorable repertory of possibilities, that is to say, it offers us different destinies. We accept the fatality and within it we decide on a destiny. Life is destiny.

I hope that no one of you will think it necessary to warn me that determinism denies liberty. I would answer that I am sorry both for determinism and for him. To put the best face on determinism, it is, or rather it was, a theory about the reality of the Universe. Although it was certain, it was no more than a theory, an interpretation, a consciously problematical thesis which had to be proven. Therefore, even though I were a determinist, I could not let that theory exercise retroactive effects on the primary and indubitable reality which we are now describing.

However deterministic the determinist may be, his living as such is relatively undetermined, and at one specific moment he made his decision between determinism and indeterminism. Thus to present that question here would be not to know what determinism is, or what is the analysis of primordial reality prior to every theory.

And do not overlook the fact that when I say life is at one and the same time fate and freedom, a possibility that though limited is still a possibility and therefore open—do not fail to note what I am saying. I myself cannot reason about it, that is to say, prove it, nor do I have to reason it out—more than that, I consciously flee from all reasoning and limit myself purely to expressing myself in concepts, to describing the basic reality which I have before me and which is assumed in every theory in all reasoning and in every proof. It was in order to forestall sad observations like that one, which I prefer not to assume in you, that I made that overly elementary observation in the beginning.

And now, parenthetically, may I note that the determinist theory as such has no existence today either in philosophy or in physics. Solid support for that statement is to be found in a sentence by one of the best modern physicists, the successor of Einstein, Hermann Weyl; in a book on the logic of physics which was published a few years ago he said, "From all the aforesaid one can judge how far is physics today—composed half of laws and half of statistics—from a position in which it could venture forth to undertake the defense of determinism." One of the mechanisms of the mental hermetism to which he alludes is that when we hear something and a very elemental objection occurs to us, we seldom think that this may also have occurred to the one who is speaking or writing, and that the truth may be that we have not understood what he has been saying. If we fail to think this, we will remain on a level lower than the person we are listening to, or the book we are reading.

So life is that paradoxical reality which consists in deciding what we are going to do, therefore in being what we not yet are, in starting to be the future. Contrary to the ways of cosmic being, the living being begins by being the creature over there, the one that comes afterwards.

This would be impossible if time were originally cosmic time. Cosmic time is only the present, because the future has not yet come, and the past no longer is. How, then, can past and future continue to be part of time? This is what makes the concept of time so difficult that it troubles philosophers.

"Our life" is set and anchored in the immediate present. But what is my life at this moment? It is not the process of saying what I am saying; what I am living this moment is not a matter of moving the lips; that is mechanical, outside my life, it pertains to the cosmic being. On the contrary, my life is the process of thinking what I am going to say; at this moment I am anticipating, I am projecting myself into the future. But in order to say this I make use of certain means—of words—and that gives me a portion of my past. My future, then, makes me discover my past in order to realize that future. The past is now real because I am re-living it, and it is when I find in the past the means of realizing my future that I discover my present. And all this happens in an instant; moment by moment life swells out into the three dimensions of the true interior time. The future tosses me back toward the past; the past toward the present, and from here I go again toward the future which throws me back to the past, and the past to another present, in a constant rotation.

We are anchored in the cosmic present, which is like the ground which our feet press while body and head reach toward the future. Nicolas of Cusa was right when he said, at the dawn of the Renaissance, *Ita nunc sive praesens complicat tempus.* The now, the present, includes all time; now, before, and after.

We live in the present, at the actual point of it, but it does not exist primarily for us; out of it, as out of the earth, we live the immediate future.

Observe that of all the points of the earth the only one which we cannot directly perceive is that which lies beneath our feet.

Before we see what surrounds us we are originally a bundle of appetites, desires, and illusions. We come into the world dowered with a system of preferences and prejudices, more or less like those of our neighbors, which each of us carries within himself like a battery of sympathies and repulsions, ready to shoot them off in favor of this or against that. The heart, that tireless machine of preferring and disdaining, is the support of our personality.

Do not, then, say that the first thing is the impression. Nothing is more important in remaking the idea of what man is than to correct the traditional perspective according to which we are supposed to want a thing for the reason that we have seen it earlier. That may seem obvious, yet it is mostly an error. He who desires material riches did not wait to want them until he saw the gold; he would seek it wherever it could be found, giving his full attention to the business side that every situation holds within itself. The artist, on the other hand, the man of esthetic preferences, will go through those same situations utterly blind to their economic side and will seek whatever there is in them of grace and beauty.

Hence the traditional belief must be turned upside down. We do not desire a thing because we have first seen it; on the contrary, we go seeking it throughout the world because in our heart of hearts we would prefer that kind of thing. Of all the sounds which are continually assaulting us and which we could hear if we tried, we hear only those to which we give our attention; that is to say, those which we favor with a special ear. And as we cannot attend to one thing without subtracting attention from another, what we do when we hear one sound that interests us is to dis-hear all the others. All seeing is a process of looking at, all hearing is in the last analysis a listening-to, all living is an incessant, original preferring and disdaining.

Nowhere, perhaps, is this clearer than in the delicate area of our love affairs. In the slumbering depth of the feminine soul, woman, when truly a woman, is always the sleeping beauty, waiting amid life's forest to be awakened by the kiss of the prince. In the depth of her soul she bears, unknowing, the preformed image of a man—not an individual image of an individual man, but a generic type of masculine perfection. And, always asleep, she moves like a sleepwalker among the men she meets, contrasting their physical and moral figures with that of her pre-existent and preferred model.

This explains two events which occur in every authentic love affair. One is the suddenness of falling in love: the woman, and the same is true of the man, finds herself suddenly, without process or transition, aflame with love. This would be inexplicable if the casual contact with this particular man had not been preceded by a secret and tacit surrender of her being to that model of a man which she has always carried within herself. The other fact is the way in which the woman, on finding herself deeply in love, not only feels that her love will be eternal, and for all future time, but seems to herself to have loved this man forever, out of the mysterious depths of the past, from time beyond measure and untold epochs of previous existence.

This eternal, and as it were, innate devotion clearly does not stem from the individual who has just appeared upon her horizon, but from that interior ideal of a man which throbbed like a promise in the depth of her quiet soul and who now, in this real being, has found realization and fulfillment.

In this extreme measure and up to such a point is human living a constant anticipation, a pre-forming of the future. We are always very perspicacious with regard to those things in which the qualities that we prefer are realized; on the other hand, we are blind to those which, though of equal or even superior perfections, belong to a type of thing that is foreign to our innate sensibility. The future comes first: incessantly we press it with eager attention so that its favorable juices may drip into our hands; and only in terms of what we demand of it, what we hope of it, do we turn our eyes toward the present and the past in order to find within them the means with which to satisfy our desires. The future is always the leader, the *Dux:* the present and the past are always aides-de-camp and soldiers. We live moving forward into our future, supported by the present, with the past, always faithful, off to the edge, a little sad, a little frail, as the moon, lighting a path through the night, goes with us step by step, shedding its pale friendship on our shoulders.

Psychologically, then, the decisive thing is not the sum of what we have been, but of what we yearn to be: the appetite, the desire, the illusion, the ambition. Whether we like it or not, our life is in its very essence futurism. Man goes being carried *du bout du nez* by his illusion—a baroque and picturesque image which is justified because the end of man's nose is, in fact, what usually goes ahead; it is the part of us which goes into the spatial "over there," the thing that anticipates and precedes us.

The process of deciding on this or that is a portion of our lives which has about it a certain breath of freedom. We are constantly deciding our future being, and to realize it we must count on the past and make use of the present as it operates on the actuality, and all of this within the "now"; because that future is not just any future, but the possible "now," and that past is not the past of someone who lived a hundred years ago, but the past up to now. Do you see? "Now" is our time, our world, our life. This flows along calm or tumultuous, a river or a torrent, through the landscape of actuality, of that unique actuality, world, and time to which we give a number, as of years after Jesus Christ. In it we go encrusted; it marks out for us an entire repertory of possibilities, of conditions, dangers, means and facilities. With its features it limits the freedom of decision which motivates our life, and in the face of that freedom it becomes our destiny.

To say that our times form our destiny is not merely a phrase. The present, in which the past—the individual and the historic past—is summarized and condensed, is that portion of fate which intervenes in our life; in this sense life always carries a fatal dimension and some hint of having fallen into a trap. Except that this trap does not strangle us, but leaves to life a margin of decision and always permits us, out of the imposed situation, to achieve an elegant solution and to forge for ourselves a beautiful life. Hence, because life is part fate, and part the freedom we need to make decisions for ourselves, there is at its very root the stuff of art; nothing symbolizes this better than the position of the poet who bases his lyric freedom on the exigencies of rhyme and rhythm. All art implies the acceptance of a shackle, of a destiny; as Nietzsche said, "The artist is he who dances in chains." The destiny which is the present is not a misfortune but a delight, the delight that the chisel feels when it encounters the resistance of the marble.

Imagine for a moment that each one of us takes only a little more care for each hour of his days, that he demands in it a little more of elegance and intensity; then, multiplying all these minute pressures toward the perfecting and deepening of each life by all the others, calculate for yourselves the gigantic enrichment, the fabulous ennobling which this process would create for human society.

This would be living at the top of one's form; instead of drifting through hours that pass like rudderless ships, we would find them moving before us, each with its new imminence and importance.

And do not say that fate does not allow us to improve our lives, for the beauty of life does not lie in the fact that destiny is or is not favorable to us, but in the grace with which we accept the challenge and out of its fatal material fashion a noble figure.

But let us gather into one clear formula our entire analysis of what, in its fundamental essence, our life is. These perceptions of fundamental facts flee one's comprehension like shy birds— and it helps to shut them into a cage fashioned from an expressive name which lets us see between the wires the idea made prisoner.

We have seen that living consists in the process of deciding what we are going to be. Heidegger says very delicately, "then life is concern"—*Sorge*—what the Latins call *cura,* from whence comes cure, procure, curiosity, and so on. In ancient Spanish the word "cuidar" (to care for, to take care) had precisely the meaning which we now find in such terms as curator, procurator, curate of souls. But I prefer to express a similar, although not identical, idea with a word which seems to me more exact: I say that life is preoccupation, and not only in moments which are difficult, but all the time; in essence it is no more than this, to be preoccupied. Every moment of the day we are having to decide what we are going to do the next moment, what it is that will occupy our lives. This is occupying ourselves in anticipation, pre-occupying ourselves.

But perhaps someone, reluctant to surrender a vigilant habit of mind, objects thus—"Sir, this is a play on words. I admit that life consists in deciding moment by moment what we are going to do, but the word preoccupation has, in the common phrase, a sense that always suggests an anxious, a difficult moment; to be preoccupied with something is to make a very serious question of it. But when we decided to come here, to spend this space of time in this fashion, there is no use pretending that we made a great question out of it. On the contrary, as you said, most of life flows by without our paying it undue attention. Why, then, use a word which is so grave, so full of pathos, if it does not coincide with what it is supposed to describe? We are no longer, fortunately, under the reign of romanticism, which fed on exaggeration and impropriety. We demand that one speak with simplicity, clarity and exactness, in words as fresh and disinfected as a surgeon's instruments."

I do not know why I assume that any one of you would make such an objection. It is, in fact, a skillful objection, and for one who is by vocation an intellectual—I pretend to nothing else, and this I am with passion—to such a one, skillful objections are the most agreeable things in the world; as an intellectual I have come into this world for no other reason but to make and to receive objections. Thus I receive them with delight, I not only receive them but I esteem them, not only do I esteem them but I solicit them. Always I know how to extract from them an excellent profit. If we go on tossing them back and forth they allot us the pleasure of victory and we can make the triumphant gesture of the good bowman who has put an arrow into the bull's-eye. If, on the contrary, the objection defeats us and even convinces us, what better fortune? It is the voluptuous pleasure of the convalescent, the awakening from a nightmare; we have given birth to a new truth and, reflecting this newborn light, the pupil widens. Therefore I accept the objection: cleanness, clarity, exactness, are the divinities to whom I, too, dedicate a trembling worship.

But it is also clear that as I have been attacked, though the attack be imaginary, I must defend myself with weapons that are effective; if I am sure that they are clean, I am not so sure that they may not also include a certain roughness.

Hypothetically, then, we are left with the assumption that some of you have come here without preoccupying yourself with what you did, without questioning it. Nothing happens more frequently, and if certain suspicions of the psychologist did not dissuade us from leaning on appearances, we would have to believe that the normal form of life is lack of preoccupation. But then, if you did not come here for a special reason of your own, because of something which preoccupied you, why did you come? The reply is inevitable—because others came.

Here is the whole secret of failure to be preoccupied. When we believe ourselves not to be preoccupied with life, we let that life float rudderless, like a buoy without anchor chains, coming and going as it is pushed by social currents. And this is what makes man common and woman mediocre, that is to say, what puts them in with the vast majority of human beings. For them, to live is to surrender to the unanimous, to let customs, prejudices, habits, topics, be installed within them, give them life, and take on the task of making them live. They are weak animals which, on sensing the weight of their own lives at a moment either dolorous or delightful, feel themselves apprehensive, and then eager to free their shoulders from the very weight which is their being and throw it on the collective group: that is to say, they are preoccupied with becoming un-preoccupied. Under their apparent indifference throbs a secret fear of having to solve for themselves the problems posed by their acts and emotions—a humble desire to be like everybody else, to renounce the responsibility of their own destiny, and dissolve it amid the multitude. This is the eternal ideal of the weak, whose preoccupation it is to do what everyone else is doing.

And if we seek an image akin to that of the eye of Horus, let us remember the rite of Egyptian burials, of that people who believed that on the other side of the grave man was summoned before a court. In that tribunal his life was judged: the first and supreme act of justice was to find the weight of his heart. In order to avoid this weighing, to deceive those powers of life and afterlife, the Egyptian had the burial squad replace the heart of flesh and blood with one made out of bronze or of black stone; he was trying to replace his life. This is what the un-preoccupied try to do—to substitute for their own being another one. This is what obsesses them. Since there is no way to escape the essential condition of living, and as living is reality, the best and most discreet course is to emphasize it, to underline it with irony; this was the elegant gesture of the fairy queen, Titania, who, in Shakespeare's enchanted forest, caressed the head of a donkey.

In the way of priests everywhere, Japanese priests curse all that is earthly, and in describing the restless futility of our world, they call it a "world of mist." In one of their poets, Isa, there appears a simple *"hai-kai"* which has stayed in my mind, and this is what it says, "A world of mist is no more than a world of mist . . . and yet . . ." And yet . . . let us accept that world of mist as the material out of which to make a life that is more complete.

José Ortega y Gasset's Major Writings

(arranged chronologically)

Obras Completas, 9 vols. Madrid: Revista de Occidente, 1962. N.B. There is some confusion on editions and dates on the *Obras Completas.* This entry does indicate, however, the most up-to-date statement on them.

Meditaciones del Quijote. Madrid: Clasica española, 1914.
  Meditations on Quixote. Tr. D. Marín. New York: Norton, 1961.
España invertebrada. Madrid: Calpe, 1922.
  Invertebrate Spain. Tr. M. Adams. New York: Norton, 1937.
El tema de nuestro tiempo. Madrid: Calpe, 1923.
  The Modern Theme. Tr. J. Cleugh. New York: Norton, 1933.
La Deshumanización del arte. Madrid: Revista de Occidente, 1925.
  The Dehumanization of Art and Notes on the Novel. Tr. H. Weyl. Princeton: Princeton University Press, 1948.
  The Dehumanization of Art and Other Writings on Art and Culture. New York: Doubleday, 1956.
La Rebelión de las masas. Madrid: Revista de Occidente, 1929.
  Revolt of the Masses. Authorized translation. New York: Norton, 1932.
Misión de la universidad. Madrid: Revista de Occidente, 1930.
  Mission of the University. Tr. H. L. Nostrand. Princeton: Princeton University Press, 1944.
En Torno a Galileo. Madrid: Revista de Occidente, 1933.
  Man and Crisis. Tr. M. Adams. New York: Norton, 1958.
Meditación de la técnica. Madrid: Revista de Occidente, 1933.
Estudios sobre el amor. Buenos Aires: Espasa-Calpe, 1939.
  On Love: Aspects of a Single Theme. Tr. T. Talbot. New York: Norton, 1957.
Del imperio romano. Madrid: Revista de Occidente, 1941.
  Concord and Liberty. Tr. H. Weyl. New York: Norton, 1946.
Tríptico: Mirabeau, o el politico; Kant; Goethe desde dentro. Buenos Aires: Espasa-Calpe, 1941.

Historia como sistema. Madrid: Revista de Occidente, 1941.
  History as a System. Tr. H. Weyl, Clark and Atkinson. New
    York: Norton, 1961.
El hombre y la gente. Madrid: Revista de Occidente, 1957.
  Man and People. Tr. W. Trask. New York: Norton, 1959.
¿Que es filosofiá? Madrid: Revista de Occidente, 1957.
  What is Philosophy? Tr. M. Adams. New York: Norton, 1964.
Le idea de principio en Leibniz y la evolución de la teoría deductiva.
  Buenos Aires: Emecé, 1958.
Origen y epílogo de la filosofía. Madrid: Revista de Occidente, 1962.
  The Origin of Philosophy. Tr. T. Talbot. New York: Norton,
    1967.

SELECTED STUDIES ABOUT ORTEGA Y GASSET
(arranged alphabetically)

Aranguren, José Luis. *La ética de Ortega.* Madrid: Taurus, 1959.

Borel, Jean Paul. *Raison et vie chez Ortega y Gasset.* Neuchâtel:
  Chaux de Fonds, 1959.

Cascalès, Charles. *L'Humanisme d'Ortega y Gasset.* Paris: Presses
  Universitaires, 1957.

Ceplecha, Christian. *The Historical Thought of José Ortega y Gasset.*
  Washington: Catholic University Press, 1958.

Cobián y Macchiavello, Alfonso. *La ontología de Ortega y Gasset.*
  Lima: Publicaciones del Instituto Riva-Agüero, 1960.

Diaz de Cerio Ruiz, Franco. *José Ortega y Gasset y la conquista de
  la conciencia historica.* Barcelona: J. Flors, 1961.

Ferrater-Mora, José. *Ortega y Gasset: An Outline of His Philosophy.*
  New Haven: Yale University Press, 1957; rev. ed. 1963.

Granell Muñiz, Manuel. *Ortega y su filosofía.* Madrid: Revista de
  Occidente, 1960.

Guy, Alain. *Ortega y Gasset, critique d'Aristote.* Paris: Presses Universitaires, 1963.

Mariás Aquilera, Julian. *Ortega.* Vol. I: *Circumstancia y vocación.*
  Madrid: Revista de Occidente, 1960.

Villaseñor, José Sanchez. *Ortega y Gasset, Existentialist.* Tr. J. Small.
  Chicago: Regnery, 1949.

Nicholas Abbagnano (1901–)

Abbagnano was born at Salerno on July 15, 1901. His father, Ulysses, was a civil lawyer who had a solid reputation as a just and diligent civic administrator. Abbagnano attended the primary and secondary schools in his hometown as well as its classical *liceo*. He then went to the University of Naples where he studied philosophy under Antonio Aliotta whose preferences were not especially sympathetic to the neo-Hegelianism then dominating the Italian philosophical scene. Aliotta worked within the Empiricist tradition and his "experimentalism" was responsible for subsequent developments in Italian philosophy such as the philosophy of science, realism, and pragmatism, all of which were regarded by the reigning idealism as philosophical abortions.

Abbagnano shared his teacher's empirical bent and sensitivity to the problems arising from contemporary science. The anti-idealism and the interest in science as a seedbed for philosophical inquiry have persisted as characteristics of his mature work. He received his degree in philosophy from Naples in 1922 with a dissertation that argued the case for the irrational sources of thought, a theme that recurs in Nietzsche.

Abbagnano won the competitive exams for the teaching of philosophy and history at the *liceo* level. From 1924 to 1936 he taught at that level in the cities of Salerno, Catania, and Naples. During these years he married and became the father of two daughters. His wife, however, became ill and died not too many years afterward. At the age of twenty-four, he completed the *libera docenza* in philosophy which enabled him to give lectures at the University of Naples. In 1936 he successfully competed for a university chair and has been professor of the history of philosophy at the University of Turin from then on. Between the years 1939 and 1956, moreover, he was professor of education at the same university.

During the years following 1923, Abbagnano studied the writings of Kierkegaard, Husserl, Jaspers, and Heidegger. But his interests were not confined to either modern or contemporary philosophy. He was profoundly interested and conversant with the writings of the Greek and medieval philosophers and produced monographs on Aristotle's conception of time and on William of Ockham. But it is the echoes of Plato and Kant that resound throughout his work, especially the Plato of the "critical dialogues" as the *Sophist,* for example.

By 1939 Abbagnano had worked out an original set of formulations in "existential analysis" and published his *Struttura dell'esistenza.* He succeeded in kindling the fires of debate among his opponents in the neo-Hegelian camp to the extent that in 1942 and 1943 the controversy was carried in the pages of *Gazetta del popolo,* a Turinese daily, and in those of *Primato,* an important Roman journal edited by the novelist Alberto Moravia.

Abbagnano was an anti-fascist. During the Second World War after the Italian surrender in 1943, he encouraged his former students and friends who were members of partisan groups and engaged in the resistance against the fascists and the German military units stationed in Italy. Not too many years after the war, he remarried. His wife, an American who had been born in Brooklyn but had spent most of her life in Europe, ran a publishing house in Turin until her death in July 1970.

Abbagnano has been to the United States under a State Department grant for "Leaders and Specialists" in order to lecture and to hold seminars in several of the large universities. He is a fellow of the Turinese Academy of Sciences and the Academy of the Lynxes, a member of the Institut International de Philosophie, and co-editor with Norberto Bobbio of the *Rivista di filosofia.*

Existentialism Is a Positive Philosophy[1]

Translated by Nino Langiulli

1. Philosophy as Problem.

Does existentialism have a character of its own with respect to traditional philosophy? And does this character justify the interest it has provoked even outside philosophical circles, and its claim to permeate literature, art, and contemporary culture in general?

Let us begin to answer this question by considering the attitude of existentialism with respect to the problem of philosophy. There has always been a problem of philosophy. This discipline could never simply *presuppose* its nature, its method and its objects, but has always had to begin with a definition of itself. Not always—in fact, rather rarely—has it succeeded in justifying its problem. This problem of *what philosophy is* has appeared more often as a provisional state of uncertainty and doubt pertinent to the very beginnings of the discipline, a state that its formation and subsequent developments should have eliminated and destroyed. Philosophy has always claimed to explain and to justify all the aspects of reality: man, the world, and God; but quite often it has forgotten or neglected to explain and justify precisely that with which it is most closely concerned—its own problem, and therefore its starting points, its progress and its conclusions, which are accompanied by the uncertainty, the instability and the doubt which repeatedly pose as a problem each of its most certain conclusions.

The fact that philosophy ought to wrestle ceaselessly for its life, that it ought to begin by giving itself a form and a feature and then fight to defend and maintain them—should this fact, or better, this destiny, rightly fall outside of philosophy, or

[1] Discourse given at the beginning of the academic year 1947–48 at the University of Turin and published as the second essay in *Esistenzialismo Positivo*.

should philosophy make of it its very heart and soul? Existentialism is born from this alternative, and on this very point marks a definitive break with philosophic naïveté. Existentialism finds those positions and systems of philosophy characterized by ignorance of this alternative impossible. When, for example, Hegel affirms the intrinsic, total and necessary identity of the real and the rational, he takes away the foundation of his own philosophy; for, if the real were identical with the rational, the problem of their identity could not arise and the philosophy that poses that problem and defends it has neither a purpose nor a significance. When, on the other hand, skepticism affirms the *equivalence* of all views or conceptions of the world, it undercuts any possible basis for its argument; for if there were equivalence, there would be no sense in demonstrating it. In a totality of equivalent prospects, each choice is justified beforehand, and the problem from which skepticism originates results in being devoid of meaning. One must ask of each philosophy whether the concept of reality that it proposes makes possible the problem from which that philosophy arises. If the concept does not make it possible, the implicit result is always the total and irremedial vacuity of the philosophy. Existentialism tries to save itself from this void. It demands that philosophy should ultimately reach a justification of its own problem and demonstrate its intrinsic possibility. This is, so to speak, the fundamental character of existentialism.

2. The Problematic Character of Philosophy.

The nature and method of existentialism derive from this character. It is evident that the first problem of such a philosophy is the one concerned with the problematic form of philosophy itself. Why is philosophy always a problem for itself? This question, in its apparent simplicity and abstractness, is rich in consequences and overtones that are not easy to perceive at first. It is at the very posing of the question, with its internal significance, that our consideration must pause. One quickly sees, then, that it is as much an answer as a question, and that it can be taken, without any change, as the very definition of philosophy. "Why is philosophy always a problem to itself?" *can* mean that philosophy *is* essentially its own problem. In this case, its problematic form is neither apparent nor provisional but substantial. Let us consider the implications of this acknowledgment. *A problem* is, in general, a state of *indetermination* wherein different contrasting possibilities are weighed. The *solution* of a problem is, in general, the choice of that possibility that justifies (or renders possible) the problem itself. These clarifications become obvious if one abandons the deeply rooted prejudice that the solution of a problem is its elimination. Actually a resolved problem is a problem justified as a problem and grounded and authenticized, therefore, by the solution itself. Insoluble problems (structurally insoluble) are not problems but puzzles, which are the delight and torment of the dilettantes of any discipline whatever. In science, for example, a resolved problem continually presents itself as a problem in the course of the investigation; it reproduces itself and lives in all its possible ramifications. In mathematics a problem is a true problem when it has been solved, that is, when its solution can be used as a solution for all the other problems to which it is applicable in and out of mathematics. These and other possible observations make clear that the solution of a problem is nothing more than the demonstration of its possibility, and that the solution, rather than eliminating, destroying, or removing the problem, gives it a foundation and justifies its authenticity.

From this viewpoint, the problematic form of philosophy does not imply that it must leave in abeyance the solution of its problem or that it must keep itself continually suspended between its possible solutions, but only that the solution, whatever it may be, should justify the possibility of the problem. This is enough to clarify, in a precise way, the subject, the object and the method of philosophy.

3. Philosophy as Existence.

It is immediately evident that, through its problematic nature, philosophy is not and cannot be a *divine knowledge* of the world. It is not, therefore, the firm, definitive and total possession of all possible knowledge; it is not even the *possession* of any knowledge whatsoever. It is, rather, the *problem* of knowledge—a problem which is continuously reborn from its own solutions. If the clarifications advanced on the nature of philosophy are accepted, every divinizing philosophy, that is, every philosophy that considers itself the activity of a pure intellect, an absolute reason, or of an intellectual intuition, must be rejected as illusory. Every philosophy of that kind makes the problem of philosophy impossible, and deprives of any significance the very inquiry on which it is founded. But with these negations one is not precipitated, as might be feared, into the abyss of irrationalism. It can still be said (though this terminology is not strictly indispensable, but only convenient and obvious) that philosophy is reason or thought, provided that one adds it is *problematic* reason or thought. Problematicity is contrasted here with the *necessity* that belongs to absolute or divinizing reason. A necessary knowledge is that which is realized as the immutable links of universal determinations, so that it can be understood and mastered by a glance that embraces the absolute totality. A knowledge so constructed excludes, by the necessity of its links, every problem from within and does not constitute a problem in its entirety. A problematic knowledge, instead, excludes necessity: it does include indetermination, doubt, decision and choice, and has *possibility* as its norm and supreme category.

A problematic knowledge is a *possible* knowledge, and this implies the possibility of nonknowledge. It is, therefore, always accompanied by *doubt*, which is precisely the recognition of the negative possibility implicit in all positive knowledge: the possibility of error, of failure and loss of possible knowledge. Necessary knowledge defines the intellectual life of an infinite being. Problematic knowledge defines the intellectual life of a finite being. Finitude here has no other meaning than *problematicity:* it but expresses the constitutive problematic character of a knowledge which is always the possibility of nonknowledge.

Man is the only thinking finite being. Problematic knowledge constitutes, therefore, the condition and the mode of man's being. If the mode of man's being is called *existence*, then problematic knowledge defines and expresses existence. We detect at this point that feature from which existentialism gets its name: the identity between existence and philosophy. This is certainly not a novelty. What else has philosophy ever been if not man's ceaseless attempt to bring a certain clarity to the being that is proper to him? But, if this attempt has always been philosophy, it has not always been the explicit *problem* of philosophy. And when it has not been the explicit problem, there has also been lacking the fundamental explanation about man: that of man's being a problem to himself. This is precisely the ultimate meaning of the recognition that philosophy is problematic knowledge that defines and expresses the condition or the mode of being of a finite being. Philosophy is immediately connected to the very constitution of man, which appears invested and illuminated by its own acknowledged problematic nature. There immediately springs from the very preliminary clarification of the nature of philosophy, the preliminary clarification regarding the nature of man. This nature is not an immobile state, nor an objective reality, nor a universal subjectivity. It is just the basic transcendental problematicity of his problems.

Philosophy, considered initially in its restricted sense and in its technical manifestations, at this point reveals itself as intimately and essentially connected with the mode of man's being —with existence. At its origin there is no gratuitous and vain *curiosity* to know, but a vital movement through which man, in the instability of his problematic nature, seeks the being which is proper to him and strives to attain it and possess it in some way. The seriousness and the value of the philosophical quest are thus guaranteed in a most resolute way. This quest is not a luxury that may be omitted or held superfluous; it is the intrinsic constitution of existence as such. On the other hand, the *technical elaboration* of philosophy (which is substantially the construction of a *language* that expresses in the most rigorous and precise form possible, the authentic philosophizing that existence is) also acquires a new significance. The intolerance and dissatisfaction generated at times by the so-called "abstruseness" of the philosophic technique are made impossible by the explicit recognition that man's experiences and fundamental attitudes find their expression and their logico-linguistic arrangement in that technique. The work of philosophers is not enclosed in their specialization, but interests all men because it finds its root in a common human condition. In virtue of this recognition, existentialism, which also avails itself of a rigorous and difficult technique, tends to surpass the narrow research of philosophers and to invest with its spirit the most varied expressions of contemporary culture.

4. Philosophy Is Not Contemplation.

The recognition of the problematic nature of philosophy quickly leads to the determination of its *subject:* this subject is man. Does it also lead to the circumscription and determination of its *object?* A preliminary question presents itself on this point: Does philosophy have, strictly speaking, an object? By object one must understand that which stands against or is in contrast to the activity that investigates it, hence, that which gives validity or truth to every type or form of knowledge. The preceding question can, therefore, take this form: Is philosophy reducible to knowledge? And in this form the question can have a negative or an affirmative answer, depending on whether it is considered possible or impossible for man to be or to become the disinterested spectator of himself.

The ideal of a disinterested self-knowledge and, therefore, of philosophy as a rigorous science of objective meanings, characterizes some currents of contemporary philosophy, above all, phenomenology. However presented or defended, this ideal constitutes, nevertheless, a grave deviation from the problematic structure of philosophy. Granted that man can become the disinterested spectator of his own I [person] and that he can contemplate his own life without being involved with it, it must be quickly recognized that we deal precisely with a *possibility,* constitutive of the problematic condition of man, which is actualized by means of a decision and a choice. Now this very problematic constitution, the possibilities that form it and the choice and decision that it makes possible, fall completely outside of a philosophy understood as science or knowledge, because these are not attitudes or experiences reducible to objective meanings. The ideal of philosophy as objective science, even as it is represented in the most modern and critical forms of phenomenology, cuts itself off from its primary moment—*the problem*—of this philosophy itself. It is, therefore, a manifestation of philosophical naïveté and a kind of philosophizing that does not achieve a critical hold on itself.

Philosophy cannot base itself on the illusion of making man a disinterested spectator of himself. Every clarification that man succeeds in attaining about himself and even that which he only deludes himself into attaining, goes immediately into forming his existence, which is consequently modified. This means that philosophy does not have an object, in the proper sense of the term; but only a *task*, and that this task consists in committing man to that form or that mode of being which he comes to consider his own. This does not imply, on the other hand, that philosophy is *practical* rather than *theoretical*, or that it concerns *action* more than *speculation*. Theory and practice, action and speculation are modes of conventional classification and are useless for philosophy, which is always concerned with man in his totality, in the problematic being proper to him, and which wholly commits him to the form or the attitude that it allows him to choose.

5. Problematicity and Problems.

To deny that philosophy is disinterested knowledge does not mean that disinterested knowledge is not possible for man. It only means that, if it is possible, it is not philosophy. It exists, certainly; therefore it is possible. But it is natural science.

The position which is at the basis of science is that man is only one of the possible objects of scientific consideration, without any title or privilege with respect to others. Man is subjected by science to the same procedures of observation and measurement to which other objects, whatever they may be, are subjected, and he has no claim to any special treatment. According to physics, for example, he is a body subject to the same laws that govern other natural bodies; for biology he is a living organism, subject, like all the others, to the requirements and the laws of organic life; even for psychology he is a center of psychophysical actions and reactions similar to those of all other animals, only more complicated. The essential characteristic of every scientific consideration and problem is that man figures as one of the possible *objects* or possible *terms*. The foundation of this characteristic is that science is, in general, *the study of the world* and, therefore, man, for science, counts only as a part or an element of the world. Disinterested knowledge, which is proper to science, is conditioned, therefore, by an attitude that is one possibility of existence: the position in which man considers himself as part of a totality that encompasses him.

We can ask to what extent this attitude is connected with human existence; the question is important because on it rests the answer to the so frequently debated question concerning the *human value* of science. The answer must be deduced from the clarifications already made about man's problematic constitution. Man exists as the very problematic nature of his problems. But these problems, whatever they may be, include him immediately as one of their terms. Every problem has, so to speak, a double aspect. It is, in the first place, a particular mode of being of man, a singular attitude of existence. In the second place it is an indeterminate or inconclusive relation between a number of possible terms. In the first sense the problem is man himself in one of his attitudes; in the second it includes man as one of its possible terms. Let us consider, for example, any scientific problem. It is, in the first place, the very life of the scientist who dedicates himself to it and makes it his dominant interest; in the second place, it is a relation of objective terms through which it reduces or can reduce the scientist himself and every other man to a physicochemical body, or an organism. This twofold dimension of a problem can be expressed simply by distinguishing the problematic character from the problem. And because the problematic character makes the problem possible, it alone is the transcendental element or, if you will, the *transcendental possibility* of every possible problem.

These clarifications show that man does not have a problematic nature unless the problems, in the very act of rooting themselves in this problematic nature, include him as one of their possible terms. This implies that scientific, like *ordinary* knowledge, which prepares and stimulates scientific research, is essentially connected to existence and is a fundamental aspect of it. The claim that man can do without science is chimerical and expresses only an adherence to a more crude and less effective form of scientific knowledge. It also implies that man cannot recognize himself in his original nature, with respect to all the other beings or things of the world, without recognizing himself in the same act as a being or thing of the world. The relationship with the world is as essential to man as his relationship with himself. The *exteriority* in which he lives forms him, no less than his *interiority* or consciousness.

It has already been said that man is a finite being precisely in virtue of his problematic constitution. Now an aspect of his finitude is clearly seen: that by which he is part and not the whole, and as a part, depends on the whole that includes him. This dependence is real even if it is not explicitly recognized. It is manifested in the corporeity of man and in the needs that bind him to the world of which he is a part. It is evident that philosophy cannot and should not close its eyes to this aspect of man's situation. It cannot insist on the pure interiority of man to himself, on his spirituality, without recognizing at the same time his exteriority and corporeity, which make him a being among other beings and, in some measure, a thing among things. The illusion of exalting man leads to his diminution; it reduces him to only one aspect of his structure, forgetting the other, without which he cannot exist.

6. Reality as Possibility.

We can review the results gleaned from the foregoing considerations in the following way: (1) The problematic form of philosophy is neither apparent nor provisional, but substantial. (2) Philosophy is, therefore, a problematic knowledge that defines and expresses the mode of being of a finite reality. This finite reality is man and his mode of being is existence. (3) Philosophy cannot be constituted as a disinterested self-contemplation of man for it is neither [absolute] knowledge nor science. (4) Knowledge and science grow together with philosophy inasmuch as the constitutive problematic character of man includes man himself among the terms of its problems. These points represent both exclusions and negations of both ancient and recent philosophic doctrines. The problematic substance of philosophy excludes every *divinizing philosophy*, that is, every philosophy that presents itself as the emanation or the expression of an absolute Spirit or Reason. The existential character of philosophy rejects the possibility that it could be organized as knowledge or science in the sense of the physicomathematical disciplines, and therefore it rejects, on the one hand, *positivism*, and on the other, *phenomenology*, which also accepts the ideal of philosophy as a logico-contemplative discipline. The unity which his relation to himself and his relation to the world achieve in the problematic nature of man excludes any personalism (*spiritualismo*)[2] that hinges exclusively on the interiority or consciousness of man.

These determinations and rejections are a step toward a positive direction for existential philosophy. A further step can be made by considering that the philosophy of existence decisively breaks the frame of necessity within which every type of dogmatic philosophy moves. The perspective that it recognizes, and within which it moves, is that of *possibilities*. The problematic nature recognized as belonging to philosophy and man, who is its unique theme, has worked this change. From the viewpoint of problematic reason, no necessitating *nature*, no immutable *datum*, no determining *law* can be perceived in man nor in any other reality that enters into a relationship with him. Only possibilities can be perceived or recognized, always individuated and singular—possibilities before which man is ceaselessly called upon to decide and to choose. Neither within nor outside himself can man ever discover anything more stable, more durable, more resolute than possibility. One possibility for him is himself, that is, his own person, which is the possible unity of his interior attitudes. Other men are possibilities for him: possibilities of concrete relations of work, of loyalty, of friendship and of love. The things of the world are possibilities for him, and precisely possibilities of utilization. So too are works of art which [however] become pieces of canvas or stone, that is, raw matter, if [a] man does not have the taste to feel and appreciate them. So

[2] The term *spiritualismo*, which is here translated by "personalism," refers to a kind of doctrine that practices philosophy as analysis of consciousness (e.g. Bergson, Lotze). W. E. Hocking and other American writers in *The Personalist* (1919) described as "personalism" what is the equivalent of the Italian *spiritualismo*. (Editor's note.)

too are the documents on which history is founded, which say nothing if man does not know how to understand the value of their testimony.

Under this aspect there is a radical difference between man and animal. In the animal, instinct is a necessitating impulse which does not recognize exceptions and which can be stifled totally or in part only by another stronger instinct. In man, even those which are called instincts are not infallible determinations, but only possibilities among which he must choose. There is no instinct so powerful that cannot be silenced, or fought against. The very aberrations to which the instincts in man sometimes succumb disclose their character of mere concrete possibilities thereby offering him alternatives from which to choose.

That man cannot cling to anything stable and definitive either within or outside of himself, that he must ceaselessly work and struggle, decide and choose, at his own risk and responsibility, is certainly the most disquieting prospect that has ever been put before men; and it is no wonder that they wince at it and seek to hide it from their eyes. Philosophy, however, cannot assume the easy and pleasant task of fondling man with illusions and assuring him with fictitious prospects. It must, instead, assume the more difficult, but also the more dignified, task of awakening him, if he is lulled to sleep by an illusory security, and of committing him to vigilance, to the struggle and to work. What it has the duty to clarify, however, is the guidance and the orientation that this prospect offers to man. This is what I shall try to illustrate quickly in what follows. And to this end it is advisable to look to the two philosophers who can offer an effective lesson in this regard: Kant and Kierkegaard.

7. The Philosophers of Possibility: Kant and Kierkegaard.

Kant is the philosopher of positive possibility. The philosophy of the German Enlightenment, from Wolff on, had found and used the method of structural and pervasive rationalism (*ragione fondante*). This method consists essentially in adducing as the foundation of a concept its possibility. Wolff and his followers, however, understood possibility in the logico-formal sense, as the absence of contradiction. Kant, for the first time, brings possibility to the level of concrete human experience; thus, he charges it with an existential meaning. Having brought knowledge back within the limits of possible experience, Kant recognizes, in the a priori forms, the possibility of experience. Having brought the moral life back within the limits of human finitude, he recognizes its possibility in the formal character of the categorical imperative, which expresses precisely the possibility of the moral person and of a community of persons. Having brought the aesthetic sense back within the limits of the intelligent animality that belongs to man, he recognizes its possibility as that of transforming man's dependence on nature to freedom from nature. For the first time, in the work of Kant, the entire world of man was expressed and founded in terms of possibilities—*transcendental* possibilities, that is, those which condition and establish. Kant's aim, in every field, was to limit, that is, to determine, authentic human possibilities by distinguishing them from those which are not authentic but purely fictitious. Hence the critical and restrictive character of his work, which is a constant polemic against theoretical dogmatism and moral fanaticism.

In Kant, however, possibility presents only one of its aspects— the positive one. Every concrete possibility, as such, always has another aspect—the negative one. It is always a *possibility-that-not* as well as a *possibility that*. The possibility of knowing, for example, is always the possibility of not knowing, that is, the possibility of doubt, of error, and of forgetting. In Kant this second aspect of possibility, as such, remains hidden, although he may have had a glimpse of it in the doctrine of radical evil. It becomes, instead, rudely disclosed in the work of Kierkegaard.

Kierkegaard is the philosopher of negative possibility. Dread is the feeling of the possible, but the possible in its annihilating and destructive force. This force is paralyzing. The "disciple of the possible," according to the expression of Kierkegaard, is one who is aware and lives under the threat of the terrifying alternatives which every concrete possibility presents for man. Kierkegaard realized the sense of the problematic nature of existence in all its force; but this problematic nature appeared to him exclusively in its negative aspect and he lived it therefore, as dread and paralyzing desperation.

Between the teachings of Kant and Kierkegaard, there is no alternative or choice. The positions are complementary. The constitutive possibility of human existence, clarified by Kant in its positive aspect, was clarified by Kierkegaard in the negative aspect to which the former is indissolubly joined. A philosophy of existence that does not care to be unilateral and does not wish to reduce existence itself to a fragment, must, in some way, continuously relate Kant to Kierkegaard and Kierkegaard to Kant. Only thus will it be able to trace, in the very problematic structure of existence, the norm and guide of existence itself.

8. The Equivalence of Possibilities: Negative Existentialism.

This is, indeed, the central problem, the only true problem of the philosophy of existence. Let us consider the condition of radical instability that this philosophy recognizes as proper to man. Man cannot perceive anything inside or outside of himself but possibilities, each of which implies a threat and a risk. How will he choose and find his way? By what sign will he recognize those that are real from those that are imaginary and how will he secure and be certain of the former?

The first response that is presented to these questions is the acknowledgment of the absolute *equivalence* of all human possibilities, an acknowledgment that implies that every choice, by the very fact of being such, is justified; and that man is essentially free, that is, indifferent, before all the possibilities that are proposed to him. This is the response of the latest French brand of existentialism (Sartre, Camus). This is undoubtedly the most obvious answer, but also the most paralyzing. A choice that is not supported by the faith in the value of what one chooses is not possible since the acknowledgment of equivalence *is* already the renunciation of choice. That acknowledgment is equivalent, therefore, to the nullification and the loss of all possibilities indiscriminately, and hence, to the negation of existence as such.

The second response to the same questions is the recognition of the equivalence of all human possibilities except one—the one which expresses and sums up the possible nullification of each and every single possibility—the possibility of *death*. This is Heidegger's response. From this point of view, the only possible choice for man is to live for death, and in the face of this, other choices are fictitious and improper. This response certainly represents a step forward from the first. It implies the possibility of a choice; but this possibility is, in effect, a necessity because there is only one possible choice. It is easy to see how, from this viewpoint, the problematic nature of existence is inverted to its contrary, that is, to necessity. The only authentic possibility of existing is the impossibility of existing. Now, impossibility is necessity, and if existence has a problematic nature, then it cannot be reduced to an impossibility. And once again existence as possibility is negated in the very act of its acknowledgment.

The third response is that all the possibilities of existence neutralize themselves through their common impossibility of being more than possibilities, that is, of grasping the being that is beyond them, transcendence. This is Jaspers' response. It is symmetrical and opposite to Heidegger's, but it leads to the same conclusion. For Heidegger existence is the impossibility to emerge from nothing and to be something; for Jaspers existence is the impossibility to be Being, to achieve transcendence. Both responses reduce existence to a fundamental impossibility; they negate, moreover, its problematic character, which makes it live and constitute itself through concrete possibilities.

The teaching that issues from the framework of these trends of contemporary existentialism is that the equivalence of the constitutive possibilities of existence, which is their common presupposition, leads to the negation of existence as possibility. *If all the possibilities that constitute existence are, for one reason or another, equivalent, then existence is impossible.* This recognition shows how much importance the consideration of value and of normativity has for existentialism although the trends cited have completely neglected this consideration. Without a positive solution of the question of value, the problematic character of existence is transformed into necessity—possibility into impossibility; existence is negated in the very act of recognition. In juxtaposition to this kind of existentialism, which can be called *negative*—not because it denies beliefs, values, or realities which are outside of its radius, but because it denies its leading principle, existence—I propose a positive direction which justifies the recognition and maintenance of existence in its fundamental problematic character, and keeps open the possibilities that constitute it. To an existentialism which lives under the exclusive sign of Kierkegaard, the philosopher of impossible possibility, one must contrast an existentialism which refers Kierkegaard to Kant and to the many other philosophers who have labored to guarantee man the legitimate possession of his own limits.

9. Theistic or Ontological Existentialism.[3]

There is no dearth of existentialist philosophies which seem, at first sight, to avoid these nullifying alternatives. They are those forms of existentialism which see in the possibilities of existence a relation with God, with Being or with Value, and they make a lever of infinity, of absoluteness, and, in a word, the omnipotence of the terminal of this relation in order to guarantee the relation itself. They recognize, therefore, in the possibilities of existence a positive character through which they seem to disclose to man the perspective of certainty.

Whether God is conceived as a *Mystery* who gives Himself to man in love rather than in rational speculation (Marcel); whether He is conceived as *Being* totally present to interior experience (Lavelle); or whether He is conceived as the supreme *Value* who gives Himself in the moral experience (Le Senne), the result of these interpretations is, in each case, that of offering man the guarantee that the possibilities of his existence are realized in the best of ways. The guarantee resides in the fact that existence is, in each case, a relation with a being (God) who has, by definition—or better who *is*, by definition—the possibility of fulfillment of all the highest human possibilities. The human possibilities are, in other words, already, from this point of view, *realized* possibilities inasmuch as they have been given or conceded to man by Being Himself, who contains them all in their full realization. Time then ceases to be a threat of destruction, and becomes a condition of realization. The success of human

[3] This selection on theistic existentialism was extracted from Abbagnano's, *Possibilità e Libertà*, and inserted here to present his complete critique of the common forms of existentialism known in the United States. (Editor's note.)

undertakings is guaranteed from the outset since, as Lavelle says, "every possibility is destined to be realized."

However consoling such a point of view may seem, still it is more the expression of wishful thinking than the result of an unbiased analysis of human existence. In reality this viewpoint cannot be of help to man in any of the particular situations in which he finds himself. If it means that *all* human possibilities, indiscriminately, are destined to be realized, then besides conflicting with the painful experience of failure, of a stalemate (*lo scacco*), of unhappiness, of suffering and of death, it offers man no criterion to distinguish between possibilities, so that all, in this case, would be equally solid, good, and happy. But if it means (which seems more consonant with the spirit of its proponents) that only some of the human possibilities are guaranteed inasmuch as they are founded on being and on value, it still clashes, and more basically, with the requirement of a criterion of choice. In this case, indeed, one *must* choose between possibilities. But how does one distinguish in particular cases the one which is founded on being and on value and is thus "destined to be realized" from the one which is not? The entire argument seems like a post-factum justification, which offers no limiting or orienting criterion in concrete existential situations. The possibilities that are realized are those founded on Being and on Value. This proposition is purely tautological. What we need to know is by what aspect or character we can recognize, beforehand, the possibilities that are realized. On this the existentialist philosophies in question say nothing.

What they do say, however, simply brings them back to that negative existentialism of which we have already spoken. There are, they say, possibilities destined to be realized, such that their nonrealization is impossible; and possibilities destined not to be realized, such that their realization is impossible. It is evident that both cases are not possibilities, since as we have seen, the property of a possibility is that it implies nothing that makes impossible its realization or its nonrealization. The property of a possibility is that it leaves the way open for either case, and where one of these ways is closed, one does not have a possibility but a necessary determination. We have here, in other words, the same surreptitious transformation to which negative existentialism submitted the notion of the possible—the transformation into the opposite concept of impossibility, that is, of necessity, which excludes freedom and choice. Their vaguely encouraging and optimistic character notwithstanding, these forms of existentialism work the same denial of existential possibilities as do the forms which appear negative and pessimistic. It too is not a *positive* existentialism.

A positive existentialism must satisfy two requirements: it must (1) maintain the notion of possibility in its twofold positive and negative aspects and avoid transforming it into a necessitating determination; (2) furnish a criterion, not infallible surely, but valid in the choice of existential possibilities.

10. Transcendental Possibility.

One must, in the first place, distinguish the *recognition* that existence is constituted by possibility from the affirmation that all these possibilities have the same value. This affirmation does not derive from that *recognition* and should not be confused with it. On the other hand, the existential possibilities cannot be catalogued and evaluated on the basis of an extrinsic criterion, a norm, or reality foreign to them and not involved with them. There is nothing—as we have said before—inside or outside of man that is not a concrete and live possibility. Consequently the same possibilities, as such, ought to have within them the criterion and measure of their value. What is this criterion?

Let us consider the importance of this question. If this criterion were lacking, neither a commitment to nor a faith in existence would be possible. Commitment and faith are, indeed, nothing more than the effective and working recognition of the value of the possibility in which man recognizes himself. Without the recognition of value, or even worse, with the acknowledgment of the equal value of all human possibilities, there is nothing left for man but to hurl himself headlong in one direction or another, yielding at random to this or that form of life, without seriousness, without faith and without reason. The problem of *faith* in existence and that of *reason* as guides and orientation for man meet at this point. We should not hesitate, however, to recognize and proclaim the truth if, unfortunately, things stood exactly so. But there are motives, and I shall try to demonstrate them, for recognizing that man has, in the very possibilities that constitute him, the norm of their evaluation.

An existential possibility can have the most diverse characteristics, but the proper and fundamental characteristic is undoubtedly that which makes it an *authentic* possibility. A possibility that is presented in the most brilliant colors, but which, once decided upon by a man and made his own, disintegrates or slips through his fingers, by withholding and denying precisely what it had promised to him, is not an authentic possibility but an impossibility. On the other hand, a possibility which, once chosen and decided upon, is consolidated *in its being* of possibility such that it makes possible again and again its own choice and decision, is an authentic, true and proper possibility. Such a possibility presents itself immediately with a *normative* character to the man who chooses it, thus making the choice obligatory. *The possibility of a possibility is the criterion and the norm of every possibility.* The possibility of possibility can be denoted with the name *transcendental possibility*. Transcendental possibility is, then, what justifies and establishes every concrete human attitude, every choice and every decision. A choice is not indeed justified because it has been made, but because it is still *possible* to make it. A decision is not good and valid because it was once made, but because it *can* still be made and still be carried out. An attitude of any kind does not derive its value from the fact that it has been assumed or can in fact be assumed, but only from the *possibility* that assuming it would not make it intrinsically impossible.

In order to be aware of the burden of these considerations, it is necessary to bear in mind that every human *attitude,* choice or decision does not concern merely the individual man who assumed it, nor is it restricted to his individuality. Thoughts, feelings, actions and all the other determinations under which we are accustomed to classify human possibilities concern other men as much as the individual to whom they belong. Thus the individual, in making a particular possibility his own or in assuming an attitude toward it, decides not only for himself, but also in the same act, his relations with others. When he is engaged in a task wherein he recognizes the possibility of concentrating and acquiring value as a person (a unity), he also engages in a whole series of possible relations between himself and others. The mere choice of any profession or work immediately puts the individual man into a complicated web of relations of loyalty, of interests, of antagonisms or friendships, of hierarchies and subordinations. But the same profession or work can be assumed or chosen in many different ways and each of these ways colors the personality of the chooser and his relations with others. Now, the criterion of transcendental possibility readily suggests that the task which I have chosen, in order to make possible the unity and equilibrium of my person, is not my true task if this unity and equilibrium are made impossible by it. And it also suggests to me that if that task tends, as does every task, to establish between others and myself a set of determined relations, it is not a true task if it denies the possibility of these relations. In this manner, every human attitude, whether simple or complex, has within itself the norm of its own possibility. This norm is not taken from without; it is inherent in the possibility that is offered to me, whatever it may be. It does not immobilize this possibility; it does not make it a reality, a datum, a fact, a necessity; it maintains it, rather, and consolidates it unmistakably in its possible being. Man, it is true, is constituted only by possibilities and has nothing more solid nor stable to hold on to. But precisely in the alternative of ceaselessly keeping open the instability which is proper to him, can he find and realize his equilibrium.

He can, *therefore he should*. But this is not to say that he is compelled to do it, nor that he always succeeds in doing it. Nothing can offer him an infallible guarantee: error is possible and everything is at his own risk. But he can, with effort and work, through doubt, error and struggle, arrive at a reasonable faith in himself, that is, in the possibility that he recognizes as his own, and in other men bound to him by this same possibility. This reasonable faith is all that can constitute his dignity and his value as man.

11. Freedom.

What has been said opens the way for an interpretation of freedom. The first observation to make in this regard is that freedom is not the indiscriminate character of every human choice or decision, of every possible attitude. It is not the condition in which man finds himself almost by right of birth and from which there is no possibility of his deviation or decline. It is not even the love of fate (*amor fati*), the pure and simple acceptance of fact, the choice of that which has already been chosen, the decision of that which has already been implicitly decided by a necessitating situation. Freedom as indifference before existential possibilities belongs to the position which affirms the absolute equality of value of these possibilities. Freedom, considered as concurrence with necessity, belongs to those positions which reduce the existential possibilities to a fundamental impossibility.

The existential possibilities are never offered to man in their indifference. Among those which he can in fact choose, only one is authentic, that is, the one that is not reduced to impossibility. He must choose this one because it alone guarantees him the possibility of choice. And this alone is freedom. It is, therefore, related to the value of possibility of the chosen possibility, that is, to transcendental possibility. And it is obvious that not every choice is free, but only the one which includes the guarantee of its own possibility. If I have freely decided what I have decided, I can ceaselessly continue to choose, because my decision guarantees itself. If I have decided badly, or even if I have erred (as is always possible), my decision backfires, tossing me into a blind alley and rendering impossible for me every relation with myself and with others. In this case I neither am free nor feel free because that form or that mode of my being that the chosen possibility deceptively outlined for me has revealed itself as impossible. Nor am I free with respect to others, since my freedom in this regard does not consist in the total absence of relations or isolation, but only in the possibility of the determinate relation I have chosen. In reality isolation (not to be confused with *solitude*) is simply *madness* for man, or else leads to forms of delinquency or moral aberration which, by denying the very possibility of any human relationship, borders on madness and is related to it. Man is free only *through* and *with* other men on the condition that his relationships with them are possible precisely because of the foundation he has chosen and decided. But for this to be possible, the decision of the individual, whatever it may be, must always include and ensure the possibility of relationship with others, and only in this case is it a free decision.

These are rather simple considerations that do not need many illustrations. I shall confine myself therefore to a single very instructive example. It is still argued, mainly after the recent sad experiences,[4] as to what must be understood by *free government* or by a free national constitution. The most obvious response, supported by the tradition of natural law, is that a free government is the one chosen by the people. But this answer is not enough, for we know that a people can choose and support a government that is not free. It must be said, therefore, that a free government is only the one which guarantees to the people the *possibility* of choice; that only this assured possibility makes it a government of free men. Once again, not every choice denotes freedom, only that choice which guarantees for itself its own possibility.

The road of freedom is the most difficult for man and he usually finds it only after many attempts, detours and errors. Much more easy and obvious is the road of nonfreedom, or of fictitious freedom, which soon after the choice turns out to be, an unbearable constriction, a split with himself and with others. Spinoza said that the free man never thinks of death; Heidegger, that the only freedom possible for man is freedom *for* death. In reality the free man neither forgets death nor lives only for it. He recognizes death as the impending risk in each of his projects or achievements, in every relation with himself and with others. He does not lose time, therefore, in getting to work on the essential things that remain to be done, nor does he neglect, at any moment, those on which the threat of death rests most gravely and menacingly. The free man remains faith-

---

[4] The Second World War. (Editor's note.)

ful to death because he remains faithful to the problematic character of his existence, which is at every instant the possibility of nonexistence. But he remains faithful to it in works and in concrete projects, that is, in the possibilities that he recognizes and makes his own. His fidelity is expressed in the duty that he feels constantly to consolidate these possibilities and in the refusal of the illusory belief that they can be kept forever secure without his own effort.

12. Time.

The recognition of the problematic character of existence implies the recognition of the *temporality* of existence itself. The philosophy of existence does not succumb to the demand of an imaginary suppression of time that is characteristic of every divinizing philosophy. Any philosophy that claims to have value as a *necessary knowledge* of the world must ignore or deny the destructive power of time and reduce it to an order of immutable determinations, that is, to eternity. But eternity is nothing but the present or simultaneity; and these are still determinations of time. Thus, the claim to ignore or suppress time results only in reducing it to one of its moments, with a neglect of the others.

The philosophy of existence starts from the explicit acknowledgment of the *reality* of time. It acknowledges, at the same time, the reality of all of its characteristics and its aspects: birth and death, preservation and destruction, permanence and change, development and decadence. These antagonistic aspects of time cannot be understood and interpreted without difficulty on the basis of just *any concept* of time. For if time is order, continuity and permanence, according to the concept which is the foundation of almost all its philosophical interpretations, then its destructive and nullifying power is not explained. If, instead, time is disorder, impermanence and destruction, according to its religious or tendentially religious interpretation, then there is no explanation for man's possibility of rescuing even bit by bit that which he cherishes and making it the patrimony of his past, of his tradition or of his history. In reality only the existential category of possibility permits an understanding of time in all the aspects of its temporality, because it permits the recognition of this temporality in the possibility which is always both positive and negative, and always implies the alternatives of order and disorder, of preservation and destruction. The temporality of time is simply the fundamental instability of the existential possibility. The threat of destruction implicit in time is but the possibility, connected to every concrete possibility, of loss and obliteration. The possibility of renewal and preservation which time possesses is that of consolidating and maintaining the concrete individual possibilities. All the aspects and dimensions of time are bound to possibility as such. The *present* of a possibility is a perspective on the *future*, which is rooted in the *past*. A possibility is always an opening toward the future, since it has in prospect the *coming to be* of that which is possible. It is, moreover, a possible connection with the past, since it only expects or projects that which, in some way, has already been. The act with which the future is problematically linked to the past and the past is pushed toward the future, is the *present* of a possibility.

As a prospect or projection of the future, every possibility includes the past and realizes some form of unity between future and past which is the present or the instant. Human existence cannot be understood, from the viewpoint of time, however, as a succession of moments. The event of succession is an event of substitution, and substitution implies *substitutibility* of the moments that succeed each other. But this *substitutibility* expresses, in its turn, the equivalence of the value of the moments and equivalence is none other than the absence of value on which preference and choice depend. Human existence can, undoubtedly, degrade itself to a pure succession of moments, that is, to an insignificant succession of possibilities which overlap and displace each other, and disappear soon after without leaving a trace. But it is undoubtedly such only when it forfeits or fails its intrinsic normative nature. It is not so when it recognizes itself in a valid possibility and concretizes and re-enforces itself in it. In that case existence is not succession, and its temporality is expressed in the possibility of safeguarding its essential aspects, and of preserving and renewing the patrimony in which it recognizes itself. The consideration of time implies, therefore, the consideration of value. Where the commitment and faith in existence are lacking, temporality appears as succession; where commitment and faith prevail, temporality is shown to be the possibility of enrichment and of preservation, and the threat of time, an alternative of success or failure.

13. History.

History is rooted in this alternative of existential temporality. It is the inquiry that commits the future to discover the truth of the past and is, therefore, a struggle to rescue what is valid and worthwhile salvaging or remembering from the destructive and nullifying power of time.

History is not an integral and, so to speak, automatic preservation of the past within the bosom of a universal or common experience or consciousness of the whole human race. Neither is it a divine *glance* cast upon human events, directed to uncover their necessary relationships and eternal simultaneity. It is, rather, a possibility and a duty for man: the possibility and duty to find and recognize in his own past authentic aspects of truth and to make them act as a norm for limiting and choosing further possibilities. Man cannot recognize and judge himself except in the [light of the] past; he must be disposed, therefore, toward recognizing his past without illusions or prejudices, with the will to discover its authentic aspect, and to avail himself in the best way of those possibilities of recall which are the sources of history. Every recognition and judgment is, however, for that very reason a commitment to the future. By judging his past and recognizing the shortcomings and the errors as well as authentic successes, he arranges the scheme of his projects to come, of his plan, in a word, of the concrete possibilities that await him. The historical investigation must, therefore, proceed always by means of a *choice* of its factors of judgment, a choice which assumes as particularly significant, for an epoch, for a personality or for a deed, individual institutions or customs, attitudes or events. But the choice is justified only if it, in some way, justifies and establishes its own possibility—if, that is, it does not make impossible that problematic character of events which is the foundation of every possible judgment or choice. Indeed, a historical evaluation that would immobilize history itself in a preconceived pattern, in a single or necessitating orientation, in an inevitably progressive or regressive order, would be a betrayal of the problematic character of history and would make judgment or evaluation impossible.

The problematic character of history is the very problematic character of existence which ceaselessly returns to itself, and seeks to recognize and strengthen its authentic possibilities. It thus forbids us optimism as well as pessimism, both of which try to tie the lot of humanity to a necessary historical order. It tells us that the order is ahead and beyond rather than behind us. It shows us in the past the elements of trust or hope as well as those of uncertainty and doubt. And in each case it commits us to work in the best way possible for that which we should cherish most, for that which is most worthy and human.

NICHOLAS ABBAGNANO'S MAJOR WRITINGS
(arranged chronologically)

Le sorgenti irrazionali del pensiero. Naples: Perrella, 1923.

Il Problema dell' arte. Naples: Perrella, 1925.

Il nuovo idealismo inglese e americano. Naples: Perrella, 1927.

La filosofia di Meyerson. Naples: Perrella, 1929.

Guglielmo di Ockham. Lanciano: Carabba, 1931.

La nozione del tempo secondo Aristotele. Lanciano: Carabba, 1933.

La fisica nuova. Naples: Guida, 1934.

Il principio della metafisica. Naples: Morano, 1935.

La struttura dell' esistenza. Turin: Paravia, 1939.

Telesio. Milan: Bocca, 1941.

Introduzione all' esistenzialismo. Milan: Bompiani, 1942.

Filosofia, Religione, Scienza. Turin: Taylor, 1947. The third chapter, "Fede, Filosofia, Religione," is translated as "Faith, Philosophy, Religion" in *Critical Existentialism*. Tr. N. Langiulli. New York: Doubleday, 1969.

Esistenzialismo Positivo. Turin: Taylor, 1948. The two essays that constitute this book are translated in *Critical Existentialism*.

Storia Della Filosofia. Turin: UTET. Vol. I, 1946; II, 1948; III, 1950. 2nd. revised edition, 1969.

Possibilita e Liberta. Turin: Taylor, 1956. Eight chapters of this book are translated in *Critical Existentialism*.

Problemi di sociologia. Turin: Taylor, 1959.

Dizionario di Filosofia. Turin: UTET, 1960.
Scritti Scelti. Turin: Taylor, 1967.
Per o contro l'uomo. Milan: Rizzoli, 1968.

Selected Studies About Abbagnano
(arranged alphabetically)

Chiodi, Pietro. *Il pensiero esistenzialista.* Milan: Garzanti, 1960.

Garin, Eugenio. *La cultura italiana tra '800 e '900.* Bari: Laterza, 1962.

Giannini, G. *L'esistenzialismo positivo di Nicola Abbagnano.* Brescia: Morcelliana, 1956.

Langiulli, Nino. "Editor's Introduction," *Critical Existentialism.* New York: Doubleday, 1969.

Paci, Enzo. *Il nulla e il problema dell' uomo.* Turin: Taylor, 1950.

Pareyson, Luigi. *Esistenza e persona.* Turin: Taylor, 1950.

Rod, W. "Der Charakter der Existenzphilosophie in Italien," in *Zeitschrift für Philosophische Forschung,* No. 2, 1958, pp. 263–277.

Romanell, Patrick. "Abbagnano," *Encyclopedia of Philosophy.* Ed. Paul Edwards. Vol. I. New York: Macmillan, 1967.

Santucci, Antonio. *Esistenzialismo e filosofia italiana.* Bologna: Mulino, 1959.

Semerari, Guiseppe. "L'Existentialisme Italien," *La Collaboration Philosophique.* Bologna: Marreggiani, 1958.

Simona, A. M. *La notion de liberté dans l'existenzialisme de Nicola Abbagnano.* Fribourg: Éditions Universitaires, 1962.

MARTIN BUBER (1878–1965)

Martin Buber was born in Vienna on February 8, 1878. His middle-class parents were divorced when he was three. He spent much of his childhood in Lemberg, Galicia (which is present-day Lvov, Ukrainian Soviet Socialist Republic), with his grandfather Salomon Buber, a well-known Hebrew scholar. While studying the Talmud with his grandfather he became acquainted with the Hasidic communities in neighboring towns. This acquaintance influenced his life in various profound ways, in his theological and philosophical reflections as well as his literary output; he collected, edited, and translated a considerable amount of Hasidic literature.

When he was thirteen, his drift from religious observance was expressed by his giving the bar mitzvah talk on Schiller rather than on a scriptural topic. He had subsequent misgivings about what he regarded as his religious slippage and apparently was tempted by suicide because of what he later termed "a mysterious and overwhelming compulsion" to understand "the limiting brink—or its limitlessness."

He was saved, he said, by reading Kant and grasping, as a result, "an eternal far removed from the finite and infinite."

He began his studies at the University of Vienna at the age of seventeen and studied philosophy and the history of art. He also attended the universities of Berlin, Zurich, and Leipzig, receiving his degree from Vienna in 1904.

At Leipzig he became acquainted with Theodor Herzl's Zionism, a movement which he found both politically and religiously satisfying. In 1901 he became editor of *Die Welt*, a Zionist journal, and met his future wife, Paula Winkler, a writer on the staff. When they were married she converted from Catholicism to Judaism. Mrs. Buber was also a novelist who used the pseudonym Georg Munk. They lived together until her death in 1958.

Buber and Herzl disagreed about the character of Zionism, Buber stressing its religious aspect while Herzl emphasized the political. The rift resulted in Buber's dropping out of active Zionism and finding a retreat among the Hasidic communities in his native Galicia. For five years he lived and studied there, learning their mystical and literary traditions.

On his return from this retreat, he became active again in Jewish journalism, editing Der Jude from 1916 to 1924. He also edited, together with a Catholic and a Protestant, the journal, Die Kreatur, between the years 1926 and 1930. During that period, i.e., 1923 to 1933, he was professor of comparative religion at the University of Frankfurt but was dismissed from his professorship by the government. He went to Palestine in 1938 where he became professor of social philosophy at Hebrew University in Jerusalem until his retirement in 1951.

Professor Buber visited the United States in 1951 and gave a series of lectures that were later published as "The Eclipse of God" and "At the Turning."

In 1963 he received the Erasmus Award in Amsterdam, presented to those who have contributed to the spiritual unity of Europe.

Besides his philosophical writing, his translations, editions, and interpretations of Hasidic literature, Buber and Franz Rosenzweig translated into German an edition of the Old Testament. Because he regarded Scripture as a dialogue between God and Israel (cf., I and Thou) rather than a set of religio-legal prescriptions and because he was not rigid in Talmudic observance, he received criticism from Orthodox quarters. But reformers also found him a source of annoyance because of his heavy dependence on Hasidic mysticism.

In his last years he lived simply in an old Arab stone house in Jerusalem with his granddaughter, Barbara Goldschmitt, who served as his housekeeper. He died there on June 13, 1965.

"Dialogue" from *Between Man and Man*

Translated by Ronald Gregor Smith

The Realms

The realms of the life of dialogue and the life of monologue do not coincide with the realms of dialogue and monologue even when forms without sound and even without gesture are included. There are not merely great spheres of the life of dialogue which in appearance are not dialogue, there is also dialogue which is not the dialogue of life, that is, it has the appearance but not the essence of dialogue. At times, indeed, it seems as though there were only this kind of dialogue.

I know three kinds. There is genuine dialogue—no matter whether spoken or silent—where each of the participants really has in mind the other or others in their present and particular being and turns to them with the intention of establishing a living mutual relation between himself and them. There is technical dialogue, which is prompted solely by the need of objective understanding. And there is monologue disguised as dialogue, in which two or more men, meeting in space, speak each with himself in strangely tortuous and circuitous ways and yet imagine they have escaped the torment of being thrown back on their own resources. The first kind, as I have said, has become rare; where it arises, in no matter how "unspiritual" a form, witness is borne on behalf of the continuance of the organic substance of the human spirit. The second belongs to the inalienable sterling quality of "modern existence". But real dialogue is here continually hidden in all kinds of odd corners and, occasionally in an unseemly way, breaks surface surprisingly and inopportunely—certainly still oftener it is arrogantly tolerated than downright scandalizing—as in the tone of a railway guard's voice, in the glance of an old newspaper vendor, in the smile of the chimney-sweeper. And the third. . . .

A *debate* in which the thoughts are not expressed in the way in which they existed in the mind but in the speaking are so pointed that they may strike home in the sharpest way, and moreover without the men that are spoken to being regarded in any way present as persons; a *conversation* characterized by the need neither to communicate something, nor to learn something, nor to influence someone, nor to come into connexion with someone, but solely by the desire to have one's own self-reliance confirmed by marking the impression that is made, or if it has become unsteady to have it strengthened; a *friendly chat* in which each regards himself as absolute and legitimate and the other as relativized and questionable; a *lovers' talk* in which both partners alike enjoy their own glorious soul and their precious experience—what an underworld of faceless spectres of dialogue!

The life of dialogue is not one in which you have much to do with men, but one in which you really have to do with those with whom you have to do. It is not the solitary man who lives the life of monologue, but he who is incapable of making real in the context of being the community in which, in the context of his destiny, he moves. It is, in fact, solitude which is able to show the innermost nature of the contrast. He who is living the life of dialogue receives in the ordinary course of the hours something that is said and feels himself approached for an answer. But also in the vast blankness of, say, a companionless mountain wandering that which confronts him, rich in change, does not leave him. He who is living the life of monologue is never aware of the other as something that is absolutely not himself and at the same time something with which he nevertheless communicates. Solitude for him can mean mounting richness of visions and thoughts but never the deep intercourse, captured in a new depth, with the incomprehensibly real. Nature for him is either an *état d'âme*, hence a "living through" in himself, or it is a passive object of knowledge, either idealistically brought within the soul or realistically alienated. It does not become for him a word apprehended with senses of beholding and feeling.

Being, lived in dialogue, receives even in extreme dereliction a harsh and strengthening sense of reciprocity; being, lived in monologue, will not, even in the tenderest intimacy, grope out over the outlines of the self.

This must not be confused with the contrast between "egoism" and "altruism" conceived by some moralists. I know people who are absorbed in "social activity" and have never spoken from being to being with a fellow-man. I know others who have no personal relation except to their enemies, but stand in such a relation to them that it is the enemies' fault if the relation does not flourish into one of dialogue.

Nor is dialogic to be identified with love. I know no one in any time who has succeeded in loving every man he met. Even Jesus obviously loved of "sinners" only the loose, lovable sinners, sinners against the Law; not those who were settled and loyal to their inheritance and sinned against him and his message. Yet to the latter as to the former he stood in a direct relation. Dialogic is not to be identified with love. But love without dialogic, without real outgoing to the other, reaching to the other, and companying with the other, the love remaining with itself—this is called Lucifer.

Certainly in order to be able to go out to the other you must have the starting place, you must have been, you must be, with yourself. Dialogue between mere individuals is only a sketch, only in dialogue between persons is the sketch filled in. But by what could a man from being an individual so really become a person as by the strict and sweet experiences of dialogue which teach him the boundless contents of the boundary?

What is said here is the real contrary of the cry, heard at times in twilight ages, for universal unreserve. He who can be unreserved with each passer-by has no substance to lose; but he who cannot stand in a direct relation to each one who meets him has a fulness which is futile. Luther is wrong to change the Hebrew "companion" (out of which the Seventy had already made one who is near, a neighbour) into "nearest". If everything concrete is equally near, equally nearest, life with the world ceases to have articulation and structure, it ceases to have human meaning. But nothing needs to mediate between me and one of my companions in the companionship of creation, whenever we come near one another, because we are bound up in relation to the same centre.

The Basic Movements

I term basic movement an essential action of man (it may be understood as an "inner" action, but it is not there unless it is there to the very tension of the eyes' muscles and the very action of the foot as it walks), round which an essential attitude is built up. I do not think of this happening in time, as though the single action preceded the lasting attitude; the latter rather has its truth in the accomplishing, over and over again, of the basic movement, without forethought but also without habit. Otherwise the attitude would have only æsthetic or perhaps also political significance, as a beautiful and as an effective lie. The familiar maxim, "An attitude must first be adopted, the rest follows of itself" ceases to be true in the circle of essential action and essential attitude—that is, where we are concerned with the wholeness of the person.

The basic movement of the life of dialogue is the turning towards the other. That, indeed, seems to happen every hour and quite trivially. If you look at someone and address him you turn to him, of course with the body, but also in the requisite measure with the soul, in that you direct your attention to him. But what of all this is an essential action, done with the essential being? In this way, that out of the incomprehensibility of what lies to hand this one person steps forth and becomes a presence. Now to our perception the world ceases to be an insignificant multiplicity of points to one of which we pay momentary attention. Rather it is a limitless tumult round a narrow breakwater, brightly outlined and able to bear heavy loads—limitless, but limited by the breakwater, so that, though not engirdled, it has become finite in itself, been given form, released from its own indifference. And yet none of the contacts of each hour is unworthy to take up from our essential being as much as it may. For no man is without strength for expression, and our turning towards him brings about a reply, however imperceptible, however quickly smothered, in a looking and sounding forth of the soul that are perhaps dissipating in mere inwardness and yet do exist. The notion of modern man that this turning to the other is sentimental and does not correspond to the compression of life today is a grotesque error, just as his affirmation that turning to the other is impractical in the bustle of this life today is only the masked confession of his weakness of initiative when confronted with the state of the time. He lets it dictate to him what is possible or permissible, instead of stipulating, as an unruffled partner, what is to be stipulated to the state of *every* time, namely, what space and what form it is bound to concede to creaturely existence.

The basic movement of the life of monologue is not turning away as opposed to turning towards; it is "reflection."

When I was eleven years of age, spending the summer on my grandparents' estate, I used, as often as I could do it unobserved, to steal into the stable and gently stroke the neck of my darling, a broad dapple-grey horse. It was not a casual delight but a great, certainly friendly, but also deeply stirring happening. If I am to explain it now, beginning from the still very fresh memory of my hand, I must say that what I experienced in touch with the animal was the Other, the immense otherness of the Other, which, however, did not remain strange like the otherness of the ox and the ram, but rather let me draw near and touch it. When I stroked the mighty mane, sometimes marvellously smooth-combed, at other times just as astonishingly wild, and felt the life beneath my hand, it was as though the element of vitality itself bordered on my skin, something that was not I, was certainly not akin to me, palpably the other, not just another, really the Other itself; and yet it let me approach, confided itself to me, placed itself elementally in the relation of *Thou* and *Thou* with me. The horse, even when I had not begun by pouring oats for him into the manger, very gently raised his massive head, ears flicking, then snorted quietly, as a conspirator gives a signal meant to be recognizable only by his fellow-conspirator; and I was approved. But once—I do not know what came over the child, at any rate it was childlike enough—it struck me about the stroking, what fun it gave me, and suddenly I became conscious of my hand. The game went on as before, but something had changed, it was no longer the same thing. And the next day, after giving him a rich feed, when I stroked my friend's head he did not raise his head. A few years later, when I thought back to the incident, I no longer supposed that the animal had noticed my defection. But at the time I considered myself judged.

Reflection is something different from egoism and even from "egotism." It is not that a man is concerned with himself, considers himself, fingers himself, enjoys, idolizes and bemoans himself; all that can be added, but it is not integral to reflection. (Similarly, to the turning towards the other, completing it, there can be added the realizing of the other in his particular existence, even the encompassing of him, so that the situations common to him and oneself are experienced also from his, the other's, end.) I term it reflection when a man withdraws from accepting with his essential being another person in his particularity—a particularity which is by no means to be circumscribed by the circle of his own self, and though it substantially touches and moves his soul is in no way immanent in it—and lets the other exist only as his own experience, only as a "part of myself." For then dialogue becomes a fiction, the mysterious intercourse between two human worlds only a game, and in the rejection of the real life confronting him the essence of all reality begins to disintegrate.

The Wordless Depths

Sometimes I hear it said that every *I and Thou* is only superficial, deep down word and response cease to exist, there is only the one primal being unconfronted by another. We should plunge into the silent unity, but for the rest leave its relativity to the life to be lived, instead of imposing on it this absolutized *I* and absolutized *Thou* with their dialogue.

Now from my own unforgettable experience I know well that there is a state in which the bonds of the personal nature of life seem to have fallen away from us and we experience an undivided unity. But I do not know—what the soul willingly imagines and indeed is bound to imagine (mine too once did it)—that in this I had attained to a union with the primal being or the godhead. That is an exaggeration no longer permitted to the responsible understanding. Responsibly—that is, as a man holding his ground before reality—I can elicit from those experiences only that in them I reached an undifferentiable unity of myself

without form or content. I may call this an original pre-
biographical unity and suppose that it is hidden unchanged beneath all biographical change, all development and complication
of the soul. Nevertheless, in the honest and sober account of the
responsible understanding this unity is nothing but the unity of
this soul of mine, whose "ground" I have reached, so much so,
beneath all formations and contents, that my spirit has no choice
but to understand it as the groundless. But the basic unity of my
own soul is certainly beyond the reach of all the multiplicity
it has hitherto received from life, though not in the least beyond
individuation, or the multiplicity of all the souls in the world
of which it is one—existing but once, single, unique, irreducible,
this creaturely one: one of the human souls and not the "soul of
the All"; a defined and particular being and not "Being"; the
creaturely basic unity of a creature, bound to God as in the
instant before release the creature is to the *creator spiritus*, not
bound to God as the creature to the *creator spiritus* in the moment of release.

The unity of his own self is not distinguishable in the man's
feeling from unity in general. For he who in the act or event
of absorption is sunk beneath the realm of all multiplicity that
holds sway in the soul cannot experience the cessation of multiplicity except as unity itself. That is, he experiences the cessation of his own multiplicity as the cessation of mutuality, as
revealed or fulfilled absence of otherness. The being which has
become one can no longer understand itself on this side of individuation nor indeed on this side of *I and Thou*. For to the
border experience of the soul "one" must apparently mean the
same as "the One".

But in the actuality of lived life the man in such a moment
is not above but beneath the creaturely situation, which is
mightier and truer than all ecstasies. He is not above but beneath dialogue. He is not nearer the God who is hidden above
I and Thou, and he is farther from the God who is turned to
men and who gives himself as the *I* to a *Thou* and the *Thou* to
an *I*, than that other who in prayer and service and life does not
step out of the position of confrontation and awaits no wordless
unity, except that which perhaps bodily death discloses.

Nevertheless, even he who lives the life of dialogue knows a lived unity: the unity of *life*, as that which once truly won is no more torn by any changes, not ripped asunder into the everyday creaturely life and the "deified" exalted hours; the unity of unbroken, raptureless perseverance in concreteness, in which the word is heard and a stammering answer dared.

Of Thinking

To all unprejudiced reflection it is clear that all *art* is from its origin essentially of the nature of dialogue. All music calls to an ear not the musician's own, all sculpture to an eye not the sculptor's, architecture in addition calls to the step as it walks in the building. They all say, to him who receives them, something (not a "feeling" but a perceived mystery) that can be said only in this one language. But there seems to cling to *thought* something of the life of monologue to which communication takes a second, secondary place. Thought seems to arise in monologue. Is it so? Is there here—where, as the philosophers say, pure subject separates itself from the concrete person in order to establish and stabilize a world for itself—a citadel which rises towering over the life of dialogue, inaccessible to it, in which man-with-himself, the single one, suffers and triumphs in glorious solitude?

Plato has repeatedly called thinking a voiceless colloquy of the soul with itself. Everyone who has really thought knows that within this remarkable process there is a stage at which an "inner" court is questioned and replies. But that is not the arising of the thought but the first trying and testing of what has arisen. The arising of the thought does not take place in colloquy with oneself. The character of monologue does not belong to the insight into a basic relation with which cognitive thought begins; nor to the grasping, limiting and compressing of the insight; nor to its moulding into the independent conceptual form; nor to the reception of this form, with the bestowal of relations, the dovetailing and soldering, into an order of conceptual forms; nor, finally, to the expression and clarification in language (which till now had only a technical and reserved symbolic function). Rather are elements of dialogue to be discovered here. It is not himself that the thinker addresses in the stages of the thought's growth, in their answerings, but as it were the basic relation in face of which he has to answer for his insight, or the order in face of which he has to answer for the newly arrived conceptual form. And it is a misunderstanding of the dynamic of the event of thought to suppose that these apostrophizings of a being existing in nature or in ideas are "really" colloquies with the self.

But also the first trying and testing of the thought, when it is provisionally completed, before the "inner" court, in the platonic sense the stage of monologue, has besides the familiar form of its appearance another form in which dialogue plays a great part, well-known to Plato if to anyone. There he who is approached for judgment is not the empirical self but the *genius*, the spirit I am intended to become, the image-self, before which the new thought is borne for approval, that is, for taking up into its own consummating thinking.

And now from another dimension which even this lease of power does not satisfy there appears the longing for a trying and testing in the sphere of pure dialogue. Here the function of receiving is no longer given over to the *Thou-I* but to a genuine *Thou* which either remains one that is thought and yet is felt as supremely living and "other", or else is embodied in an intimate person. "Man", says Wilhelm von Humboldt in his significant treatise on *The Dual Number* (1827), "longs even for the sake of his mere thinking for a *Thou* corresponding to the *I*. The conception appears to him to reach its definiteness and certainty only when it reflects from another power of thought. It is produced by being torn away from the moving mass of representation and shaped in face of the subject into the object. But the objectivity appears in a still more complete form if this separation does not go on in the subject alone, if he really sees the thought outside himself; and this is possible only in another being, representing and thinking like himself. And between one power of thought and another there is no other mediator but speech." This reference, simplified to an aphorism, recurs with Ludwig Feuerbach in 1843: "True dialectic is not a monologue of the solitary thinker with himself, it is a dialogue between *I* and *Thou*."

But this saying points beyond that "reflecting" to the fact that even in the original stage of the proper act of thought the inner action might take place in relation to a genuine and not merely an "inward" (Novalis) *Thou*. And where modern philosophy is most earnest in the desire to ask its questions on the basis of human existence, situation and present, in some modifications an important further step is taken. Here it is certainly no longer just that the *Thou* is ready to receive and disposed to philosophize along with the *I*. Rather, and pre-eminently, we have the *Thou* in opposition because we truly have the other who thinks other things in another way. So, too, it is not a matter of a game of draughts in the tower of a castle in the air, but of the binding business of life on the hard earth, in which one is inexorably aware of the otherness of the other but does not at all contest it without realizing it; one takes up its nature into one's own thinking, thinks in relation to it, addresses it in thought.

This man of modern philosophy, however, who in this way no longer thinks in the untouchable province of pure ideation, but thinks in reality—does he think in reality? Not solely in a reality framed by thought? Is the other, whom he accepts and receives in this way, not solely the other framed by thought, and therefore unreal? Does the thinker of whom we are speaking hold his own with the bodily fact of otherness?

If we are serious about thinking between *I* and *Thou* then it is not enough to cast our thoughts towards the other subject of thought framed by thought. We should also, with the thinking, precisely with the thinking, live towards the other man, who is not framed by thought but bodily present before us; we should live towards his concrete life. We should live not towards another thinker of whom we wish to know nothing beyond his thinking but, even if the other is a thinker, towards his bodily life over and above his thinking—rather, towards his person, to which, to be sure, the activity of thinking also belongs.

When will the action of thinking endure, include, and refer to the presence of the living man facing us? When will the dialectic of thought become dialogic, an unsentimental, unrelaxed dialogue in the strict terms of thought with the man present at the moment?

Eros

The Greeks distinguished between a powerful, world-begetting Eros and one which was light and whose sphere was the soul; and also between a heavenly and a profane Eros. Neither seems to me to indicate an absolute distinction. For the primal god Desire from whom the world is derived, is the very one who in the form of a "tender elfin spirit" (Jacob Grimm) enters into the sphere of souls and in an arbitrary daimonic way carries out here, as mediator of the pollination of being, his cosmogonic work: he is the great pollen-bearing butterfly of psychogenesis. And the Pandemos (assuming it is a genuine Eros and not a Priapos impudently pretending to be the higher one) needs only to stir his wings to let the primal fire be revealed in the body's games.

Of course, the matter in question is whether Eros has not forfeited the power of flight and is now condemned to live among tough mortals and govern their mortality's paltry gestures of love. For the souls of lovers do to one another what they do; but lame-winged beneath the rule of the lame-winged one (for his power and powerlessness are always shown in theirs) they cower where they are, each in his den, instead of soaring out each to the beloved partner and there, in the beyond which has come near, "knowing".

Those who are loyal to the strong-winged Eros of dialogue know the beloved being. They experience his particular life in simple presence—not as a thing seen and touched, but from the innervations to his movements, from the "inner" to his "outer". But by this I mean nothing but the bipolar experience, and—more than a swinging over and away in the instant—a contemporaneity at rest. That inclination of the head over there—you feel how the soul enjoins it on the neck, you feel it not on your neck but on that one over there, on the beloved one, and yet you yourself are not as it were snatched away, you are here, in the feeling self-being, and you receive the inclination of the head, its injunction, as the answer to the word of your own silence. In contemporaneity at rest you make and you experience dialogue. The two who are loyal to the Eros of dialogue, who love one another, receive the common event from the other's side as well, that is, they receive it from the two sides, and thus for the first time understand in a bodily way what an event is.

The kingdom of the lame-winged Eros is a world of mirrors and mirrorings. But where the winged one holds sway there is no mirroring. For there I, the lover, turn to this other human being, the beloved, in his otherness, his independence, his self-reality, and turn to him with all the power of intention of my own heart. I certainly turn to him as to one who is there turning to me, but in that very reality, not comprehensible by me but rather comprehending me, in which I am there turning to him. I do not assimilate into my own soul that which lives and faces me, I vow it faithfully to myself and myself to it, I vow, I have faith.

The Eros of dialogue has the simplicity of fulness; the Eros of monologue is manifold. Many years I have wandered through the land of men, and have not yet reached an end of studying the varieties of the "erotic man" (as the vassal of the broken-winged one at times describes himself). There a lover stamps around and is in love only with his passion. There one is wearing his differentiated feelings like medal-ribbons. There one is enjoying the adventures of his own fascinating effect. There one is gazing enraptured at the spectacle of his own supposed surrender. There one is collecting excitement. There one is displaying his "power". There one is preening himself with borrowed vitality. There one is delighting to exist simultaneously as himself and as an idol very unlike himself. There one is warming himself at the blaze of what has fallen to his lot. There one is experimenting. And so on and on—all the manifold mono-logists with their mirrors, in the apartment of the most intimate dialogue!

I have spoken of the small fry, but I have had more in mind the leviathans. There are some who stipulate to the object they propose to devour that both the doing as a holy right and the suffering as a sacred duty are what is to be called heroic love. I know of "leaders" who with their grip not only cast into confusion the plasma of the growing human being but also disinte-grate it radically, so that it can no longer be moulded. They relish this power of their influence, and at the same time deceive themselves and their herd into imagining they are moulders of youthful souls, and call on *Eros*, who is inaccessible to the *profanum vulgus*, as the tutelary god of this work.

They are all beating the air. Only he who himself turns to the other human being and opens himself to him receives the world in him. Only the being whose otherness, accepted by my being, lives and faces me in the whole compression of existence, brings the radiance of eternity to me. Only when two say to one another with all that they are, "It is *Thou*", is the indwelling of the Present Being between them.

Community

In the view customary to-day, which is defined by politics, the only important thing in groups, in the present as in history, is what they aim at and what they accomplish. Significance is ascribed to what goes on within them only in so far as it influences the group's action with regard to its aim. Thus it is conceded to a band conspiring to conquer the state power that the comradeship which fills it is of value, just because it strengthens the band's reliable assault power. Precise obedience will do as well, if enthusiastic drill makes up for the associates remaining strangers to one another; there are indeed good grounds for preferring the rigid system. If the group is striving even to reach a higher form of society then it can seem dangerous if in the life of the group itself something of this higher form begins to be realized in embryo. For from such a premature seriousness a suppression of the "effective" impetus is feared. The opinion apparently is that the man who whiles away his time as a guest on an oasis may be accounted lost for the project of irrigating the Sahara.

By this simplified mode of valuation the real and individual worth of a group remains as uncomprehended as when we judge a person by his effect alone and not by his qualities. The perversion of thought grows when chatter is added about sacrifice of being, about renunciation of self-realization, where possible with a reference to the favourite metaphor of the dung. Happiness, possession, power, authority, life can be renounced, but sacrifice of being is a sublime absurdity. And no moment, if it has to vouch for its relation to reality, can call upon any kind of later, future moments for whose sake, in order to make them fat, it has remained so lean.

The feeling of community does not reign where the desired change of institutions is wrested in common, but without community, from a resisting world. It reigns where the fight that is fought takes place from the position of a community struggling for its own reality as a community. But the future too is decided here at the same time; all political "achievements" are at best auxiliary troops to the effect which changes the very core, and which is wrought on the unsurveyable ways of secret history by the moment of realization. No way leads to any other goal but to that which is like it.

But who in all these massed, mingled, marching collectivities still perceives what that is for which he supposes he is striving—what community is? They have all surrendered to its counterpart. Collectivity is not a binding but a bundling together: individuals packed together, armed and equipped in common, with only as much life from man to man as will inflame the marching step. But community, growing community (which is all we have known so far) is the being no longer side by side but *with* one another of a multitude of persons. And this multitude, though it also moves towards one goal, yet experiences everywhere a turning to, a dynamic facing of, the other, a flowing from I to *Thou*. Community is where community happens. Collectivity is based on an organized atrophy of personal existence, community on its increase and confirmation in life lived towards one other. The modern zeal for collectivity is a flight from community's testing and consecration of the person, a flight from the vital dialogic, demanding the staking of the self, which is in the heart of the world.

The men of the "collective" look down superciliously on the "sentimentality" of the generation before them, of the age of the "youth movement". Then the concern, wide-ranging and deeply-pondered, was with the problem of all life's relations, "community" was aimed at and made a problem at the same time. They went round in circles and never left the mark. But now there is commanding and marching, for now there is the "cause". The false paths of subjectivity have been left behind and the road of objectivism, going straight for its goal, has been reached. But as there existed a pseudo-subjectivity with the former, since the elementary force of being a subject was lacking, so with the latter there exists a pseudo-objectivism, since one is here fitted not into a world but into a worldless faction. As in the former all songs in praise of freedom were sung into the void, because only freeing from bonds was known, but not freeing to responsibility, so in the latter even the noblest hymns on authority are a misunderstanding. For in fact they strengthen only the semblance of authority which has been won by speeches and cries; behind this authority is hidden an absence of consistency draped in the mighty folds of the attitude. But genuine authority, celebrated in those hymns, the authority of the genuine charismatic in his steady response to the lord of Charis, has remained unknown to the political sphere of the present. Superficially the two generations are different in kind to the extent of contradiction, in truth they are stuck in the same chaotic condition. The man of the youth movement, pondering his problems, was concerned (whatever the particular matter at different times) with his very own share in it, he "experienced" his I without pledging a self—in order not to have to pledge a self in response and responsibility. The man of the collective undertaking, striding to action, succeeded beforehand in getting rid of himself and thus radically escaping the question of pledging a self. Progress is nevertheless to be recorded. With the former monologue presented itself as dialogue. With the latter it is considerably simpler, for the life of monologue is by their desire driven out from most men, or they are broken of the habit; and the others, who give the orders, have at least no need to feign any dialogic.

Dialogue and monologue are silenced. Bundled together, men march without *Thou* and without *I*, those of the left who want to abolish memory, and those of the right who want to regulate it: hostile and separated hosts, they march into the common abyss.

Conversation with the Opponent

I hope for two kinds of readers for these thoughts: for the *amicus* who knows about the reality to which I am pointing with a finger I should like to be able to stretch out like Grünewald's Baptist; and for the *hostis* or *adversarius* who denies this reality and therefore contends with me, because I point to it (in his view misleadingly) as to a reality. Thus he takes what is said here just as seriously as I myself do, after long waiting writing what is to be written—just as seriously, only with the negative sign. The mere *inimicus*, as which I regard everyone who wishes to relegate me to the realm of ideology and there let my thoughts count, I would gladly dispense with.

I need say nothing at this point to the *amicus*. The hour of common mortality and the common way strikes in his and in my ears as though we stood even in the same place with one another and knew one another.

But it is not enough to tell the *adversarius* here what I am pointing at—the hiddenness of his personal life, his secret, and that, stepping over a carefully avoided threshold, he will discover what he denies. It is not enough. I dare not turn aside his gravest objection. I must accept it, as and where it is raised, and must answer.

So now the *adversarius* sits, facing me in his actual form as he appears in accordance with the spirit of the time, and speaks, more above and beyond me than towards and to me, in accents and attitude customary in the universal duel, free of personal relation.

"In all this the actuality of our present life, the conditioned nature of life as a whole, is not taken into account. All that you speak of takes place in the never-never-land, not in the social context of the world in which we spend our days, and by which if by anything our reality is defined. Your 'two men' sit on a solitary seat, obviously during a holiday journey. In a big city office you would not be able to let them sit, they would not reach the 'sacramental' there. Your 'interrupted conversation' takes place between intellectuals who have leisure a couple of months before the huge mass event to spin fantasies of its prevention through a spiritual influence. That may be quite interesting for people who are not taken up with any duty. But is the business employee to 'communicate himself without reserve' to his colleagues? Is the worker at the conveyor belt to 'feel himself addressed in what he experiences'? Is the leader of a gigantic technical undertaking to 'practise the responsibility of dialogue'? You demand that we enter into the situation which approaches us, and you neglect the enduring situation in which everyone of us, so far as we share in the life of community, is elementally placed. In spite of all references to concreteness, all that is pre-war individualism in a revised edition."

And I, out of a deep consciousness of how almost impossible it is to think in common, if only in opposition, where there is no common experience, reply.

Before all, dear opponent, if we are to converse with one another and not at and past one another, I beg you to notice that I do not demand. I have no call to that and no authority for it. I try only to say that there is something, and to indicate how it is made: I simply record. And how could the life of dialogue be demanded? There is no ordering of dialogue. It is not that you *are* to answer but that you *are able*.

You are really able. The life of dialogue is no privilege of intellectual activity like dialectic. It does not begin in the upper story of humanity. It begins no higher than where humanity begins. There are no gifted and ungifted here, only those who give themselves and those who withhold themselves. And he who gives himself to-morrow is not noted to-day, even he himself does not know that he has it in himself, that we have it in ourselves, he will just find it, "and finding be amazed".

You put before me the man taken up with duty and business. Yes, precisely him I mean, him in the factory, in the shop, in the office, in the mine, on the tractor, at the printing-press: man. I do not seek for men. I do not seek men out for myself, I accept those who are there, I have them, I have him, in mind, the yoked, the wheel-treading, the conditioned. Dialogue is not an affair of spiritual luxury and spiritual luxuriousness, it is a matter of creation, of the creature, and he is that, the man of whom I speak, he is a creature, trivial and irreplaceable.

In my thoughts about the life of dialogue I have had to choose the examples as "purely" and as much in the form of paradigm as memory presented them to me in order to make myself intelligible about what has become so unfamiliar, in fact so sunk in oblivion. For this reason I appear to draw my tales from the province which you term the "intellectual", in reality only from the province where things succeed, are rounded off, in fact are exemplary. But I am not concerned with the pure; I am concerned with the turbid, the repressed, the pedestrian, with toil and dull contrariness—and with the break-through. With the break-through and not with a perfection, and moreover with the break-through not out of despair with its murderous and renewing powers; no, not with the great catastrophic break-through which happens once for all (it is fitting to be silent for a while about that, even in one's own heart), but with the breaking through from the status of the dully-tempered disagreeableness, obstinacy, and contrariness in which the man, whom I pluck at random out of the tumult, is living and out of which he can and at times does break through.

Whither? Into nothing exalted, heroic or holy, into no Either and no Or, only into this tiny strictness and grace of every day, where I have to do with just the very same "reality" with whose duty and business I am taken up in such a way, glance to glance, look to look, word to word, that I experience it as reached to me and myself to it, it as spoken to me and myself to it. And now, in all the clanking of routine that I called my reality, there appears to me, homely and glorious, the effective reality, creaturely and given to me in trust and responsibility. We do not find meaning lying in things nor do we put it into things, but between us and things it can happen.

It is not sufficient, dear opponent, first of all to ascribe to me the pathos of "all or nothing" and then to prove the impossibility of my alleged demand. I know neither what all nor what nothing is, the one appears to me to be as inhuman and contrived as the other. What I am meaning is the simple *quantum satis* of that which this man in this hour of his life is able to fulfil and to receive—if he gives himself. That is, if he does not let himself be deceived by the compact plausibility that there are places excluded from creation, that he works in such a place and is able to return to creation when his shift is over; or that creation is outstripped, that it once was but is irrevocably over, now there is business and now it is a case of stripping off all romanticism, gritting the teeth and getting through with what is recognized as necessary. I say—if he does not let himself be deceived.

No factory and no office is so abandoned by creation that a

creative glance could not fly up from one working-place to another, from desk to desk, a sober and brotherly glance which guarantees the reality of creation which is happening—*quantum satis*. And nothing is so valuable a service of dialogue between God and man as such an unsentimental and unreserved exchange of glances between two men in an alien place.

But is it irrevocably an alien place? Must henceforth, through all the world's ages, the life of the being which is yoked to business be divided in two, into alien "work" and home "recovery"? More, since evenings and Sundays cannot be freed of the workday character but are unavoidably stamped with it, must such a life be divided out between the business of work and the business of recovery without a remainder of directness, of unregulated surplus—of freedom? (And the freedom I mean is established by no new order of society.)

Or does there already stir, beneath all dissatisfactions that can be satisfied, an unknown and primal and deep dissatisfaction for which there is as yet no recipe of satisfaction anywhere, but which will grow to such mightiness that it dictates to the technical leaders, the promoters, the inventors, and says, "Go on with your rationalizing, but humanize the rationalizing *ratio* in yourselves. Let it introduce the living man into its purposes and its calculations, him who longs to stand in a mutual relation with the world." Dear opponent, does the longing already stir in the depths—an impulse to great construction or a tiny spark of the last revolution—to fill business with the life of dialogue? That is, in the formulation of the *quantum satis*, the longing for an order of work in which business is so continually soaked in vital dialogic as the tasks to be fulfilled by it allow? And of the extent to which they can allow it there is scarcely an inkling to-day, in an hour when the question which I put is at the mercy of the fanatics, blind to reality, who conform to the time, and of the heralds, blind to possibility, of the impervious tragedy of the world.

Be clear what it means when a worker can experience even his relation to the machine as one of dialogue, when, for instance, a compositor tells that he has understood the machine's humming as "a merry and grateful smile at me for helping it to set aside the difficulties and obstructions which disturbed and bruised and pained it, so that now it could run free". Must even you not think then of the story of Androclus and the Lion?

But when a man draws a lifeless thing into his passionate longing for dialogue, lending it independence and as it were a soul, then there may dawn in him the presentiment of a world-wide dialogue, a dialogue with the world-happening that steps up to him even in his environment, which consists partly of things. Or do you seriously think that the giving and taking of signs halts on the threshold of that business where an honest and open spirit is found?

You ask with a laugh, can the leader of a great technical undertaking practise the responsibility of dialogue? He can. For he practises it when he makes present to himself in its concreteness, so far as he can, *quantum satis*, the business which he leads. He practises it when he experiences it, instead of as a structure of mechanical centres of force and their organic servants (among which latter there is for him no differentiation but the functional one), as an association of persons with faces and names and biographies, bound together by a work that is represented by, but does not consist of, the achievements of a complicated mechanism. He practises it when he is inwardly aware, with a latent and disciplined fantasy, of the multitude of these persons, whom naturally he cannot separately know and remember as such; so that now, when one of them for some reason or other steps really as an individual into the circle of his vision and the realm of his decision, he is aware of him without strain not as a number with a human mask but as a person. He practises it when he comprehends and handles these persons as persons—for the greatest part necessarily indirectly, by means of a system of mediation which varies according to the extent, nature and structure of the undertaking, but also directly, in the parts which concern him by way of organization. Naturally at first both camps, that of capital and that of the proletariat, will decry his masterly attitude of fantasy as fantastic nonsense and his practical attitude to persons as dilettantist. But just as naturally only until his increased figures of production accredit him in their eyes. (By this of course is not to be implied that those increases necessarily come to pass: between truth and success there is no pre-stabilized harmony.) Then, to be sure, something worse will follow. He will be pragmatically imitated, that is, people will try to use his "procedure" without his way of thinking and imagining. But this demoniac element inherent in spiritual history (think only of all the magicizing of religion) will, I think, shipwreck here on the power of discrimination in men's souls. And meanwhile it is to be hoped that a new generation will arise, learning from what is alive, and will take all this in real seriousness as he does.

Unmistakably men are more and more determined by "circumstances". Not only the absolute mass but also the relative might of social objectives is growing. As one determined partially by them the individual stands in each moment before concrete reality which wishes to reach out to him and receive an answer from him; laden with the situation he meets new situations. And yet in all the multiplicity and complexity he has remained Adam. Even now a real decision is made in him, whether he faces the speech of God articulated to him in things and events—or escapes. And a creative glance towards his fellow-creature can at times suffice for response.

Man is in a growing measure sociologically determined. But this growing is the maturing of a task not in the "ought" but in the "may" and in "need", in longing and in grace. It is a matter of renouncing the pantechnical mania or habit with its easy "mastery" of every situation; of taking everything up into the might of dialogue of the genuine life, from the trivial mysteries of everyday to the majesty of destructive destiny.

The task becomes more and more difficult, and more and more essential, the fulfilment more and more impeded and more and more rich in decision. All the regulated chaos of the age waits for the break-through, and wherever a man perceives and responds, he is working to that end.

Buber's Major Writings
(arranged chronologically)

A. Edition of the *Works*

Werke. Munich & Heidelberg: Kösel & L. Schneider. Erster Band: *Schriften zur Philosophie*, 1962; Zweiter Band: *Schriften zur Bibel*, 1964; Dritter Band: *Schriften zum Chassidismus*, 1963.

B. The Individual Works and Translations

Die Geschichten des Rabbi Nachman. Frankfurt a. M.: Rütten & Loening, 1906.

   The Tales of Rabbi Nachman. Tr. M. Friedman. New York: Horizon, 1956.

Die Legende des Baalschem. Frankfurt a. M.: Rütten & Loening, 1908.

   The Legend of the Baal-Shem. Tr. M. Friedman. New York: Harper, 1955.

Ekstatische Konfessionen. Jena: Eugen Diedrichs, 1909.

Chinesische Geister- und Liebesgeschichten. Frankfurt a. M.: Rütten & Loening, 1911.

Drei Reden über das Judentum. Frankfurt a. M.: Rütten & Loening, 1911.

   Included in *Addresses on Judaism.* Tr. Eva Jospe. New York: Schocken, 1966.

Daniel: Gespräche von der Verwirklichung. Leipzig: Insel, 1913.

   Daniel: Dialogues on Realization. Ed. & tr. M. Friedman. New York: Holt, Rinehart & Winston, 1964.

Reden und Gleichnisse des Tschuang-Tse. Leipzig: Insel, 1914.

Die jüdische Bewegung: Gesammelte Aufsätze und Ansprachen. Vol. I: 1900–1914; Vol. II: 1916–1920. Berlin: Jüdischer Verlag, 1916 & 1921.

Vom Geist des Judentums. Leipzig: K. Wolff, 1916.

Ereignisse und Begegnungen. Leipzig: Insel, 1917.

Mein Weg zum Chassidismus: Erinnerungen. Frankfurt a. M.: Rütten & Loening, 1918. [Later included in *Hinweise*]

Cheruth: Ein Rede über Jugend und Religion. Vienna & Berlin: R. Lowit, 1919.

Worte an die Zeit. Vol. I: Grundsätze; Vol. II: *Gemeinschaft.* Munich: Dreiländer, 1919.

Der Heilige Weg. Frankfurt a. M.: Rütten & Loening, 1919.

Die Rede, die Lehre, und das Lied. Leipzig: Insel, 1920.

Der Grosse Maggid und seine Nachfolge. Frankfurt a. M.: Rütten & Loening, 1922.

Ich und Du. Leipzig: Insel, 1923; *Nachworterweiterte.* Heidelberg: L. Schneider, 1958.

   I and Thou. Tr. R. G. Smith. Edinburgh: T & T Clark, 1937; second edition with Postscript. New York: Scribners, 1958.

Das verborgene Licht. Frankfurt a. M.: Rütten & Loening, 1924.

Rede über das Erzieherische. Berlin: L. Schneider, 1926.

"Education," in *Between Man and Man*. Tr. R. G. Smith. London: Routledge & Kegan Paul, 1947.

Das Baal-Schem-Tow: Unterweisung im Umgang mit Gott. Hellerau: J. Hegner, 1927.

Die chassidischen Bücher, Gesamtausgabe. Hellerau: J. Hegner, 1928. [A collection including *Die Geschichten des Rabbi Nachman, Die Legende des Baalschem, Man Weg zur Chassidismus, Der grosse Maggid und seine Nachfolge*, and *Das Verborgene Licht*.]

    Tales of the Hasidim: The Early Masters. Tr. Olga Marx. New York: Schocken, 1947.

    Tales of the Hasidim: The Later Masters. Tr. Olga Marx. New York: Schocken, 1948.

Hundert chassidische Geschichten. Berlin: Schocken, 1930.

Das Kommende: Untersuchungen der Entstehungsgeschichte des messianischen Glaubens. Vol. I: *Königtum Gottes*. Berlin: Schocken, 1932; 2nd enlarged ed., 1936; 3rd rev. ed., Heidelberg: L. Schneider, 1956.

    The Kingship of God. Tr. R. Scheiman. New York: Harper, 1966.

Zwiesprache. Berlin: Schocken, 1932.

    "Dialogue," in *Between Man and Man*.

Kampf um Israel: Reden und Schriften (1921–1932). Berlin: Schocken, 1933.

    Israel and the World: Essays in a Time of Crisis. New York: Schocken, 1948; expanded edition, 1963.

Erzählungen von Engeln, Geistern, und Dämonen. Berlin: Schocken, 1934.

    Tales of Angels, Spirits, and Demons. Tr. D. Astin & J. Rothenberg. New York: Hawk's Well, 1958.

Deutung des Chassidismus. Berlin: Schocken, 1935.

    Mamre: Essays in Religion. Tr. G. Hort. London: Oxford University Press, 1946. [Also included are five essays from *Kampf um Israel*.]

Die Frage an den Einzelman. Berlin: Schocken, 1936.

    "The Question to the Single One," in *Between Man and Man*.

Die Stunde und die Erkenntnis: Reden und Aufsätze, 1933–1935. Berlin: Schocken, 1936.

Zion als Ziel und Aufgabe. Berlin: Schocken, 1936.

Worte an die Jugend. Berlin: Schocken, 1938.

Gog und Magog [in Hebrew], serially in *Davar*, Oct. 23, 1941–January 10, 1942.

    Gog und Magog: Eine Chronik. Heidelberg: L. Schneider, 1949.

    For the Sake of Heaven. Tr. from German of *Gog und Magog* by

L. Lewisohn. Philadelphia: Jewish Publication Society, 1945; New York: Harper, 1953.

Torat ha neviim. Jerusalem: Mosad Bialik, 1942.
  The Prophetic Faith. Tr. C. Wilton-Davies. New York: Macmillan, 1949.

Be pfardes ha hasidut. Tel-Aviv: Mosad Bialik, 1945.
  Hasidism. Tr. Greta Hort et al. New York: Philosophical Library, 1948.

Darko shel Adam (meolam ha hassidut). Jerusalem: Mosad Bialik, 1945.
  The Way of Man, According to the Teachings of Hasidism. [Tr. not given.] London: Routledge & Kegan Paul, 1950. Reprinted in *Hasidism and Modern Man.* Ed. & tr. M. Friedman. New York: Horizon, 1958.

Moshe. Jerusalem: Schocken, 1945.
  Moses. Oxford: East & West Library, 1946.

Or ha-ganuz. Tel-Aviv: 1946.
  Ten Rungs: Hasidic Sayings. Tr. Olga Marx. New York: Schocken, 1947.

Netivot be utopiyah. Tel-Aviv: Am Oved, 1947.
  Paths in Utopia. Tr. R. F. Hull. London: Routledge & Kegan Paul, 1949.

Das Problem des Menschen. Heidelberg: L. Schneider, 1948.
  "What is Man," in *Between Man and Man.*

Israel und Palästina: Zur Geschichte einer Idee. Ed. W. Rüegg. Zürich: Artemis, 1950.
  Israel and Palestine: The History of an Idea. Tr. S. Godman. New York: Farrar, Straus & Young, 1952.

Zwei Glaubensweisen. Zürich: Manesse, 1950.
  Two Types of Faith. Tr. N. P. Goldhawk. London: Routledge & Kegan Paul, 1951.

Urdistanz und Beziehung. Heidelberg: L. Schneider, 1951.
  "Distance and Relation." Tr. R. G. Smith. *The Hibbert Journal,* Vol. XLIX [January, 1951], pp. 105–113; later included in *The Knowledge of Man.* Ed. M. Friedman. New York: Harper, 1965.

An der Wende: Reden über das Judentum. Cologne: J. Hegner, 1952.
  At the Turning: Three Addresses on Judaism. [Tr. not given.] New York: Farrar, Straus & Young, 1952; also included in *Addresses on Judaism.* Tr. Eva Jospe. New York: Schocken, 1966.

Bilder von Gut und Böse. Cologne: J. Hegner, 1952.
  Images of Good and Evil. Tr. M. Bullock. London: Routledge &

Kegan Paul, 1952; also in *Good and Evil: Two Interpretations*. New York: Scribners, 1953.

Die chassidische Botschaft. Heidelberg: L. Schneider, 1952. Partly translated in *The Origin and Meaning of Hasidism*. Ed. & tr. M. Friedman. New York: Horizon, 1960.

Gottesfinsternis. Zürich: Manesse, 1953.

Eclipse of God: Studies in the Relation between Religion and Philosophy. Tr. M. Friedman et al. New York: Harper, 1952. [The English version was published earlier.]

Recht und Unrecht: Deutung einiger Psalmen. Basel: Klosterberg, 1952.

Right and Wrong: An Interpretation of Some Psalms. Tr. R. G. Smith. London: S.C.M. Press, 1952; also found in *Good and Evil*.

Zwischen Gesellschaft und Staat. Heidelberg: L. Schneider, 1952.

"Society and the State," in *Pointing the Way: Collected Essays*. Tr. & ed. M. Friedman. New York: Harper, 1957.

Einsichten. Aus den Schriften gesammelt. Wiesbaden: Insel, 1953.

Hinweise: Gesammelte Aufsätze (1909–1953). Zürich: Manesse, 1953. Most of these essays are translated in *Pointing the Way*.

Reden über Erziehung. Heidelberg: L. Schneider, 1953.

Die Schriften über das dialogische Prinzip. Heidelberg: L. Schneider, 1954.

The "Nachwort" translated as "The History of the Dialogical Principle," by M. Friedman in the revised edition of *Between Man and Man*. New York: Macmillan, 1965.

Die Mensch und sein Gebild. Heidelberg: L. Schneider, 1955.

"Man and His Image-Work." Tr. M. Friedman, in *The Knowledge of Man*.

Das Sehertum: Anfang und Ausgang. Cologne: J. Hegner, 1955. One of the essays, "Abraham the Seer," was translated by Sophie Meyer in *Judaism*. Vol. 5, No. 4 [Fall 1956].

Das Buch der Preisungen. Cologne: J. Hegner, 1958.

Bücher der Kündung. Cologne: J. Hegner, 1958.

Schuld und Schuldgefühle. Heidelberg: L. Schneider, 1958.

"Guilt and Guilt Feelings." Tr. M. Friedman, in *The Knowledge of Man*.

Be Sod Siach. Jerusalem: Mosad Bialik, 1959 [Dialogical writings].

Begegnung: Autobiographische Fragmente. Ed. P. Schilpp & M. Friedman. Stuttgart: Kohlhammer, 1960.

"Autobiographical Fragments," *The Philosophy of Martin Buber*. Ed. P. Schilpp & M. Friedman. La Salle: Open Court, 1967.

Am ve' olam. Jerusalem: Sifriah Zionit, 1961. [*A People and the World.*]

Logos: Zwei Reden. Heidelberg: L. Schneider, 1962.

Elija: Ein Mysterienspiel. Heidelberg: L. Schneider, 1963. "Elijah: A Mystery Play." Tr. M. Friedman, in *Judaism,* Vol. 14, No. 3 [Summer, 1965].

Der Jude und sein Judentum: Gesammelte Aufsätze und Reden. Cologne: J. Melzer, 1963.

Nachlese. Heidelberg: L. Schneider, 1965.

Selected Studies About Buber
(arranged alphabetically)

A. Bibliography

Friedman, Maurice. "Bibliography of the Writings of Martin Buber." *The Philosophy of Martin Buber.* Ed. P. Schilpp & M. Friedman. La Salle: Open Court, 1967.

B. Monographs and Articles

Berkovits, Elieser. *A Jewish Critique of the Philosophy of Martin Buber.* New York: Yeshiva University Press, 1962.

Blumenfeld, Walter. *La antropologia filosófica de Martin Buber y la filosofía antropologica, un ensayo.* Lima: Santa Rosa, 1951.

Cohen, Arthur. *Martin Buber.* New York: Hillary House, 1957.

Diamond, Malcolm. *Martin Buber: Jewish Existentialist.* New York: Oxford University Press, 1960.

Friedman, Maurice. *Martin Buber: The Life of Dialogue.* Chicago: University of Chicago Press, 1955.

Grünfeld, Werner. *Der Begegnungscharackter der Wirklichkeit in Philosophie und Pädagogik Martin Bubers.* Düsseldorf: Henn, 1965.

Kohn, Hans. *Martin Buber, sein Werk und seine Zeit. Ein Versuch über Religion und Politik.* Hellerau: J. Hegner, 1930.

Schaeder, Grete. *Martin Buber. Hebräischer Humanismus.* Göttingen: Vandenhoeck & Ruprect, 1966.

Schilpp, P. & Friedman, M. (eds.). *The Philosophy of Martin Buber.* La Salle: Open Court, 1967.

Wodehouse, Helen. "Martin Buber's 'I and Thou.'" *Philosophy,* XX [1945], 17–30.

GABRIEL MARCEL (1889–)

Marcel was born in Paris on December 7, 1889. His mother, Laure Meyer, died when he was four. His father, Henri, was a state counsellor, French minister to Sweden, and director of the *Beaux Arts, Bibliothéque nationale,* and the *Musées nationaux.* The widower married his wife's sister and it was she who raised Marcel, playing an important role in his development. His father's esteem for the realm of the esthetic rubbed off on him and expressed itself in Marcel's love of music and the theater.

Marcel was an only child. He overcame his loneliness by inventing imaginary characters and conversing with them and then by placing them in the dramas he began writing at an early age. His formal education was a distress to him both because of parental pressure to achieve high marks and what he believed was dry, detached, and impersonal training. He attended the *Lycée Carnot* and the Sorbonne, attaining his *Agrégation de philosophie* in 1910. He did not, however, complete his doctoral dissertation which was to be on the necessary conditions for the intelligibility of religious thought.

For several years, Marcel taught philosophy at various *lycées* but ceased teaching on a regular basis after 1922. He worked for two Paris publishers, Plon and Grasset, and since 1927 has been Plon's editor of a collection of translations from notable contemporary authors. Unable to enter military service because of his health, he served as a Red Cross official. His work included obtaining news of wounded, killed, and missing soldiers and informing their families. Philosophy that abstracted from empirical or concrete particular events received a shattering blow from these war experiences such that he mentions them with respect to his philosophical formation.

In 1919 Marcel married Jacqueline Boegner, a devout Protestant. Marcel himself had been raised in an ethical, but non-religious atmosphere; his father had abandoned Catholicism and remained a lifelong agnostic as did his second wife, Marcel's aunt. In 1929, however, he became a Catholic, goaded, among other influences, by an open letter by François Mauriac challenging him to admit that he belonged to the Catholic Church. Twelve years later, his wife also converted.

Marcel's undergraduate thesis had made a comparison between Coleridge and Schelling (whose later work is classed as "Existentialist" by some historians of philosophy) and his early writings indicate a profound (and unusual for a Frenchman) acquaintance with Anglo-American philosophy of the early part of this century. F. H. Bradley's thesis of internal relations impressed him, as did Josiah Royce's concept of the social world. Marcel also held W. E. Hocking's thinking on social and religious matters in high regard. Among the philosophers associated with the Existentialist tradition it is Scheler for whom Marcel has deep respect to the extent that he devoted positive critical comment to Scheler's phenomenology of resentment. The writings of his fellow Frenchman, Jean-Paul Sartre, however, have received several vigorous attacks from Marcel.

Besides his work in philosophy, he has written several dramas and has also written a good deal of literary criticism. Marcel won the *Grand Prix de Littérature de l'Académie Français* in 1948, the Goethe Prize in 1956, and the *Grand Prix National des Lettres* in 1958, gave the Gifford Lectures in 1949–1950 at Aberdeen, Scotland and the William James Lectures at Harvard University in 1961. He belongs to the Institut de France and is an officer of the *Légion d'Honneur*.

"An Outline of a Concrete Philosophy"
from *Creative Fidelity*

Translated by Robert Rosthal

The ideas developed in the present chapter are not only difficult
to grasp but are virtually incapable of exposition in any strict
sense. Few ideas, I should think, are as ill-adapted to a didactic
exposition; and in any case, I should like to avoid a didactic approach. This, however, is not the only difficulty: the title of the
chapter which I chose without previous reflection, introduces a
further complication into an already complex situation. The
title was chosen because of its generality, for I did not wish to
become involved in details I could not cope with before I knew
how to present my theme. At the present time it seems to me
that the title is overly ambitious, inadequate, and to a certain
extent, misleading. Thus the reader may infer that I wanted to
enter a plea in behalf of a particular philosophical doctrine.
This is not quite true. To be sure, I shall describe a certain
kind of reaction to the official philosophy which, while chiefly a
personal one, is not peculiar to me. But putting aside all modesty
which would be inappropriate in the present context, I shall
from the outset speak exclusively for myself, not knowing to
what extent other philosophers with whom I am in general agreement would accept what I propound. The reader will readily
note that I become more directly and more personally involved
as I go along; some readers will find this shocking, but I do not
believe that such readers can be useful or even understanding
adepts of a concrete philosophy as I conceive it.

After explaining in what I admit to be a highly polemical
and eristic fashion what I mean by a concrete philosophy, I
shall indicate—and this will be the most difficult section—my
own main points of view. After this I shall try to lead you via
a number of rather precipitous detours to vantage points from
which it will be possible to survey certain characteristic spiritual
landscapes as I should like to call them. A friend once told me

in connection with *Etre et avoir* that the book had given him an unsurpassed feeling for the developing movement of thought. Nothing, I believe, has greater significance than this, but I am afraid that it is infinitely more difficult to convey such a feeling when one must do it in expository form. If I have any success in this connection, I will not be as disappointed as I first anticipated.

The first question which may occur to the reader is: "Do you believe that the concrete philosophy to which you refer is a philosophy which has existed in the past? Where and at what period do you place it?" It is absolutely impossible to reply to this question. Or, rather, the most that can be said with respect to the past is that there have been places and times where and when concrete philosophical thought has blossomed; but this thought has always or almost always tended to degenerate either into a scholasticism or into a series of devitalized commentaries which fatally tended to sterilize and blind the really deep and fresh intuition about which they proliferated. Expend, restore: these two verbs which express the two successive but related moments of every living process of becoming, can also be applied here. Here, expenditure is also exploitation; but a mysterious event occurs on the level of philosophical thought which is contrary to what occurs on the technical or practical level: the exploitation of a thought tends to obnubilate, alter and degrade it. This is what I venture to call the peculiar danger of "isms." Cartesianism versus Descartes, Kantianism versus Kant, Bergsonism versus Bergson, are so many possible themes for a historian of thought. There is a lot of material for reflection here, the details of which I cannot now enter into. What I should simply like to indicate is, that if the expression "concrete philosophy" has any meaning, it is primarily because it embodies a rejection in principle of all "isms," including a certain kind of academicism.

On reflection, it seems to me that the form of my philosophical thought has been shaped in response to the demands of such refusal; it is a form which has been imposed on me—since I cannot truthfully say that I willed it. From the outset before the war, my plan had rather been to write a work which would be traditional in form; while unlike Hamelin's *Essai* which had always repelled me because of its rigorously systematic character, it would hopefully be similar to the *Contingence des lois de la nature*,[1] for example. From the start, the *Journal métaphysique* was destined to be a series of notes taken down day by day, which could be developed at some time or other into an organic whole. It was curious to see how, as my ideas became clearer, or rather, as my mind apprehended more directly the concrete nature of its contents, I perceived more clearly the difficulty of moving from the first to the second level; furthermore, this insight was progressively accompanied by a more critical reflection on the very notion of a system. I do not think it is an exaggeration to say that the revulsion evoked in me by the idea of a system, which I was able to formulate more clearly as time went on, has played a considerable role in this context. This point should be elaborated somewhat. What we are concerned with at present is the idea of *my* system; hence the relation signified by this expression between the system and the person who considers himself its inventor and patent-holder. It has become increasingly evident to me that the claim to "encapsule the universe" in a set of formulas which are more or less rigorously related, is absurd. And doubtless, this has been the source of the extraordinary annoyance I have always felt whenever certain amiable individuals, animated by the very best intentions, ask me questions about *my* philosophy. The attempt to imprison me in this sort of shell which I am supposed to have secreted, is, I think, all that is required to make me find it uninhabitable. Philosophy has increasingly appeared to me an open inquiry; here the possessive index is divested of a meaning which when construed in terms of results, of what is already acquired, seems to me intolerable or inconceivable; I understand very well why people should ask me about my research since it is indeed my own; however, insofar as I admit that it is completed, it on the contrary no longer belongs to me. "There is nothing less patentable than philosophy, nothing more difficult to appropriate." I have affirmed as much on a previous occasion. The philosopher is just the opposite of a property owner, which does not imply that he feels no temptation to claim certain privileges;

[1] [Émile Boutroux, 1874. Transl. note.]

but he should recognize the temptation for what it is. The same can be said of the artist, but here the problem is somewhat different.

Under these circumstances it is clear why the *Journal métaphysique* increasingly became an instrument of research and even an integral part of that research. This is why I often took the opportunity to write: "We must investigate, search, continue on;" in the same way as the adventurer indicates a path to follow, the explorer the trails he has not been able to take. I believe that my concern has never been and that it never will be, self-exploitation.

What does it mean to philosophize concretely? This question does not at all imply a return to empiricism; this point is extremely important: the most pernicious and dehumanized philosophies such as Spencerism, together with the speculation associated with it, have been based to my mind on empirical foundations.

We are nearer to the truth if we say that it is to philosophize *hic et nunc*. I want to clarify what I mean by this, but I can only do so in a polemical manner, i.e., by opposing a certain official philosophy or pseudo-philosophy. First of all, with respect to the attitude with which one approaches the history of philosophy: we witness today, and have witnessed for more than twenty years—fortunately a reaction is taking place—the resignation of philosophy in behalf of the history of philosophy, a resignation which threatens to have the most dangerous repercussions on history itself. When confronted with a certain problem, for example, one first tries to determine how it appeared in history, in such or such a system; that is, the problem is treated as an entity which has evolved in a certain way; when one has reluctantly reached the final chapter or rather, epilogue, and is compelled to ask the fatal question: *Quid nunc?*—and now what?— the temptation is to let the problem evaporate, or reduce it to ashes. The crematorium is a more or less faithful image of such a conclusion. There is no task which would be of greater use nor any more delicate, than that of a phenomenological analysis of that *we others*, expressed in epilogues with an apparent modesty mingled with the extraordinary presumption typical of those who plume themselves on their scientific attitude. It is undeniable that the ideal for the majority of such philosophers (I use the term "philosopher" reluctantly), consists in a kind of general elimination of problems. We presumably pay the necessary respect to them in studying their historical development, but we must substitute for them the positive inquiries typical of the empirical sciences such as psychology or sociology. However, we must examine the significance of this attempt to absorb the former. No theme is more crucial to our inquiry.

We can now introduce the subject of what is scientifically verifiable, where team-work is required. The extent to which the image of the factory and the laboratory have obsessed philosophers is difficult to assess. A number of connected themes should be examined. The inferiority complex of the philosopher, say, when he compares himself to the scientist—but of the philosopher who betrays himself. The philosopher of integrity is not converted. This gives rise to still further questions. We must understand the cause of the betrayal; the weakness which leads to a disownment. A number of related factors intervene, beginning with the development of democratic superstitions (as Scheler has demonstrated, it is likely that this development itself has its source in an inferiority complex). Take the democratic notion of value: the "I think" which is degraded into thought in general, and thought in general which in turn is degraded to the rank of the impersonally democratic "one."

What I have called concrete philosophy must adopt a position which is completely opposed to this attitude.

First, with respect to the history of philosophy. Of course, a philosopher should "know" the history of philosophy, but to my mind he should know it more or less in the sense in which a composer knows harmony; that is, possessing the tools of harmony without ever becoming their slave. From the moment he is their slave, he is no longer a creator or an artist. Similarly, the philosopher who has surrendered to the history of philosophy is, to that extent, not a philosopher. It should be added—and this implies an important distinction—that whoever has not lived a philosophical problem, who has not been gripped by it, cannot understand what this problem meant for those who lived before him; roles are reversed in this respect, and the history of philosophy presupposes philosophy and not conversely.

However, an objection may arise: how can the philosopher be compared to the musician? The latter invents, the former claims to understand. Are not the values inspiring artistic creation and philosophical inquiry irreducibly distinct? This is a large problem which I can only touch on here. I should simply like to affirm that the two do converge despite their differences.

Separate out certain structures: one finds that there is a limiting zone of invention and discovery which is not to be identified with production. If I am not mistaken, it was Paul Valéry who wrote that "Artistic genius acts like those extremely high temperatures which have the power to dissociate combinations of atoms and regroup them in accordance with a completely different order of another type."

Nobody would care to deny that the function of the philosopher is similar, and even those who are located at the antipodes of what I have called concrete philosophy, Bertrand Russell, for example, have understood this.

However, there is another factor or aspect of the situation which seems to me just as important. Whoever philosophizes *hic et nunc,* is, it may be said, a prey of reality; he will never become completely accustomed to the fact of existing; existence is inseparable from a certain astonishment. The child, in this sense, is close to existence; we all know children who have asked extremely metaphysical questions at the age of six; but this astonishment usually disappears, the surprise dies away. The majority of licensed philosophers who are known—I will not cite any names—do not show the least trace of it. There is room for extended analysis here too. A reader of Mr. Piaget or Mr. Levy-Bruhl will not fail to relate metaphysical astonishment to heaven knows what prelogical mentality, and melancholically deplore its survival in certain backward contemporaries. However, we must closely examine the nature of this habituation to reality which is considered typical of the adult attitude. Habituation to reality, but actually, the word "reality" is inappropriate in this context. Whatever our level of approach, there can be no apprehension of reality which is not accompanied by a certain shock. Doubtless such a shock can only be felt intermittently by definition. Only the habituated mind, or more accurately, the mind which is established in its daily routine, cannot feel it any more, or else finds some way of eliminating the memory it has of it—whereas a metaphysical mind never wholly resigns itself to this routine, viewing it as a state of sleep. This is not merely a minor difference: for it implies an absolute incompatibility in the mode of evaluation.

Personally, I am inclined to deny that any work is philosophical if we cannot discern in it what may be called the sting of reality. I may add that in the development of any philosophy, there is always a point, unfortunately, at which the dialectical instrument tends to operate all by itself in a vacuum. Any philosopher who makes judgments or otherwise functions in his capacity as philosopher, cannot be distrusted enough. For he makes a distinction with respect to his own reality which mutilates it and which irremediably tends to falsify his thought; I believe that the role of the most vivifying philosophical minds of the last century, of a Kierkegaard perhaps, but certainly of a Schopenhauer or a Nietzsche, has properly consisted in revealing, directly or indirectly, that dialectic whereby the philosopher may be led to surpass himself as a simple *Fachmensch*, as a simple specialist.

It may be said in this respect that no concrete philosophy is possible without a constantly renewed yet creative tension between the I and those depths of our being in and by which we are; nor without the most stringent and rigorous reflection, directed on our most intensely lived experience.

I just mentioned the *I:* I do not believe that I, anymore than Mr. Le Senne,[2] can dispense with this word which has been so philosophically discredited up to the present time. However, it must be understood that I do not mean by this the ideal subject of knowledge. In general, the *cogito* in its idealist interpretation —I shall not decide whether it can be taken in any other sense —does not seem to me a likely point of departure for a possible metaphysics.

In a footnote to *Etre et avoir*, I affirmed: "The Incarnation, central datum of metaphysics. The incarnation, situation of a being which appeared to itself as tied to a body . . . A

2 Rene Le Senne (1882–1954), a philosopher who taught at the Sorbonne [Editor's note].

fundamental situation which cannot strictly speaking be disposed of, surmounted or analyzed. Properly speaking, it is not a fact but rather the datum with respect to which a fact becomes possible."[3] Whereas between the *cogito* and any fact, there is a hiatus which it is probably impossible to fill.

One of the axes of my philosophical inquiries, beginning with the second part of the *Journal métaphysique*, undoubtedly passes through this point; in returning to this passage, I was surprised to find that in 1928 I used the same expressions Jaspers later used in his own system. A pure coincidence, but one based on the very character of this kind of philosophy. The importance of the terms *situation* and *commitment* which appeared in a note written at the same period, cannot be overstressed. I have always strongly emphasized the fact that a philosophy which begins with the *cogito*, i.e. with non-commitment even if construed as an act, runs the risk of never getting back to being. "The incarnation is the datum with respect to which a fact becomes a possible"; it is not a form, and it cannot be maintained that it is a pure and simple relation. It is a datum which is not transparent to itself. The truth is that the seductiveness of the *cogito* for philosophers lies precisely in its apparent transparency. It is always appropriate to ask, however, whether this isn't a false supposition of transparency. This, I believe, creates a dilemma: either this supposition of transparency is false, and there is, as I believe, in the *cogito* itself, an element of obscurity which cannot be elucidated—or, if the *cogito* is really transparent to itself, we can never infer existence from it no matter what logical procedure we use.

At this point opacity and the conditions which cause it should become the object of our reflections. I have been increasingly compelled to adopt the paradoxical thesis that it is always the self which creates its own obscurity, its opacity deriving from the fact that the self places itself between the I and the other. "The obscurity of the external world is a function of my own obscurity; the world has no intrinsic obscurity."[4] This observation will crop up again shortly. But we must first return to the

[3] P. 11.
[4] *Etre et avoir*, p. 13.

other term of that tension which to my mind is the very source
of a concrete philosophy. What are we to understand by "these
depths of being in and by which we are?"

I want to maintain that there is something which is inexhaustibly concrete at the heart of reality or of human destiny the
understanding of which does not proceed by successive stages as
in the case of the empirical sciences. Each of us gains access to
this inexhaustible reality only through the purest and most
unblemished part of himself. The obstacles in the way are enormous. Indeed experience reveals that those pure parts of oneself
which alone can make contact with being are concealed from
the outset by a mass of accretions and encrustations; it is only
through a long and painful task of cleansing, or more accurately,
of purification, and by a painful self-discipline, that we succeed in ridding ourselves of them; while this is being accomplished, the dialectical instrument which is an integral part of
philosophical thought, and which that thought should always
control, is being forged. Here we touch on a central but highly
difficult theme which has priority over all the others. I have to
cite one of the passages in my book which I believe is essential
although I am afraid it is not the most obvious, for it will give
me the chance to lay bare what I believe is the hinge on which
metaphysics turns. I am afraid that this passage will give you
an extremely vague impression of what I mean. However, it will
be clarified in the sequel where I take the detours I mentioned
earlier, and where, I believe, you will be able to grasp somewhat better the meaning and implication of this extremely abstract passage:

> Reflection on the question: *What am I?* and its impli-
> cations. When I reflect on the implications of the question
> *what am I?*, considered in its comprehensive sense, I un-
> derstand it to mean: what qualifications do I have to an-
> swer this question? hence any answer to this question
> *which comes from me,* should be mistrusted.
>
> Can somebody else supply me with the answer, how-
> ever? At once an objection arises: it is I who discern the
> qualifications the other person has to answer me, the final
> validity of his statements; but what qualifications do I have
> which would allow me to exercise this discrimination? If I

wish to avoid self-contradiction I must rely on an absolute judgment which is more private to me than my own judgment; indeed, so far as I construe that judgment as something external to me, I necessarily reopen the question of whether it is valid, of how it is to be appraised. Hence the question as such cannot really be asked and is converted instead into an appeal. Insofar as I become aware of this *appeal qua appeal*, however, I come to understand that it is possible only because there is something deep within me besides my own self, something more private to me than myself, and as soon as this occurs, the significance of the appeal is altered.

There will be an objection: this appeal, taken in the first of the above senses, need not have any real object; it can be lost in the dark, so to speak. What, however, is the import of this objection? that I haven't perceived any answer to this "question," i.e., that "someone else hasn't answered." In this case I remain on the level of the assertion or non-assertion of a fact; but I am thereby restricted to the circle of the problematic (i.e. of what is placed *before* me).[5]

I will add to this passage another note written two months later, but with the same orientation:

In no circumstances can an assertion ever appear to generate the reality of that which it asserts. The proper formulation here is: I assert it because it is. Now this expresses the results of a previous reflection, but at this stage, the *this is* seems to be external to the assertion and prior to it; the assertion refers to something given. A secondary reflection, however, immediately follows. By reflecting itself, the assertion encroaches on the hallowed ground reserved to the *this is*. Hence I must infer: *this is* itself presupposes an assertion. An infinite regress therefore follows unless I am willing to lay down the affirmation itself as origin, but we will not press the point. Let us admit that being has besieged the self, as it were; and by *self*, I mean in this context, the subject who affirms. Such a subject still mediates between being and the assertion; hence the problem I raised

[5] *Ibid.*, pp. 180–182.

in my notes of January 19, is raised again; for I am compelled to question the ontological status of this self with respect to the being which besieges it. Is the self submerged by it, or does the self somehow govern it instead? If it governs it, however, what confers this power on it, and what exactly is its significance?[6]

This brings us to a distinction which I regard as fundamental, and which at the present time seems a presupposition of my entire philosophical thought, although it was not explicitly formulated until October 1932:

"The distinction between the mysterious and the problematic." A problem is something which one runs up against, which bars the way. It is before me in its entirety. A mystery, however, is something in which I find myself involved, whose essence therefore, is not to be completely before me. On this level it seems as though the distinction between the *in me* and the *before me* loses its meaning.[7]

Considered in these terms, many metaphysical problems appear as degraded mysteries. The clearest example of this degradation is the problem of evil as it has been traditionally formulated; we are asked to consider evil as the malfunctioning of a certain mechanism, the universe itself, which is to be examined from the outside just as a mechanic takes apart a motorcycle which doesn't run. In so doing, I consider myself not only immune to its illness or infirmity, but also external to a universe which I claim mentally at least to be able to reconstruct in its totality. Hence I adopt a position which is completely false and which is incompatible with my real situation. What is inappropriately called the problem of freedom provides us with another example. I have defined a mystery as "a problem which encroaches on its own immanent conditions of possibility," and this encroachment is particularly obvious in the case of freedom. For freedom is a ground of that very thought which tries to conceive it.

What is more, I can say without hesitation that the act of thought itself must be acknowledged a mystery; for it is the func-

6 *Ibid.*, pp. 203–204.
7 *Ibid.*, p. 145.

tion of thought to show that any objective representation, abstract schema, or symbolical process, is inadequate. This is the answer that we can make to the objection that the non-problematizable cannot really be thought. For this objection is based on a postulate which must be rejected, and which consists in holding that there is an essential commensurability between thought and its object.

Before going any further into the question of what I have called the inexhaustibly concrete, I should like to make one more preliminary remark.

Ultimately, any attempt to problematize implies the notion of a certain continuity of experience which must be preserved. But the experience which concerns us in this context, whatever scientific interpretation we give it, is really *my* experience, *my* system, the extension however remote, of an original datum which in the final analysis, is my body. In the case of a mystery, however, I am by definition led beyond any "system for me." I am involved *in concreto* in an order which by definition can never become an order or a system for me, but only for a mind which transcends and includes me, and with which I cannot even ideally identify myself. The terms *beyond, transcendence,* here take on their full meaning. I might add in passing that this is the main point of disagreement between Mr. Le Senne and myself.

If we now consider being as something inexhaustibly concrete, we will note first that it cannot function as a datum, properly speaking, that it cannot be observed but only acknowledged—I am even tempted to say, if the term did not have a foreign ring to the philosophical ear—not so much acknowledged as greeted.

The given is always presented to us as something which in principle can be catalogued, something which some procedure or other can fully account for; doubtless there is a further implication that this composite of qualities must have been built up by a process of addition and juxtaposition, and that I can mentally reproduce the procedure whereby that addition or juxtaposition actually occurred. Viewing it in this way, however, clearly involves a kind of manipulation which allows me to exercise control over something which I may to that extent consider as inert; and it is undeniable that a certain joy morally accompanies the exercise of this control.

Why, then, did I write: "Whatever can be catalogued is an occasion for despair?" an observation which I believe is very important since in it may be discerned the root of what I had been led to call the tragedy of having. The explanation of this paradox seems to me to lie in the fact that this power or control which is in principle infinite, is applied to something that surpasses it in every respect: more concretely, it is here we shall find what I am tempted to call a feeling of anguished expectation, a hanging over the void. At this point we must offer by way of illustration a number of particular experiences which will at first seem rather rudimentary.

For some time I have been in a place whose resources at first seemed to me to be inexhaustible; bit by bit, however, I have gone through all the streets, seen all the "places of interest;" and now I am overcome with a certain impatience, boredom, and distaste. I feel as if I were in prison. The place where I was staying was one where a certain number of experiences were to be had, and these experiences have already transpired. Moreover, I cannot communicate my state of mind to anyone who has lived there for a number of years, anyone who participates in its life and in what it contains of what is inexpressible and therefore impossible to exhaust. It is quite clear that a certain living relationship has grown up between him and this place, this region, which I should like to call a creative interchange; as far as I am concerned, however, nothing of this sort occurs; I have come there only to increase what I have with a certain number of additional properties.

I realize that the above is only a schema, but it is one to which I attach all the more significance because I have to admit against my will that I too have tended to behave during my life like a collector. Why? What is the reason for this impatience? It is clear that at the root of this avarice there is chiefly an awareness of time which passes, of the irrevocable; life is short, first this and then that, must be obtained. However, when I reflect at the same time on the value of this accumulation, it seems to me absurd: what weight can what I was able to know or annex to myself have, when compared with what I have not seen or assimilated? Once again despair overcomes me, hems me in, so to speak; again it is as though I were a prisoner.

If we investigate this further I think we shall find that wherever there is a creative interchange with its implication of genuine rootedness, the term "datum" tends to lose its meaning, and the sphere of the problematic is at the same time transcended. Perhaps this connection between the datum and the problematic will emerge more clearly if we take another example, one relating this time to the experience we have of others.

It is clear that I can consider a certain person as a mineral from which I can extract a certain amount of usable metal. The rest is waste matter; I reject it. The criterion of interest that is used is essential to the situation, although this expression need not be interpreted necessarily in a strictly utilitarian sense. The proliferation of inquiries and interviews has certainly contributed to the false belief that a being has value to the extent that he is "interesting."

Here again the notion of a collection is the heart of the matter. With or within myself I establish a sort of library or museum in which the interesting elements that I have been able to extract from my conversation with the other, are to be incorporated. A conversation to which I contribute nothing, where I confide nothing—except whatever is required to evoke the responses I want. This is tantamount to saying that my interlocutor is not treated as a being in this context; in fact, he is not even an other, since in such a non-lived, fictional relationship, I myself do not intervene as a being, as someone real.

"The other as other exists for me only insofar as I am open to him (insofar as he is a thou), but I am only open to him insofar as I cease to form a circle with myself within which I somehow place the other, or rather, the idea of the other; for in so doing, the other becomes the idea of the other, and the idea of the other is no longer the other as such, but the other *qua* related to me, as fragmented, as parceled out or in the process of being parceled out."[8]

At the moment when communication is established between me and the other, however, we pass from one world into an-

8 *Ibid.*, p. 155.

other; we emerge into a region where one is not merely one among others, where transcendence takes on the aspect of love. The category of the given is transcended; "never enough, always more, always closer"; these are the simple expressions which clearly indicate the change of perspective I am trying to evoke; the change involved is only partial, moreover. However, there is a sense in which the thou is given to me—and here we remain in the sphere of the problematic with all that it implies of uncertainty, doubt, jealousy—a degraded state which is based on the fact that the thou is not maintained as a thou. There is a sense, however, in which it cannot be (*Albertine Disparue* for example, should be read, in the light of these relations between the given and the problematic. For Proust, the thou is instantly converted into an it. The immanent structure of experience, moreover, ruthlessly tends to favor such a conversion)—Absence and death play a crucial role in this context.

Certain readers will be surprised at the role played by death, suicide, betrayal, in all of my writings; I do not think we can ever ascribe enough importance to these, and any philosophy which tries to elude them or conjure them away, is guilty of the worst possible kind of betrayal; it is, moreover, inevitably punished for it, in that it loses its footholds, to borrow an analogy from mountain climbing. We can push the analogy still further, but an important difference should be emphasized. For while dizziness is an obstacle to the climber, it is a positive condition of any metaphysical thought which is worthy of its name. Indeed, a certain awareness of, or attraction for, the void is perhaps necessary if being in all its plenitude is to be forcefully affirmed.

Absence, death, are construed as tests in both *Etre et avoir* and the *Mystere ontologique*. The notion of a test is fundamental in this context[9]—and I should like to indicate its meaning—particularly because a certain kind of religious preaching has perhaps unknowingly tended to obliterate it. Mr. Le Senne, in his *Obstacle et valeur,* has returned to the idea of a test; I believe that I agree with him in large part, but the agreement can-

[9] [An alternate translation is *trial*. The French term is *épreuve*. Transl. note.]

not be extended to an identity of views. I do not propose to start here with a definition since this should rather be the goal of our inquiry. Here I ascribe to the word "test" the meaning it has *grosso modo* in expressions such as "submit a work or feeling to the test of time." I shall follow my customary procedure here, i.e. analyze some example which is as concretely expressed as possible. Two young people are in love, but are not certain of the sincerity of their feelings; actually such uncertainty is rather intimated by the people who form their circle of acquaintances; but this is not of any importance in the present case. They decide (or someone decides for them) that they will live apart from each other for a while so that time and the separation can have their effects; if their love endures this test, they will conclude—(or someone will conclude for them)—that they can now reasonably be married. Time and the separation are not merely obstacles, resistant to their purposes, here; rather what resists them is used, and a functional value is conferred on it; such value consists in making possible what we may call an inner confrontation. The feelings of the two young people had been established as an absolute; but reflection (whether theirs or their parents') has intervened to give a hypothetical character to that absolute: aren't you deceived? aren't you misled with respect to the nature and *real* power of your feelings? *Real;* this word must be stressed. The question of reality, identified with value or sincerity in the present context, is raised; and it is to this question that the test provides a response. We must not be taken in by words; time in itself, or separation, do not by themselves, decide the issue; but they do clarify our awareness and help to guide it in its relations with itself; the young people meet a year later; they recognize one another. . . .

This analysis, I believe, will help to advance our inquiry. We discover that the test implies a challenge to immediate experience; a conditional challenge at least, I would maintain: of course, it seems as though I am completely involved in my feelings at this moment; but this could be an illusion; I am not in a position to decide on the answer; I succeed however in detaching myself from my immediate feeling to ask the question. The proper function of the trial is to make a reflective judgment possible which would let us modify as to its reality the affirmation of immediacy made at the beginning. Something else of fundamental importance should also be noted, namely that in this context everything is a function of freedom and freedom alone. It is an essential characteristic of the test that it is possible to be unaware of it as such; perhaps our two young people, because of obstinacy or the simple play of vanity, refuse to acknowledge that their feelings have not withstood the test, assert that nothing has changed, and that they will get married whatever anyone thinks.

Here we are on a level where the data are relatively simple; for in the example chosen, we can confidently identify duration and reality. The test of time enables us to discern whether the feeling was or was not a durable one.

This subject, however, is open to indefinite exploration. If we wish to apply the notion of a test to suffering or to death, new data are introduced—and here certain precautions have to be taken which have occasionally been ignored by indiscrete apologists. Take an invalid who has been confined to his bed for a number of years, and who can only forsee death as the end of his suffering. A priest with the best intentions in the world, comes to his bedside and says: "Thank God for the grace he has bestowed on you. This suffering has been laid on you to give you the opportunity to merit the heavenly beatitude." I am afraid that assurances which are presented in this manner will only develop an attitude of revolt and negation in the invalid. Let us forget for the moment that we are concerned with "someone else." Put yourself in the state of mind of the invalid: what sort of God is this who tortures me for my own benefit? What right has he? And what of yourself? What right do you have to be the interpreter of such a cruel and hypocritical God? The only reason you can do so is because you cannot imagine my suffering, because it is not yours—and you have the right to say what you did only if you suffered as I do, with me. . . .

I should now like to elucidate this in terms of what I have called concrete philosophy. First of all, we have to overcome this exteriority; the philosopher must sympathize with the invalid to the extent that he *becomes* the invalid; the latter must hear his words as if they came from the depths of his own consciousness. Thought in this context can assume only a personal form, that of meditation. To be sure, I can abandon myself purely and simply to my suffering, identify myself with it, and this too, is a terrible temptation. I can reconcile myself to my suffering which I proclaim to be completely meaningless; however, since it is the center of my world, the world itself, centered on something meaningless, also becomes absolutely meaningless. This is not just an abstract possibility but a temptation which at times is almost irresistible; however limited the sphere of my action may be, my affirmation is no less one of universal meaninglessness, and it is my role to prolong, extend, verify or confirm it; to help impose it even on those who had not at first consented to it. It is clear that I have the ability to effectively increase the share of meaninglessness in the world. We can go even further: we should acknowledge that the world accepts this condemnation of itself and lends itself to it; in a sense it even invokes it insofar as it seems justified. Is this the inevitable result of my situation? I do not find this conclusion tenable. A choice, however indistinct it may be, seems to be open to me; to be sure, nobody can force me to assign a meaning to my suffering, I cannot be *taught* that it has meaning; it has been observed that such a pretension to teach it always threatens to release a corrosive spirit of contradiction. However, I myself can try to understand or create that meaningfulness within myself. I am using the words "understand" and "create" indistinguishably since their meanings coincide in the present case. One thing should be understood at the outset if I am to accomplish this: strictly speaking, I cannot affirm that my suffering is meaningless; a meaning is not something that can be affirmed; hence the absence of meaning cannot be affirmed either; a meaning can only be recreated by an act of mind. Hence to say: my suffering is meaningless, is really to refuse to admit to oneself that it has meaning; more precisely, it is to show one's inadequacy in a situation where something was in the process of being created. We can make this clearer to a certain extent if we consider a situation where suffering exposes me to others; it can then be an occasion for stiffening or contracting, for focussing my attention on myself, or it can, on the contrary, open my eyes to the suffering of others which I was unable to imagine before. Here the meaning of test becomes obvious. Our concern here is one of creative interpretation. I can refuse, once again, to treat suffering as a test, to subject my reality to the test of suffering. I can do so. But at what price? We must not be taken in by words. In the case of such a refusal, I affirm myself, but what qualities does this self possess? I set myself up as an innocent source of protest against a world which is cruel and meaningless. Reflection discloses, however, that it is rather my situation itself that is meaningless. Every protest presupposes a remedy to which it is directed; here the remedy is inconceivable and the protest is immediately canceled in the same way as a protest made by someone who thought he was addressing somebody else, is stifled, when he perceives that he is alone.

At this point someone will be inclined, I should think, to raise an objection. It will be maintained that the test so understood, is only conceivable under extreme circumstances which, if they are not compelling, nevertheless encourage me to ask myself what I am; and here we have a concrete example of the dialectic I described at the beginning of my exposition. For does not our life go on under average, normal conditions, without being in such jeopardy?

I believe that our reply must first of all be—but we should not be satisfied with the reply—that on reflection, the opposition between normal and extreme conditions is untenable. The extreme circumstance, *par excellence*, is the immediate nearness of death, and nobody can be really sure that his death is not imminent. If, as we must concede, the point of view of the philosopher coincides with that of the man who is fully alert to his state, we can then hold that he should view the world in the light of that threat, for the normal state is an extreme state. To be sure this is only a part, an aspect of the truth, so to speak; and it is no less true and perhaps even more essential for us to affirm that we should live and work every moment as though we had an eternity before us. This represents an antinomy for which there is no dearth of examples and which is connected with the mysterious relation between my being and my life. At this point I should like to say a few words about one of the most significant yet hidden of all the relationships I have tried to illuminate in my work.

The person who gives up his life for a cause is aware of giving all, of making a *total* sacrifice; but even if he is going to a certain death, his act is not a suicide, and there is, metaphysically speaking, a gap between the act of sacrificing his life and that of killing himself. Why? Here we must introduce the notions of disposability and indisposability. Doubtless, the person who gives up his life gives up everything, but he does it for something else that he asserts means more, that is worth more; he puts his life at the disposal of that higher reality; he extends to the ultimate that disposability which is exemplified in the fact of dedicating oneself to a person, to a cause. In so doing, he has, if I may say so, proved that he has placed or situated his being beyond life. There is not and cannot be any sacrifice without hope, and hope is suspended in the ontological realm. Suicide, on the other hand, is basically negation. If there is any exclamation which signifies the intention of the suicide, it is the word: enough! If killing oneself does not mean the deliberate desire to make oneself indisposable, it in any case means that one does not care whether he remains disposable for others. Suicide is essentially a refusal; it is a resignation. Sacrifice is essentially attachment (and every secular critic of asceticism has ignored this characteristic and thereby failed in his purpose).

To be sure, these observations are phenomenological, but they clear the way for a hyperphenomenological reflection which is identical with metaphysics itself. Whether or not he actually believes in eternal life, the person who sacrifices himself acts as if he believed; the suicide acts as if he did not believe. The philosopher, however, cannot be satisfied with the use of the expression "as if" in this context. Whatever Vahinger may have thought, every philosophy of the "as if" is self-contradictory; every authentic philosophy is the active negation of the "as if." In this connection a preliminary reflection will be of help. Nothing is less able to illuminate a being for us, less able to show his worth or what he is, than knowing what his opinions are; opinions do not count, and if I had the time, I would be glad to demonstrate this in detail, and to exhibit what is entailed by such a demonstration, particularly in connection with those implications of a political complexion. The question which then arises is whether, contrary to the atheistic, unmeaning justifications that the nonbeliever offers or claims to offer of his sacrifice, the latter does not actually confirm the truth of that which the nonbeliever denies. Consider the passage of Proust in *Le Prison-nière*, which I will cite in an abridged form: "All these obligations which have not their sanction in our present life, seem to belong to a different world . . . , a world entirely different from this which we leave in order to be born into this world, before perhaps returning to the other to live once again beneath the sway of those unknown laws which we have obeyed because we bore their precepts in our hearts, knowing not whose hand had traced them there—those laws to which every profound work of the intellect brings us nearer and which are invisible only—and still!—to fools. So that the idea that Bergotte was not wholly and permanently dead is by no means improbable."[10] Here we have one of those Platonic intuitions—so rare in Proust's work—which contradicts the general tenor of his work.

If such a hyperphenomenological reflection is possible, however, it is because we penetrate here into the zone of the meta-problematic. The views I have expressed in *Etre et avoir* on fidelity, faith, hope, are completely unintelligible if the distinction between a problem and a mystery is not understood. A philosopher friend once said to me with respect to this book: "It is more moving, more compressed than the *Journal méta-physique*, but it seems to me to be less positive." I shall ignore everything involving the emotions evoked by the book since this is clearly not for me to judge; however, I can say that if the reader does not see that this is the most positive book he can find, the essence of it has entirely eluded him. To be truthful, I see clearly what the reply will be; and this will afford me the opportunity of explaining myself with respect to a particularly delicate point insofar as it is possible to do so. Somebody will maintain: "This book is positive to the extent that it is obviously written by a Catholic; but those who do not participate in your faith will be brought by your reflection up against a wall which for them is unsurmountable. In this sense your friend

[10] Marcel Proust, *The Captive*, Part I, *Remembrance of Things Past*. Transl. C. K. Scott Moncrieff (N.Y.: Random House, 1927), vol. II, p. 150.

was right. And generally, the anguished question in the minds of those who read your book is the relation between a concrete philosophy and a Christian philosophy. Is it your view that one passes imperceptibly from one to the other? How is this possible, however, without sophistry? Moreover, from the Christian point of view, wouldn't this imply a kind of rationalization or naturalization of the supernatural? Even the use of the term 'mystery' is misleading."

This question in its own right deserves to be developed in much greater detail. I can only reply in a general way.

First of all, two things are clear.

It is plain that an adept of concrete philosophy as I conceive it, is not necessarily a Christian; strictly speaking, it cannot even be said that he is embarked on a path which should logically lead him to Christianity; on the other hand, I believe that the Christian who is also a philosopher and can dig under the scholastic formulas on which he is frequently nourished, would almost inevitably rediscover the fundamental data of what I have called concrete philosophy (whereas he will certainly never find the idealism of Brunschvicg nor doubtless even that of Hamelin). Such an answer, however, is still beside the point.

In the first place, I must say that at least to my mind, a concrete philosophy cannot fail to be magnetically attracted to the data of Christianity, perhaps without knowing it. And I do not think that this fact should shock anyone. For the Christian, there is an essential agreement between Christianity and human nature. Hence the more deeply one penetrates into human nature, the more one finds oneself situated on the axes of the great truths of Christianity. An objection will be raised: You affirm this as a Christian, not as a philosopher. Here, I can only repeat what I said at the beginning: the philosopher who compels himself to think only as a philosopher, places himself on the hither side of experience in an infrahuman realm; but philosophy implies an exaltation of experience, not a castration of it.

With respect to the ambiguity of the word "mystery," I can only say this: insofar as it seems a disturbing fact to me that one should grant that the mysteries of faith are superimposed on a completely problematizable world, hence one stripped of ontological thickness; on a world penetrable to reason as a crystal is to light; so it seems to me if not rational, then at least reasonable to think that this world is itself rooted in being, hence that it transcends in every way those localized problems with their similarly localized solutions which permit the insertion of the technical into things. I have referred to the incarnation in a purely philosophical sense; this incarnation, mine and yours, is to that other Incarnation, to the dogma of the Incarnation, as philosophical mysteries are to revealed mysteries.

"Doubtless, the recognition of the ontological mystery which I perceive as the main bastion of metaphysics, is only possible through the fructifying radiation of revelation itself, which can also be realized in the depths of those souls for whom every positive religion is alien; this recognition, which occurs in certain higher modes of human experience, does not imply any adhesion to a determinate religion, but it does permit the person who rises up to it, to forsee the possibility of a revelation quite differently from someone who, never having passed beyond the boundaries of the problematizable, remains on the hither side of the line where the mystery of being can be perceived and proclaimed. An irresistible movement impels such a philosophy towards an encounter with a light of which it already has a presentiment and whose hidden stimulus and future energy it already feels in its heart."[11]

MARCEL'S MAJOR WRITINGS

(arranged chronologically)

A. Philosophical Writings

Journal métaphysique. Paris: Gallimard, 1927.
  Metaphysical Journal. Tr. Bernard Wall. Chicago: Regnery, 1952.
Être et avoir. Paris: Aubier, 1935.
  Being and Having. Tr. Katherine Farrer. Westminister: Dacre, 1949.
Du Refus à l'invocation. Paris: Gallimard, 1940.
  Creative Fidelity. Tr. Robert Rosthal. New York: Farrar, Straus & Giroux, 1964.
Homo Viator: Prolégomènes à une métaphysique de l'espérance. Paris: Aubier, 1945.

  [11] *Le Monde cassé* (Paris: Desclée de Brouwer, 1933), p. 301.

Homo Viator: Introduction to a Metaphysics of Hope. Chicago: Regnery, 1952.

La métaphysique de Royce. Paris: Aubier, 1945.

   Royce's Metaphysics. Tr. Virginia & Gordon Ringer. Chicago: Regnery, 1956.

"Regard en arrière," in Gilson, E., et al. *Existentialisme chrétien: Gabriel Marcel.* Paris: Plon, 1947.

   "An Essay in Autobiography," *The Philosophy of Existence.* Tr. Manya Harari. London: Harvill, 1948.

Positions et approches concrètes du mystère ontologique. Louvain: Nauwelaerts; Paris: Vrin, 1949.

   "On the Ontological Mystery," in *The Philosophy of Existence.*

Le mystère de l'être. 2 vols. Paris: Aubier, 1951.

   The Mystery of Being. Vol. I: Tr. G. S. Fraser; Vol. II: Tr. R. Hague. Chicago: Regnery, 1951.

Les Hommes contre l'humain. Paris: La Colombe, 1951.

   Man Against Mass Society. Tr. G. S. Fraser. Chicago: Regnery, 1952.

Le Déclin de la sagesse. Paris: Plon, 1954.

   The Decline of Wisdom. Tr. M. Harari. New York: Philosophical Library, 1955.

L'Homme Problématique. Paris: Aubier, 1955.

   Problematic Man. Tr. B. Thompson. New York: Herder & Herder, 1967.

Présence et immortalité. Paris: Flammarion, 1959.

   Presence and Immortality. Tr. M. A. Machado. Pittsburgh: Duquesne University Press, 1967.

Fragments philosophiques 1909–1914. Louvain: Nauwelaerts, 1962.

   Philosophical Fragments 1909–1914. Tr. L. Blain. South Bend: University of Notre Dame Press, 1965.

The Existential Background of Human Dignity [Wm. James Lectures 1961]. Cambridge: Harvard University Press, 1963.

Auf der Suche nach Wahrheit und Gerechtigkeit. Frankfurt a. M.: Knecht, 1964.

   Searchings. Tr. Anonymous. Westminister: Newman, 1967.

Paix sur la terre; deux discours, une tragédie. Paris: Aubier, 1965.

Essai de philosophie concrète. Paris: Gallimard, 1967.

Pour une sagesse tragique et son au-delà. Paris: Plon, 1968.

B. Drama and Criticism

Le Seuil Invisible [*La Grâce; Le Palais de Sable*]. Paris: Grasset, 1914.

Le coeur des autres. Paris: Grasset, 1921.

L'Iconoclaste. Paris: Stock, 1923.

Un Homme de Dieu. Paris: Grasset, 1925.
> *A Man of God*. Tr. M. Gabain, in *Three Plays*. New York: Hill and Wang, 1958.

Le Quatuor en fa dièse. Paris: Plon, 1929.

Trois Pièces [*Le Regard neuf; La Mort de demain; La Chapelle ardente*]. Paris: Plon, 1931.
> *La Chapelle ardente* was translated as *The Funeral Pyre* by R. Heywood in *Three Plays*.

Le Monde cassé. Paris: Desclée de Brouwer, 1933.

Le Dard. Paris: Plon, 1936.

Le Fanal. Paris: Stock, 1936.
> *The Lantern*, in *Cross Currents*, VIII, No. 2 [Spring 1958].

Le Chemin de crête. Paris: Grasset, 1936.
> *Ariadne*. Tr. R. Heywood, in *Three Plays*.

La Soif. Paris: Desclée de Brouwer, 1938. [Republished as *Les Cours avides*. Paris: Le Table Ronde, 1951.]

L'Horizon. Paris: Aux Étudiants de France, 1945.

Théâtre comique [*Colombyre ou le Brasier de la Paix; Le Double expertise; Les Points sur les I; Le Divertissement posthume*]. Paris: Albin Michel, 1947.

Vers un autre royaume [*L'Émissaire; Le Signe de la Croix*]. Paris: Plon, 1949.

La Fin des temps. Paris: Réalités, No. 56 [1950].

Rome n'est plus dans Rome. Paris: La Table Ronde, 1951.

Mon Temps n'est pas le vôtre. Paris: Plon, 1955.

Croissez et multipliez. Paris: Plon, 1955.

La Dimension Florestan [including the essay "La crépuscule du sens commun"]. Paris: Plon, 1958.

Théâtre et religion. Lyon: Vitte, 1959.

L'Heure théâtrale: de Giraudoux à Jean-Paul Sartre. Paris: Plon, 1959.

Selected Studies About Marcel
(arranged alphabetically)

Bagot, Jean Pierre. *Connaissance et amour; Essai sur la philosophie de Gabriel Marcel*. Paris: Beauchesne, 1958.

Bernard, Michel. *La philosophie religieuse de Gabriel Marcel*. Paris: Les Cahiers du Nouvel Humanisme, 1952.

Cain, Seymour. *Gabriel Marcel*. New York: Hillary House, 1963.

Collins, James. "Gabriel Marcel and the Mystery of Being," *Thought.* XVIII [Dec. 1943], 665–693.

De Corte, Marcel. *La philosophie de Gabriel Marcel.* Paris: Chez Pierre Tequi, no date.

Gallagher, Kenneth. *The Philosophy of Gabriel Marcel.* New York: Fordham University Press, 1962.

Gilson, Étienne, et al. *Existentialisme chrétienne: Gabriel Marcel.* Paris: Plon, 1947.

Hocking, William E. "Marcel and the Ground Issues of Metaphysics," *Philosophy and Phenomenological Research.* XIV, 439–469.

Prini, Pietro. *Gabriel Marcel e la metodologia dell' inverificabile.* Rome: Editrice Studium Christi, 1950.

Ricoeur, Paul. *Gabriel Marcel et Karl Jaspers; Philosophie du mystère et philosophie du paradox.* Paris: Éditions due Temps Présent, 1947.

Troisfontaines, Roger. *De l'existence à l'être.* 2 vols. Paris: Vrin, 1953.

NICHOLAS BERDYAEV (1874–1948)

Berdyaev was born on March 6, 1874, in Kiev. His father had come from a military family and was himself an officer in the Imperial Guards. His mother, Princess Kudashev, was half French, but also belonged to Polish nobility. The family religion was Orthodox.

Early in his life he developed a *tic douloureux* which caused him both discomfort and embarrassment throughout his life. He attended the Military Cadet Corps of Pages and spent six years there finding both the regimentation and the "worldly society of the upper class" distasteful.

When Berdyaev entered the University of Kiev in 1894, he did so as a law student. He became involved in Marxist activities, was arrested, then exiled in 1898 to Vologda. His expulsion from the university ended a formal course of education. Although he studied at other universities, he never earned a degree. His first book was written during his exile and indicated a trend away from Marxism toward personalism.

Upon his return from exile in 1901, Berdyaev became acquainted with Sergius Bulgakov, a former Marxist and professor of economics at Kiev. Bulgakov awakened his religious interests. The two became lifelong friends.

Berdyaev then spent a term at the University of Heidelberg in 1903 in order to hear the philosophy lectures of Wilhelm Windelband. When he returned to Russia, he married Lydia Yudifovna and settled in St. Petersburg, where for two years he helped Bulgakov edit *Novi Put* (*The New Way*), a journal of literary, political, and philosophical analysis. In 1907 he traveled to Paris to find out about the current religious and philosophical movements going on there. He moved to Moscow on his return and joined a religio-philosophical society there, founded in honor of Vladimir Solovyev. During the fourteen years he spent in Moscow, he participated in the religious and cultural revival going on in Russia at the time. Moreover, he became a loyal though nonconformist member of the Orthodox Church. Brought to civil trial in 1914 because of an article criticizing the Holy Governing Synod, he escaped sentence in 1917 when World War I and the Communist Revolution intervened.

The Free Academy of Spiritual Culture which Berdyaev founded in 1918 possessed semiofficial status at first, but government displeasure and repression increased to the point where Berdyaev was prohibited from publishing his lectures there, and announcements of its activities were forbidden. Yet in 1920 he received an appointment to the chair of philosophy at the University of Moscow. Berdyaev then and afterwards had mixed views of the revolution. Although he condemned the crimes and violence of the Soviet order, he believed, unlike most of his fellow emigrées, that the seeds of messianism were present in post-revolutionary Russia. Nevertheless he was expelled in 1922 from the U.S.S.R., together with a number of other Russian intellectuals.

After spending two years in Berlin where he lectured at the newly founded Russian Scientific Institute and where he established the Religious-Philosophical Academy, Berdyaev, his wife, and sister-in-law moved to Clamart outside Paris, which had replaced Berlin as the center of the Russian community abroad. He re-established the Academy in Paris and founded a monthly journal *Put* (*The Way*) devoted to religious philosophy. The journal was continued until the beginning of World War II. Berdyaev was also reunited with Bulgakov, who had become the dean of the newly founded Russian Theological Academy.

In 1939 an invitation to lecture at the Sorbonne was extended to Berdyaev and the revised French edition of his *Freedom and the Spirit* won an award from the French Academy. The years of the German occupation of France during World

War II were not extremely difficult for him despite the fact that the Gestapo questioned him several times. Two years after the war ended, Cambridge University conferred an honorary doctorate of divinity upon him. The following year, 1948, three years after the death of his wife, he died on March 23 (some accounts report the 24th). There were no children.

"The Problem of Being and Existence"
from *The Beginning and the End*

Translated by R. M. French

> 1. *Being as objectification. Being and the existent, that which exists. Being and non-being. Being as concept. Being and value. Being and spirit.* 2. *The supremacy of freedom over being. The determinism of being and freedom. Being and primary passion. Being as congealed freedom and congealed passion. Being as nature and being as history*

1

From ancient times philosophers have sought for the knowledge of being (*ousia, essentia*). The construction of an ontology has been philosophy's highest claim. And at the same time the possibility of achieving this has raised doubts among the philosophers. At times it has appeared as though human thought was in this respect pursuing a phantom.

The transition from the many to the One, and from the One to the many was a fundamental theme in Greek philosophy. In a different way the same topic has been fundamental in Indian philosophy also. Indian thought has been disquieted by the question: how does being arise out of non-being? It has to a large extent been focussed upon the problem of nothingness, non-being and illusion. It has been occupied with the discovery of the Absolute and deliverance from the relative, which meant salvation. Indian thought has tried to place itself on the other side of being and non-being, and has revealed a dialectic of being and non-being. It is this that has made it important.[1]

The Greeks sought for ἀρχή—the primordial. They meditated upon the unchangeable; they were disquieted by the problem of the relation of the unchangeable to the changing; they desired to explain how becoming arises out of being. Philosophy has sought to rise above the deceptive world of the senses and to penetrate behind this world of plurality and change to the One. Doubts were felt even about the reality of movement. If man breaks through to the knowledge of being he will reach the summit of knowledge, and, it was sometimes thought, he will attain salvation through having achieved union with the primary source. Yet at the same time Hegel says that the concept of being is quite futile, while Lotze says that being is indefinable and can only be experienced.[2]

Heidegger, in claiming to construct a new ontology, says that the concept of being is very obscure. Pure being is an abstraction and it is in an abstraction that men seek to lay hold upon primary reality, primary life. Human thought is engaged in the pursuit of its own product. It is in this that the tragedy of philosophical learning lies, the tragedy, that is, of all abstract philosophy. The problem which faces us is this: is not being a product of objectification? Does it not turn the subject matter of philosophical knowledge into objects in which the noumenal world disappears? Is not the concept of being concerned with being quâ concept, does being possess existence?

Parmenides is the founder of the ontological tradition in philosophy, a highly significant and important tradition in connection with which the efforts of reason have reached the level of genius. To Parmenides being is one and unchanging. There is no non-being, there is only being. To Plato, who carried on this ontological tradition, true being is the realm of ideas which he sees behind the moving and multiple world of the senses. But at the same time Plato maintains the supremacy of the good and beneficent over being, and from that it is possible to go on to an-

[1] See R. Grousset: Les philosophies indiennes. O. Strauss: Indische Philosophie. A. Schweitzer: Les grands penseurs de l'Inde.

[2] See Lotze: Metaphysik.

other tradition in philosophy. In Plato the unity of perfection is the highest idea, and the idea of being is being itself. Eckhardt held that *Esse* is *Deus*. Husserl, after passing through a phase of idealism and asserting the primacy of the mind, came to carry on the tradition of Platonism in the contemplation of ideal being, *Wesenheiten*.

In the processes of thought the human mind sought to rise above this world of sense which presents itself to us, and in which everything is unstable, above a world which is a world of becoming, rather than of being. But by that very fact the search for being was made to depend upon thinking, and the impress of thought lay upon it. Being became an object of thought and thereby came to denote objectification. What reason finds is its own product. Reality is made to depend upon the fact that it becomes the subject matter of knowledge, in other words an object. But in actual fact the reverse is true, reality is not in front of the knowing subject but 'behind' him, in his existentiality.

The erroneous character of the old realism is particularly clear in the case of Thomism, the philosophy of the common or of sound common sense. It regards the products of thinking, the hypostatization of thought, as objective realities.[3] And so St Thomas Aquinas supposes that the intellect, and the intellect alone, comes into touch with being. Being is received from without. This is to make the average normal consciousness, which is also regarded as unchangeable human nature, absolute. That kind of ontology is a clear example of naturalistic metaphysics, and it does not recognize the antinomies to which the reason gives birth. The nature of the intellectual apprehension of being is settled by the fact that being was already beforehand the product of intellectualization. In the Thomist view being comes before thought; but this being was already fabricated by thought. Being is secondary not primary.

In mediaeval philosophy the question of the relation between *essentia* and *existentia* played a great part. Being is *essentia*. But the question remains: does *essentia* possess an *existentia* of its own? In present day philosophy, for example in Heidegger and

[3] See Garrigou-Lagrange: *Le sens commun*.

Jaspers, this question assumes a new form, that of the relation between *Sein* and *Dasein*.[4] Aristotle and the scholastics admitted a classification in logic of the same sort as in zoology and in this classification the concept of being took its place as the broadest and highest. Brunschvicg points out with truth that it was Descartes who broke with this naturalism in logic and metaphysics.[5] But ontology has never been able to cut itself off entirely from the naturalistic spirit.

Hegel introduced a new element into the concept of being. He introduced the idea of non-being, nothingness, without which there is no becoming, no emergence of what is new. Being itself is empty and the equivalent of non-being. The initial fact is being-non-being, unity, being and nothingness. Being is nothingness, indeterminate and unqualified being. *Dasein* in Hegel is the union of being and nothingness, becoming, determinate being. Truth is in the transition from being to nothingness, and from nothingness to being. Hegel wants to put life into numbed and ossified being. He seeks to pass from the concept to concrete being. This is attained by way of recognizing the ontological nature of the concept itself, it is being which is filled with interior life. "Identity", says Hegel, "is a definition of only simple, immediate, dead being, whereas contradiction is the root of all movement and vitality. It is only in so far as nothingness has within itself its contradiction that it has movement and attains a state of wakefulness and activity."[6] Dialectic is real life.

But Hegel does not attain to real concreteness. He remains under the sway of object-ness. Vladimir Soloviëv, who was much under the influence of Hegel, makes a very valuable and important distinction between being and the existent. Being is the predicate of the existent, which is the subject. We say: "this creature is" and "that sensation is". A hypostatization of the predicate takes place.[7] Various kinds of being are formed through the abstraction and hypostatization of attributes and

[4] Heidegger: *Sein und Zeit*. Jaspers: *Philosophie*, 3 vols.

[5] See L. Brunschvicg: *Spinose et ses contemporains*, and *Le progrès de la conscience dans la philosophie occidentale*.

[6] See Hegel: *The Science of Logic*. Vol. II.

[7] See Soloviëv: *Critique of Abstract Principles*, and *The Philosophical Principles of Pure Knowledge*.

qualities. In this way ontologies have been built up which have constituted a doctrine of abstract being, rather than of the concrete existent. But the real subject-matter of philosophy ought to be, not being in general, but that to which and to whom being belongs, that is, the existent, that which exists. A concrete philosophy is an existential philosophy, and that Soloviëv did not arrive at, he remained an abstract metaphysician. The doctrine of the all-in-one is ontological monism.[8]

It is not true to say that being is: only the existent is, only that which exists. What being tells of a thing is that something is, it does not speak about *what* is. The subject of existence confers being. The concept of being is logically and grammatically ambiguous, two meanings are confused in it. Being means that something is, and it also means that which is. This second meaning of "being" ought to have been discarded. Being appears as both a subject and a predicate, in the grammatical sense of those words. In point of fact, being is a predicate only. Being is the common, the universal. But the common has no existence and the universal is only within that which exists, in the subject of existence, not in the object. The world is multiple, everything in it is individual and single. The universally-common is nothing but the attainment of the quality of unity and commonness in this plurality of individualities. There is some degree of truth in what Rickert says, that being is a judgment of value, that the real is the subject-matter of judgment. From this the mistaken conclusion is drawn that truth is obligation, rather than being; the transcendent is only *Geltung*. *Geltung* refers to value not to reality.

When the primacy of obligation over being is asserted, this may seem like the Platonic primacy of the good over being. But Soloviëv says that that which obliges to be in this world is the eternally existent in another sphere. A fundamental question arises: does meaning, the ideal value, exist and if so in what sense does it exist? Does a subject of meaning, value, and idea exist? My answer to this question is that it does, it exists as spirit. Spirit moreover is not abstract being, it is that which concretely exists. Spirit is a reality of another order than the reality

[8] See S. Frank: *The Unfathomable.*

of "objective" nature or the "objectivity" which is born of reason. Ontology should be replaced by pneumatology. Existential philosophy departs from the "ontological" tradition, in which it sees unconscious objectification. When Leibniz sees in the monad a simple substance which enters into a complex organization, his teaching is about the world harmony of monads, and what he is most interested in is the question of simplicity and complexity, he is still in the power of naturalistic metaphysics and an objectified ontology.

It is essential to grasp the inter-relations of such concepts as truth, being, and reality. Of these terms, reality is the least open to doubt and the most independent of schools of philosophical terminology, in the meaning which it has acquired. But originally it was connected with *res*, a thing, and the impress of an objectified world has been stamped upon it. Truth again is not simply that which exists, it is an attained quality and value, truth is spiritual. That which is, is not to be venerated simply because it is. The error of ontologism leads to an idolatrous attitude towards being. It is Truth that must be venerated, not being. Truth moreover exists concretely not in the world but in the Spirit. The miracle of Christianity consists in the fact that in it the incarnation of Truth, of the Logos, of Meaning, appeared, the incarnation of that which is unique, singular and unrepeatable; and that incarnation was not objectification, but an abrupt break with objectification. It must be constantly reiterated that spirit is never an object and that there is no such thing as objective spirit. Being is only one among the offspring of spirit. But only the trans-subjective is that which exists, the existent. Whereas being is merely a product of hypostatized existence.

Pure ontologism subordinates value to being. To put it in another way, it is compelled to regard being as a unique scale and criterion of value and of truth, of the good and the beautiful. Being, the nature of being, indeed *is* goodness, truth and beauty. The one and only meaning of goodness, truth and beauty is in this, that they are—being. And the reverse side of the matter is similar, the sole evil, falsehood and ugliness, is non-being, the denial of being. Ontologism has to recognize being as God, to deify being and to define God as being. And this is characteristic of the kataphatic doctrine of God, and distinguishes it in principle from the apophatic which regards God not as being, but as supra-being.

Schelling says that God is not being, but life.[9] "Life"—it is a better word than "being". But ontological philosophy has a formal likeness to the philosophy of life, to which "life" is the sole standard of truth, goodness and beauty; life at its maximum is to it the supreme value. The highest good, the highest value is defined as the maximum of being or the maximum of life. And there is no disputing the fact that one must be, one must live, before the question of value and good can be raised at all. There is nothing more sad and barren than that which the Greeks expressed by the phrase οὐκ ὄν, which is real nothingness. The words μὴ ὄν conceal a potentiality, and this therefore is only half being or being which is not realized.

Life is more concrete and nearer to us than being. But the inadequacy of the philosophy of life consists in this, that it always has a biological flavour: Nietzsche, Bergson and Klages illustrate the point. Being indeed is abstract and has no interior life. Being can possess the highest qualities, but it may also not possess them, it can be also the very lowest. And therefore being cannot be a standard of quality and value. The situation is always saved when the phrase "real and true" is added. But then "reality and truth" become the highest standard and appraisal. It is the attainment of "real and true" being which is the aim, not the affirmation of being at its maximum. This only underlines the truth that ontologism is a hypostatization of predicates and qualities. Being acquires an axiological sense. Value, goodness, truth and beauty are a vision of quality in existence and rise above being.

But there is something else still more important in characterizing ontologism in philosophy. The recognition of being as the supreme good and value means the primacy of the common over what is individual and this is the philosophy of universals. Being is the world of ideas which crushes the world of the individual, the unique, the unrepeatable. The same thing happens

[9] See Schelling: *Philosophie der Offenbarung.*

when matter is regarded as the essence of being. Universalist ontologism cannot recognize the supreme value of personality: personality is a means, a tool of the universally common.

In the most living reality *essentia* is individual in its existentiality, while the universal is a creation of reason (Duns Scotus). The philosophy of ideal values is characterized by the same crushing of personality, nor has it any need to oppose the philosophy of abstract being. Real philosophy is the philosophy of the concrete living entity and entities and it is that which corresponds most closely to Christianity. It is also the philosophy of concrete spirit, for it is in spirit that value and idea are to be found. Meaning also is something which exists and by its existence is communicated to those that exist. Being and becoming must have a living carrier, a subject, a concrete living entity. That which concretely exists is more profound than value and comes before it, and existence goes deeper than being.

Ontologism has been the metaphysics of intellectualism. But the words "ontology" and "ontologism" are used in a broad sense and not rarely are identified with metaphysical realism as a whole. Hartmann says that the irrational in ontology lies deeper than the irrational in mysticism, for it is beyond the bounds not only of what can be known, but also of what can be experienced.[10] But in this way ontological depth is assigned a higher (or deeper) level than the possibility of experience, that is, than existence. This ontological depth is very like the Unknowable of Spencer. In Fichte being exists for the sake of reason and not the other way about. But being is the offspring of reason and reason moreover is a function of primary life or existence. Pascal goes deeper when he says that man is placed between nothingness and infinity. This is the existential position of man, and not an abstraction of thought.

Attempts have been made to stabilize being and strengthen its position between nothingness and infinity, between the lower abyss and the higher, but this has been merely an adjustment of reason and consciousness to the social conditions of existence in the objectified world. But infinity breaks through from below and from above, acts upon man, and overthrows stabilized being

[10] N. Hartmann: *Grundzüge einer Metaphysik der Erkenntnis.*

and established consciousness. It gives rise to the tragic feeling of life and to the eschatological outlook.

And this accounts for the fact that what I call eschatological metaphysics (which is also an existential metaphysics) is not ontology. It denies the stabilization of being and foresees the end of being, because it regards it as objectification. In this world indeed being is change, not rest. That is what is true in Bergson.[11] I have already said that the problem of the relation between thinking and being has been put in the wrong way. The actual statement of the problem has rested upon failure to understand the fact that knowledge is the kindling of light within being, not taking up a position in front of being as an object.

Apophatic theology is of immense importance for the understanding of the problem of being. It is to be seen in Indian religious philosophy and, in the West, principally in Plotinus, in the Neo-platonists in pseudo-Dionysius the Areopagite, in Eckhardt, in Nicholas of Cusa and in German speculative mysticism. Kataphatic theology rationalized the idea of God. It applied to God the rational categories which were worked out in relation to the object world. And so it has been light-heartedly asserted, as a basic truth, that God is being. The kind of thinking which is adapted to the knowledge of being has been applied to him, the sort of thinking which is stamped with the indelible impress of the phenomenal, natural and historical world. This cosmomorphic and sociomorphic knowledge of God has led to the denial of the fundamental religious truth that God is mystery and that mystery lies at the heart of all things.

The teaching of kataphatic theology to the effect that God is being and that he is knowable in concepts is an expression of theological naturalism. God is interpreted as nature and the attributes of nature are transferred to him (almightiness, for example); just as in the same sociomorphic way the properties of power are communicated to him. But God is not nature, and not being, he is Spirit. Spirit is not being, it stands higher than being and is outside objectification. The God of kataphatic theology is a God who reveals himself in objectification. It is a

11 Bergson: *L'Évolution créatrice*.

doctrine about what is secondary not about what is primary. The important religious process in the world is one of spiritualizing the human idea of God.[12] The teaching of Eckhardt about *Gottheit* as of greater depth than *Gott* is profound. *Gottheit* is mystery and the concept of creator of the world is not applicable to *Gottheit*. God, as the first thing and the last, is the non-being which is supra-being.

Negative theology recognizes that there is something higher than being. God is not being. He is greater and higher, more mysterious than our rationalized concept of being. Knowledge of being is not the last thing, nor the first. The One in Plotinus is on the other side of being. The depth of the apophatic theology of Plotinus, however, is distorted by monism according to which the separate entity issues from the addition of non-being. This would be true, if by "non-being" we understood freedom as distinct from nature. Eckhardt's teaching is not pantheism, it cannot be turned into the language of rational theology, and those who propose to call it theo-pantheism have a better case. Otto is right when he speaks of the supra-theism not the anti-theism of Sankhara and Eckhardt.[13] One must rise higher than being.

The relation which subsists among God, the world and man is not to be thought of in terms of being and necessity. It must be conceived by thought which is integrated in the experience of spirit and freedom. In other words it must be thought of in a sphere which lies beyond all objectification, all object power, authority, cause, necessity and externality, outside all ejection into the external. The sun outside me denotes my fall, it ought to have been within me and to send out its rays from within me.

This is above all of cosmological significance, and it means that man is a microcosm.[14] But in the problem which concerns the relations which subsist between man and God, it certainly should not be taken to mean pantheistic identity. That is always evidence of rationalistic thinking about being in which everything is either relegated to a place outside, or identified with,

[12] See R. Otto: *Das Heilige.*
[13] See Otto: *West-Oestliche Mystik.*
[14] See my *The Meaning of the Creative Act.*

something. God and man are not external to each other, nor outside one another; neither are they identified, the one nature does not disappear in the other. But it is impossible to work out adequate concepts about this, it can be expressed only in symbols. Symbolic knowledge which throws a bridge across from one world to the other, is apophatic.

Knowledge by concepts which are subject to the restraining laws of logic, is suitable only to being, which is a secondary objectified sphere, and does not meet the needs of the realm of the spirit, which is outside the sphere of being or of supra-being. The concept of being has been a confusion of the phenomenal world with the noumenal, or the secondary with the primary, and of predicate with subject. Indian thought took the right view in asserting that being depends upon act. Fichte also maintains the existence of pure act. Being is postulated as an act of spirit, it is derivative. What is true does not mean what belongs to being, as mediaeval scholastic philosophy would have it. *Existentia* is not apprehended by the intellect, whereas *essentia* is so apprehended, simply because it is a product of the intellect. What is true does not mean what belongs to being, but what belongs to the spirit.

A matter of great importance in the question of the relation between kataphatic and apophatic theology, is the working out of the idea of the Absolute, and this has been in the main the business of philosophy, rather than of religion. The Absolute is the boundary of abstract thought, and what men wish is to impart a positive character to its negative character. The Absolute is that which is separate and self-sufficient, there is in the Absolute no relation to any other. In this sense God is not the Absolute, the Absolute cannot be the Creator, and knows no relation to anything else. The God of the Bible is not the Absolute. It might be put in a paradoxical way by saying that God is the Relative, because God has a relation to his other, that is to say to man and to the world, and he knows the relation of love. The perfection of God is the perfection of his relation; paradoxically speaking, it is the absolute perfection of that relation. Here the state of being absolute is the predicate not the subject. It is doubtful whether the distinction can be allowed which Soloviëv draws between the Absolute Existent and the Absolute which is becoming; there is no becoming in the Absolute. The Absolute is the unique, and the thinking mind can assert this of the *Gottheit*, though it says it very poorly.

A real, not verbal, proof of the being of God is in any case impossible because God is not being, because being is a term which belongs to naturalism, whereas the reality of God is a reality of spirit, of the spiritual sphere which is outside what belongs to being or to supra-being. God cannot in any sense whatever be conceived as an object, not even as the very highest object. God is not to be found in the world of objects. Ontological proof shares in the weakness of all ontologism. The service which Husserl rendered by his fight against all forms of naturalistic metaphysics must be acknowledged.[15] Naturalism understands the fullness of being in terms of the form of a material thing, the naturalization of the mind regards the mind as a part of nature. But existence bears different meanings in different spheres. Husserl draws a distinction between the being of a thing and the being of the mind. In his view the mind is the source of all being, and in this respect he is an idealist. It is the being of consciousness with which he is concerned.

It is rightly pointed out that there is a difference between Husserl and Descartes, in that the latter was not concerned with an investigation into the various meanings of existence. But Husserl is concerned with that, and seeks to pass on from a theory of knowledge to a theory of being. But he preserves the ontologism which comes down from Plato. It is upon being that he keeps his attention fixed. But there is this further to be said, that not only things but even *Wesenheiten* also exist for the mind only, and that means that they are exposed to the process of objectification. Behind this lies a different sphere, the sphere of the spirit. Spirit is not being, but the existent, that which exists and possesses true existence, and it is not subject to determination by any being at all. Spirit is not a principle, but personality, in other words the highest form of existence.

Those idealists who have taught that God is not being, but existence and value, have simply been teaching, though in a dis-

---

[15] See Levinas: *La théorie de l'intuition dans la phénoménologie de Husserl.*

torted and diminished form, the eschatological doctrine of God. God reveals himself in this world and he is apprehended eschatologically. . . . I stand by a philosophy of spirit, but it differs from the traditional "spiritualist" metaphysics. Spirit is understood not as substance, nor as another nature comparable with material nature. Spirit is freedom, not nature: spirit is act, creative act; nor is it being which is congealed and determined, albeit after a different fashion. To the existential philosophy of spirit the natural material world is a fall, it is the product of objectification, self-alienation within existence. But the form of the human body and the expression of the eyes belong to spiritual personality and are not opposed to spirit.

2

Ontological philosophy is not a philosophy of freedom. Freedom cannot have its source in being, nor be determined by being: it cannot enter into a system of ontological determinism. Freedom does not suffer the determining power of being, nor that of the reason. When Hegel says that the truth of necessity is freedom he denies the primary nature of freedom and entirely subordinates it to necessity. And in no degree does it help when Hegel asserts that the finite condition of the world is consciousness of freedom of the spirit, and the ultimate aim is the actualization of freedom. Freedom is represented as the outcome of a necessary world process—as a gift of necessity. But then, it has to be said that in Hegel even God is an outcome of the world process; he becomes within the world-order. The choice has to be made—either the primacy of being over freedom, or the primacy of freedom over being. The choice settles two types of philosophy. The acceptance of the primacy of being over freedom is inevitably either open or disguised determinism. Freedom cannot be a kind of effect of the determining and begetting agency of anything or anybody; it flees into the inexplicable depth, into the bottomless abyss. And this is acknowledged by a philosophy which takes as its starting point the primacy of freedom over being, freedom which precedes being and all that belongs to it.

But most of the schools of philosophical thought are under the sway of determined and determining being. And that kind of philosophizing is in the power of objectification, that is of the ejection of human existence into the external. "In the beginning was the Logos." But in the beginning also was freedom. The Logos was in freedom and freedom was in the Logos. That, however, is only one of the aspects of freedom. It has another aspect, one in which freedom is entirely external to the Logos and a clash between the Logos and Freedom takes place. Thus it is that the life of the world is a drama, it is full of the sense of tragedy, the antagonism of diametrically opposed principles occurs in it. There is an existential dialectic of freedom: it passes into necessity, freedom not only liberates, it also enslaves. There is no smooth development in the process of reaching perfection. The world lives in stresses of passion, and the basic theme of its life is freedom. The philosophical doctrines of freedom give little satisfaction for the most part. They shrink from coming into contact with the mystery of it, and fear to penetrate into that mystery.

There was real genius in Boehme's teaching about the *Ungrund*. It was a vision rather than a rational doctrine. Boehme was one of the first to break away from the intellectualism of Greek and scholastic philosophy, and his voluntarism is a revelation of the possibility of freedom for philosophy. He reveals an interior life and process within the Deity itself. It is an eternal birth of God, a self-begetting. The denial of this theogonic process is a denial of the life of the Godhead. Franz Baader also says the same.[16] It was Boehme's view, as it was that of Heraclitus, that the life of the world is embraced by fire, which is the fundamental element. Streams of fire flow through the cosmos: there is a conflict between light and darkness, between good and evil. The contradictory, suffering, and flamingly tragic character of the life of the world is accounted for by the fact that before being and deeper than being lies the *Ungrund*, the bottomless abyss, irrational mystery, primordial freedom, which is not derivable from being. I reproduce here what I wrote in my essay on "The Doctrine of the *Ungrund* and Freedom in Jacob Boehme". "The doctrine of the *Ungrund* answers the need

---

[16] See Franz von Baader's *Complete Works*: Vol. XIII. *Vorlesungen und Erläuterungen zu Jacob Boehme's Lehre*. p. 65.

which Boehme felt to come to grips with the mystery of freedom, the emergence of evil, the conflict between light and darkness," Boehme says: "Ausser der Natur ist Gott ein Mysterium, verstehet in dem Nichts; denn ausser der Natur ist das Nichts, das ist ein Auge der Ewigkeit, ein ungründlich Auge, das in Nichts stehet oder siehet, denn es ist der Ungrund und dasselbe Auge ist ein Wille, verstehet ein Sehen nach der Offenbarung, das Nichts zu finden."[17]

The *Ungrund,* then, is nothingness, the groundless eye of eternity; and at the same time it is will, not grounded upon anything, bottomless, indeterminate will. But this is a nothingness which is *"Ein Hunger zum Etwas"*.[18] At the same time the *Ungrund* is freedom.[19] In the darkness of the *Ungrund* a fire flames up and this is freedom, meonic, potential freedom. According to Boehme freedom is opposed to nature, but nature emanated from freedom. Freedom is like nothingness, but from it something emanates. The hunger of freedom, of the baseless will for something, must be satisfied.

"Das Nichts macht sich in seiner Lust aus der Freiheit in der Finsternis des Todes offenbar, denn das Nichts will nicht ein Nichts sein, und kann nicht ein Nichts sein."[20]

The freedom of the *Ungrund* is neither light nor darkness, it is neither good nor evil. Freedom lies in the darkness and thirsts for light; and freedom is the cause of light.

"Die Freiheit ist und stehet in der Finsternis, und gegen der finstern Begierde nach des Lichts Begierde, sie ergreifet mit dem ewigen Willen die Finsternis; und die Finsternis greifet nach dem Lichte der Freiheit und kann es nicht erreichen denn sie schliesst sich mit Begierde selber in sich zu, und macht sich in sich selber zur Finsternis."[21]

Apophatically and by way of antinomy, Boehme describes the mystery which comes to pass within that depth of being which makes contact with the original nothingness. Fire flames up in the darkness and the light begins to dawn. Nothingness becomes

---

[17] See Jacob Boehme's *Sämmtliche Werke* edited by Schiller. Vol. IV. pp. 284–5. *Vom dreifachen Leben des Menschen.*
[18] Ibid. Vol. IV. p. 286.   [19] Ibid. Vol. IV. pp. 287–9.
[20] Ibid. Vol. IV. p. 406.   [21] Ibid. p. 428.

something, groundless freedom gives birth to nature. For the first time perhaps in the history of human thought, Boehme saw that at the basis of being and superior to being lies groundless freedom, the passionate desire of nothing to become something, the darkness in which fire and light begin to kindle into flame. In other words he is the founder of metaphysical voluntarism which was unknown alike to mediaeval thought and to the thought of the ancient world.

Will, that is, freedom, is the beginning of everything. But Boehme's thought would seem to suggest that the *Ungrund*, the ungrounded will, lies in the depth of the Godhead and precedes the Godhead. The *Ungrund* is indeed the Godhead of apophatic theology and at the same time, the abyss, the free nothingness which precedes God and is outside God. Within God is nature, a principle distinct from him. The Primary Godhead, the Divine Nothingness is on the further side of good and evil, of light and darkness. The divine *Ungrund*, before its emergence, is in the eternity of the Divine Trinity. God gives birth to himself, realizes himself out of the Divine Nothingness. This is a way of thinking about God akin to that in which Meister Eckhardt draws a distinction between *Gottheit* and *Gott*. *Gott* as the Creator of the world and man is related to creation. He comes to birth out of the depth of *Gottheit*, of the ineffable Nothingness. This idea lies deep in German mysticism.

Such a way of thinking about God is characteristic of apophatic theology. Nothingness is deeper down and more original than some-thing. Darkness, which is not in this case evil, is deeper down and more original than light, and freedom deeper and more original than all nature. The God of kataphatic theology, on the other hand, is already some-thing and means thinking about what is secondary.

"Und der Grund derselben Tinktur ist die göttliche Weisheit; und der Grund der Weisheit ist die Dreiheit der ungründlichen Gottheit, und der Grund der Dreiheit ist der einige unerforschliche Wille, und des Willens Grund ist das Nichts."[22]

Here indeed, we have the theogonic process, the process of

[22] See Jacob Boehme's *Sämmtliche Werke* edited by Schiller. Vol. IV. *Von der Gnadenwahl*. p. 504.

the birth of God in eternity, in eternal mystery, and it is described according to the method of apophatic theology. Boehme's contemplation goes deeper than all the affirmations of secondary and rationalized kataphatic doctrines. Boehme establishes the path from the eternal basis of nature, from the free will of the *Ungrund,* that is groundlessness, to the natural basis of the soul.[23] Nature is secondary and derivative. Freedom, the will, is not nature. Freedom is not created. God is born everywhere and always, he is at once ground and groundlessness. The *Ungrund* must be understood above all as freedom, freedom in the darkness.

"Darum so hat sich der ewige frei Wille in Finsternis, und Qual, sowohl auch durch die Finsternis in Feuer und Lichte, und in ein Fremdenreich eingeführet, auf dass das Nichts in Etwas erkannt werde, und dass es ein Spiel habe in seinem Gegenwillen, dass ihm der freie Wille des Ungrundes im Grunde offenbar sei, denn ohne Böses mochte kein Grund sein."[24]

Freedom has its roots in nothingness, in the meon, it is in fact the *Ungrund.* "Der frei Wille ist aus keinem Anfange, auch aus keinem Grunden nichts gefasset, oder durch etwas geformet . . . Sein rechter Urstand ist im Nichts."[25] Here *Nichts* does not mean a void; it is more primary than being, since being is secondary. From this the primacy of freedom over being follows. The freedom of the will contains within it both good and evil, both love and wrath. Light and darkness alike are also contained in it. Free will in God is the *Ungrund* in God, the nothingness in him. Boehme gives a profound exposition of the truth about the freedom of God, which traditional Christian theology also recognizes. His teaching about the freedom of God goes deeper than that of Duns Scotus.

"Der ewige Göttliche Verstand ist ein freier Wille, nicht von Etwas oder durch Etwas entstanden, er ist sein Selbst eigener Sitz und wohnet einig und allein in sich Selber; unergriffen von etwas, denn ausser und vor ihm ist Nichts, doch auch Selber als ein Nichts. Er ist ein einiger Wille des Ungrundes,

---

23 Ibid. Vol. IV. p. 607.
24 Ibid. Vol. V. *Misterium Magnum.* p. 162.
25 Ibid. Vol. V. p. 164.

und ist weder nahe noch ferne, weder hoch noch niedrig, sondern er ist Alles, und doch als ein Nichts."[26]

To Boehme, chaos is the root of nature, chaos, that is to say, freedom. The *Ungrund*, the will, is an irrational principle. In the Godhead itself there is a groundless will, in other words, an irrational principle. Darkness and freedom in Boehme are always correlative and coinherent. Freedom even is God himself and it was in the beginning of all things. It would appear that Boehme was the first in the history of human thought to locate freedom in the primary foundation of being, at a greater and more original depth than any being, deeper and more primary than God himself. And this was pregnant with vast consequences in the history of thought. Such an understanding of the primordial nature of freedom would have filled both Greek philosophers and mediaeval scholastics with horror and alarm. It reveals the possibility of an entirely different theodicy and anthropodicy. The primordial mystery is the kindling of light within dark freedom, within nothingness, and the consolidation of the world out of that dark freedom. Boehme writes marvellously about this in *Psychologia vera*: "Denn in der Finsternis ist der Blitz, und in der Freiheit das Licht mit der Majestät. Und ist dieses nur das Scheiden, dass die Finsternis materialisch macht, da doch auch kein Wesen einer Begreiflichkeit ist; sondern finster Geist und Kraft, eine Erfüllung der Freiheit in sich selber, verstehe in Begehren, und nicht ausser: denn ausser ist die Freiheit."[27]

There are two wills, one in the fire and the other in the light. Fire and light are basic symbols in Boehme. Fire is the beginning of everything, without it nothing would be, there would be only *Ungrund*. "Und wäre Alles ein Nichts und Ungrund ohne Feuer."[28] The transition from non-being to being is accomplished through the kindling of fire out of freedom. In eternity there is the original will of the *Ungrund* which is outside nature and before it. The philosophical ideas of Fichte and Hegel, Schopenhauer and E. Hartmann emanated from this, although

[26] Ibid. Vol. V. p. 193.

[27] See Jacob Boehme's *Sämmtliche Werke* edited by Schiller. Vol. VI. p. 14.

[28] Ibid. Vol. VI. p. 60.

they de-Christianized Boehme. German idealist metaphysics pass directly from the idea of *Ungrund,* of the unconscious, from the primordial act of freedom, to the world process, not to the Divine Trinity as in Boehme. The primary mystery of being, according to Boehme, consists in this, that nothingness seeks something.

"Der Ungrund ist ein ewig Nichts, und machet aber einen ewigen Anfang, als eine Sucht; denn das Nichts ist eine Sucht nach Etwas: und da doch auch Nichts ist, das Etwas gebe, sondern die Sucht ist selber das Geben dessen, das doch auch Nichts ist bloss eine begehrende Sucht."[29]

In Boehme's teaching freedom is not the ground of moral responsibility in man. Nor is it freedom that controls his relations to God and his neighbour. Freedom is the explanation of the genesis of being and at the same time of the genesis of evil: it is a cosmological mystery. Boehme gives no rational doctrine expressed in pure concepts of the *Ungrund* and of freedom. He uses the language of symbol and myth, and it may be just for that reason that he succeeds in letting in some light upon that depth the knowledge of which is not attainable in rational philosophy. Boehme had a vision of the *Ungrund* and that vision became a fertilizing element in German metaphysics, which tried to rationalize it.

German metaphysics, as contrasted with Latin and Greek, was to see an irrational principle in the primary fount of being, not reason, which floods the world with light as the sun does, but will, act. This comes from Boehme, and beneath the surface his influence is to be traced in Kant, Fichte, Schelling, Hegel and Schopenhauer. The possibility of a philosophy of freedom was brought to light, a philosophy which rests upon the primacy of freedom over being. Hegel does not remain true to the philosophy of freedom, but in him also the principle enunciated by Boehme may be seen; he too is bent upon what lies beyond the boundaries of ontologism. Kant must be counted as a founder of the philosophy of freedom.

Everything leads us to the conclusion that being is not the ultimate depth, that there is a principle which precedes the emergence of being and that freedom is bound up with that

[29] Ibid. Vol. VI. *Mysterium pansophicon.* p. 413.

principle. Freedom is not ontic but meonic. Being is a secondary product and it is always the case that in it freedom is already limited, and even disappears altogether. Being is congealed freedom, it is a fire which has been smothered and has cooled: but freedom at its fountain head is fiery. This cooling of the fire, this coagulation of freedom is in fact objectification. Being is brought to birth by the transcendental consciousness as it turns to the object. Whereas the mystery of primary existence with its freedom, with its creative fire, is revealed in the direction of the subject. Glimpses of the elements of a philosophy of freedom can already be seen in the greatest of the schoolmen, Duns Scotus, although he was still in chains. The influence of Boehme is of fundamental importance in Kant. It is also a basic theme in Dostoyevsky, whose creative work is of great significance in metaphysics.

The world and man are not in the least what they look like to the majority of professional metaphysicians, wholly concentrated as these are upon the intellectual side of life and the process of knowing. It is only a few of them who have broken through towards the mystery of existence, and philosophers belonging to particular academic traditions least of all. Being has been understood as idea, thought, reason, *nous, ousia, essentia,* because it was indeed a product of reason, thought, idea. Spirit has seemed to philosophers to be *nous,* because out of it the primordial breath of life was drawn and upon it lay the stamp of objectifying thought. Kant did not bring to light the transcendental feelings, volitions and passions which condition the objective world of appearances. I am not referring to psychological passions nor psychological volitions, but to transcendental, which condition the world of phenomena from out of the noumenal world.

Transcendental will and passion are capable of being transformed, and turned into another direction, they can reveal a world within the depth of the subject, in the mind before it is rationalized and objectified. And then being itself may appear to us as cooled passion and congealed freedom. Primary passion lies in the depth of the world, but it is objectified, it grows cold, it becomes stabilized, and self-interest is substituted for it. The world as passion is turned into the world as a struggle for life.

Nicholas Hartmann, a typical academic philosopher, defines the irrational in a negatively epistemological manner, as that which became part of knowledge. But the irrational has also a different, an existential meaning. New passion is needed, a new passionate will, to melt down the congealed, determinate world and bring the world of freedom to light. And such a passion, such a passionate will can be set aflame on the summits of consciousness, after all the testing enquiries of reason. There is a primary, original passion, the passionate will, which is also the final and ultimate will. I call it messianic. It is only by messianic passion that the world can be transformed and freed from slavery.

Passion is by nature twofold, it can enslave and it can liberate. There is fire which destroys and reduces to ashes, and there is fire which purifies and creates. Jesus Christ said that he came to bring down fire from heaven and desired that it might be kindled. Fire is the great symbol of a primordial element in human life and in the life of the world. The contradictions of which the life of the world and of man is made up are akin to the fiery element, which is present even in our thinking. Creative thought, which experiences opposition and is set in motion by it, is fiery thought. Hegel understood this in the sphere of logic. But the flaming fiery basis of the world, to which men but rarely break through because of their dull prosaic everyday life and to which men of genius do break through, gives rise to suffering. Suffering may ruin men, but there is depth in it, and it can break through the congealed world of day-to-day routine.

Fire is a physical symbol of spirit. According to Heraclitus and Boehme the world is embraced by fire, and Dostoyevsky felt that the world was volcanic. And this fire is both in cosmic life and in the depth of man. Boehme revealed a longing, the longing of nothingness to become something, the primordial will out of the abyss. In Nietzsche, the dionysiac will to power, although it was expressed in an evil form, was the same fusing and flaming fire. Bergson's *élan vital*, although it is given too academic a form and smacks of biology, tells us that the metaphysical ground of the world is creative impulse and life. Frobenius, in the more restricted sphere of the philosophy of culture, speaks of alarm, the grip of emotion, and shock as creative springs of culture.[30] Shestov always speaks of a shock as a source of real philosophy. And in very truth shock is a source of strength in perceiving the mystery of human existence and of the existence of the world, the mystery of destiny. Pascal and Kierkegaard were people who had been subject to shocks of that kind. But their words were words of horror and almost of despair. But if it is in a state of horror and despair that man moves on his way, yet horror and despair are not a definition of what the world and man are in their primary reality and original life. The primary reality, the original life is creative will, creative passion, creative fire. Out of this first source suffering, horror and despair do indeed arise. In the objective world and in appearances we already see the cooling process, and the realm of necessity and law. Man's answer to the call of God should have been creative act, in which the fire was still conserved. But the fall of man had as its result that the only possible response took the form of law.

In this the mystery of divine-human relations is hidden, and it is to be understood not in an objectified, but in an existential manner. But the creative passion is preserved in man even in his fallen state. It is most clearly seen in creative genius, and it remains unintelligible to the vast masses of mankind, submerged as they are in the daily dull routine. In the depth of man is hidden the creative passion of love and sympathy, the creative passion to know and give names to things (Adam gave names to things), the creative passion for beauty and power of expression. Deep down in man is a creative passion for justice, for taking control of nature: and there is a general creative passion for a vital exulting impulse, and ecstasy. On the other hand, the fall of the object world is the stifling of creative passion and a demand that it shall cool down.

The primary reality and original life shows itself to us in two forms: in the world of nature, and in the world of history. We shall see later on that these two forms of the world, as appearances, are linked with different sorts of time. While life in nature flows on in cosmic time, life in history moves forward in historical time. To metaphysics of the naturalistic type being is

[30] See L. Frobenius: *Le destin des civilisations*.

nature, not necessarily material, but also spiritual nature. Spirit is naturalized and understood as substance. That being so, history which is pre-eminently movement in time is subordinated to nature, and turned into a part of cosmic life. But the fundamental position of historiosophy, in opposition to the predominating naturalist philosophy, consists in just this, that it is not history which is a part of nature, but nature which is a part of history. In history the destiny and meaning of world life is brought to light.

It is not in the cycle of cosmic life that meaning can be revealed, but in movement within time, in the realization of the messianic hope. The sources of the philosophy of history are not to be found in Greek philosophy but in the Bible. Metaphysical naturalism, which regards spirit as nature and substance, is static ontologism. It makes use of the spatial symbolism of a hierarchical conception of the cosmos, not of symbols which are associated with time. But on the other hand to interpret the world as history, is to take a dynamic view of it, and this view understands the emergence of what is new.

Here there is a clash between two types of *Weltanschauung*, one of which may be described as cosmocentricism and the other as anthropocentricism. But nature and history are under the power of objectification. The only possible way out from this objectification is through history, through the self-revelation in it of metahistory. It is not found by submerging it in the cycle of nature. The way out is always bound up with a third kind of time, with existential time, the time of inward existence. It is only a non-objectified existential philosophy which can arrive at the mystery and meaning of the history of the world and of man. But when it is applied to history existential philosophy becomes eschatological.

The philosophy of history, which did not exist so far as Greek philosophy was concerned, cannot fail to be Christian. History has a meaning simply because meaning, the Logos, appeared in it; the God-man became incarnate, and it has meaning because it is moving towards the realm of God-Manhood. The theme of what in a derivative sense is called "being" is concerned with the encounter and the reciprocal action between primordial passionate will, primordial creative act, primordial freedom, and the Logos, Meaning. And these are flashes of freedom, will, longing and passion shining through by the power of the Logos-Meaning, through the acquisition of spirituality and a sense of spiritual freedom. Passion in cosmic life is irrational in character and subconscious, and it has to be transformed and become supra-rational and supra-conscious. We are told about the destructive nature of passion, and men assign a supremacy over the passion to reason and prudence. But the victory over evil and enslaving passions is also a passionate victory, it is the victory of radiant light, the light of a sun, not of objectifying reason. Is the absence of passion a mistake in nomenclature, or is it a mistaken idea? The spiritual sun is not dispassionate. The seed springs up out of the earth when the sun rays fall on it.

The latest attempt to construct an ontology is the work of Heidegger, and he claims that his ontology is existential.[31] It cannot be denied that Heidegger's thought displays great intensity of intellectual effort, concentration and originality. He is one of the most serious and interesting philosophers of our time. His chasing after new phrases and a new terminology is a little irritating, although he is a great master in this respect. In every metaphysical question he rightly takes the whole of metaphysics into view. One cannot but think it a revealing and astonishing thing that the latest ontology, at which this very gifted philosopher of the West has arrived, is not a theory of being, but of non-being, of nothingness. And the most up to date wisdom on the subject of the life of the world is expressed in the words "Nichts nichtet". The fact that Heidegger raises the problem of nothingness, of non-being, and that as contrasted with Bergson, he recognizes its existence, must be regarded as a service which we owe to him. In this respect a kinship with Boehme's teaching about the Ungrund may be noted.[32] Without nothingness there would be neither personal existence nor freedom.

But Heidegger is perhaps the most extreme pessimist in the history of philosophical thought in the West. In any case his pessimism is more extreme and more thorough-going than Schopenhauer's, for the latter was aware of many things which

[31] See his Sein und Zeit.
[32] See Heidegger: Was ist Metaphysik?

were a consolation to him. Moreover, he does not in actual fact give us either a philosophy of being, or a philosophy of *Existenz*, but merely a philosophy of *Dasein*. He is entirely concerned with the fact that human existence is cast out into the world. But this being cast out into the world, into *das man*, is the fall. In Heidegger's view the fall belongs to the structure of being, being strikes its very roots into commonplace existence. He says that anxiety is the structure of being. Anxiety brings being into time.

But from what elevation can all this be seen? What intelligible meaning can one give it? Heidegger does not explain whence the power of getting to know things is acquired. He looks upon man and the world exclusively from below, and sees nothing but the lowest part of them. As a man he is deeply troubled by this world of care, fear, death and daily dullness. His philosophy, in which he has succeeded in seeing a certain bitter truth, albeit not the final truth, is not existential philosophy, and the depth of existence does not make itself felt in it.

This philosophy remains under the sway of objectification. The state of being cast out into the world, into *das man*, is in fact objectification. But in any case this essay in ontology has almost nothing in common with the ontological tradition which descends from Parmenides and Plato. Nor is it a matter of chance, it is indeed full of significance, that this latest of ontologies finds its support in nothingness which reduces to nothing.

Does this not mean that it is necessary to reject ontological philosophy and go over to an existential philosophy of the spirit, which is not being but which is not non-being either?

BERDYAEV'S MAJOR WRITINGS

(arranged chronologically)

N. B. The transliterations of the Russian titles was arrived at by comparing those of Spinka & Vallon. See bibliography.

Subyektivismus i indivualismus v obshchestvennoi filosofii (Subjectivism and Individualism in Social Philosophy). St. Petersburg: Popov, 1901.

Sub specie aeternitatis: Opyty filosofskiye, sotsialniye i literaturniye (In the Light of Eternity: Philosophical, Social and Literary Essays). St. Petersburg: Pirozhkov, 1907.

Novoe religioznoe soznanie i obshchestvennost (The New Religious Consciousness and Society). St. Petersburg: Pirozhkov, 1907.

Dukhovny krizis inteligentsii (The Spiritual Crisis of the Intelligentsia). St. Petersburg: Obschestvennaya Polza, 1910.

Filosofiya svobody (Philosophy of Freedom). Moscow: Put, 1911.

Dusha Rosii (The Soul of Russia). Moscow: Put, 1911.

Aleksei Stepanovich Khomyakov. Moscow: Put, 1912.

Smysl tvorchestva. Moscow: Leman & Sakharov, 1916.
   The Meaning of the Creative Act. Tr. D. Lowrie. New York: Harper, 1955.

Sudba Rosii (The Fate of Russia). Moscow: Leman & Sakharov, 1918.

Smysl istorii. Berlin: Obelisk, 1923.
   The Meaning of History. Tr. G. Reavey. New York: Scribners, 1936.

Mirosozertsanie Dostoevskago. Prague: Y.M.C.A. Press, 1923.
   Dostoevsky. Tr. D. Attwater. New York: Sheed & Ward, 1934.

Filosofiya neravenstva (The Philosophy of Inequality). Berlin: Obelisk, 1923.

Russkaya religioznaya ideya (The Russian Religious Idea). Berlin: Obelisk, 1924.

Novoye srednovyekovie (The New Middle Ages). Berlin: Obelisk, 1924.
   The End of Our Time. Tr. D. Attwater. New York: Sheed & Ward, 1933.

Problemy russkago religioznago soznaniya (Russian Religious Consciousness). Paris: Y.M.C.A. Press, 1924.

Konstantin Leontyev. Paris: Y.M.C.A. Press, 1926.
   Leontiev. Tr. G. Reavey. Toronto: Saunders, 1940.

Filosofiya svobodnago dukha (Philosophy of the Free Spirit). 2 vols. Paris: Y.M.C.A. Press, 1927.
   Freedom and the Spirit. Tr. O. F. Clarke. New York: Scribners, 1935.

O dostoinstvye Khristianstva i nedostoinstvye Khristian. Warsaw, 1928.
   "The Worth of Christianity and the Unworthiness of Christians," in The Bourgeois Mind and Other Essays. Tr. Countess Bennigsen & D. Attwater. New York: Sheed & Ward, 1933.

Marksizm i religiya (Marxism and Religion). Warsaw, 1929.

Khristianstvo i aktivnost chelovieka. Paris: Y.M.C.A. Press, 1929.

"Christianity and Human Activity," in *The Bourgeois Mind and Other Essays*.

O naznachenii chelovyeka. Paris: Y.M.C.A. Press, 1931.
   The Destiny of Man. Tr. N. Duddington. New York: Scribners, 1937.

O samoubiistvye. Paris: Y.M.C.A. Press, 1931.

Russkaya religioznaya psikhologiya i kommunistichesky ateizm. Paris: Y.M.C.A. Press, 1931.
   Russian Religious Psychology and Communist Atheism. Tr. D. Attwater. New York: Macmillan, 1932.
   The Russian Revolution. Tr. [from manuscripts] D. B. London: Sheed & Ward, 1931.

Khristianstvo i klassovaya borba. Paris: Y.M.C.A. Press, 1931.
   Christianity and the Class War. Tr. D. Attwater. New York: Sheed & Ward, 1933.

Khristianstvo pered sovremennoi deistvitelsnostyu (Christianity and Modern Reality). Paris: Y.M.C.A. Press, 1932.

Chelovyek i mashina. Paris: Y.M.C.A. Press, 1933.
   "Man and the Machine," in *The Bourgeois Mind and Other Essays*.

Sudba chelovyeka v sovremennom mire. Paris: Y.M.C.A. Press, 1934.
   The Fate of Man in the Modern World. Tr. D. Lowrie. Milwaukee: Morehouse-Gorham, 1935.

Ya i mir obyektov (I and the World of Objects). Paris: Y.M.C.A. Press, 1934.
   Solitude and Society. Tr. G. Reavey. New York: Scribners, 1937.

Dukh i realnost. Paris: Y.M.C.A. Press, 1937.
   Spirit and Reality. Tr. G. Reavey. New York: Scribners, 1939.
   The Origin of Russian Communism. Tr. R. M. French. New York: Scribners, 1937.
   War and the Christian Conscience. Tr. not given. London: J. Clarke, 1938.

O rabstvye i svobodye chelovyeka. Paris: Y.M.C.A. Press, 1939.
   Slavery and Freedom. Tr. R. M. French. New York: Scribners, 1944.

Khristianstvo i antisemitizm. Paris: Editeurs réunis, 1939.
   Christianity and Anti-Semitism. Tr. A. Spears & V. Kanter. New York: Philosophical Library, 1954.

Russkaya ideya. Paris: Y.M.C.A. Press, 1946.
   The Russian Idea. Tr. R. M. French. New York: Macmillan, 1948.

Opyt eskatologicheskoi metafiziki (Essay on Eschatological Metaphysics). Paris: Y.M.C.A. Press, 1946.
   The Beginning and the End. Tr. R. M. French. New York: Harper, 1952.

Dialectique existentielle du divin et de l'humain. Paris: Jarrin, 1947.
  The Divine and the Human. Tr. R. M. French. New York: Macmillan, 1949.
Au seuil de la nouvelle époque. Neuchâtel: Delachaux & Niestlé, 1948.
  Toward a New Epoch. Tr. O. F. Clarke. London: Geoffrey Bles, 1949.
Samopoznanie (Self-knowledge). Paris: Y.M.C.A. Press, 1949.
  Dream and Reality. Tr. K. Lampert. New York: Macmillan, 1951.
Tsarstvo dukha i tsarstvo kesaria. Paris: Y.M.C.A. Press, 1951.
  The Realm of Spirit and the Realm of Caesar. Tr. D. Lowrie. London: Gollancz, 1952.
  Truth and Revelation. Tr. R. M. French. London: Bles, 1953.

SELECTED STUDIES ABOUT BERDYAEV

(arranged alphabetically)

Allen, E. L. *Freedom in God: A Guide to the Thought of Nicholas Berdyaev.* London: Hodden & Stoughton, 1950.
Calian, Carnegie. *The Significance of Eschatology in the Thought of Nicholas Berdyaev.* Leiden: Brill, 1965.
Clarke, Oliver F. *Introduction to Berdyaev.* London: Bles, 1950.
Lavelle, Louis. *Le moi et son destin.* Paris: Aubier, 1936.
Nucho, Fuad. *Berdyaev's Philosophy: The Existential Paradox of Freedom and Necessity.* New York: Doubleday, 1966.
Rössler, R. *Das Weltbild Nicolai Berdjajews.* Göttingen: Vanderhoek & Ruprecht, 1956.
Seaver, George. *Nicholas Berdyaev. An Introduction to His Thought.* New York: Harper, 1950.
Spinka, Matthew. *Nicholas Berdyaev: Captive of Freedom.* Philadelphia: Westminster, 1950.
Tancini, F. "Il personalismo di Nicola Berdyaev," *Filosofi contemporanei.* Milan: Istituto di studi filosofici di Torino, 1943.
Tillich, Paul. "Nicholas Berdyaev," *Religion in Life.* Vol. VII [Summer 1938], pp. 407–415.
Vallon, Michel. *An Apostle of Freedom: Life and Teachings of Nicholas Berdyaev.* New York: Philosophical Library, 1960.

Jean-Paul Sartre (1905–)

Sartre was born on June 21, 1905, in Paris. His father, Jean-Baptiste, was a naval officer and his mother, Anne-Marie Schweitzer, was a cousin of Albert Schweitzer. The father died because of fever contracted in Cochin when Sartre was an infant. He was subsequently reared in the home of his maternal grandfather who taught German at the Lycée Henri IV in Paris. The religious background of the household was mixed; his father, mother, and grandmother were Catholics, but the grandfather was Lutheran with an anticlerical bent. He himself had received Catholic religious instruction but soon drifted from religion to become a professed atheist.

Sartre attended the Lycée de la Rochelle, the Lycée Henri IV and the Lycée Louis-le-Grand before entering the École Normale Supérieure in 1924 where he pursued the study of literature and philosophy. He failed his final examinations on the first attempt but passed on the second and took his *Agrégation de Philosophie* in 1929. Sartre was something of a hero to the students of the École Normale for outmaneuvering the administration in its attempt to discipline those who were contemptuous of school ritual. Merleau-Ponty was among the benefactors of Sartre's shrewdness and their friendship began at that time.

Sartre did his military duty in the Meterological Corps between the years 1929 and 1931. Upon his discharge, he taught philosophy at the Lycée in Le Havre between 1931 and 1932, then spent the next two years in Germany at the Institut Français in Berlin for the purpose of studying contemporary German philosophy. Sartre stayed chiefly in Berlin the first year and devoted his time to the works of Husserl, Scheler, Jaspers, and Heidegger. He then went to Freiburg for the winter semester of 1933–1934, the very period in which Heidegger was Rector Magnificus of the University. The book that impressed him deeply was Husserl's *Ideas*. Sartre's essay, *The Transcendence of the Ego,* illustrates Husserl's influence upon him, although it is not an unreserved influence, given Sartre's rejection of a fundamental argument in Husserl, namely, the reality of the "transcendental ego." His first major philosophical study, *Being and Nothingness,* however, shows him struggling with Heidegger's formulations in *Being and Time.* The differences between himself and Heidegger are patently clear insofar as Sartre retains the very oppositions which Heidegger's work intends to overcome, i.e., oppositions such as man-world; consciousness-being; subject-object; etc. Sartre does not allow Heidegger to tempt him to denounce his Cartesian origins and in this he proved to be more in sympathy with Husserl.

Sartre's writing career extends considerably beyond philosophical essays into novels, short stories, plays, and literary criticism. Having studied American novelists like Faulkner and Hemingway, he produced a first-rate novel, *Nausea,* which was published in 1938. It reproduces remarkably the theme of Rilke's *The Notes of Malte Laurids Brigge.*

Sartre returned from Germany and taught again at Le Havre from 1934 to 1936, at Laon from 1936 to 1937, and then at the Lycée Pasteur in Paris from 1937 to 1939. When the Second World War began, he was mobilized as a private and sent to defend the Maginot Line. Captured there, he was a prisoner of war in Germany for nine months but was released in 1941 whereupon he served in the Resistance Movement from 1941 to 1944, writing for the underground newspapers, *Combat* and *Les Lettres Françaises.* During this period he was associated again with the Lycée Pasteur and from 1942 to 1944 with the Lycée Condorcet. From 1944 on, however, he has been free to pursue his career as a full-time writer.

When the war ended, Sartre continued his political activity by founding a party of the non-Communist left, the French Rally of Revolutionary Democrats. It proved to be an unsuccessful venture. His relationship to the Communists is ambiguous. He shares their political views but is not a party member. At the theoretical level he moved closer to Marxism as is evident from his second major philosophical writing, *Critique de la raison dialectique*. His association and friendship with Merleau-Ponty were ruptured over Marxism and the Communist Party, inasmuch as he maintained that critical attacks on the Party would prove to be a betrayal of political allies while Merleau-Ponty maintained that naive acceptance of Marxism and alliance with the Party were not intellectually possible. Yet Sartre also believes that his head will be among the first to roll if the Party comes to power in France.

During the late forties Sartre, his friend and companion, Simone de Beauvoir, a then unknown philosophy teacher, and their associates frequented the Café de Flore. This was the occasion for the notoriety of Existentialist philosophy. Existentialism made the pages of *Life* magazine and Sartre's "headquarters," the Café de Flore, became a tourist attraction.

In 1945 he traveled to the United States and lectured at Columbia, Harvard, Princeton, and Yale. In the same year he was awarded the French Legion d'honneur but refused it. He also refused the 1964 Nobel Prize for Literature, claiming that "A writer who takes political, social, or literary positions must act only with the means that are his. Those means are the written word. A writer must not accept official rewards because he would be adding the influence of the institution that crowned his work to the power of his pen. This is not fair to the reader."

Sartre has lent his support to various causes in the late fifties and sixties—to the revolution in Cuba (*Sartre on Cuba*), to the Black movement (Introduction to Franz Fanon's *Wretched of the Earth*), to the events of May 1968 that tore France apart and led to the fall of President Charles de Gaulle, and lately (May 1970) to a publication of young Maoists entitled *The People's Cause*. When two editors of the paper were arrested and later convicted on charges of inciting murder, pillage, and arson, Sartre took over as editor but was disappointed that he, too, was not put on trial. In an article in *Le Monde* he even warned that "May 1968 was not a blaze without a tomorrow."

There are some who regard his recent actions as those of an authentic hero committed to the causes of freedom, justice, and equality while others regard them as examples of his attachment to melodrama and romanticism, and they believe that the *enfant terrible* has become an old fool.

Existentialism Is a Humanism

Translated by Philip Mairet

My purpose here is to offer a defence of existentialism against several reproaches that have been laid against it.

First, it has been reproached as an invitation to people to dwell in quietism of despair. For if every way to a solution is barred, one would have to regard any action in this world as entirely ineffective, and one would arrive finally at a contemplative philosophy. Moreover, since contemplation is a luxury, this would be only another bourgeois philosophy. This is, especially, the reproach made by the Communists.

From another quarter we are reproached for having underlined all that is ignominious in the human situation, for depicting what is mean, sordid or base to the neglect of certain things that possess charm and beauty and belong to the brighter side of human nature: for example, according to the Catholic critic, Mlle. Mercier, we forget how an infant smiles. Both from this side and from the other we are also reproached for leaving out of account the solidarity of mankind and considering man in isolation. And this, say the Communists, is because we base our doctrine upon pure subjectivity—upon the Cartesian "I think": which is the moment in which solitary man attains to himself; a position from which it is impossible to regain solidarity with other men who exist outside of the self. The *ego* cannot reach them through the *cogito*.

From the Christian side, we are reproached as people who deny the reality and seriousness of human affairs. For since we ignore the commandments of God and all values prescribed as eternal, nothing remains but what is strictly voluntary. Everyone can do what he likes, and will be incapable, from such a point of view, of condemning either the point of view or the action of anyone else.

It is to these various reproaches that I shall endeavour to reply to-day; that is why I have entitled this brief exposition "Existentialism and Humanism." Many may be surprised at the mention of humanism in this connection, but we shall try to see in what sense we understand it. In any case, we can begin by saying that existentialism, in our sense of the word, is a doctrine that does render human life possible; a doctrine, also, which affirms that every truth and every action imply both an environment and a human subjectivity. The essential charge laid against us is, of course, that of over-emphasis upon the evil side of human life. I have lately been told of a lady who, whenever she lets slip a vulgar expression in a moment of nervousness, excuses herself by exclaiming, "I believe I am becoming an existentialist." So it appears that ugliness is being identified with existentialism. That is why some people say we are "naturalistic," and if we are, it is strange to see how much we scandalise and horrify them, for no one seems to be much frightened or humiliated nowadays by what is properly called naturalism. Those who can quite well keep down a novel by Zola such as *La Terre* are sickened as soon as they read an existentialist novel. Those who appeal to the wisdom of the people—which is a sad wisdom—find ours sadder still. And yet, what could be more disillusioned than such sayings as "Charity begins at home" or "Promote a rogue and he'll sue you for damage, knock him down and he'll do you homage"?[1] We all know how many common sayings can be quoted to this effect, and they all mean much the same—that you must not oppose the powers-that-be; that you must not fight against superior force; must not meddle in matters that are above your station. Or that any action not in accordance with some tradition is mere romanticism; or that any undertaking which has not the support of proven experience is foredoomed to frustration; and that since experience has shown men to be invariably inclined to evil, there must be firm rules to restrain them, otherwise we shall have anarchy. It is, however, the people who are forever mouthing these dismal proverbs and, whenever they are told of some more or less repulsive action, say "How like human nature!"—it is these very people, always harp-

---

[1] *Oignez vilain il vous plaindra, poignez vilain il vous oindra.*

ing upon realism, who complain that existentialism is too gloomy a view of things. Indeed their excessive protests make me suspect that what is annoying them is not so much our pessimism, but, much more likely, our optimism. For at bottom, what is alarming in the doctrine that I am about to try to explain to you is—is it not?—that it confronts man with a possibility of choice. To verify this, let us review the whole question upon the strictly philosophic level. What, then, is this that we call existentialism?

Most of those who are making use of this word would be highly confused if required to explain its meaning. For since it has become fashionable, people cheerfully declare that this musician or that painter is "existentialist." A columnist in *Clartés* signs himself "The Existentialist," and, indeed, the word is now so loosely applied to so many things that it no longer means anything at all. It would appear that, for the lack of any novel doctrine such as that of surrealism, all those who are eager to join in the latest scandal or movement now seize upon this philosophy in which, however, they can find nothing to their purpose. For in truth this is of all teachings the least scandalous and the most austere: it is intended strictly for technicians and philosophers. All the same, it can easily be defined.

The question is only complicated because there are two kinds of existentialists. There are, on the one hand, the Christians, amongst whom I shall name Jaspers and Gabriel Marcel, both professed Catholics;[2] and on the other the existential atheists, amongst whom we must place Heidegger[3] as well as the French existentialists and myself. What they have in common is simply the fact that they believe that *existence* comes before *essence*—or, if you will, that we must begin from the subjective. What exactly do we mean by that?

If one considers an article of manufacture—as, for example,

[2] Sartre is wrong on two counts here. Jaspers could hardly be classified as a Christian philosopher at all, much less a Catholic. The religious background of his family is, in fact, Protestant (Editor's note).

[3] Sartre is also mistaken about Heidegger. Although the matter is a complex one, Heidegger has explicitly protested the label "atheist" that has been applied to him. See *Letter on Humanism*, p. 204 (Editor's note).

a book or a paper-knife—one sees that it has been made by an artisan who had a conception of it; and he has paid attention, equally, to the conception of a paper-knife and to the pre-existent technique of production which is a part of that conception and is, at bottom, a formula. Thus the paper-knife is at the same time an article producible in a certain manner and one which, on the other hand, serves a definite purpose, for one cannot suppose that a man would produce a paper-knife without knowing what it was for. Let us say, then, of the paper-knife that its essence—that is to say the sum of the formulae and the qualities which made its production and its definition possible—precedes its existence. The presence of such-and-such a paper-knife or book is thus determined before my eyes. Here, then, we are viewing the world from a technical standpoint, and we can say that production precedes existence.

When we think of God as the creator, we are thinking of him, most of the time, as a supernal artisan. Whatever doctrine we may be considering, whether it be a doctrine like that of Descartes, or of Leibnitz himself, we always imply that the will follows, more or less, from the understanding or at least accompanies it, so that when God creates he knows precisely what he is creating. Thus, the conception of man in the mind of God is comparable to that of the paper-knife in the mind of the artisan: God makes man according to a procedure and a conception, exactly as the artisan manufactures a paper-knife, following a definition and a formula. Thus each individual man is the realisation of a certain conception which dwells in the divine understanding. In the philosophic atheism of the eighteenth century, the notion of God is suppressed, but not, for all that, the idea that essence is prior to existence; something of that idea we still find everywhere, in Diderot, in Voltaire and even in Kant. Man possesses a human nature; that "human nature," which is the conception of human being, is found in every man; which means that each man is a particular example of an universal conception, the conception of Man. In Kant, this universality goes so far that the wild man of the woods, man in the state of nature and the bourgeois are all contained in the same definition and have the same fundamental qualities. Here again, the essence of man precedes that historic existence which we confront in experience.

Atheistic existentialism, of which I am a representative, declares with greater consistency that if God does not exist there is at least one being whose existence comes before its essence, a being which exists before it can be defined by any conception of it. That being is man or, as Heidegger has it, the human reality. What do we mean by saying that existence precedes essence? We mean that man first of all exists, encounters himself, surges up in the world—and defines himself afterwards. If man as the existentialist sees him is not definable, it is because to begin with he is nothing. He will not be anything until later, and then he will be what he makes of himself. Thus, there is no human nature, because there is no God to have a conception of it. Man simply is. Not that he is simply what he conceives himself to be, but he is what he wills, and as he conceives himself after already existing—as he wills to be after that leap towards existence. Man is nothing else but that which he makes of himself. That is the first principle of existentialism. And this is what people call its "subjectivity," using the word as a reproach against us. But what do we mean to say by this, but that man is of a greater dignity than a stone or a table? For we mean to say that man primarily exists—that man is, before all else, something which propels itself towards a future and is aware that it is doing so. Man is, indeed, a project which possesses a subjective life, instead of being a kind of moss, or a fungus or a cauliflower. Before that projection of the self nothing exists; not even in the heaven of intelligence: man will only attain existence when he is what he purposes to be. Not, however, what he may wish to be. For what we usually understand by wishing or willing is a conscious decision taken—much more often than not—after we have made ourselves what we are. I may wish to join a party, to write a book or to marry—but in such a case what is usually called my will is probably a manifestation of a prior and more spontaneous decision. If, however, it is true that existence is prior to essence, man is responsible for what he is. Thus, the first effect of existentialism is that it puts every man in possession of himself as he is, and places the entire responsibility for his existence squarely upon his own shoulders. And, when we say that man is responsible for himself, we do not mean that he is responsible only for his own individuality, but that he is responsible for all men. The word "subjectivism" is to be understood in two senses, and our adversaries play upon only one of them. Subjectivism means, on the one hand, the freedom of the individual subject and, on the other, that man cannot pass beyond human subjectivity. It is the latter which is the deeper meaning of existentialism. When we say that man chooses himself, we do mean that every one of us must choose himself; but by that we also mean that in choosing for himself he chooses for all men. For in effect, of all the actions a man may take in order to create himself as he wills to be, there is not one which is not creative, at the same time, of an image of man such as he believes he ought to be. To choose between this or that is at the same time to affirm the value of that which is chosen; for we are unable ever to choose the worse. What we choose is always the better; and nothing can be better for us unless it is better for all. If, moreover, existence precedes essence and we will to exist at the same time as we fashion our image, that image is valid for all and for the entire epoch in which we find ourselves. Our responsibility is thus much greater than we had supposed, for it concerns mankind as a whole. If I am a worker, for instance, I may choose to join a Christian rather than a Communist trade union. And if, by that membership, I choose to signify that resignation is, after all, the attitude that best becomes a man, that man's kingdom is not upon this earth, I do not commit myself alone to that view. Resignation is my will for everyone, and my action is, in consequence, a commitment on behalf of all mankind. Or if, to take a more personal case, I decide to marry and to have children, even though this decision proceeds simply from my situation, from my passion or my desire, I am thereby committing not only myself, but humanity as a whole, to the practice of monogamy. I am thus responsible for myself and for all men, and I am creating a certain image of man as I would have him to be. In fashioning myself I fashion man.

This may enable us to understand what is meant by such terms—perhaps a little grandiloquent—as anguish, abandonment and despair. As you will soon see, it is very simple. First, what do we mean by anguish? The existentialist frankly states that man is in anguish. His meaning is as follows—When a man commits himself to anything, fully realising that he is not only choosing what he will be, but is thereby at the same time a legislator deciding for the whole of mankind—in such a moment a man cannot escape from the sense of complete and profound responsibility. There are many, indeed, who show no such anxiety. But we affirm that they are merely disguising their anguish or are in flight from it. Certainly, many people think that in what they are doing they commit no one but themselves to anything: and if you ask them, "What would happen if everyone did so?" they shrug their shoulders and reply, "Everyone does not do so." But in truth, one ought always to ask oneself what would happen if everyone did as one is doing; nor can one escape from that disturbing thought except by a kind of self-deception. The man who lies in self-excuse, by saying "Everyone will not do it" must be ill at ease in his conscience, for the act of lying implies the universal value which it denies. By its very disguise his anguish reveals itself. This is the anguish that Kierkegaard called "the anguish of Abraham." You know the story: An angel commanded Abraham to sacrifice his son: and obedience was obligatory, if it really was an angel who had appeared and said, "Thou, Abraham, shalt sacrifice thy son." But anyone in such a case would wonder, first, whether it was indeed an angel and secondly, whether I am really Abraham. Where are the proofs? A certain mad woman who suffered from hallucinations said that people were telephoning to her, and giving her orders. The doctor asked, "But who is it that speaks to you?" She replied: "He says it is God." And what, indeed, could prove to her that it was God? If an angel appears to me, what is the proof that it is an angel; or, if I hear voices, who can prove that they proceed from heaven and not from hell, or from my own subconsciousness or some pathological condition? Who can prove that they are really addressed to me?

Who, then, can prove that I am the proper person to impose, by my own choice, my conception of man upon mankind? I shall never find any proof whatever; there will be no sign to convince me of it. If a voice speaks to me, it is still I myself who must decide whether the voice is or is not that of an angel. If I regard a certain course of action as good, it is only I who choose to say that it is good and not bad. There is nothing to show that I am Abraham: nevertheless I also am obliged at every instant to perform actions which are examples. Everything happens to every man as though the whole human race had its eyes fixed upon what he is doing and regulated its conduct accordingly. So every man ought to say, "Am I really a man who has the right to act in such a manner that humanity regulates itself by what I do." If a man does not say that, he is dissembling his anguish. Clearly, the anguish with which we are concerned here is not one that could lead to quietism or inaction. It is anguish pure and simple, of the kind well known to all those who have borne responsibilities. When, for instance, a military leader takes upon himself the responsibility for an attack and sends a number of men to their death, he chooses to do it and at bottom he alone chooses. No doubt he acts under a higher command, but its orders, which are more general, require interpretation by him and upon that interpretation depends the life of ten, fourteen or twenty men. In making the decision, he cannot but feel a certain anguish. All leaders know that anguish. It does not prevent their acting, on the contrary it is the very condition of their action, for the action presupposes that there is a plurality of possibilities, and in choosing one of these, they realise that it has value only because it is chosen. Now it is anguish of that kind which existentialism describes, and moreover, as we shall see, makes explicit through direct responsibility towards other men who are concerned. Far from being a screen which could separate us from action, it is a condition of action itself.

And when we speak of "abandonment"—a favorite word of Heidegger—we only mean to say that God does not exist, and that it is necessary to draw the consequences of his absence right to the end. The existentialist is strongly opposed to a certain type of secular moralism which seeks to suppress God at the least possible expense. Towards 1880, when the French professors endeavoured to formulate a secular morality, they said something like this:—God is a useless and costly hypothesis, so we will do without it. However, if we are to have morality, a society and a law-abiding world, it is essential that certain values should be taken seriously; they must have an *à priori* existence ascribed to them. It must be considered obligatory *à priori* to be honest, not to lie, not to beat one's wife, to bring up children and so forth; so we are going to do a little work on this subject, which will enable us to show that these values exist all the same, inscribed in an intelligible heaven although, of course, there is no God. In other words—and this is, I believe, the purport of all that we in France call radicalism—nothing will be changed if God does not exist; we shall re-discover the same norms of honesty, progress and humanity, and we shall have disposed of God as an out-of-date hypothesis which will die away quietly of itself. The existentialist, on the contrary, finds it extremely embarrassing that God does not exist, for there disappears with Him all possibility of finding values in an intelligible heaven. There can no longer be any good à priori, since there is no infinite and perfect consciousness to think it. It is nowhere written that "the good" exists, that one must be honest or must not lie, since we are now upon the plane where there are only men. Dostoievsky once wrote "If God did not exist, everything would be permitted"; and that, for existentialism, is the starting point. Everything is indeed permitted if God does not exist, and man is in consequence forlorn, for he cannot find anything to depend upon either within or outside himself. He discovers forthwith, that he is without excuse. For if indeed existence precedes essence, one will never be able to explain one's action by reference to a given and specific human nature; in other words, there is no determinism—man is free, man *is* freedom. Nor, on the other hand, if God does not exist, are we provided with any values or commands that could legitimise our behaviour. Thus we have neither behind us, nor before us in a luminous realm of values, any means of justification or excuse. We are left alone, without excuse. That is what I mean when I say that man is condemned to be free. Condemned, because he did not create himself, yet is nevertheless at liberty, and from the moment that he is thrown into this world he is responsible for everything he does. The existentialist does not believe in the power of passion. He will never regard a grand passion as a destructive torrent upon which a man is swept into certain actions as by fate, and which, therefore, is an excuse for them. He thinks that man is responsible for his passion. Neither will an existentialist think that a man can find help through some sign being vouchsafed upon earth for his orientation: for he thinks that the man himself interprets the sign as he chooses. He thinks that every man, without any support or help whatever, is condemned at every instant to invent man. As Ponge has written in a very fine article, "Man is the future of man." That is exactly true. Only, if one took this to mean that the future is laid up in Heaven, that God knows what it is, it would be false, for then it would no longer even be a future. If, however, it means that, whatever man may now appear to be, there is a future to be fashioned, a virgin future that awaits him—then it is a true saying. But in the present one is forsaken.

As an example by which you may the better understand this state of abandonment, I will refer to the case of a pupil of mine, who sought me out in the following circumstances. His father was quarrelling with his mother and was also inclined to be a "collaborator"; his elder brother had been killed in the German offensive of 1940 and this young man, with a sentiment somewhat primitive but generous, burned to avenge him. His mother was living alone with him, deeply afflicted by the semi-treason of his father and by the death of her eldest son, and her one consolation was in this young man. But he, at this moment, had the choice between going to England to join the Free French Forces or of staying near his mother and helping her to live. He fully realised that this woman lived only for him and that his disappearance—or perhaps his death—would plunge her into despair. He also realised that, concretely and in fact, every action he performed on his mother's behalf would be sure of effect in the sense of aiding her to live, where as anything he did in order to go and fight would be an ambiguous action which might vanish like water into sand and serve no purpose. For instance, to set out for England he would have to wait indefinitely in a Spanish camp on the way through Spain; or, on arriving in England or in Algiers he might be put into an office to fill up forms. Consequently, he found himself confronted by two very different modes of action; the one concrete, immediate, but directed towards only one individual; and the other an action addressed to an end infinitely greater, a national collectivity, but for that very reason ambiguous—and it might be frustrated on the way. At the same time, he was hesitating between two kinds of morality; on the one side the morality of sympathy, of personal devotion and, on the other side, a morality of wider scope but of more debatable validity. He had to choose between those two. What could help him to choose? Could the Christian doctrine? No. Christian doctrine says: Act with charity, love your neighbour, deny yourself for others, choose the way which is hardest, and so forth. But which is the harder road? To whom does one owe the more brotherly love, the patriot or the mother? Which is the more useful aim, the general one of fighting in and for the whole community, or the precise aim of helping one particular person to live? Who can give an answer to that *à priori*? No one. Nor is it given in any ethical scripture. The Kantian ethic says, Never regard another as a means, but always as an end. Very well; if I remain with my mother, I shall be regarding her as the end and not as a means: but by the same token I am in danger of treating as means those who are fighting on my behalf; and the converse is also true, that if I go to the aid of the combatants I shall be treating them as the end at the risk of treating my mother as a means.

If values are uncertain, if they are still too abstract to determine the particular, concrete case under consideration, nothing remains but to trust in our instincts. That is what this young man tried to do; and when I saw him he said, "In the end, it is feeling that counts; the direction in which it is really pushing me is the one I ought to choose. If I feel that I love my mother enough to sacrifice everything else for her—my will to be avenged, all my longings for action and adventure—then I stay with her. If, on the contrary, I feel that my love for her is not enough, I go." But how does one estimate the strength of a feeling? The value of his feeling for his mother was determined precisely by the fact that he was standing by her. I may say that I love a certain friend enough to sacrifice such or such a sum of money for him, but I cannot prove that unless I have done it. I may say, "I love my mother enough to remain with her," if actually I have remained with her. I can only estimate the strength of this affection if I have performed an action by which it is defined and ratified. But if I then appeal to this affection to justify my action, I find myself drawn into a vicious circle.

Moreover, as Gide has very well said, a sentiment which is

play-acting and one which is vital are two things that are hardly distinguishable one from another. To decide that I love my mother by staying beside her, and to play a comedy the upshot of which is that I do so—these are nearly the same thing. In other words, feeling is formed by the deeds that one does; therefore I cannot consult it as a guide to action. And that is to say that I can neither seek within myself for an authentic impulse to action, nor can I expect, from some ethic, formulae that will enable me to act. You may say that the youth did, at least, go to a professor to ask for advice. But if you seek counsel—from a priest, for example—you have selected that priest; and at bottom you already knew, more or less, what he would advise. In other words, to choose an adviser is nevertheless to commit oneself by that choice. If you are a Christian, you will say, Consult a priest; but there are collaborationists, priests who are resisters and priests who wait for the tide to turn: which will you choose? Had this young man chosen a priest of the resistance, or one of the collaboration, he would have decided beforehand the kind of advice he was to receive. Similarly, in coming to me, he knew what advice I should give him, and I had but one reply to make. You are free, therefore choose—that is to say, invent. No rule of general morality can show you what you ought to do: no signs are vouchsafed in this world. The Catholics will reply, "Oh, but they are!" Very well; still, it is I myself, in every case, who have to interpret the signs. Whilst I was imprisoned, I made the acquaintance of a somewhat remarkable man, a Jesuit, who had become a member of that order in the following manner. In his life he had suffered a succession of rather severe setbacks. His father had died when he was a child, leaving him in poverty, and he had been awarded a free scholarship in a religious institution, where he had been made continually to feel that he was accepted for charity's sake, and, in consequence, he had been denied several of those distinctions and honors which gratify children. Later, about the age of eighteen, he came to grief in a sentimental affair; and finally, at twenty-two—this was a trifle in itself, but it was the last drop that overflowed his cup—he failed in his military examination. This young man, then, could regard himself as a total failure: it was a sign—but a sign of what? He might have taken refuge in bitterness or despair. But

he took it—very cleverly for him—as a sign that he was not intended for secular successes, and that only the attainments of
religion, those of sanctity and of faith, were accessible to him.
He interpreted his record as a message from God, and became a
member of the Order. Who can doubt but that this decision as
to the meaning of the sign was his, and his alone? One could
have drawn quite different conclusions from such a series of
reverses—as, for example, that he had better become a carpen-
ter or a revolutionary. For the decipherment of the sign, however, he bears the entire responsibility. That is what "abandonment" implies, that we ourselves decide our being. And with
this abandonment goes anguish.

As for "despair," the meaning of this expression is extremely
simple. It merely means that we limit ourselves to a reliance
upon that which is within our wills, or within the sum of the
probabilities which render our action feasible. Whenever one
wills anything, there are always these elements of probability. If
I am counting upon a visit from a friend, who may be coming
by train or by tram, I presuppose that the train will arrive at the
appointed time, or that the tram will not be derailed. I remain
in the realm of possibilities; but one does not rely upon any
possibilities beyond those that are strictly concerned in one's action. Beyond the point at which the possibilities under consideration cease to affect my action, I ought to disinterest myself.
For there is no God and no prevenient design, which can adapt
the world and all its possibilities to my will. When Descartes
said, "Conquer yourself rather than the world," what he meant
was, at bottom, the same—that we should act without hope.

Marxists, to whom I have said this, have answered: "Your
action is limited, obviously, by your death; but you can rely
upon the help of others. That is, you can count both upon what
the others are doing to help you elsewhere, as in China and in
Russia, and upon what they will do later, after your death, to
take up your action and carry it forward to its final accomplish-
ment which will be the revolution. Moreover you must rely
upon this; not to do so is immoral." To this I rejoin, first, that I
shall always count upon my comrades-in-arms in the struggle, in
so far as they are committed, as I am, to a definite, common
cause; and in the unity of a party or a group which I can more

or less control—that is, in which I am enrolled as a militant and whose movements at every moment are known to me. In that respect, to rely upon the unity and the will of the party is exactly like my reckoning that the train will run to time or that the tram will not be derailed. But I cannot count upon men whom I do not know, I cannot base my confidence upon human goodness or upon man's interest in the good of society, seeing that man is free and that there is no human nature which I can take as foundational. I do not know whither the Russian revolution will lead. I can admire it and take it as an example in so far as it is evident, to-day, that the proletariat plays a part in Russia which it has attained in no other nation. But I cannot affirm that this will necessarily lead to the triumph of the pro-letariat: I must confine myself to what I can see. Nor can I be sure that comrades-in-arms will take up my work after my death and carry it to the maximum perfection, seeing that those men are free agents and will freely decide, to-morrow, what man is then to be. To-morrow, after my death, some men may decide to establish Fascism, and the others may be so cowardly or so slack as to let them do so. If so, Fascism will then be the truth of man, and so much the worse for us. In reality, things will be such as men have decided they shall be. Does that mean that I should abandon myself to quietism? No. First I ought to commit myself and then act my commitment, according to the time-honoured formula that "one need not hope in order to undertake one's work." Nor does this mean that I should not belong to a party, but only that I should be without illusion and that I should do what I can. For instance, if I ask myself "Will the social ideal as such, ever become a reality?" I cannot tell, I only know that whatever may be in my power to make it so, I shall do; beyond that, I can count upon nothing.

Quietism is the attitude of people who say, "let others do what I cannot do." The doctrine I am presenting before you is pre-cisely the opposite of this, since it declares that there is no reality except in action. It goes further, indeed, and adds, "Man is nothing else but what he purposes, he exists only in so far as he realises himself, he is therefore nothing else but the sum of his actions, nothing else but what his life is." Hence we can well understand why some people are horrified by our teaching. For many have but one resource to sustain them in their misery, and that is to think, "Circumstances have been against me, I was worthy to be something much better than I have been. I admit I have never had a great love or a great friendship; but that is because I never met a man or a woman who were worthy of it; if I have not written any very good books, it is because I had not the leisure to do so; or, if I have had no children to whom I could devote myself it is because I did not find the man I could have lived with. So there remains within me a wide range of abilities, inclinations and potentialities, unused but perfectly viable, which endow me with a worthiness that could never be inferred from the mere history of my actions." But in reality and for the existentialist, there is no love apart from the deeds of love; no potentiality of love other than that which is manifested in loving; there is no genius other than that which is expressed in works of art. The genius of Proust is the totality of the works of Proust; the genius of Racine is the series of his tragedies, outside of which there is nothing. Why should we attribute to Racine the capacity to write yet another tragedy when that is precisely what he did not write? In life, a man commits himself, draws his own portrait and there is nothing but that portrait. No doubt this thought may seem comfortless to one who has not made a success of his life. On the other hand, it puts everyone in a position to understand that reality alone is reliable; that dreams, expectations and hopes serve to define a man only as deceptive dreams, abortive hopes, expectations unfulfilled; that is to say, they define him negatively, not positively. Nevertheless, when one says, "You are nothing else but what you live," it does not imply that an artist is to be judged solely by his works of art, for a thousand other things contribute no less to his definition as a man. What we mean to say is that a man is no other than a series of undertakings, that he is the sum, the organisation, the set of relations that constitute these undertakings.

In the light of all this, what people reproach us with is not, after all, our pessimism, but the sternness of our optimism. If people condemn our works of fiction, in which we describe characters that are base, weak, cowardly and sometimes even frankly evil, it is not only because those characters are base, weak, cowardly or evil. For suppose that, like Zola, we showed that the behaviour of these characters was caused by their heredity, or by the action of their environment upon them, or by determining factors, psychic or organic. People would be reassured, they would say, "You see, that is what we are like, no one can do anything about it." But the existentialist, when he portrays a coward, shows him as responsible for his cowardice. He is not like that on account of a cowardly heart or lungs or cerebrum, he has not become like that through his physiological organism; he is like that because he has made himself into a coward by his actions. There is no such thing as a cowardly temperament. There are nervous temperaments; there is what is called impoverished blood, and there are also rich temperaments. But the man whose blood is poor is not a coward for all that, for what produces cowardice is the act of giving up or giving way; and a temperament is not an action. A coward is defined by the deed that he has done. What people feel obscurely, and with horror, is that the coward as we present him is guilty of being a coward. What people would prefer would be to be born either a coward or a hero. One of the charges most often laid against the *Chemins de la Liberté* is something like this—"But, after all, these people being so base, how can you make them into heroes?" That objection is really rather comic, for it implies that people are born heroes: and that is, at bottom, what such people would like to think. If you are born cowards, you can be quite content, you can do nothing about it and you will be cowards all your lives whatever you do; and if you are born heroes you can again be quite content; you will be heroes all your lives, eating and drinking heroically. Whereas the existentialist says that the coward makes himself cowardly, the hero makes himself heroic; and that there is always a possibility for the coward to give up cowardice and for the hero to stop being a hero. What counts is the total commitment, and it is not by a particular case or particular action that you are committed altogether.

We have now, I think, dealt with a certain number of the reproaches against existentialism. You have seen that it cannot be regarded as a philosophy of quietism since it defines man by his action; nor as a pessimistic description of man, for no doctrine is more optimistic, the destiny of man is placed within himself. Nor is it an attempt to discourage man from action since it tells him that there is no hope except in his action, and that the one thing which permits him to have life is the deed. Upon this level therefore, what we are considering is an ethic of action and self-commitment. However, we are still reproached, upon these few data, for confining man within his individual subjectivity. There again people badly misunderstand us.

Our point of departure is, indeed, the subjectivity of the individual, and that for strictly philosophic reasons. It is not because we are bourgeois, but because we seek to base our teaching upon the truth, and not upon a collection of fine theories, full of hope but lacking real foundations. And at the point of departure there cannot be any other truth than this, *I think, therefore I am*, which is the absolute truth of consciousness as it attains to itself. Every theory which begins with man, outside of this moment of self-attainment, is a theory which thereby suppresses the truth, for outside of the Cartesian *cogito*, all objects are no more than probable, and any doctrine of probabilities which is not attached to a truth will crumble into nothing. In order to define the probable one must possess the true. Before there can be any truth whatever, then, there must be an absolute truth, and there is such a truth which is simple, easily attained and within the reach of everybody; it consists in one's immediate sense of one's self.

In the second place, this theory alone is compatible with the dignity of man, it is the only one which does not make man into an object. All kinds of materialism lead one to treat every man including oneself as an object—that is, as a set of pre-determined reactions, in no way different from the patterns of qualities and phenomena which constitute a table, or a chair or a stone. Our aim is precisely to establish the human kingdom as a pattern of values in distinction from the material world. But the subjectivity which we thus postulate as the standard of truth is no narrowly individual subjectivism, for as we have demonstrated, it is not only one's own self that one discovers in the *cogito*, but those of others too. Contrary to the philosophy of Descartes, contrary to that of Kant, when we say "I think" we are attaining to ourselves in the presence of the other, and we are just as certain of the other as we are of ourselves. Thus the man who discovers himself directly in the *cogito* also discovers all the others, and discovers them as the condition of his own existence. He recognises that he cannot be anything (in the sense in which one says one is spiritual, or that one is wicked or jealous) unless others recognise him as such. I cannot obtain any truth whatsoever about myself, except through the mediation of another. The other is indispensable to my existence, and equally so to any knowledge I can have of myself. Under these conditions, the intimate discovery of myself is at the same time the revelation of the other as a freedom which confronts mine, and which cannot think or will without doing so either for or against me. Thus, at once, we find ourselves in a world which is, let us say, that of "inter-subjectivity." It is in this world that man has to decide what he is and what others are.

Furthermore, although it is impossible to find in each and every man a universal essence that can be called human nature, there is nevertheless a human universality of *condition*. It is not by chance that the thinkers of to-day are so much more ready to speak of the condition than of the nature of man. By his condition they understand, with more or less clarity, all the *limitations* which *à priori* define man's fundamental situation in the universe. His historical situations are variable: man may be born a slave in a pagan society, or may be a feudal baron, or a proletarian. But what never vary are the necessities of being in the world, of having to labour and to die there. These limitations are neither subjective nor objective, or rather there is both a subjective and an objective aspect of them. Objective, because we meet with them everywhere and they are everywhere recognisable: and subjective because they are *lived* and are nothing if man does not live them—if, that is to say, he does not freely determine himself and his existence in relation to them. And, diverse though man's purposes may be, at least none of them is wholly foreign to me, since every human purpose presents itself as an attempt either to surpass these limitations, or to widen them, or else to deny or to accommodate oneself to them. Consequently every purpose, however individual it may be, is of universal value. Every purpose, even that of a Chinese, an Indian or a Negro, can be understood by a European. To say it can be understood, means that the European of 1945 may be striving out of a certain situation towards the same limitations in the same way, and that he may re-conceive in himself the purpose of the Chinese, of the Indian or the African. In every purpose there is universality, in this sense that every purpose is comprehensible to every man. Not that this or that purpose defines man for ever, but that it may be entertained again and again. There is always some way of understanding an idiot, a child, a primitive man or a foreigner if one has sufficient information. In this sense we may say that there is a human universality, but it is not something given; it is being perpetually made. I make this universality in choosing myself; I also make it by understanding the purpose of any other man, of whatever epoch. This absoluteness of the act of choice does not alter the relativity of each epoch.

What is at the very heart and centre of existentialism, is the absolute character of the free commitment, by which every man realises himself in realising a type of humanity—a commitment always understandable, to no matter whom in no matter what epoch—and its bearing upon the relativity of the cultural pattern which may result from such absolute commitment. One must observe equally the relativity of Cartesianism and the absolute character of the Cartesian commitment. In this sense you may say, if you like, that every one of us makes the absolute by breathing, by eating, by sleeping or by behaving in any fashion whatsoever. There is no difference between free being—being as self-committal, as existence choosing its essence—and absolute being. And there is no difference whatever between being as an absolute, temporarily localised—that is, localised in history—and universally intelligible being.

This does not completely refute the charge of subjectivism. Indeed that objection appears in several other forms, of which the first is as follows. People say to us, "Then it does not matter what you do," and they say this in various ways. First they tax us with anarchy; then they say, "You cannot judge others, for there is no reason for preferring one purpose to another"; finally, they may say, "Everything being merely voluntary in this choice of yours, you give away with one hand what you pretend to gain with the other." These three are not very serious objections. As to the first, to say that it matters not what you choose is not correct. In one sense choice is possible, but what is not possible is not to choose. I can always choose, but I must know that if I do not choose, that is still a choice. This, although it may appear merely formal, is of great importance as a limit to fantasy and caprice. For, when I confront a real situation—for example, that I am a sexual being, able to have relations with a being of the other sex and able to have children—I am obliged to choose my attitude to it, and in every respect I bear the responsibility of the choice which, in committing myself, also commits the whole of humanity. Even if my choice is determined by no *à priori* value whatever, it can have nothing to do with caprice: and if anyone thinks that this is only Gide's theory of the *acte gratuit* over again, he has failed to see the enormous difference between this theory and that of Gide. Gide does not know what a situation is, his "act" is one of pure caprice. In our view, on the contrary, man finds himself in an organised situation in which he is himself involved: his choice involves mankind in its entirety, and he cannot avoid choosing. Either he must remain single, or he must marry without having children, or he must marry and have children. In any case, and whichever he may choose, it is impossible for him, in respect of this situation, not to take complete responsibility. Doubtless he chooses without reference to any pre-established values, but it is unjust to tax him with caprice. Rather let us say that the moral choice is comparable to the construction of a work of art.

But here I must at once digress to make it quite clear that we are not propounding an aesthetic morality, for our adversaries are disingenuous enough to reproach us even with that. I mention the work of art only by way of comparison. That being understood, does anyone reproach an artist when he paints a picture for not following rules established *à priori*? Does one ever ask what is the picture that he ought to paint? As everyone knows, there is no pre-defined picture for him to make; the artist applies himself to the composition of a picture, and the picture that ought to be made is precisely that which he will have made. As everyone knows, there are no aesthetic values *à priori*, but there are values which will appear in due course in the coherence of the picture, in the relation between the will to create and the finished work. No one can tell what the painting of to-morrow will be like; one cannot judge a painting until it is done. What has that to do with morality? We are in the same creative situation. We never speak of a work of art as irresponsible; when we are discussing a canvas by Picasso, we understand very well that the composition became what it is at the time when he was painting it, and that his works are part and parcel of his entire life.

It is the same upon the plane of morality. There is this in common between art and morality, that in both we have to do with creation and invention. We cannot decide *à priori* what it is that should be done. I think it was made sufficiently clear to you in the case of that student who came to see me, that to whatever ethical system he might appeal, the Kantian or any other, he could find no sort of guidance whatever; he was obliged to invent the law for himself. Certainly we cannot say that this man, in choosing to remain with his mother—that is, in taking sentiment, personal devotion and concrete charity as his moral foundations—would be making an irresponsible choice, nor could we do so if he preferred the sacrifice of going away to England. Man makes himself; he is not found ready-made; he makes himself by the choice of his morality, and he cannot but choose a morality, such is the pressure of circumstances upon him. We define man only in relation to his commitments; it is therefore absurd to reproach us for irresponsibility in our choice.

In the second place, people say to us, "You are unable to judge others." This is true in one sense and false in another. It is true in this sense, that whenever a man chooses his purpose and his commitment in all clearness and in all sincerity, whatever that purpose may be it is impossible to prefer another for him. It is true in the sense that we do not believe in progress. Progress implies amelioration; but man is always the same, facing a situation which is always changing, and choice remains always a choice in the situation. The moral problem has not changed since the time when it was a choice between slavery and anti-slavery—from the time of the war of Secession, for example, until the present moment when one chooses between the M.R.P.[4] and the Communists.

We can judge, nevertheless, for, as I have said, one chooses

[4] Mouvement Républicain Populaire.

in view of others, and in view of others one chooses himself. One can judge, first—and perhaps this is not a judgment of value, but it is a logical judgment—that in certain cases choice is founded upon an error, and in others upon the truth. One can judge a man by saying that he deceives himself. Since we have defined the situation of man as one of free choice, without excuse and without help, any man who takes refuge behind the excuse of his passions, or by inventing some deterministic doctrine, is a self-deceiver. One may object: "But why should he not choose to deceive himself?" I reply that it is not for me to judge him morally, but I define his self-deception as an error. Here one cannot avoid pronouncing a judgment of truth. The self-deception is evidently a falsehood, because it is a dissimulation of man's complete liberty of commitment. Upon this same level, I say that it is also a self-deception if I choose to declare that certain values are incumbent upon me; I am in contradiction with myself if I will these values and at the same time say that they impose themselves upon me. If anyone says to me, "And what if I wish to deceive myself?" I answer, "There is no reason why you should not, but I declare that you are doing so, and that the attitude of strict consistency alone is that of good faith. Furthermore, I can pronounce a moral judgment. For I declare that freedom, in respect of concrete circumstances, can have no other end and aim but itself; and when once a man has seen that values depend upon himself, in that state of forsakenness he can will only one thing, and that is freedom as the foundation of all values. That does not mean that he wills it in the abstract: it simply means that the actions of men of good faith have, as their ultimate significance, the quest of freedom itself as such. A man who belongs to some communist or revolutionary society wills certain concrete ends, which imply the will to freedom, but that freedom is willed in community. We will freedom for freedom's sake, and in and through particular circumstances. And in thus willing freedom, we discover that it depends entirely upon the freedom of others and that the freedom of others depends upon our own. Obviously, freedom as the definition of a man does not depend upon others, but as soon as there is a commitment, I am obliged to will the liberty of others at the same time as mine. I cannot make liberty my aim unless I make that of others equally my aim. Consequently, when I recognise, as entirely authentic, that man is a being whose existence precedes his essence, and that he is a free being who cannot, in any circumstances, but will his freedom, at the same time I realise that I cannot not will the freedom of others. Thus, in the name of that will to freedom which is implied in freedom itself, I can form judgments upon those who seek to hide from themselves the wholly voluntary nature of their existence and its complete freedom. Those who hide from this total freedom, in a guise of solemnity or with deterministic excuses, I shall call cowards. Others, who try to show that their existence is necessary, when it is merely an accident of the appearance of the human race on earth,—I shall call scum. But neither cowards nor scum can be identified except upon the plane of strict authenticity. Thus, although the content of morality is variable, a certain form of this morality is universal. Kant declared that freedom is a will both to itself and to the freedom of others. Agreed: but he thinks that the formal and the universal suffice for the constitution of a morality. We think, on the contrary, that principles that are too abstract break down when we come to defining action. To take once again the case of that student; by what authority, in the name of what golden rule of morality, do you think he could have decided, in perfect peace of mind, either to abandon his mother or to remain with her? There are no means of judging. The content is always concrete, and therefore unpredictable; it has always to be invented. The one thing that counts, is to know whether the invention is made in the name of freedom.

Let us, for example, examine the two following cases, and you will see how far they are similar in spite of their difference. Let us take *The Mill on the Floss*. We find here a certain young woman, Maggie Tulliver, who is an incarnation of the value of passion and is aware of it. She is in love with a young man, Stephen, who is engaged to another, an insignificant young woman. This Maggie Tulliver, instead of heedlessly seeking her own happiness, chooses in the name of human solidarity to sacrifice herself and to give up the man she loves. On the other hand, La Sanseverina in Stendhal's *Chartreuse de Parme*, believing that it is passion which endows man with his real value, would have declared that a grand passion justifies its sacrifices, and must be preferred to the banality of such conjugal love as would unite Stephen to the little goose he was engaged to marry. It is the latter that she would have chosen to sacrifice in realising her own happiness, and, as Stendhal shows, she would also sacrifice herself upon the plane of passion if life made that demand upon her. Here we are facing two clearly opposed moralities; but I claim that they are equivalent, seeing that in both cases the overruling aim is freedom. You can imagine two attitudes exactly similar in effect, in that one girl might prefer, in resignation, to give up her lover whilst the other preferred, in fulfilment of sexual desire, to ignore the prior engagement of the man she loved; and, externally, these two cases might appear the same as the two we have just cited, while being in fact entirely different. The attitude of La Sanseverina is much nearer to that of Maggie Tulliver than to one of careless greed. Thus, you see, the second objection is at once true and false. One can choose anything, but only if it is upon the plane of free commitment.

The third objection, stated by saying, "You take with one hand what you give with the other," means, at bottom, "your values are not serious, since you choose them yourselves." To that I can only say that I am very sorry that it should be so; but if I have excluded God the Father, there must be somebody to invent values. We have to take things as they are. And moreover, to say that we invent values means neither more nor less than this; that there is no sense in life à priori. Life is nothing until it is lived; but it is yours to make sense of, and the value of it is nothing else but the sense that you choose. Therefore, you can see that there is a possibility of creating a human community. I have been reproached for suggesting that existentialism is a form of humanism: people have said to me, "But you have written in your Nausée that the humanists are wrong, you have even ridiculed a certain type of humanism, why do you now go back upon that?" In reality, the word humanism has two very different meanings. One may understand by humanism a theory which upholds man as the end-in-itself and as the supreme value. Humanism in this sense appears, for instance, in Cocteau's story Round the World in 80 Hours, in which one of the characters declares, because he is flying over mountains in an aeroplane, "Man is magnificent!" This signifies that although I, personally, have not built aeroplanes I have the benefit of those particular inventions and that I personally, being a man, can consider myself responsible for, and honoured by, achievements that are peculiar to some men. It is to assume that we can ascribe value to man according to the most distinguished deeds of certain men. That kind of humanism is absurd, for only the dog or the horse would be in a position to pronounce a general judgment upon man and declare that he is magnificent, which they have never been such fools as to do—at least, not as far as I know. But neither is it admissible that a man should pronounce judgment upon Man. Existentialism dispenses with any judgment of this sort: an existentialist will never take man as the end, since man is still to be determined. And we have no right to believe that humanity is something to which we could set up a cult, after the manner of Auguste Comte. The cult of humanity ends in Comtian humanism, shut-in upon itself, and—this must be said —in Fascism. We do not want a humanism like that.

But there is another sense of the word, of which the fundamental meaning is this: Man is all the time outside of himself: it is in projecting and losing himself beyond himself that he makes man to exist; and, on the other hand, it is by pursuing transcendent aims that he himself is able to exist. Since man is thus self-surpassing, and can grasp objects only in relation to his self-surpassing, he is himself the heart and centre of his transcendence. There is no other universe except the human universe, the universe of human subjectivity. This relation of transcendence as constitutive of man (not in the sense that God is transcendent, but in the sense of self-surpassing) with subjectivity (in such a sense that man is not shut up in himself but forever present in a human universe)—it is this that we call existential humanism. This is humanism, because we remind man that there is no legislator but himself; that he himself, thus abandoned, must decide for himself; also because we show that it is not by turning back upon himself, but always by seeking, beyond himself, an aim which is one of liberation or of some particular realisation, that man can realise himself as truly human.

You can see from these few reflections that nothing could be more unjust than the objections people raise against us. Existentialism is nothing else but an attempt to draw the full conclusions from a consistently atheistic position. Its intention is not in the least that of plunging men into despair. And if by despair one means—as the Christians do—any attitude of unbelief, the despair of the existentialists is something different. Existentialism is not atheist in the sense that it would exhaust itself in demonstrations of the non-existence of God. It declares, rather, that even if God existed that would make no difference from its point of view. Not that we believe God does exist, but we think that the real problem is not that of His existence; what man needs is to find himself again and to understand that nothing can save him from himself, not even a valid proof of the existence of God. In this sense existentialism is optimistic, it is a doctrine of action, and it is only by self-deception, by confusing their own despair with ours that Christians can describe us as without hope.

SARTRE'S MAJOR WRITINGS
(arranged chronologically)

A. Philosophy

"La transcendence de l'égo," *Recherches philosophiques*, 6 [1936], 85–123.
   The Transcendence of the Ego. Tr. Forest Williams and Robert Kirkpatrick. New York: The Noonday Press, 1957.
L'imagination. Paris: Alcan, 1936.
   Imagination. Tr. Forest Williams. Ann Arbor: University of Michigan Press, 1962.
"Une idée fondamentale de la phénoménologie de Husserl: l'intentionalité," *Nouvelle Revue Francaise.* [January 1939]; reprinted in *Situations*, Vol. I, pp. 31–35.
Esquisse d'une théorie des émotions. Paris: Hermann, 1939.
   The Emotions: Outline of a Theory. Tr. Bernard Frechtman. New York: Philosophical Library, 1948.
L'imaginaire: Psychologie phénoménologique de l'imagination. Paris: Gallimard, 1940.

Psychology of the Imagination. Tr. Bernard Frechtman. New York: Philosophical Library, 1948.

L'être et le néant: Essai d'ontologie phénoménologique. Paris: Gallimard, 1943.

    Being and Nothingness. Tr. Hazel Barnes. New York: Philosophical Library, 1956.

L'existentialisme est un humanisme. Paris: Nagel, 1946.

    Existentialism and Humanism. Tr. Philip Mairet. London: Methuen, 1948.

    Existentialism. Tr. Bernard Frechtman. New York: Philosophical Library, 1947.

Situations [6 vols.]. Paris: Gallimard, 1947–1965.

    Partly translated in:

    Literary and Philosophical Essays. Tr. Annette Michelson. New York: Criterion Books, 1959.

    What is Literature? Tr. Bernard Frechtman. New York: Philosophical Library, 1949.

    Essays in Aesthetics. Tr. Wade Baskin. New York: Philosophical Library, 1963.

    Situations. Tr. Benita Eisler. New York: Braziller, 1965.

Réflexions sur la question juive. Paris: Mortihien, 1946.

    Anti-Semite and Jew. Tr. George J. Becker. New York: Schocken Books, 1948.

    Baudelaire. Tr. Martin Turnell. New York: New Directions, 1950.

Saint Genet: comédien et martyr. Paris: Gallimard, 1952.

    Saint Genet: Actor and Martyr. Tr. Bernard Frechtman. New York: Braziller, 1963.

Critique de la raison dialectique. Paris: Gallimard, 1960.

    Partly translated in:

    Search for a Method. Tr. Hazel Barnes. New York: Knopf, 1963.

B. Novels, Stories, and Plays

La Nausée. Paris: Gallimard, 1938.

    Nausea. Tr. Lloyd Alexander. New York: New Directions, 1949.

Le Mur. Paris: Gallimard, 1939.

    The Wall and Other Stories. Tr. Lloyd Alexander. New York: New Directions, 1948.

Les Mouches. Paris: Gallimard, 1943.

    The Flies. Tr. Stuart Gilbert. New York: Knopf, 1948.

Les Chemins de la Liberté:

  I. *L'âge de raison.* Paris: Gallimard, 1945.

      The Age of Reason. Tr. Eric Sutton. New York: Knopf, 1947.

II. *Les sursis.* Paris: Gallimard, 1945.
   The Reprieve. Tr. Eric Sutton. New York: Knopf, 1947.
III. *La mort dans l'âme.* Paris: Gallimard, 1947.
   Troubled Sleep. Tr. Gerard Hopkins. New York: Knopf, 1950.

Les Jeux sont Faits. Paris: Nagel, 1947.
   The Chips Are Down. Tr. Louise Varèse. New York: Lear, 1948.
Huis Clos. Paris: Gallimard, 1947.
   No Exit. Tr. Stuart Gilbert. New York: Knopf, 1948.
Morts sans sépulture. Paris: Gallimard, 1947.
   The Victors. Tr. Lionel Abel. New York: Knopf, 1949.
La Putain respectueuse. Paris: Gallimard, 1947.
   The Respectful Prostitute. Tr. Lionel Abel. New York: Knopf, 1949.
Les mains sales. Paris: Gallimard, 1948.
   Dirty Hands. Tr. Lionel Abel. New York: Knopf, 1949.
L'engrenage. Paris: Nagel, 1949.
   In the Mesh. Tr. Mervyn Savill. London: Dakers, 1954.
Le Diable et le bon dieu. Paris: Gallimard, 1951.
   The Devil and the Good Lord. Tr. Kitty Black. New York: Knopf, 1960.
Kean, ou désordre et génie. Paris: Gallimard, 1954.
   Kean, or Disorder and Genius. Tr. Kitty Black. New York: Knopf, 1960.
Nekrassov. Paris: Gallimard, 1956.
   Nekrassov. Tr. Sylvia & George Leeson. London: Hamish Hamilton, 1956.
Les séquestrés d'Altone. Paris: Gallimard, 1960.
   The Condemned of Altona. Tr. Sylvia & George Leeson. New York: Knopf, 1961.

C. Autobiography

Les Mots. Paris: Gallimard, 1964.
   The Words. Tr. Bernard Frechtman. New York: Braziller, 1964.

SELECTED STUDIES ABOUT SARTRE

(arranged alphabetically)

Ayer, A. J. "Novelist-Philosophers: J. P. Sartre," *Horizon,* XII [1945], 12–26, 101–110.
Belkind, Allen. *Jean-Paul Sartre: Sartre* and *Existentialism in Eng-*

lish, *A Bibliographical Guide*. Kent, Ohio: Kent State University Press, 1970.

Champigny, Robert. *Stages on Sartre's Way*. Bloomington: Indiana University Press, 1959.

Desan, Wilfrid. *The Tragic Finale. An Essay on the Philosophy of Jean-Paul Sartre*. Cambridge: Harvard University Press, 1954.

————. *The Marxism of Jean-Paul Sartre*. New York: Doubleday, 1965.

Greene, Norman. *Jean-Paul Sartre: The Existentialist Ethic*. Ann Arbor: University of Michigan Press, 1960.

Gurwitch, Aron. "A Non-Egological Conception of Consciousness," *Philosophy and Phenomenological Research*, I [1941], 325–338.

Hartmann, Klaus. *Sartre's Ontology*. Evanston: Northwestern University Press, 1966.

Jolivet, Regis. *Sartre: The Theology of the Absurd*. Tr. Wesley Piersol. Westminster: Newman, 1967.

Kern, Edith. *Sartre: A Collection of Critical Essays*. Englewood Cliffs: Prentice Hall, 1962.

Manser, Anthony. *Sartre: A Philosophic Study*. London: Athlone, 1966.

Marcuse, Herbert. "Existentialism: Remarks on J. P. Sartre's *L'Être et le néant*," *Philosophy and Phenomenological Research*, VIII [1948], 309–336.

McGill, V. J. "Sartre's Doctrine of Freedom," *Revue international de philosophie*, IX [1949], 329–359.

Merleau-Ponty, Maurice. *Les aventures de la dialectique*. Paris: Gallimard, 1953.

Molnar, Thomas. *Sartre: Ideologue of our Time*. New York: Funk & Wagnalls, 1968.

Murdock, Iris. *Sartre: Romantic Rationalist*. New Haven: Yale University Press, 1953.

Natanson, Maurice. *A Critique of Jean-Paul Sartre's Ontology*. Lincoln: University of Nebraska Press, 1951.

Schuetz, Alfred. "Sartre's Theory of the Alter Ego," *Philosophy and Phenomenological Research*, IX [1948], 181–199.

Salvan, Jacques. *The Scandalous Ghost. Sartre's Existentialism as related to Vitalism, Humanism, Mysticism, and Marxism*. Detroit: Wayne State University Press, 1967.

Varet, Gilbert. *L'Ontologie de Sartre*. Paris: Presses Universitaires, 1948.

Warnock, Mary. *The Philosophy of Sartre*. London: Hutchinson, 1965.

Maurice Merleau-Ponty (1908–1961)

Merleau-Ponty was born in Rochefort-sur-Mer in the district of Charente Maritime on March 14, 1908. His father died before the First World War. He and his brother and sister were reared by his mother; Merleau-Ponty frequently recalled his happy childhood despite the absence of a father.

He was brought up in his mother's religious tradition, Catholicism, and was a practicing member of that faith into his adult life. As with Heidegger, Merleau-Ponty's earliest publications appeared in a Catholic journal of opinion. But late in the thirties he apparently ceased being an active Catholic. He refused to be regarded as an atheist although from certain perspectives he could be considered one.

Merleau-Ponty attended the Lycée Louis le Grand and then the École Normale Supérieur in Paris where he first met Jean-Paul Sartre, who later became his friend and associate. After taking his *Agrégation de Philosophie* in 1931, he taught at a *lycée* in Beauvais, received a grant from Caisse de la Recherche Scientifique for a year, and then taught again at the *lycée* in Chartres. In 1935 he returned to the École Normale as an *agrégré repetiteur*, i.e., as a junior member of the faculty. He later received an appointment to the Lycée Carnot in Paris with which he was associated until 1944.

It was in the latter half of the 1930s that Merleau-Ponty studied and assimilated the writings of Husserl, Scheler, Heidegger, and Marcel, all of whom were important influences in his development away from traditional French philosophy, i.e., Cartesianism, and toward his own formulations of the problems of behavior and perception. His work also bears the stamp of

Hegel upon it—of Hegel highlighted by the interpretations of Alexandre Kojève, who taught at the École des Hautes Études from 1933 to 1939. When the Second World War erupted in 1939, Merleau-Ponty entered the army and served as an infantry lieutenant. Upon France's defeat by Germany, he was demobilized and returned to teaching. At the same time, he wrote his most important full-fledged book, *Phénoménologie de la perception*. While teaching at the Lycée Condorcet in Paris in 1944 near the end of the war in France, he and Jean-Paul Sartre decided to found a journal devoted to artistic, political, and philosophical matters. They called it *Les Temps modernes*. Merleau-Ponty was its political editor from 1945 to 1952 when he resigned. Coinciding with the resignation was the termination of his friendship with Sartre. Although the co-editors were both on what is usually called the left of the political spectrum, they disagreed profoundly about Marxism, as well as the methods of the Communist parties of Russia and of France. Merleau-Ponty was critical of the historical inevitability in Marxism, the purges and labor camps in Russia, and the opportunism of the French Communists. Sartre, although neither a Marxist nor a Communist, has moved ever closer to the former and has regarded public criticism of Communists as ammunition for the common enemy—bourgeois capitalism.

In the meantime he had moved from the Lycée Condorcet to the Lycée Saint Quentin and from there to the University of Lyon and professor of philosophy between 1949 and 1950. Then he transferred in 1950 to the Sorbonne as professor of psychology and pedagogy. He remained at that post for two years until he received an appointment to fill the chair of philosophy at the Collège de France. He was the youngest philosopher ever to obtain this position—an eminent one in French academic circles. Merleau-Ponty held it until his death on May 4, 1961, caused by a coronary thrombosis. He was survived by his wife, a physician and psychiatrist who was prominent in her own right, and his daughter.

"Interrogation and Intuition"
from *The Visible and the Invisible*

Edited by Claude LeFort and translated by Alphonso Lingis

Philosophy does not raise questions and does not provide answers that would little by little fill in the blanks. The questions
are within our life, within our history: they are born there, they
die there, if they have found a response, more often than not
they are transformed there; in any case, it is a past of experience
and of knowledge that one day ends up at this open wondering.
Philosophy does not take the context as given; it turns back upon
it in order to seek the origin and the meaning of the questions
and of the responses and the identity of him who questions, and
it thereby gains access to the interrogation that animates all the
questions of cognition, but is of another sort than they.

Our ordinary questions—"Where am I?" "What time is it?"—
are the lack and the provisional absence of a factor of a positive
statement, holes in a fabric of things or of indicatives that we
are sure is continuous, since there is a time, a space, and since
the only question is at what point of this space and of this time
we are. Philosophy, at first sight, only generalizes this type of
question. When it asks if space, if time, if movement, if the
world exist, the field of the question is more ample, but like the
natural question it is still but a semi-question, included within a
fundamental faith: there is something, and the only question is
if it is really this space, this time, this movement, this world
that we think we see or feel. The destruction of beliefs, the symbolic murder of the others and of the world, the split between
vision and the visible, between thought and being do not, as
they claim, establish us in the negative; when one has subtracted
all that, one installs oneself in what remains, in sensations,
opinions. And what remains is not nothing, nor of another sort
than what has been struck off: what remains are mutilated fragments of the vague *omnitudo realitatis* against which the doubt

was plied, and they regenerate it under other names—appearance, dream, Psyche, representation.

It is in the name and for the profit of these floating realities that the solid reality is cast into doubt. One does not quit the something, and doubt as a destruction of certitudes is not a doubt. It is no different when the doubt is made methodic, when it is no longer a fluidification of the certitudes but a deliberate withdrawal, a refusal to embody them. This time one no longer contests that there are evidences and that for the moment they are irresistible; and if one holds them in suspense it is for the sole motive that they are our own, caught up in the flux of our life, and that in order to retain them more than an instant we should have to trust in the obscure time equipment of our internal works, which perhaps gives us only coherent illusions. This deceiving nature, this opaque something that would shut us up in our lights, is only a phantasm of our rigorism, a perhaps. If this possible suffices to hold in check our evidences, it is because we give weight to it by the decision to tacitly presuppose nothing. If, in its name, we feign to nullify lights we could not nullify really, take what is only conditional to be false, make of an eventual divergence between the evident and the true an infinite distance, and of a speculative doubt the equivalent of a condemnation, it is because, as passive beings, we feel ourselves caught up in a mass of Being that escapes us, or even maneuvered by an evil agent, and we oppose to this adversity the desire for an absolute evidence, delivered from all facticity.

Thus the methodic doubt, that which is carried out within the voluntary zone of ourselves, refers to Being, since it resists a factual evidence, represses an involuntary truth which it acknowledges to be already there and which inspires the very project of seeking an evidence that would be absolute. If it remains a doubt, it can do so only by reviving the equivocations of scepticism, by omitting to mention the borrowings it makes from Being, or by evoking a falsity of Being itself, a Great Deceiver, a Being that actively conceals itself and pushes before itself the screen of our thought and of its evidences, as if this elusive being were nothing. The philosophical interrogation therefore would not go all the way through with itself if it limited itself to generalizing the doubt, the common question of

the *an sit*, to extending them to the world or to Being, and
would define itself as doubt, non-knowing or non-belief. Things
are not so simple. In being extended to everything, the common
question changes its meaning. Philosophy elects certain beings—
"sensations," "representation," "thought," "consciousness," or
even a deceiving being—in order to separate itself from all being.
Precisely in order to accomplish its will for radicalism, it would
have to take as its theme the umbilical bond that binds it always
to Being, the inalienable horizon with which it is already and
henceforth circumvented, the primary initiation which it tries
in vain to go back on. It would have to no longer deny, no
longer even doubt; it would have to step back only in order to
see the world and Being, or simply put them between quotation
marks as one does with the remarks of another, to let them
speak, to listen in. . . .

Then, if the question can no longer be that of the *an sit*, it
becomes that of the *quid sit*; there remains only to study what
the world and truth and being are, in terms of the complicity
that we have with them. At the same time that the doubt is renounced, one renounces the affirmation of an absolute exterior,
of a world or a Being that would be a massive individual; one
turns toward that Being that doubles our thoughts along their
whole extension, since they are thoughts of something and
since they themselves are not nothing—a Being therefore that is
meaning, and meaning of meaning. Not only that meaning that
is attached to words and belongs to the order of statements and
of things said, to a circumscribed region of the world, to a certain
type of Being—but universal meaning, which would be capable
of sustaining logical operations and language and the unfolding
of the world as well. It will be *that without which* there would
be neither world nor language nor anything at all—it will be the
essence.

When it looks back from the world to what makes it a world,
from beings to what makes them be, the pure gaze, which involves nothing implicit (which does not, like the gaze of our
eyes, have the darkness of a body and a past behind itself),
could apply itself only to something that would be before it
without restriction or condition: to what makes the world
be a world, to an imperative grammar of Being, to indecomposable

nuclei of meaning, systems of inseparable properties. The essences are this intrinsic sense, these necessities by principle. However may be the realities in which they are compounded and confused (but where their implications constantly make themselves no less felt), they are the sole legitimate or authentic being, which has the pretension and the right to be and which is affirmative of itself, because it is the system of everything that is possible before the eyes of a pure spectator, the diagram or pattern of what, at all the levels, is *something*—something in general, or something material, or something spiritual, or something living.

Through the question *quid sit,* more effectively than through the doubt, philosophy succeeds in detaching itself from all beings, because it changes them into their meaning. This is already the procedure of science, when, to respond to the questions of life which are only a hesitation between the yes and the no, it casts the prevailing categories into question, invents new types of Being, a new heaven of essences. But it does not terminate this labor: it does not entirely disengage its essences from the world; it maintains them under the jurisdiction of the facts, which can tomorrow call for another elaboration. Galileo gives but a rough draft of the material thing, and the whole of classical physics lives on an essence of *Physis* that is perhaps not the true essence: must one maintain its principles, and, by means of some auxiliary hypothesis, reduce wave mechanics to them however one can? Or, on the contrary, are we in sight of a new essence of the material world? Must we maintain the Marxist essence of history and treat the facts that seem to call it into question as empirical and confused variants, or, on the contrary, are we at a turning point where, *beneath* the Marxist essence of history, a more authentic and more complete essence shows through?

The question remains unsettled in scientific knowing because in it truths of fact and truths of reason overlap and because the carving out of the facts, like the elaboration of the essences, is there conducted under presuppositions that remain to be interrogated, if we are to know fully what science means. Philosophy would be this same reading of meaning carried out to its conclusion, an exact science, the sole exact one, because it alone goes all the way in the effort to know what Nature and History and the World and Being *are*, when our contact with them is not only the partial and abstract contact of the physical experiment and calculation, or of the historical analysis, but the total contact of someone who, living in the world and in Being, means to see his life fully, particularly his life of knowledge, and who, an inhabitant of the world, tries to think himself in the world, to think the world in himself, to unravel their jumbled essences, and to form finally the signification "Being."*

When philosophy finds beneath the doubt a prior "knowing," finds around the things and the world as facts and as doubtful facts a horizon that encompasses our negations as our affirmations, and when it penetrates into this horizon, certainly it must define anew this new something. Does it define it well or sufficiently by saying that it is the *essence?* Is the question of the essence the ultimate question? With the essence and the pure spectator who sees it, are we really at the source? The essence is certainly dependent. The inventory of the essential necessities is always made under a supposition (the same as that which recurs so often in Kant): if this world is to exist for us, or if there is to be a world, or if there is to be something, then it is necessary that they observe such and such a structural law. But whence do we get the hypothesis, whence do we know that there is something, that there is a world?

This knowing is beneath the essence, it is the experience of which the essence is a part and which it does not envelop. The being of the essence is not primary, it does not rest on itself, it is not it that can teach us what Being is; the essence is not *the* answer to the philosophical question, the philosophical question is not posed in us by a pure spectator: it is first a question as to how, upon what ground, the pure spectator is established, from what more profound source he himself draws. Without the necessities by essence, the unshakable connections, the irresistible implications, the resistant and stable structures, there would be neither a world, nor something in general, nor Being; but their authority as essences, their affirmative power, their dignity

---

* What is true here: what is not nothing is *something*, but: this something is not hard as a diamond, not unconditioned, *Erfahrung*.

as principles are not self-evident. We do not have the right to say that the essences we find give the primitive meaning of Being, that they are the possible in itself, the whole possible, and to repute as impossible all that does not obey their laws, nor to treat Being and the world as their consequence: they are only its manner or its style, they are the *Sosein* and not the *Sein*. And if we are justified in saying that every thought respects them as well as does our own, if they have universal value, this is so inasmuch as another thought founded on other principles must, if it is to make itself known to us, to enter into communication with us, adapt itself to the conditions of our own thought, of our experience, take its place in our world, and inasmuch as, finally, all the thinkers and all the essences possible open upon one sole experience and upon the same world.

We are no doubt using essences in order to establish and state this; the necessity of this conclusion is a necessity of essence. But it only crosses over the limits of one thought and imposes itself upon all, it indeed only survives my own intuition of the moment and is valid for me as a durable truth because my own experience interconnects within itself and connects with that of the others by opening upon one sole world, by inscribing itself in one sole Being. It is to experience therefore that the ultimate ontological power belongs, and the essences, the necessities by essence, the internal or logical possibility, solid and incontestable as they may be under the gaze of the mind, have finally their force and their eloquence only because all my thoughts and the thoughts of the others are caught up in the fabric of one sole Being. The pure spectator in me, which elevates each thing to the essence, which produces its ideas, is assured that it touches Being with them only because it emerges within an actual experience surrounded by actual experiences, by the actual world, by the actual Being, which is the ground of the predicative Being. The possibilities by essence can indeed envelop and dominate *the facts;* they themselves derive from another, and more fundamental, possibility: that which works over my experience, opens it to the world and to Being, and which, to be sure, does not find them before itself as *facts* but animates and organizes *their facticity*. When philosophy ceases to be doubt in order to make itself disclosure, explicitation, the field it opens to itself is indeed made up of significations or of essences—since it has detached itself from the facts and the beings—but these significations or essences do not suffice to themselves, they overtly refer to our acts of ideation which have lifted them from a brute being, wherein we must find again in their wild state what answers to our essences and our significations.

When I ask myself what the something or the world or the material thing is, I am not yet the pure spectator I will become through the act of ideation; I am a field of experience where there is only sketched out the family of material things and other families and the world as their common style, the family of things said and the world of speech as their common style, and finally the abstract and fleshless style of something in general. In order to pass from this to the essences, it is necessary for me to actively intervene, to vary the things and the field, not through some manipulation, but, without touching them, by supposing changed or putting out of circuit such and such a relationship or such and such a structure, noting how this would affect the others, so as to locate those relationships and structures that are separable from the thing, and those on the contrary that one could not suppress or change without the thing ceasing to be itself. It is from this test that the essence emerges—it is therefore not a positive being. It is an in-variant, it is exactly that whose change or absence would alter or destroy the thing; and the solidity, the essentiality of the essence is exactly measured by the power we have to vary the thing. A pure essence which would not be at all contaminated and confused with the facts could result only from an attempt at total variation. It would require a spectator himself without secrets, without latency, if we are to be certain that nothing be surreptitiously introduced into it.

In order to really reduce an experience to its essence, we should have to achieve a distance from it that would put it entirely under our gaze, with all the implications of sensoriality or thought that come into play in it, bring it and bring ourselves wholly to the transparency of the imaginary, think it without the support of any ground, in short, withdraw to the bottom of nothingness. Only then could we know what moments positively make up the being of this experience.

But would this still be an experience, since I would be soaring over it? And if I tried to maintain a sort of adhesion to it in thought, is it properly speaking an essence that I would see? Every ideation, because it is an ideation, is formed in a space of existence, under the guarantee of my duration, which must turn back into itself in order to find there again the same idea I thought an instant ago and must pass into the others in order to rejoin it also in them. Every ideation is borne by this tree of my duration and other durations, this unknown sap nourishes the transparency of the idea; behind the idea, there is the unity, the simultaneity of all the real and possible durations, the cohesion of one sole Being from one end to the other. Under the solidity of the essence and of the idea there is the fabric of experience, this flesh of time, and this is why I am not sure of having penetrated unto the hard core of being: my incontestable power to give myself leeway (*prendre du champ*), to disengage the possible from the real, does not go as far as to dominate all the implications of the spectacle and to make of the real a simple variant of the possible; on the contrary it is the possible worlds and the possible beings that are variants and are like doubles of the actual world and the actual Being.

I have leeway enough to replace such and such moments of my experience with others, to observe that this does not suppress it—therefore to determine the inessential. But does what remains after these eliminations belong necessarily to the Being in question? In order to affirm that I should have to soar over my field, suspend or at least reactivate all the sedimented thoughts with which it is surrounded, first of all my time, my body—which is not only impossible for me to do in fact but would deprive me of that very cohesion in depth (*en épaisseur*) of the world and of Being without which the essence is subjective folly and arrogance. There is therefore for me something inessential, and there is a zone, a hollow, where what is not inessential, not impossible, assembles; there is no positive vision that would definitively give me the essentiality of the essence.

Shall we say then that we *fall short of* the essence, that we have it only in principle, that it lies at the limit of an always imperfect idealization? This double thinking that opposes the principle and the fact saves with the term "principle" only a presumption of the essence, although this is the moment to decide if it is justified, and to save the presumption it entrenches us in relativism, although by renouncing the essence that is intemporal and without locality we would perhaps obtain a true thought with regard to the essence.

It is on account of having begun with the antithesis of the fact and the essence, of what is individuated in a point of space and time and what is from forever and nowhere, that one is finally led to treat the essence as a limit idea, that is, to make it inaccessible. For this is what obliged us to seek the being of the essence in the form of a second positivity beyond the order of the "facts," to dream of a variation of the thing that would eliminate from it all that is not authentically itself and would make it appear all naked whereas it is always clothed—to dream of an impossible labor of experience on experience that would strip it of its facticity as if it were an impurity. Perhaps if we were to re-examine the anti-thesis of fact and essence, we would be able on the contrary to redefine the essence in a way that would give us access to it, because it would be not beyond but at the heart of that coiling up (*enroulement*) of experience over experience which a moment ago constituted the difficulty.

Only a thought that looks at being from elsewhere, and as it were head-on, is forced into the bifurcation of the essence and the fact. If I am *kosmotheoros,* my sovereign gaze finds the things each in its own time, in its own place, as absolute individuals in a unique local and temporal disposition. Since they participate in the same significations each from its own place, one is led to conceive another dimension that would be a transversal to this flat multiplicity and that would be the system of significations without locality or temporality. And then, since it is indeed necessary to connect the two and to comprehend how the two orders are connected up through us, one arrives at the inextricable problem of the intuition of essences. But am I *kosmotheoros*? More exactly: is being *kosmotheoros* my ultimate reality? Am I primitively the power to contemplate, a pure look which fixes the things in their temporal and local place and the essences in an invisible heaven; am I this ray of knowing that would have to arise from nowhere? But even while I am installing myself at this zero point of Being, I know very well that it has a mysterious tie with locality and temporality: tomorrow, in a moment, this aerial view, with everything it encompasses, will fall at a certain date of the calendar; I will assign to it a certain point of apparition on the earth and in my life. One has to believe that time has continued to flow on beneath and that the earth has continued to exist. Since, however, I had crossed over to the other side, instead of saying that I am in time and in space, or that I am nowhere, why not rather say that I am everywhere, always, by being at this moment and at this place?

For the visible present is not *in* time and space, nor, of course, *outside* of them: there is nothing before it, after it, about it, that could compete with its visibility. And yet it is not alone, it is not everything. To put it precisely, it stops up my view, that is, time and space extend beyond the visible present, and at the same time they are *behind* it, in depth, in hiding. The visible can thus fill me and occupy me only because I who see it do not see it from the depths of nothingness, but from the midst of itself; I the seer am also visible. What makes the weight, the thickness, the flesh of each color, of each sound, of each tactile texture, of the present, and of the world is the fact that he who grasps them feels himself emerge from them by a sort of coiling up or redoubling, fundamentally homogeneous with them; he feels that he is the sensible itself coming to itself and that in return the sensible is in his eyes as it were his double or an extension of his own flesh. The space, the time of the things are shreds of himself, of his own spatialization, of his own temporalization, are no longer a multiplicity of individuals synchronically and diachronically distributed, but a relief of the simultaneous and of the successive, a spatial and temporal pulp where the individuals are formed by differentiation. The things —here, there, now, then—are no longer in themselves, in their own place, in their own time; they exist only at the end of those rays of spatiality and of temporality emitted in the secrecy of my flesh. And their solidity is not that of a pure object which the mind soars over; I experience their solidity from within insofar as I am among them and insofar as they communicate through me as a sentient thing. Like the memory screen of the psychoanalysts, the present, the visible counts so much for me and has an absolute prestige for me only by reason of this immense latent content of the past, the future, and the elsewhere, which it announces and which it conceals.

There is therefore no need to add to the multiplicity of spatio-temporal atoms a transversal dimension of essences—what there is is a whole architecture, a whole complex of phenomena "in tiers," a whole series of "levels of being,"[1] which are differentiated by the coiling up of the visible and the universal over a certain visible wherein it is redoubled and inscribed. Fact and essence can no longer be distinguished, not because, mixed up in our experience, they in their purity would be inaccessible and would subsist as limit-ideas beyond our experience, but because—Being no longer being *before me*, but surrounding me and in a sense traversing me, and my vision of Being not forming itself from elsewhere, but from the midst of Being—the alleged facts, the spatio-temporal individuals, are from the first mounted on the axes, the pivots, the dimensions, the generality of my body, and the ideas are therefore already encrusted in its joints. There is no emplacement of space and time that would not be a variant of the others, as they are of it; there is no individual that would not be representative of a species or of a family of beings, would not have, would not be a certain style, a certain manner of managing the domain of space and time over which it has competency, of pronouncing, of articulating that domain, of radiating about a wholly virtual center—in short, a certain manner of being, in the active sense, a certain *Wesen*, in the sense that, says Heidegger, this word has when it is used as a verb.[2]

[1] Jean Wahl, "Sein, Wahrheit, Welt," Revue de métaphysique et de morale, LXV, No. 2 [April–June, 1960], 187–94.

[2] The high school building, for us who return to it, thirty years later, as for those who occupy it today, is not so much an object which it would be useful or possible to describe by its characteristics, as it is a certain odor, a certain affective texture which holds sway over a certain vicinity of space. This velvet, this silk, are under my fingers a certain manner of resisting them and of yielding to them, a rough, sleek, rasping power, which respond for an X-spot of my flesh, lend themselves to its movement of muscled flesh, or tempt it in its inertia (*Einführung in die Metaphysik* [Tübingen, 1953], p. 26). [English translation by Ralph Manheim, *Introduction to Metaphysics* (Garden City, N. Y., 1961), pp. 27–28.]

In short, there is no essence, no idea, that does not adhere to a domain of history and of geography. Not that it is *confined* there and inaccessible for the others, but because, like that of nature, the space or time of culture is not surveyable from above, and because the communication from one constituted culture to another occurs through the wild region wherein they all have originated. Where in all this is the essence? Where is the existence? Where is the *Sosein,* where the *Sein?* We never have before us pure individuals, indivisible glaciers of beings, nor essences without place and without date. Not that they exist elsewhere, beyond our grasp, but because we are experiences, that is, thoughts that feel behind themselves the weight of the space, the time, the very Being they think, and which therefore do not hold under their gaze a serial space and time nor the pure idea of series, but have about themselves a time and a space that exist by piling up, by proliferation, by encroachment, by promiscuity —a perpetual pregnancy, perpetual parturition, generativity and generality, brute essence and brute existence, which are the nodes and antinodes of the same ontological vibration.

And if one were to ask what is this indecisive milieu in which we find ourselves once the distinction between fact and essence is rejected, one must answer that it is the very sphere of our life, and of our life of knowledge. Now would be the time to reject the myths of inductivity and of the *Wesenschau,* which are transmitted, as points of honor, from generation to generation. It is nonetheless clear that Husserl himself never obtained one sole *Wesenschau* that he did not subsequently take up again and rework, not to disown it, but in order to make it say what at first it had not quite said. Thus it would be naïve to seek solidity in a heaven of ideas or in a *ground (fond)* of meaning—it is neither above nor beneath the appearances, but at their joints; it is the tie that secretly connects an experience to its variants.

It is clear also that pure inductivity is a myth. Let us set aside the domain of physics, to show later that the psychoanalysis of objective knowledge is interminable, or rather that, like every psychoanalysis, it is destined not to suppress the past, the phantasms, but to transform them from powers of death into poetic productivity, and that the very idea of objective knowledge and the idea of algorithm as a spiritual automaton and finally the idea of an object that informs itself and knows itself are, as much as any other ideas, and more than any other, supported by our reveries. Let us leave that aside for the moment. In any case, as soon as it is a question of the living being and of the body, and a fortiori of man, it is indeed clear that no fruitful research is pure inductivity, a pure inventorying of constants in themselves, that psychology, ethnology, sociology have taught us something only by putting the morbid or archaic or simply different experience in contact with our experience, by clarifying the one by the other, criticizing the one by the other, by organizing the *Ineinander,* and finally, by practicing that eidetic variation which Husserl was wrong to reserve primarily for the solitary imagination and vision of the philosopher, whereas it is the support and the very locus of that *opinio communis* we call science. Along this route, at least, it is indeed certain that we gain access to objectivity, not by penetrating into an In Itself, but by disclosing, rectifying each by the other, the exterior datum and the internal double of it that we possess insofar as we are sensible-sentients (*sentants-sensibles*), archetypes and variants of humanity and of life, that is, insofar as we are within life, within the human being and within Being, and insofar as it is in us as well, and insofar as we live and know not halfway between opaque facts and limpid ideas, but at the point of intersection and overlapping where families of facts inscribe their generality, their kinship, group themselves about the dimensions and the site of our own existence.

This environment of brute existence and essence is not something mysterious: we never quit it, we have no other environment. The facts and the essences are abstractions: what there is are worlds and a world and a Being, not a sum of facts or a system of ideas, but the impossibility of meaninglessness or ontological void, since space and time are not the sum of local and temporal individuals, but the presence and latency behind each of all the others, and behind those of still others—and what they are we do not know, but we do know at least that they are determinable in principle. This world, this Being, facticity and ideality undividedly, is not one in the sense that being one applies to the individuals it contains, and still less is it two or several in that sense. Yet it is nothing mysterious: it is, whatever we may say, this world, this Being that our life, our science, and our philosophy inhabit.[3]

We shall render explicit the cohesion of time, of space, of space and time, the "simultaneity" of their parts (literal simultaneity in space, simultaneity in the figurative sense in time) and the intertwining (*entrelacs*) of space and time. And we shall render explicit the cohesion of the obverse and the reverse of my body which is responsible for the fact that my body—which is visible, tangible like a thing—acquires this view upon itself, this contact with itself, where it doubles itself up, unifies itself, in such a way that the objective body and the phenomenal body turn about one another or encroach upon one another. For the moment it suffices to show that the unique Being, the dimensionality to which these moments, these leaves, and these dimensions belong, is beyond the classical essence and existence and renders their relationship comprehensible.

Before the essence as before the fact, all we must do is situate ourselves within the being we are dealing with, instead of looking at it from the outside—or, *what amounts to the same thing*, what we have to do is put it back into the fabric of our life, attend from within to the dehiscence (analogous to that of my own body) which opens it to itself and opens us upon it, and which, in the case of the essence, is the dehiscence of the speaking and the thinking. As my body, which is one of the visibles, sees itself also and thereby makes itself the natural light opening its own interior to the visible, in order for the visible there to become my own landscape, realizing (as it is said) the miraculous promotion of Being to "consciousness," or (as we prefer to say) the segregation of the "within" and the "without"; so also speech (*la parole*)—which is sustained by the thousands of ideal relations of the particular language (*la langue*), and which, therefore, in the eyes of science, is, as a constituted language

---

[3] EDITOR: Here, in the course of the text itself, are inserted these lines: "in this labor of experience on experience which is the carnal context of the essence, it is necessary to draw attention particularly to the labor of speech (take up again the paragraph under discussion, and the apprehension of the essence as a spread between words [*écart des paroles*])."

(*langage*), a certain region in the universe of significations—is also the organ and the resonator of all the other regions of signification and consequently coextensive with the thinkable.

Like the flesh of the visible, speech is a total part of the significations, like it, speech is a relation to Being through a being, and, like it, it is narcissistic, eroticized, endowed with a natural magic that attracts the other significations into its web, as the body feels the world in feeling itself. In reality, there is much more than a parallel or an analogy here, there is solidarity and intertwining: if speech, which is but a region of the intelligible world, can be also its refuge, this is because speech prolongs into the invisible, extends unto the semantic operations, the belongingness of the body to being and the corporeal relevance of every being, which for me is once and for all attested by the visible, and whose idea each intellectual evidence reflects a little further. In a philosophy that takes into consideration the operative world, functioning, present and coherent, as it is, the essence is not at all a stumbling block: it has its place there as an operative, functioning, essence. No longer are there essences above us, like positive objects, offered to a spiritual eye; but there is an essence beneath us, a common nervure of the signifying and the signified, adherence in and reversibility of one another—as the visible things are the secret folds of our flesh, and yet our body is one of the visible things.

As the world is behind my body, the operative essence is behind the operative speech also, the speech that possesses the signification less than it is possessed by it, that does not speak *of it,* but speaks *it,* or speaks *according to it,* or lets it speak and be spoken within me, breaks through my present. If there is an ideality, a thought that has a future in me, that even breaks through my space of consciousness and has a future with the others, and finally, having become a writing, has a future in every possible reader, this can be only that thought that leaves me with my hunger and leaves them with their hunger, that betokens a generalized buckling of my landscape and opens it to the universal, precisely because it is rather an *unthought.* Ideas that are too much possessed are no longer ideas; I no longer think anything when I speak of them, as if it were essential to the essence that it be for tomorrow, as if it were only a tacking thread in the fabric of the words. A discussion is not an exchange or a confrontation of ideas, as if each formed his own, showed them to the others, looked at theirs, and returned to correct them with his own. . . . Someone speaks, and immediately the others are now but certain divergencies by relation to his words, and he himself specifies his divergence in relation to them. Whether he speaks up or hardly whispers, each one speaks with all that he is, with his "ideas," but also with his obsessions, his secret history which the others suddenly lay bare by formulating them as ideas.

Life becomes ideas and the ideas return to life, each is caught up in the vortex in which he first committed only measured stakes, each is led on by what he said and the response he received, led on by his own thought of which he is no longer the sole thinker. No one thinks any more, everyone speaks, all live and gesticulate within Being, as I stir within my landscape, guided by gradients of differences to be observed or to be reduced if I wish to remain here or to go yonder. Whether in discussion or in monologue, the essence in the living and active state is always a certain vanishing point indicated by the arrangement of the words, their "other side," inaccessible, save for him who accepts to live first and always in them.

As the nervure bears the leaf from within, from the depths of its flesh, the ideas are the texture of experience, its style, first mute, then uttered. Like every style, they are elaborated within the thickness of being and, not only in fact but also by right, could not be detached from it, to be spread out on display under the gaze.

The philosophical interrogation is therefore not the simple expectation of a signification that would come to fill it. "What is the world?" or, better, "what is Being?"—these questions become philosophical only if, by a sort of diplopia, at the same time that they aim at a state of things, they aim at themselves as questions—at the same time that they aim at the signification "being," they aim at the being of signification and the place of signification within Being. It is characteristic of the philosophical questioning that it return upon itself, that it ask itself also what to question is and what to respond is. Once this question to the second power is raised, it cannot be effaced. Henceforth nothing can continue to be as if there had never been any question. The forgetting of the question, the return to the positive would be possible only if the questioning were a simple absence of meaning, a withdrawal into the nothingness that is nothing.

But he who questions is not nothing, he is—and this is something quite different—a being that questions himself; the negative in him is borne by an infrastructure of being, it is therefore not a nothing that eliminates itself from the account. We said that the doubt is a clandestine positivism and that it is necessary to go beyond it toward the something it negates and yet affirms. But conversely if we wished to go beyond it unto a sphere of absolute certitude that would be the sphere of significations or essences, this absolute positivism would mean that he who questions had distanced Being and the world from himself so much that he was of them no longer. Like the negativism of the doubt, the positivism of the essences says secretly the contrary of what it says openly. The intent to reach the absolutely hard being of the essence conceals the mendacious pretension to be nothing. No question goes toward Being: if only by virtue of its being as a question, it has already frequented Being, it is returning to it. As the view that the question be a real rupture with Being, a lived nothingness, is precluded, also precluded is the view that it be an ideal rupture, an absolutely pure gaze directed upon an experience reduced to its signification or its essence.

As is precluded the view that the question be without response, be a pure gaping toward a transcendent Being, also precluded is the view that the response be immanent to the question and that, as Marx said, humanity raise only the questions it can resolve. And these two views are precluded for the same reason, which is that in both hypotheses there would finally be no question, and that in both these views our initial situation is ignored—either, cut off from Being, we would not even have enough of the positive to raise a question, or, already caught up in Being, we would be already beyond every question. The questions of essence to which one wishes to reduce philosophy are not of themselves more philosophical than the questions of fact, and the questions of fact, when the occasion arises, no less philosophical than they. The dimension of philosophy cuts across that of the essence and the [fact].[4] To question oneself about the essence of time and of space is not yet to do philosophy, if one does not then question oneself about the relations of time itself and of space itself with their essence. And in a sense the questions of fact go further than the truths of reason.

> From time to time, a man lifts his head, sniffs, listens, considers, recognizes his position: he thinks, he sighs, and, drawing his watch from the pocket lodged against his chest, looks at the time. *Where am I?* and *What time is it?*—such is the inexhaustible question turning from us to the world. . . .[5]

Inexhaustible, because the time and the place change continually, but especially because the question that arises here is not at bottom a question of knowing in what spot of a space taken as given, at what hour of a time taken as given, we are—but first what is this indestructible tie between us and hours and places, this perpetual taking of our bearings on the things, this continual installation among them, through which first it is necessary that I be at a time, at a place, whatever they be. Positive information, a statement whatever it be, only defer that question and beguile our hunger. They refer us to some sort of law of our being that lays down that after a space there is a space, that after a time there is a time, but it is this law itself that our questions of fact are reaching for. If we could scrutinize their ultimate motivation, we would find beneath the questions *where am I?* and *what time is it?* a secret knowledge of space and time as beings to be questioned, a secret knowledge of interrogation as the ultimate relation to Being and as an ontological organ. The necessities by essence will not be the "answer" philosophy calls for, any more than are the facts. The "answer" is higher than the "facts," lower than the "essences," in the wild Being where they were, and—behind or beneath the cleavages of our acquired culture—continue to be, undivided.

[4] EDITOR: We reintroduce between brackets the term "fact" erased by error.

[5] Claudel, *Art poétique* (Paris, 1951), p. 9.

What we propose here, and oppose to the search for the essence, is not the return to the immediate, the coincidence, the effective fusion with the existent, the search for an original integrity, for a secret lost and to be rediscovered, which would nullify our questions and even reprehend our language. If co-incidence is lost, this is no accident; if Being is hidden, this is itself a characteristic of Being, and no disclosure will make us comprehend it. A lost immediate, arduous to restore, will, if we do restore it, bear within itself the sediment of the critical pro-cedures through which we will have found it anew; it will therefore not be the immediate. If it is to be the immediate, if it is to retain no trace of the operations through which we ap-proach it, if it is Being itself, this means that there is no route from us to it and that it is inaccessible by principle.

The visible things about us rest in themselves, and their natural being is so full that it seems to envelop their perceived being, as if our perception of them were formed within them. But if I express this experience by saying that the things are in their place and that we fuse with them, I immediately make the experience itself impossible: for in the measure that the thing is approached, I cease to be; in the measure that I am, there is no thing, but only a double of it in my "camera obscura." The moment my perception is to become pure perception, thing, Being, it is extinguished; the moment it lights up, already I am no longer the thing. And likewise there is no real coinciding with the being of the past: if the pure memory is the former present preserved, and if, in the act of recalling, I really become again what I was, it becomes impossible to see how it could open to me the dimension of the past. And if in being inscribed within me each present loses its flesh, if the pure memory into which it is changed is an invisible, then there is indeed a past, but no coinciding with it—I am separated from it by the whole thick-ness of my present; it is mine only by finding in some way a place in my present, in making itself present anew.

As we never have at the same time the thing and the con-sciousness of the thing, we never have at the same time the past and the consciousness of the past, and for the same reason: in an intuition by coincidence and fusion, everything one gives to Being is taken from experience, everything one gives to experience is taken from Being. The truth of the matter is that the experience of a coincidence can be, as Bergson often says, only a "partial coincidence." But what is a coincidence that is only partial? It is a coincidence always past or always future, an experience that remembers an impossible past, anticipates an impossible future, that emerges from Being or that will incorporate itself into Being, that "is of it" but is not it, and therefore is not a coincidence, a real fusion, as of two positive terms or two elements of an alloyage, but an overlaying, as of a hollow and a relief which remain distinct.

Coming after the world, after nature, after life, after thought, and finding them constituted before it, philosophy indeed questions this antecedent being and questions itself concerning its own relationship with it. It is a return upon itself and upon all things but not a return to an immediate—which recedes in the measure that philosophy wishes to approach it and fuse into it. The immediate is at the horizon and must be thought as such; it is only by remaining at a distance that it remains itself. There is an experience of the visible thing as pre-existing my vision, but this experience is not a fusion, a coincidence: because my eyes which see, my hands which touch, can also be seen and touched, because, therefore, in this sense they see and touch the visible, the tangible, from within, because our flesh lines and even envelops all the visible and tangible things with which nevertheless it is surrounded, the world and I are within one another, and there is no anteriority of the *percipere* to the *percipi*, there is simultaneity or even retardation. For the weight of the natural world is already a weight of the past.

Each landscape of my life, because it is not a wandering troop of sensations or a system of ephemeral judgments but a segment of the durable flesh of the world, is qua visible, pregnant with many other visions besides my own; and the visible that I see, of which I speak, even if it is not Mount Hymettus or the plane trees of Delphi, is numerically the same that Plato and Aristotle saw and spoke of. When I find again the actual world such as it is, under my hands, under my eyes, up against my body, I find much more than an object: a Being of which my vision is a part, a visibility older than my operations or my acts.

But this does not mean that there was a fusion or coinciding of me with it: on the contrary, this occurs because a sort of dehiscence opens my body in two, and because between my body looked at and my body looking, my body touched and my body touching, there is overlapping or encroachment, so that we must say that the things pass into us as well as we into the things.

Our intuition, said Bergson, is a reflection, and he was right; his intuition shares with the philosophies of reflection a sort of supralapsarian bias: the secret of Being is in an integrity that is behind us. Like the philosophies of reflection, what Bergson lacks is the double reference, the identity of the retiring into oneself with the leaving of oneself, of the lived through with the distance. The return to the immediate data, the deepening of experience on the spot, are certainly the hallmark of philosophy by opposition to naïve cognitions. But the past and the present, the essence and the fact, space and time, are not *given* in the same sense, and none of them is given in the sense of coincidence. The "originating"[6] is not of one sole type, it is not all behind us; the restoration of the true past, of the pre-existence is not all of philosophy; the lived experience is not flat, without depth, without dimension, it is not an opaque stratum with which we would have to merge.

The appeal to the originating goes in several directions: the originating breaks up, and philosophy must accompany this break-up, this non-coincidence, this differentiation. The difficulties of coincidence are not only factual difficulties which would leave the principle intact. Already with respect to the intuition of essences we have encountered this system of double truth, which is also a system of double falsity: for what is true *in principle* never being true *in fact,* and conversely the factual situation never committing the principles, each of the two instances condemns the other, and condemns it with reprieve, by leaving to it competency in its own order. If the coincidence is never but partial, we must not define the truth by total or effective coincidence. And if we have the idea of the thing itself

6 TRANSLATOR: We are translating *originaire* by "originating," to be taken in an active sense. Merleau-Ponty says it means "fundamental and inaugural."

and of the past itself, there must be something in the factual order that answers to it.

It is therefore necessary that the deflection (*écart*), without which the experience of the thing or of the past would fall to zero, be also an openness upon the thing itself, to the past itself, that it enter into their definition. What is given, then, is not the naked thing, the past itself such as it was in its own time, but rather the thing ready to be seen, pregnant—in principle as well as in fact—with all the visions one can have of it, the past such as it was one day *plus* an inexplicable alteration, a strange distance—bound in principle as well as in fact to a recalling that spans that distance but does not nullify it. What there is is not a coinciding by principle or a presumptive coinciding and a factual non-coinciding, a bad or abortive truth, but a privative non-coinciding, a coinciding from afar, a divergence, and something like a "good error."

It is by considering language that we would best see how we are to and how we are not to return to the things themselves. If we dream of finding again the natural world or time through coincidence, of being identical to the O-point which we see yonder, or to the pure memory which from the depths of ourselves governs our acts of recall, then language is a power for error, since it cuts the continuous tissue that joins us vitally to the things and to the past and is installed between ourselves and that tissue like a screen. The philosopher speaks, but this is a weakness in him, and an inexplicable weakness: he should keep silent, coincide in silence, and rejoin in Being a philosophy that is there ready-made. But yet everything comes to pass as though he wished to put into words a certain silence he hearkens to within himself. His entire "work" is this absurd effort. He wrote in order to state his contact with Being; he did not state it, and could not state it, since it is silence. Then he recommences. . . . One has to believe, then, that language is not simply the contrary of the truth, of coincidence, that there is or could be a language of coincidence, a manner of making the things themselves speak—and this is what he seeks. It would be a language of which he would not be the organizer, words he would not assemble, that would combine through him by virtue of a natural intertwining of their meaning, through the occult trading of the metaphor—where what counts is no longer the manifest meaning of each word and of each image, but the lateral relations, the kinships that are implicated in their transfers and their exchanges. It is indeed a language of this sort that Bergson himself required for the philosopher. But we have to recognize the consequence: if language is not necessarily deceptive, truth is not coincidence, nor mute.

We need only take language too in the living or nascent state, with all its references, those behind it, which connect it to the mute things it interpellates, and those it sends before itself and which make up the world of things said—with its movement, its subtleties, its reversals, its life, which expresses and multiplies tenfold the life of the bare things. Language is a life, is our life and the life of the things. Not that *language* takes possession of life and reserves it for itself: what would there be to say if there existed nothing but things said? It is the error of the semantic philosophies to close up language as if it spoke only of itself: language lives only from silence; everything we cast to the others has germinated in this great mute land which we never leave.

But, because he has experienced within himself the need to speak, the birth of speech as bubbling up at the bottom of his mute experience, the philosopher knows better than anyone that what is lived is lived-spoken, that, born at this depth, language is not a mask over Being, but—if one knows how to grasp it with all its roots and all its foliation—the most valuable witness to Being, that it does not interrupt an immediation that would be perfect without it, that the vision itself, the thought itself, are, as has been said, "structured as a language,"[7] are *articulation* before the letter, apparition of something where there was nothing or something else.

Hence the problem of language is, if one likes, only a regional problem—that is, if we consider the ready-made language, the secondary and empirical operation of translation, of coding and decoding, the artificial languages, the technical relation between a sound and a meaning which are joined only by express convention and are therefore ideally isolable. But if, on the contrary, we consider the speaking word, the assuming of the

[7] Jacques Lacan.

conventions of his native language as something natural by him who lives within that language, the folding over within him of the visible and the lived experience upon language, and of language upon the visible and the lived experience, the exchanges between the articulations of his mute language and those of his speech, finally that operative language which has no need to be translated into significations and thoughts, that language-thing which counts as an arm, as action, as offense and as seduction because it brings to the surface all the deep-rooted relations of the lived experience wherein it takes form, and which is the language of life and of action but also that of literature and of poetry—then this logos is an absolutely universal theme, it is the theme of philosophy.

Philosophy itself is language, rests on language; but this does not disqualify it from speaking of language, nor from speaking of the pre-language and of the mute world which doubles them: on the contrary, philosophy is an operative language, that language that can be known only from within, through its exercise, is open upon the things, called forth by the voices of silence, and continues an effort of articulation which is the Being of every being.

We would err as much by defining philosophy as the search for the essences as by defining it as the fusion with the things, and the two errors are not so different. Whether we orient ourselves upon the essences, which are the more pure in the measure that he who sees them has no part in the world, in the measure, consequently, that we look out from the depths of nothingness, or whether we seek to merge with the existing things, at the very point and at the very instant that they are, this infinite distance, this absolute proximity express in two ways —as a soaring over or as fusion—the same relationship with the thing itself. They are two positivisms.

Whether one installs oneself at the level of statements, which are the proper order of the essences, or in the silence of the things, whether one trusts in speech absolutely, or whether one distrusts it absolutely—the ignorance of the problem of speech is here the ignoring of all mediation. Philosophy is flattened to the sole plane of ideality or to the sole plane of existence. On both sides one wants something—internal adequation of the idea or self-identity of the thing—to come stop up the look, and one excludes or subordinates the thought of the far-offs, the horizonal thought. That every being presents itself at a distance, which does not prevent us from knowing it, which is on the contrary the guarantee for knowing it: this is what is not considered. That the presence of the world is precisely the presence of its flesh to my flesh, that I "am of the world" and that I am not it, this is what is no sooner said than forgotten: metaphysics remains coincidence. That there is this thickness of flesh between us and the "hard core" of Being, this does not figure in the definition: this thickness is ascribed to me, it is the sheath of non-being that the subjectivity always carries about itself. Infinite distance or absolute proximity, negation or identification: our relationship with Being is ignored in the same way in both cases.

In both cases, one misses it because one thinks one will ensure it more effectively by approaching the essence or the thing as closely as possible. One forgets that this frontal being before us —whether we posit it, whether it posits itself within us qua being-posited—is second by principle, is cut out upon a horizon which is not nothing, and which for its part is not by virtue of com-position. One forgets that our openness, our fundamental relationship with Being, that which makes it impossible for us to feign to not be, could not be formed in the order of the being-posited, since it is this openness precisely that teaches us that the beings-posited, whether true or false, are not nothing, that, whatever be the experience, an experience is always contiguous upon an experience, that our perceptions, our judgments, our whole knowledge of the world can be changed, crossed out, Husserl says, but not nullified, that, under the doubt that strikes them appear other perceptions, other judgments more true, because we are within Being and because there is something.

Bergson had indeed said that the fundamental knowing is not that which wishes to take hold of time as between forceps, wishes to fix it, to determine it by the relations between its parts, to measure it; and that on the contrary time offers itself to him who wishes only to "see it,"[8] and who, precisely because he has given up the attempt to seize it, rejoins, by vision, its internal propulsion. But more often than not the idea of fusion or of coincidence serves as a substitute for these indications, which would call for a theory of the philosophical view or vision as a maximum of true proximity to a Being in dehiscence. . . . We should have to return to this idea of proximity through distance, of intuition as auscultation or palpation in depth, of a view which is a view of self, a torsion of self upon self, and which calls "coincidence" in question.

And thereby we would see finally what the philosophical questioning is. Not the *an sit* and the doubt, where Being is tacitly understood, and not the "I know that I know nothing," where already the absolute certitude of the ideas breaks through, but a true "what do I know?" which is not quite that of Montaigne. For the "what do I know?" could be a simple appeal for the elucidation of the things that we know, without any examination of the idea of knowing. In that case it would be one of those questions of cognition (as can also be the "where am I?") where we are hesitating only about what to call entities—space, knowledge—which are taken as evident in themselves. But already when I say "what do I know?" in the course of a phrase,[9] another sort of question arises: for it extends to the idea of knowing itself; it invokes some intelligible place where the facts, examples, ideas I lack, should be found; it intimates that the interrogative is not a mode derived by inversion or by reversal of the indicative and of the positive, is neither an affirmation nor a negation veiled or expected, but an original manner of aiming at something, as it were a *question-knowing*, which by principle no statement or "answer" can go beyond and which perhaps therefore is the proper mode of our relationship with Being, as though it were the mute or reticent interlocutor of our questions.

"What do I know?" is not only "what is knowing?" and not only "who am I?" but finally: "what is there?" and even: "what

[8] *La Pensée et le mouvant* (Paris, 1934), p. 10. [English translation by Mabelle L. Andison, *The Creative Mind* (New York, 1946), p. 13.]

[9] TRANSLATOR: *Que sais-je?*—an idiomatic exclamatory turn of phrase in French.

is the *there is?*" These questions call not for the exhibiting of
something said which would put an end to them, but for the
disclosure of a Being that is not posited because it has no need
to be, because it is silently behind all our affirmations, negations,
and even behind all formulated questions, not that it is a matter
of forgetting them in its silence, not that it is a matter of im-
prisoning it in our chatter, but because philosophy is the recon-
version of silence and speech into one another: "It is the experience . . . still mute which we are concerned with leading to
the pure expression of its own meaning."[10]

MAURICE MERLEAU-PONTY'S MAJOR WRITINGS
(arranged chronologically)

La structure du comportement. Paris: Presses Universitaires de France,
    1942.

  The Structure of Behavior. Tr. Alden Fisher. Boston: Beacon Press,
      1963.

Phénoménologie de la perception. Paris: Gallimard, 1945.

  Phenomenology of Perception. Tr. Colin Smith. London: Rout-
      ledge & Kegan Paul, 1962.

"Le primat de la perception et ses conséquences philosophiques," *Bul-
    letin de la Société francaise de philosophie,* 4 [1947], 119–153.

  "The Primacy of Perception and its Philosophical Consequences."
      Tr. J. Edie, in *The Primacy of Perception and Other Essays.*
      Ed. J. Edie. Evanston: Northwestern University Press, 1964.

Sens et Non-Sens. Paris: Nagel, 1948.

  Sense and Non-Sense. Tr. H. L. Dreyfus & P. A. Dreyfus. Evans-
      ton: Northwestern University Press, 1964.

Humanisme et terreur. Paris: Gallimard, 1947.

  Humanism and Terror. Tr. J. O'Neill. Boston: Beacon, 1970.

Les sciences de l'homme et la phénoménologie. Paris: Les Cours de
    Sorbonne, 1951.

  "Phenomenology and the Sciences of Man." Tr. J. Wild, in *The
      Primacy of Perception and Other Essays.*

Les relations avec autrui chez l'enfant. Paris: Les Cours de Sorbonne,
    1951.

---

[10] Husserl, *Meditations cartésiennes,* French translation (Paris,
1947), p. 33. [English translation by Dorion Cairns, *Cartesian Meditations* (The Hague, 1960), pp. 38–39.]

"The Child's Relations with Others." Tr. W. Cobb, in *The Primacy of Perception and Other Essays.*

Éloge de la philosophie. Paris: Gallimard, 1953.

  In Praise of Philosophy. Tr. J. Wild & J. Edie. Evanston: Northwestern University Press, 1963.

Les aventures de la dialectique. Paris: Gallimard, 1955.

Signes. Paris: Gallimard, 1960.

  Signs. Tr. R. C. McCleary. Evanston: Northwestern University Press, 1964.

"L'oeil et l'esprit," *Art de France,* Vol. I, No. 1 [January 1961].

  "Eye and Mind." Tr. C. Dallery, in *The Primacy of Perception and Other Essays.*

Le Visible et l'invisible. Suivi de notes de travail par Merleau-Ponty. Ed. Claude Lefort. Paris: Gallimard, 1964.

  The Visible and the Invisible. Tr. A. Lingis. Evanston: Northwestern University Press, 1968.

Résumés de cours, College de France 1952–1960. Paris: Gallimard, 1968.

  Themes from the Lectures at the College de France 1952–1960. Tr. J. O'Neill. Evanston: Northwestern University Press, 1970.

Selected Studies About Merleau-Ponty
(arranged alphabetically)

Bannan, John. *The Philosophy of Merleau-Ponty.* New York: Harcourt, Brace, 1967.

Barral, Mary Rose. *Merleau-Ponty: The Role of the Body-Subject in Interpersonal Relations.* Pittsburgh: Duquesne University Press, 1965.

Bayer, Raymond. *Merleau-Ponty's Existentialism.* Buffalo: University of Buffalo Studies, 1951.

Carr, David. "Maurice Merleau-Ponty: Incarnate Consciousness," *Existential Philosophers: Kierkegaard to Merleau-Ponty.* Ed. G. Schrader. New York: McGraw-Hill, 1967.

Centineo, Ettore. *Una fenomenologia della storia: L'esistenzialismo di M. Merleau-Ponty.* Palermo: Palumbo, 1959.

De Waelhens, Alphonse. *Une philosophie de l'ambiguité: L'Existentialisme de Maurice Merleau-Ponty.* Louvain: Publications Universitaires de Louvain, 1951.

Hyppolite, Jean. *Sens et existence dans la philosophie de Maurice Merleau-Ponty.* Oxford: The Clarendon Press, 1963.

Kaelin, Eugene. *An Existentialist Aesthetic: The Theories of Sartre and Merleau-Ponty*. Madison: University of Wisconsin Press, 1962.

Kwant, Remy. *The Phenomenological Philosophy of Merleau-Ponty*. Pittsburgh: Duquesne University Press, 1963.

————. *From Phenomenology to Metaphysics: An Inquiry into the Last Period of Merleau-Ponty's Philosophy*. Pittsburgh: Duquesne University Press, 1966.

Langan, Thomas. *Merleau-Ponty's Critique of Reason*. New Haven: Yale University Press, 1966.

Rabil, Albert. *Merleau-Ponty: Existentialist of the Social World*. New York: Columbia University Press, 1967.

Sartre, Jean-Paul. *Situations*. Tr. Benita Eisler. New York: Braziller, 1965.

Semerari, Giuseppe. "Esistenzialismo e marxismo nella fenomenologia della percezione," *Revista di filosofia*, 52:2 [April 1961], 167–190; 52:3 [July 1961], 330–353.

Viano, Carlo. "Esistenzialismo e umanesimo in Maurice Merleau-Ponty," *Rivista di filosofia*, 44:1 [January 1953], 39–60.

ALBERT CAMUS (1913–1960)

Camus was born on November 7, 1913, in Mondovi, Algeria.
His father, Lucien, a laborer of Alsatian origin, was killed during
military services at the battle of the Marne in 1914. His mother,
Katherine Sintès Camus, who was of Spanish descent, moved
together with her two sons to Algiers where she worked as a
cleaning woman. A childhood illness had left her deaf and with
a speech impediment. But the stark and painful course of
Camus's childhood was partially assuaged by the stark beauty
and climate of North Africa.

At elementary school, one of Camus's teachers, Louis Germain
—to whom he dedicated his Nobel Prize acceptance speech—
prepared him for a scholarship to the *lycée* of Algiers. His
studies, however, were compromised by his passion for athletics,
especially as a soccer goalkeeper. It was a rude shock when he
suffered a serious attack of tuberculosis in 1930, which cur-
tailed, thereafter, his athletic pursuits.

In that same year he was attending the University of Algiers
as a philosophy student. His mentor and friend there was Jean
Grenier, who had also been his philosophy teacher at the *lycée*
of Algiers. Tuberculosis not only limited his athletic activity
but prevented his preparation for a college teaching career because of the required medical examination he would have to
pass.

For the next few years he took various odd jobs: clerking in
an import-export firm, selling automobile parts, forecasting
weather, and private tutoring. In 1934 he married Simone Hie,
the daughter of an Algiers doctor. The marriage lasted only a
year. The brevity of his first marriage was matched by the

brevity of his membership in the Communist Party during 1934.

Camus completed his dissertation under René Poirier on the topic of Plotinus' influence on St. Augustine and received the *diplôme d'études supérieures* in 1936. During the mid-thirties he was also involved as an actor-writer-director for an amateur theater group called *La Théâtre du travail* and later *Le Théâtre de l'equipe*. He also worked as an actor for Radio-Algiers for about a year. Then in 1938 he settled into journalism as a reporter for *Alger-Républicain*.

When World War II began, he tried to volunteer for the armed services but was rejected because of his health. He went to Paris in 1940 to work as a rewrite for *Paris-Soir* after *Alger-Républicain* closed down. Camus left Paris just before the German invasion and settled in Lyon where he married his second wife, Francine Faure, who had been born and raised in Oran. In 1945 twins were born to them in Paris.

At the end of 1942, Camus joined a group in the French resistance movement in Lyon and edited its clandestine news sheet, *Combat*. The sheet gave information about the war, called for citizens to join the underground, published data about German reprisals, deportations, and executions, and encouraged the French toward the expectation of a liberated France. He moved to Paris again in 1943 to continue his responsibilities for *Combat* while working ostensibly as a reader for the publisher Gallimard, a position he retained after the war. He was awarded the Medal of the Liberation for his part in the cause.

Camus was already quite well known by the time the war ended, and in the winter of 1946–1947 he lectured in the United States and in 1949 in various countries in South America. During the same span of years, Camus's criticism of the Communist Party became open. He had become increasingly suspicious of the Communists in his alliance with them in the Resistance, so that by 1950 he not only rejected Marxist historical and social necessitarianism but also the repressive character of the Soviet Union exhibited by the Siberian labor camps.

Their respective positions on Marxism and the Communist Party led Camus and Jean-Paul Sartre into a bitter controversy. The two had been friends, and when Sartre attempted in 1947 to create a non-communist left, Camus was sympathetic. When the attempt failed, Sartre concluded that effective social action could be achieved only through the Communist Party and he regarded Camus's criticisms of the Party as reactionary bourgeois sentiment. The break between the two occurred in 1952 after Sartre's bitter review in *Les Temps modernes* of Camus's *L'Homme révolté*.

By 1953 Camus returned to an activity he had enjoyed before the war—the theater. He became involved as a director and playwright in various productions and festivals of the French theater. In 1959 he was appointed as director of the new state-supported experimental theater by André Malraux, who was then in charge of France's cultural activities. Camus had already received widespread renown, having been awarded the Nobel Prize for literature for 1957.

On January 4, 1960, Camus was killed in an automobile accident while returning to Paris from Lourmarin, a village in the South of France where he had recently purchased a house.

"The Myth of Sisyphus" from *The Myth of Sisyphus*

Translated by Justin O'Brien

The gods had condemned Sisyphus to ceaselessly rolling a rock to the top of a mountain, whence the stone would fall back of its own weight. They had thought with some reason that there is no more dreadful punishment than futile and hopeless labor.

If one believes Homer, Sisyphus was the wisest and most prudent of mortals. According to another tradition, however, he was disposed to practice the profession of highwayman. I see no contradiction in this. Opinions differ as to the reasons why he became the futile laborer of the underworld. To begin with, he is accused of a certain levity in regard to the gods. He stole their secrets. Ægina, the daughter of Æsopus, was carried off by Jupiter. The father was shocked by that disappearance and complained to Sisyphus. He, who knew of the abduction, offered to tell about it on condition that Æsopus would give water to the citadel of Corinth. To the celestial thunderbolts he preferred the benediction of water. He was punished for this in the underworld. Homer tells us also that Sisyphus had put Death in chains. Pluto could not endure the sight of his deserted, silent empire. He dispatched the god of war, who liberated Death from the hands of her conqueror.

It is said also that Sisyphus, being near to death, rashly wanted to test his wife's love. He ordered her to cast his unburied body into the middle of the public square. Sisyphus woke up in the underworld. And there, annoyed by an obedience so contrary to human love, he obtained from Pluto permission to return to earth in order to chastise his wife. But when he had seen again the face of this world, enjoyed water and sun, warm stones and the sea, he no longer wanted to go back to the infernal darkness. Recalls, signs of anger, warnings were of no avail. Many years more he lived facing the curve of the gulf, the sparkling sea, and the smiles of earth. A decree of the gods was necessary. Mercury came and seized the impudent man by the collar and, snatching him from his joys, led him forcibly back to the underworld, where his rock was ready for him.

You have already grasped that Sisyphus is the absurd hero. He *is*, as much through his passions as through his torture. His scorn of the gods, his hatred of death, and his passion for life won him that unspeakable penalty in which the whole being is exerted toward accomplishing nothing. This is the price that must be paid for the passions of this earth. Nothing is told us about Sisyphus in the underworld. Myths are made for the imagination to breathe life into them. As for this myth, one sees merely the whole effort of a body straining to raise the huge stone, to roll it and push it up a slope a hundred times over; one sees the face screwed up, the cheek tight against the stone, the shoulder bracing the clay-covered mass, the foot wedging it, the fresh start with arms outstretched, the wholly human security of two earth-clotted hands. At the very end of his long effort measured by skyless space and time without depth, the purpose is achieved. Then Sisyphus watches the stone rush down in a few moments toward that lower world whence he will have to push it up again toward the summit. He goes back down to the plain.

It is during that return, that pause, that Sisyphus interests me. A face that toils so close to stones is already stone itself! I see that man going back down with a heavy yet measured step toward the torment of which he will never know the end. That hour like a breathing-space which returns as surely as his suffering, that is the hour of consciousness. At each of those moments when he leaves the heights and gradually sinks toward the lairs of the gods, he is superior to his fate. He is stronger than his rock.

If this myth is tragic, that is because its hero is conscious. Where would his torture be, indeed, if at every step the hope of succeeding upheld him? The workman of today works every day in his life at the same tasks, and this fate is no less absurd. But it is tragic only at the rare moments when it becomes conscious. Sisyphus, proletarian of the gods, powerless and rebellious, knows the whole extent of his wretched condition: it is what he thinks of during his descent. The lucidity that was to constitute his torture at the same time crowns his victory. There is no fate that cannot be surmounted by scorn.

If the descent is thus sometimes performed in sorrow, it can also take place in joy. This word is not too much. Again I fancy Sisyphus returning toward his rock, and the sorrow was in the beginning. When the images of earth cling too tightly to memory, when the call of happiness becomes too insistent, it happens that melancholy rises in man's heart: this is the rock's victory, this is the rock itself. The boundless grief is too heavy to bear. These are our nights of Gethsemane. But crushing truths perish from being acknowledged. Thus, Œdipus at the outset obeys fate without knowing it. But from the moment he knows, his tragedy begins. Yet at the same moment, blind and desperate, he realizes that the only bond linking him to the world is the cool hand of a girl. Then a tremendous remark rings out: "Despite so many ordeals, my advanced age and the nobility of my soul make me conclude that all is well." Sophocles' Œdipus, like Dostoevsky's Kirilov, thus gives the recipe for the absurd victory. Ancient wisdom confirms modern heroism.

One does not discover the absurd without being tempted to write a manual of happiness. "What! by such narrow ways—?"

There is but one world, however. Happiness and the absurd are two sons of the same earth. They are inseparable. It would be a mistake to say that happiness necessarily springs from the absurd discovery. It happens as well that the feeling of the absurd springs from happiness. "I conclude that all is well," says Œdipus, and that remark is sacred. It echoes in the wild and limited universe of man. It teaches that all is not, has not been, exhausted. It drives out of this world a god who had come into it with dissatisfaction and a preference for futile sufferings. It makes of fate a human matter, which must be settled among men.

All Sisyphus' silent joy is contained therein. His fate belongs to him. His rock is his thing. Likewise, the absurd man, when he contemplates his torment, silences all the idols. In the universe suddenly restored to its silence, the myriad wondering little voices of the earth rise up. Unconscious, secret calls, invitations from all the faces, they are the necessary reverse and price of victory. There is no sun without shadow, and it is essential to know the night. The absurd man says yes and his effort will henceforth be unceasing. If there is a personal fate, there is no higher destiny, or at least there is but one which he concludes is inevitable and despicable. For the rest, he knows himself to be the master of his days. At that subtle moment when man glances backward over his life, Sisyphus returning toward his rock, in that slight pivoting he contemplates that series of unrelated actions which becomes his fate, created by him, combined under his memory's eye and soon sealed by his death. Thus, convinced of the wholly human origin of all that is human, a blind man eager to see who knows that the night has no end, he is still on the go. The rock is still rolling.

I leave Sisyphus at the foot of the mountain! One always finds one's burden again. But Sisyphus teaches the higher fidelity that negates the gods and raises rocks. He too concludes that all is well. This universe henceforth without a master seems to him neither sterile nor futile. Each atom of that stone, each mineral flake of that night-filled mountain, in itself forms a world. The struggle itself toward the heights is enough to fill a man's heart. One must imagine Sisyphus happy.

CAMUS'S MAJOR WRITINGS
(arranged chronologically)

A. There are two editions of Camus's collected writings:

Oeuvres complètes. Ed. Roger Quilliot. [Bibliothèque de la Pléiades] Paris: Gallimard, I: *Théâtre, récits, nouvelles,* 1962; II: *Essais,* 1965.

Oeuvres complètes. Paris: Imprimerie nationale Sauret, I: *Récits et romans,* 1961; II: *Essais littéraires,* 1962; III: *Essais philosophiques,* 1962; IV: *Essais politiques,* 1962; V: *Théâtre,* 1962; VI: *Adaptations et traductions,* 1962.

B. Notebooks

Carnets: mars 1935–février 1942. Paris: Gallimard, 1962.
    The Notebooks: 1935–1942. Tr. P. Thody. New York: Knopf, 1963.
Carnets II: janvier 1942–mars 1951. Paris: Gallimard, 1964.
    The Notebooks: 1942–1951. Tr. P. Thody. New York: Knopf, 1965.

C. Essays

L'Envers et l'endroit. Algiers: Charlot, 1936.
Noces. Algiers: Charlot, 1938.
Le Mythe de Sisyphe. Paris: Gallimard, 1942.
    The Myth of Sisyphus. Tr. J. O'Brien. New York: Knopf, 1955.
Lettres à un ami allemand. Paris: Gallimard, 1945.
    Resistance, Rebellion, and Death. Tr. J. O'Brien. New York: Knopf, 1961.
Prométhée aux enfers. Paris: Palimugre, 1947.
Actuelles I, II, III. Paris: Gallimard, 1950, 1953, 1958. These chronicles are partially translated in *Resistance, Rebellion, and Death.*
Le Minotaure ou la halte d'Oran. Algiers: Charlot, 1950.
    The Myth of Sisyphus and other Essays. Tr. J. O'Brien. New York: Vintage, 1960.
L'Homme révolté. Paris: Gallimard, 1951.
    The Rebel. Tr. A. Bower. New York: Knopf, 1954.
L'Été. Paris: Gallimard, 1954.

C. Novels and Stories

L'Étranger. Paris: Gallimard, 1942.
    The Stranger. Tr. S. Gilbert. New York: Knopf, 1946.

La Peste. Paris: Gallimard, 1947.
   The Plague. Tr. S. Gilbert. New York: Knopf, 1948.
La Chute. Paris: Gallimard, 1956.
   The Fall. Tr. J. O'Brien. New York: Knopf, 1957.
L'Exil et le royaume. Paris: Gallimard, 1957.
   Exile and the Kingdom. Tr. J. O'Brien. New York: Knopf, 1958.

D. Plays

La Révolte dans les Asturies: Essai de création collective. Algiers:
   Charlot, 1936.
Le Malentendu suivi de Caligula. Paris: Gallimard, 1944.
   Caligula and Cross-Purpose. Tr. S. Gilbert. Norfolk: New Direc-
   tions, 1949: *Caligula and Three Other Plays.* Tr. S. Gilbert.
   New York: Knopf, 1958.
L'État de siège. Paris: Gallimard, 1948. Translated in *Caligula and
   Three Other Plays.*
Les Justes. Paris: Gallimard, 1950. Translated in *Caligula and Three
   Other Plays.*

SELECTED STUDIES ABOUT CAMUS

(arranged alphabetically)

A. Bibliography

Roeming, R. F. *Camus: A Bibliography.* Madison: University of
   Wisconsin Press, 1968.

B. Monographs and Articles

Arendt, Hannah. "La Philosophie de L'Existence," *Deucalion,* No. 2
   [1947], 214–245; 247–252.
Ayer, A. J. "Albert Camus," *Horizon,* XIII, No. 75 [March 1946],
   155–168.
Brée, Germaine. *Camus.* New Brunswick: Rutgers University Press,
   1959.
—— (ed.). *Camus: A Collection of Critical Essays.* Englewood Cliffs:
   Prentice Hall, 1962.
Cox, Richard. "Ideology, History, and Political Philosophy: Camus'
   L'Homme Révolté," *Social Research,* XXXII, No. 1 [Spring
   1965], 71–97.
Cruickshank, John. *Albert Camus and the Literature of Revolt.* Lon-
   don: Oxford, 1959.
Gargan, Edward. "Revolution and Morale in the Formative Thought

of Albert Camus," *Review of Politics,* Vol. 25 [October 1963],
483–496.

Hanna, Thomas. *The Thought and Art of Albert Camus.* Chicago:
Regnery, 1958.

Rhein, Phillip. *Albert Camus.* New York: Twayne, 1969.

Sartre, Jean-Paul. *Literary and Philosophical Essays.* Tr. Annette
Michelson. New York: Criterion, 1955.

Spiegelberg, Herbert. "French Existentialism: Its Social Philosophies,"
Kenyon Review, XVI, No. 3 [Summer 1954], 446–462.

Thody, Philip. *Albert Camus, 1913–1960.* London: Hamish Hamilton, 1961.

Tillich, Paul. "Existential Philosophy," *Journal of the History of
Ideas,* V, No. 1 [January 1944], 44–70.

Wolheim, Richard. "The Political Philosophy of Existentialism,"
Cambridge Journal, VII, No. 1 [October 1953], 3–19.

Selected Bibliographies

Selected Bibliographies of Existentialism in General

Bollnow, O. F. *Deutsche Existenzphilosophie*. Bern: Francke, 1953.

Brown, R. H. "Existentialism. A Bibliography," *Modern Schoolman*, Vol. 31 [November 1953], 19–33.

Burton, A. & Lunde, D. *Bibliographic Sources of Existential Thought*. California: Agnews State Hospital, 1961.

Douglas, Kenneth. *A Critical Bibliography of Existentialism (The Paris School)*. New Haven: Yale French Studies, Special Monograph No. 1 [1950].

Gérard, J.; De Waelhens, A.; Le Meere, J. *"Bibliographie* sur l'existentialisme," *Revue international de philosophie* [July 1949], 343–359.

"Addendum à la bibliographie des ouvrages italiens sur l'existentialisme," *Revue international de philosophie* [October 1949], 502–506.

Selected Studies About Existentialism in General

Abbagnano, Nicola. *Storia della Filosofia*. 2nd ed. Turin: U.T.E.T., 1969. Vol. III, pp. 824–885.

Allen, E. L. *Existentialism from Within*. London: Routledge & Kegan Paul, 1953.

Astrada, Carlos. *La Revolución Existencialista*. Buenos Aires: Ediciones Nuevo Destino, 1952.

Barnes, Hazel. *Humanistic Existentialism: The Literature of Possibility*. Lincoln: University of Nebraska, 1959.

Barrett, William. *Irrational Man*. New York: Doubleday, 1958.

——. *What is Existentialism?* New York: Grove Press, 1964.

Blackham, H. J. *Six Existentialist Thinkers*. London: Routledge & Kegan Paul, 1951.

Bochenski, I. *Contemporary European Philosophy*. Berkeley: University of California Press, 1957.

Bollnow, Otto. *Existenzphilosophie*. Stuttgart: Kohlhammer, 1949.

Brock, Werner. *An Introduction to Contemporary German Philosophy*. Cambridge: Cambridge University Press, 1935.

Chiodi, Pietro. *Existenzialismo e fenomenologia*. Milan: Edizioni di Communità, 1963.

Collins, James. *The Existentialists*. Chicago: Regnery, 1952.

Copleston, F. C. *Contemporary Philosophy*. Westminster: Newman, 1956.

Foulquie, Paul. *Existentialism*. Tr. K. Raine. New York: Roy, 1950.

Grene, Marjorie. *Introduction to Existentialism*. Chicago: University of Chicago, 1959. First published in 1948 under the title *Dreadful Freedom*.

Heinemann, F. H. *Existentialism and the Modern Predicament*. New York: Harper, 1953.

Kaufmann, Walter. *From Shakespeare to Existentialism*. Revised edition. New York: Doubleday, 1960.

Kuhn, Helmut. *Encounter with Nothingness, An Essay on Existentialism*. London: Methuen, 1951.

La Croix, J. *Marxisme, existentialisme, personalisme*. Paris: Presses Universitaires de France, 1950.

Lee, E. & Mandelbaum, M. (eds.). *Phenomenology and Existentialism*. Baltimore: Johns Hopkins, 1967.

Löwith, Karl. *Nature, History, and Existentialism*. Evanston: Northwestern University Press, 1966.

Lukács, Georgy. *Existentialisme ou marxisme?* Tr. E. Kelemen. Paris: Nagel, 1948.

Michalson, Carl. *Christianity and the Existentialists*. New York: Scribner's, 1956.

Molina, Fernando. *Existentialism as Philosophy*. Englewood Cliffs: Prentice Hall, 1962.

Mounier, Emmanuel. *Existentialist Philosophies*. London: Rockcliff, 1948.

Odajnyk, Walter. *Marxism and Existentialism*. New York: Doubleday, 1965.

Olafson, Frederick. *Principles and Persons: An Ethical Interpretation of Existentialism*. Baltimore: Johns Hopkins, 1967.

Pareyson, Luigi. *Studi sull' esistenzialismo*. Florence: Sansoni, 1943.

Patka, Frederick. *Existentialist Thinkers and Thought*. New York: Citadel, 1962.

Reinhardt, Kurt. *The Existentialist Revolt*. Milwaukee: Bruce, 1952.

Rintelen, Fritz von. *Beyond Existentialism*. Tr. H. Graef. London: Allen & Unwin, 1962.

Roubiczek, Paul. *Existentialism*. New York: Cambridge University Press, 1964.

Sanborn, Patricia. *Existentialism*. New York: Pegasus, 1968.

Schrader, George. *Existential Philosophers: Kierkegaard to Merleau-Ponty*. New York: McGraw-Hill, 1967.

Smith, Colin. *Contemporary French Philosophy*. New York: Barnes & Noble, 1964.

Spiegelberg, Herbert. *The Phenomenological Movement*. 2 vols. The Hague: Nijhoff, 1960.

Ussher, Arland. *Journey Through Dread*. New York: Devin-Adair, 1955.

Wahl, Jean. *Les philosophies de l'existence*. Paris: Colin, 1954.

Warnock, Mary. *Existential Ethics*. New York: St. Martin's, 1967.

Wild, John. *The Challenge of Existentialism*. Bloomington: Indiana University Press, 1955.